Exceptional Children

IN TODAY'S SCHOOLS — Fourth Edition

What Teachers Need to Know

Edward L. Meyen
University of Kansas

Yvonne N. Bui
University of San Francisco

LOVE PUBLISHING COMPANY®
Denver • London • Sydney

 Published by Love Publishing Company
P.O. Box 22353
Denver, Colorado 80222
www.lovepublishing.com

Fourth Edition

Library of Congress Control Number: 2006920935

Contents

3 Early Intervention and Secondary Transition: Family and Community Partnerships   57
by Keith Storey & Jane Squires

Part II   Students With Mild to Moderate Disabilities (High-Incidence)   79

4 Specific Learning Disabilities   83
by Mary Brownell, Martha A. League, & Seonjin Seo

5 Emotional/Behavior Disorders   105
by Stephen W. Smith & T. Rowand Robinson

6 Speech/Language Impairments and Communication Disorders 125

by Cindy H. T. Lian

7 Physical and Health Disabilities 147

by Donna Lehr

8 Gifted and Talented 167

by Kimberley Chandler

9 Mild to Moderate Disabilities Instructional Perspectives 185

by Yvonne N. Bui & Edward L. Meyen

Part III Students With Moderate to Severe Disabilities (Low-Incidence) 221

10 Cognitive and Developmental Disabilities 223
by Sean J. Smith

11 Autism Spectrum Disorders 245
*by Brenda Smith Myles, Anastasia Hubbard,
Terri Cooper Swanson, Ronda L. Schelvan,
& Alison Simonelli*

12 Hearing Loss 259
by Sally Roberts

16 Professional Expectations for the Profession   367

by Mary Brownell, Anne G. Bishop, Dimple Malik, & Lisa K. Langley

Preface

This new edition of *Exceptional Children in Today's Schools* provides an exciting learning experience for students in introduction to special education courses, taking into account the importance of interactivity, efficiency and effectiveness, and varying learner preferences. Information science has moved beyond access and storage of information to interactive systems for teaching and learning. The population of students enrolled in introductory courses includes a much larger proportion of individuals who are enrolled in alternative teacher education programs, pursuing certification while also employed in a related career. Emerging policies such as those embedded in No Child Left Behind carry greater accountability implications for general education, and the public is becoming more assertive in communicating its expectations about public education to policy makers. Aspiring teachers like you in special education today have many pressing matters competing for your time, and your teaching and learning preferences vary. This new edition is designed to help future teachers learn new skills and acquire needed knowledge, in the way that suits you best.

Our responses to the changing preferences in how adult learners prefer investing their time and energy in professional preparation and the conditions surrounding the education of students with exceptional learning needs are evident as you begin to use the many resources designed as integral features of this edition. We updated policies and concerns related to public enlightenment. We integrated content throughout the chapters to reflect the growing number of students from culturally and linguistically diverse backgrounds in our schools, as changes in student demographics have implications for how teachers plan for instruction and collaborate with parents and families. Challenges presented by advancements in information science in the form of instructional technology and the changing needs of those aspiring to be special education teachers were difficult but interesting, allowing the author team to be creative and to step out and experiment with some ideas whose time had come. And we put you, the aspiring teacher, in the driver's seat.

This new edition includes both the print copy and the companion e-book with a wide array of activities, handouts, self-tests, interactive features, case studies, glossary items, and audio recordings of each chapter. The print version contains updated content and a focus on what beginning teachers need to know, opening the door to a broader set of resources in the form of the e-book. All of the content in the print version is included in the e-book, but the e-book is far more than a digital text. What is most significant about the e-book is that it is in an online self-instructional format. You can assess your understanding at any time with practice tests, search for definitions, apply what you have learned by responding to training activities, modify prepared notes, review content whenever you wish, and access any aspect of the e-book by a mere click on the table of contents. You can print out any part of the e-book, building your own customized print version in the sequence and manner that serves you best now as a student and later as a teacher. And because you have the print version in your hands now, you can decide the balance you wish to find with this book, the e-book version, and anything you create from both models.

After researching the experience of adults engaged in online instruction to learn from them what features enhance their learning, we designed a print version and an e-book with maximum options to match your learning styles. You can access the content of *Exceptional Children in Today's Schools* in four forms—the hard-copy textbook, an illustrated text version with direct links to all features in the e-book, a multimedia version that allows you to listen to the text being read aloud while you view picture slides, and a download of the MP3 files for your own player. And across all options, when you move from one mode to another, the content remains the same. But with the companion e-book the content is enhanced, supplemented, and made more accessible depending on your choices of use. You control your own learning.

Welcome to the fourth edition. We have designed it for you.

Ed Meyen and *Yvonne Bui*

Acknowledgments

The creation of instructional resources for introductory courses on the education of children and youth with exceptional learning needs represents a major challenge. Beginning teachers must understand the characteristics and attributes of the learners and the legislative mandates that ensure the rights of these children. They must also be introduced to best practices and understand their professional responsibilities. Our primary commitment in conceiving the book in your hands and the online e-book has been to assemble a group of authors whose experience, talent, and knowledge merge to provide the context and insights essential for such a team effort. We express our appreciation to each team member for joining us in this endeavor.

Due to the companion e-book design, this project was much more than a typical multiauthored book. Contributors were called upon to develop a number of resources that they normally would not create if they were only writing a book chapter. We were committed to making this edition an informative resource for beginning teachers, but we also wanted to push the technology as far as we could to maximize the use of the e-book and enhance learning for as many users as possible. As the instructional features were designed, each added to the demand on the authors. They willingly worked with us to fulfill these objectives. Without their patience, ideas, and significant work, our goals would not have been achieved.

Of equal importance is the acknowledgment of a very talented group of individuals that worked with us in designing the e-book. We believe our product is far more than a digital text. It is a dynamic set of resources that interact to accommodate a wide array of instructional preferences. Each individual who labored with us on the technical aspects of the e-book has left his or her mark on these resources. We are indebted to these colleagues for their many contributions that make the e-book a unique, comprehensive but expandable, approach to learning. Above all, we thank them for the personal pride they took in making something new work and for staying with us whenever it appeared that a solution could be a little daunting. These colleagues include Barbara Alves, Ron Aust, Rachel Castor, Chih-Jung Lin, Kevin Osborn, Satha Phongsatha, Thanawan Phongsatha, Mitch Sandow, Bradley Scott, Joel Shaw, Thomas Shorock, Dan Spurgin, Shiau Yan Tan, Meng Yew Tee, and Natalie Yeh.

To Stan Love, Susan Warhover, and Robin Finelli at Love Publishing Company, we cannot thank you enough for your willingness to allow us the flexibility to carry out this project. There is always a risk when a project breaks new ground, as we hope our e-book does. We know that this effort placed additional demands on you. It was a great experience and we thank you.

Meet the Authors

Edward L. Meyen is a professor of special education and co-director of the e-Learning Design Lab at the University of Kansas. Meyen has published extensively in areas related to instruction, curriculum, and programming for students with exceptional learning needs. In recent years, his research, teaching, and publishing have centered on e-learning with a focus on evaluation and designing and teaching online instruction. Meyen is currently involved in the development of online lessons and tutorials related to standards-based instruction and statewide assessments. His current research interests are in the areas of online instructional design, assessment, content managements processes, and knowledge object instructional development systems.

Yvonne N. Bui is an assistant professor and chairperson of the Department of Learning & Instruction at the University of San Francisco (USF). Bui has published in areas related to curriculum and instruction for students with disabilities, particularly those in urban areas. In recent years her research, teaching, and publishing have focused on developing instructional strategies for low-performing students from culturally and linguistically diverse backgrounds. Bui is currently the project director for a personnel preparation grant from the Office of Special Education Programs at USF. The credential/masters program prepares candidates to teach in special education settings in urban school districts with a focus on mild to moderate disabilities.

Meet the Contributors

Chapter 1: The Emergence of Special Education
Yvonne N. Bui, University of San Francisco
Edward L. Meyen, University of Kansas

Chapter 2: Cultural, Linguistic, and Instructional Diversity
Yvonne N. Bui, University of San Francisco
Alicia Moore, Southwestern Texas University
LaVonne Neal, University of Colorado at Colorado Springs

Chapter 3: Early Intervention and Secondary Transition: Family and Community Partnerships
Keith Storey, Touro University
Jane Squires, University of Oregon

Chapter 4: Specific Learning Disabilities
Mary Brownell, University of Florida
Martha A. League, University of Florida
Seonjin Seo, University of Florida

Chapter 5: Emotional/Behavior Disorders
Stephen W. Smith, University of Florida
T. Rowand Robinson, University of Wisconsin–Whitewater

Chapter 6: Speech/Language Impairments and Communication Disorders
Cindy H. T. Lian, Ph.D., CCC-SLP

Chapter 7: Physical and Health Disabilities
Donna Lehr, Boston University

Chapter 8: Gifted and Talented
Kimberley Chandler, College of William and Mary

Chapter 9: Mild to Moderate Disabilities Instructional Perspectives
Yvonne N. Bui, University of San Francisco
Edward L. Meyen, University of Kansas

Part I

INTRODUCTION TO SPECIAL EDUCATION

One would think that in a country where mandatory school attendance is couched in public policy, the education of children and youth with exceptional learning needs would never be an issue. Unfortunately, that is not the case. Historically, the establishment of a free and appropriate education for students with disabilities has not been interpreted as being central to the provisions governing public education in this country. Consequently, parents, professionals, advocates, and persons with disabilities themselves have gone through a long and arduous process to achieve the civil rights of individuals with disabilities and making what we have today, in the form of special education, public policy.

Understanding the process and the efforts behind it to bring about these public policies, along with their educational implications, is an important part of the knowledge base necessary to be an effective teacher. Although policies do not result in effective instruction, they create the conditions under which teachers and others must operate to make a difference in the lives of children, youth, and adults with disabilities. It becomes your responsibility as a practicing professional to ensure that you know what your obligations are and that you possess the knowledge and skills required to fulfill them.

To fully understand the potential impact of disability on the lives of individuals with disabilities and their families, it is important to keep in perspective what is occurring in the larger society. With advances in medical science, for example, more children survive who earlier might not have lived due to the severity of their medical condition. However, although they have survived, many require treatment, services, and resources that are essential to their quality of life. Further, shifts in the economy can create employment conditions that can greatly restrict opportunities for employment or resources central to their daily lives. Finally, changing demographics can make a difference in what communities are able or willing to do to ensure that the needs of persons with disabilities are accommodated across the life span.

While much has been achieved in this country to bring about equality for many groups, including those with disabilities, it is a constant struggle. As circumstances change, policy makers must be constantly aware of how changing circumstances impact all groups. Further, advocates, families, and professionals must be vigilant in monitoring societal changes and pursue equity for all.

As a beginning teacher your role in achieving equity is no less than that of other advocates and policy makers. In fact, in many ways your role will be more strategic. You will find yourself responsible for implementing many public policies and for monitoring others. At the same time you are uniquely responsible for becoming an effective teacher in an educational system where resources are often insufficient and available interventions are sometimes not as powerful as necessary. Yet your role is central to the accountability called for in education by public policy today.

The complexities that surround the education of children and youth with disabilities make the decision about what to cover first in an introductory text difficult at best. Some might argue that beginning teachers should first be introduced to the pedagogy of how to teach students with exceptional learning needs. Others may take the view that because of the numerous ways in which conditions that cause disabilities affect learning and behavioral attributes, these should take center stage, beginning with a chapter on each disability and associated learning characteristics.

Amidst these varying opinions, we are of the conviction that it is important for individuals preparing to be teachers to have a foundation in the policies that undergird special education and the role of the teacher. We also believe that having a perspective on the programmatic contributions that education can make to students' quality of life across the life span is essential early in the study of special education.

The rationale for the emphasis on foundations is most evident. Early advocacy efforts were directed at ensuring educational equity. For the most part, that was interpreted to mean access to education with a concern for the appropriateness of the education provided across the different categories of learners with disabilities. As access was eventually gained, it soon became apparent that education during the traditional school-age years was not sufficient to prepare students with disabilities for the challenges to be faced later in life in terms of employment, independent living, and so on. Specifically, it became clear that there was a need for early intervention and special preparation in the form of transition programs at the secondary level and beyond. Just as educational equity generalized across disability groups, the same was true for early intervention and transition. Finally, in recent years the impact of cultural, linguistic, and instructional diversity on all disability groups has become a significant issue among educators and policy makers.

Each of these topics warrants serious consideration by all teachers. In most teacher preparation programs their importance is reinforced by coursework devoted to the study of them. In this book we have positioned the study of early intervention, transition and diversity early on to provide readers insight into the programmatic needs of children and youth with disabilities while creating a framework for the study of specific disability groups.

The Emergence of Special Education

1

Yvonne N. Bui & Edward L. Meyen

ost readers of this book are preparing to enter the teaching profession with a goal of teaching students who have exceptional learning needs. Some may have begun teaching while continuing their studies in special education. If you are among the latter group, you probably are spending some time in classrooms observing students as they respond to their teachers and to their classmates. If you are already teaching, you remember your first day as a teacher. Etched in your mind are the faces of the children and your anticipation of what was about to unfold. You may even remember the sounds of students interacting with each other or the expressions on their faces when they mastered a new concept. Those are the moments we remember as teachers.

I remember vividly my first day of teaching. The students were not much younger than I was. There were only nine of them. This was a self-contained class for students who at the time were labeled as "educable mentally retarded." Three were from families belonging to the migrant workforce that came to work in the fields each spring. Two were from very poor families and had always attended special classes. One had a history of uncontrollable behavioral outbursts. The other students were considered nonachievers, and the special class was assumed to be the best place for them. The classroom was located in a junior high school. Except for Johnny, who was a couple of years older than his peers, the students spent the entire school day with me. Johnny, a excellent athlete, participated in physical education and played sports.

The principal met me at the school on the Saturday before school was to start on Monday to give me the curriculum. It consisted of an assortment of outdated textbooks and several workbooks that he thought I could use to create worksheets on the ditto machine.

While that scenario may seem totally inappropriate today, at the time it represented state-of-the-art practices in public education. Indeed, prior to that time, students like mine either dropped out of school or were socially promoted without the benefit of any special instruction to meet their needs. In fact, the boy with the behavioral difficulties was 13 and had only recently been allowed to attend school. That reflected the status of public policy with regard to the education of students with disabilities, or "handicapped," as they were referred to at that time.

Much has changed in public policy over the last four decades. You likely grew up having classmates with disabilities of various types, unaware that the situation was ever any different. Although the world is not perfect for students with exceptional learning needs today, improvements are being made in response to emerging public policies. As you begin your teaching career, public policies will continue to change. You will play a major role in implementing those policies and ensuring that they have the intended impact on the children with exceptional learning needs whom you will be responsible for teaching.

As you will soon learn through your study of students with exceptional learning needs, the design of special education programs and the determination of who is eligible for those programs is highly controlled by public policy. One might think that this would result in uniformity in teaching methods, organization of classes, and the way teachers go about meeting their professional responsibilities in the classroom when teaching students with exceptional learning needs. This is not necessarily the case. Yes, common criteria are used in identifying students with exceptional learning needs, and similarities are found in how instruction and related services are made available to students with disabilities. But you also will find that schools vary in how they meet the requirements of the law in providing special education services. That is good, as this variance across schools and teaching practices contributes to the knowledge base on how best to enhance the achievement of these students.

As a professional new to the field of special education, you will have to develop your own understanding of what special education means to you within the context of public policy and the realities of your personal experience. The goal is to make a significant difference in the lives of students whose needs differ from those of peers who do not experience exceptional learning needs related to their disabilities. The most significant difference you can make as a teacher will be to help them achieve their potential and to develop the self-confidence necessary for a productive life.

This chapter will provide you with a frame of reference on public policies that constitute the foundation for special education. As you read subsequent chapters and complete your teacher education program, you will build on this knowledge. Moreover, you will continue to build on it as you pursue your teaching career and policies continue to evolve.

Historical Context

A brief look at the early development of special education is important for you to understand the changes occurring today in the education of exceptional children. The earliest attempts to educate children with what was at the time referred to as "handicapping conditions" did not take place in the public schools. In the 19th century most of these children were educated in private residential settings known as "institutions" or "asylums." The first of these, the American Asylum for the Deaf, was established in 1817 in West Hartford, Connecticut. In 1831, the Perkins School for the Blind opened in Watertown, Massachusetts. As public acceptance of residential programs grew, institutions for individuals with mental retardation came into being and, by the 1880s, were common in several states (Gearheart, 1980).

Public school classes for students with mental retardation or students who were deaf or blind did not become popular until the early 1900s. Programs for students with mental retardation increased in 1916 with the revision of the Stanford–Binet Intelligence Scale, which made it possible to differentiate students by ability level. Thus, schools could identify children as having mental retardation or as underachieving (performing at a level lower than their tested ability).

Intelligence Testing

Intelligence testing subsequently became popular and provided the impetus for many practices in the schools beyond setting admissions criteria for certain special education programs. This type of testing came under considerable scrutiny later, and its fairness for some populations of learners was questioned. This questioning continues periodically, as intelligence tests are revised in response to the criticisms that they discriminate against individuals from certain cultures and do not always measure what is important to teachers when planning instructional programs.

> **Note**
>
> Although intelligence testing used to be widely used and accepted, its legitimacy and fairness is now questioned. Many professionals use other forms of assessment in addition to or in place of intelligence testing.

Nevertheless, intelligence tests remain a major factor in the diagnosis and placement of many exceptional children into special education programs. Other forms of assessment used today, such as authentic assessments, are emerging and are yielding much more usable information for educational planning.

Self-Contained Classes

Until the late 1950s, public school services for exceptional children were limited primarily to children identified as having mild mental retardation, hearing or visual impairments, emotional disturbance, or physical disabilities. These children were served in self-contained special education classes, segregated from other students in the same building or in special schools. Many of them were excluded from attending school altogether, and several groups that today receive special services attended schools that paid little attention to their special needs.

No state or federal special financial assistance existed for school districts that provided special education, and only a few states had established eligibility criteria to guide the organization of programs. Students with special needs were grouped by disability and, to the extent possible, by age. Their educational needs were defined largely by their characteristics and the obvious implications of their disabilities.

As educational programs for these children became more prevalent, teachers began to receive special training, curricula were developed for special students, and program standards began to evolve. At the same time, districts became sensitive to the increased cost of providing special education programs, if for no other reason than the low pupil-teacher ratio for special education, which added to the cost.

The 1970s

The decade of the 1970s was a landmark era in the history of special education. Most of the public policies that undergird special education today were the consequences of actions occurring in the 1970s. The remainder of this chapter addresses policies and practices that are an outgrowth of events that took place in this decade. This will be evident as the education of students with exceptional learning needs is discussed in subsequent chapters. Central to making this period a landmark era were two court cases, each of which was instrumental in changing the scene in special education and the result of major advocacy efforts by parents.

PARC

The first landmark case was the *Pennsylvania Association for Retarded Children (PARC) v. The Commonwealth of Pennsylvania* (1972). This suit was brought against the State for failing to provide access to public education for all children with mental retardation. The lawsuit resulted in a court order to develop educational services for children with mental retardation in the state. The court decreed that these children be educated in a program as similar as possible to that provided to students without disabilities.

Mills

The second landmark case was *Mills v. Washington D.C. Board of Education* (1972). In the Mills case, parents brought a class action suit against the District of Columbia for failing to provide a publicly supported education for all children. Again, the court ordered that educational opportunity include students with disabilities.

Normalization

At the time these historical court cases were being heard in the courts, the principle of normalization was being introduced (Wolfensberger, 1972). This set the stage for improvement of public attitudes toward persons with disabilities. The principle of normalization called for emphasizing normal environments and behavior. The incorporation of normalization as a public policy had a significant impact on deinstitutionalization (Murdick, Garten, & Crabtree, 2002) and the growth in special education programs, and created the conditions that escalated the framing of public policies in the education of children and youth that persist today.

Equal Rights

Important!

The legislative history of establishing equal rights for persons with disabilities was characterized by a targeted, systematic, and sustained effort on the part of advocacy groups at both state and national levels. The goal was to establish laws that would result in more equitable and nondiscriminatory policies and practices. In many ways this history has paralleled the civil rights movement for racial equality.

An example of a civil rights case that influenced subsequent legislation on behalf of persons with disabilities was the *Brown v. Board of Education* (Topeka, Kansas) court decree in 1954. This decree established the right to equal educational opportunity based upon the Fourteenth Amendment. It recognized that education of any "class of children" separately, even if done in equal facilities, is intrinsically unequal because of the stigma attached to segregation and because of the denial of association with children from other classes.

The Focus on Public Policy

Central to public policies underlying the education of children and youth with disabilities in the United States is a commitment to compulsory public education for all and the need for nondiscriminatory practices. Historically, students whose learning attributes varied from the norm were often overlooked in the implementation of these principles. That has been particularly true of young people with disabilities. In fact, circumstances did not begin to improve until parents and others with particular interests in the educational needs of these children and youth realized that public policy was not going to change until policy makers understood the need for public policy directed to the specific needs of persons with disabilities.

As a way of stimulating the development of special education programs, in the 1950s states began to subsidize local districts that elected to provide special services. To ensure accountability, states established eligibility criteria for access to special education services and for receipt of special state financial aid. In sparsely populated rural areas, where a district might have only three or four students with similar disabilities, several districts joined together so they had a sufficient number of children to justify establishing a class. In some states, multicounty cooperative units were organized to create a sufficient population base to support the provision of comprehensive special education services. Indeed, to this day cooperative models are an effective means of delivering services to students with exceptional learning needs in some rural areas.

As special education services increased, the demand for specially trained teachers emerged. Teaching programs began to expand, and colleges and universities started to offer summer programs in teaching methods so practicing teachers could receive emergency certificates to teach in special education.

Today, public policy is specific at state and federal levels alike in terms of the nature of the educational programs and services that students with disabilities are entitled to receive. And due process procedures are in place to ensure that students with disabilities and their families have proper recourse if the public policies are not fully implemented by their local schools.

The Framework for Structuring and Implementing Public Policy

Public policy governing the education of children and youth with disabilities is set by acts of Congress. Because of state and local responsibilities for public education, the process is very much a partnership. Thus, all levels of the educational structure have obligations for framing and implementing public policy. As a teacher, you will be expected to understand the public policies that your state and district have translated into procedures and practices. Professional development opportunities and resources will be made available to you, along with consultation from specialists in your district, to assist you in adhering to these policies in your teaching role.

Briefly, four levels in the organizational structure are involved in implementing public policy in the delivery of special education services and programs:

1. Office of Special Education Programs in the Department of Education at the federal level
2. State Education Agencies (SEAs)
3. Intermediate Education Units (IEUs)
4. Local Education Agencies (LEAs)

4 levels in organizational structure to implement pub. policy

Each state has a department of education, the SEA, with a unit dedicated to special education programs, but the LEAs have the primary responsibility for delivering educational services. Table 1.1 gives a description of the services provided at each level.

It is important to keep in mind that, though the name of the Office of Special Education Programs at the federal level has changed over the years, there is only one such office, and once the name has changed, it remains constant until restructuring occurs. The names of SEA, IEU, and LEA, however, vary by state. For example, in your state the SEA may be called the State Department of Public Instruction or some similar name.

An IEU is an organizational structure between the local education agency and the state education agency. In several states IEUs are set up by county boundaries. Others encompass several counties. Still other states ignore county lines and allow adjoining districts to organize as IEUs. IEUs provide varied services. Some have taxing powers, and others obtain funds from SEAs and by contracting with LEAs. Some states created IEUs specifically to serve special education programs. Other states developed IEUs to offer broader educational services. IEUs also vary in the name given to them.

TABLE 1.1	
Responsibilities of Education Agencies	
Agency	**Function**
U.S. Department of Education Office of Special Education and Rehabilitative Services (OSERS) Office of Special Education Programs (OSEP)	■ Serves as a resource to Congress in legislation ■ Enforces implementation of federal laws ■ Administers federal funds to state and local education agencies ■ Provides leadership in stimulating research and personnel training
State education agency (SEA)	■ Establishes rules and regulations for the approval of local educational programs serving exceptional children and youth ■ Serves as resource to the state legislature on matters relating to special education ■ Provides leadership in statewide planning to ensure equal educational opportunity ■ Serves as the major source for appeal in disputes involving the education of exceptional children and youth ■ Serves in a liaison role in coordinating services to families ■ Monitors compliance of local districts in meeting state and federal requirements ■ Provides leadership inservice training
Local education agency (LEA)	■ Provides appropriate educational programs and services for all exceptional children and youth ■ Implements programs in compliance with state and federal regulations ■ Conducts inservice training to ensure that all educational personnel are effective in meeting the needs of exceptional students ■ Maintains due process procedures ■ Serves as liaison with community agencies in coordinating programs for exceptional children and youth
Intermediate education unit (IEU)	■ May provide direct services to exceptional children and youth ■ Complies with state and federal regulations governing the education of exceptional children and youth ■ Often contracts with LEAs to provide transportation for special exceptional children and youth ■ Generally operates inservice training programs as part of an instructional materials center (IMC)

Contemporary Legislation

Although state and local educational agencies have the primary responsibility for implementing public policies, federal legislation provides the laws with which the state and local educational agencies must comply. This legislation is summarized here.

Section 504 of the Rehabilitation Act of 1973

The amended Section 504 of the Rehabilitation Act of 1973 was the first civil rights law that specifically prohibited discrimination against children and adults with disabilities (Turnbull, Turnbull, Shank, Smith, & Leal, 2002). The law specified that

> *No otherwise qualified individual with a disability in the United States...shall, solely by reason of her or his handicap, be excluded from participation in, be denied the benefits of, or be subjected to discrimination under any program or activity receiving Federal financial assistance....—29 U.S.C. § 794(a)*

Section 504 made a significant impact on a broad array of programs or activities such as states and school districts that received federal monies to educate students with disabilities. Other important provisions included equal access to programs and services such as architectural accessibility (e.g., ramps) for individuals with disabilities and the provision of auxiliary aids such as an interpreter for a student who is deaf.

Under Section 504, public programs that received federal funding were required to make "reasonable accommodations" for individuals with disabilities (Yell, 1998). For example, a school might have to give a student with exceptional learning needs extended time to complete a test. This in part resulted from the possibility of losing federal funds as a consequence of noncompliance. Also, some of the provisions of the act focused on requirements that were very public.

For example, the requirements related to architectural accessibility included policies that were observable (e.g., absence of curb cuts). Thus, many individuals who did not have a disability as defined by the law also benefited from the elimination of architectural barriers. This caused the public to begin seeing the universal value derived from meeting the needs of persons with disabilities.

Americans with Disabilities Act of 1990

Although Section 504 mandated that "reasonable accommodations" be made for students with exceptional needs, it was limited in scope because its provisions for individuals with disabilities applied only to public programs and activities that received federal financial assistance. Programs and activities in the private sector were not prohibited from discriminating against individuals with disabilities. To try to cover this gap, the Americans with Disabilities Act (ADA) was passed in 1990 as the second civil rights law (it went into effect in 1992). ADA remains the most encompassing antidiscrimination law to specifically guarantee the rights of individuals with disabilities because it extended the provisions of Section 504 by prohibiting discrimination for persons of all ages and types of disabilities in the private sector as well (Yell, 1998).

The private and public sectors covered under ADA were employment (e.g., jobs at privately owned companies), transportation (e.g., buses), state and local government activities and programs (e.g., prisons), places of public accommodations (e.g.,

[Handwritten margin notes:]
504 required:
"reasonable accommodations" (public domain only)

ADA:
all ages ÷ types of disabilities covered; but in private sector as well as public.

restaurants), and telecommunication services (e.g., pay phones). For example, employers could not discriminate against individuals with disabilities during the application process or pay them differently than others. Like Section 504, the ADA had broad application for the public. The ADA did not focus just on educational or public agencies. It had major implications for the business world and it raised the concern of the public to the needs of persons with disabilities. The ADA also yielded benefits to the public beyond those specific to persons with disabilities such as ramps and elevators in movie theaters.

handicapped accessibility!

Education for All Handicapped Children Act of 1975 (PL 94-142)

Although Section 504 and ADA prohibited discrimination on the basis of disability, these laws did not guarantee educational opportunities for students with exceptional needs. In response to this need, in 1975 Congress passed PL 94-142, the Education for All Handicapped Children Act, declaring that public schools must provide an equal educational opportunity to all students with disabilities, including students with severe and profound disabilities (implementation of PL 94-142 began in 1978). These fundamental changes were accompanied by a philosophical shift among educators away from advocacy of separate programs for students with disabilities toward advocacy of integration for students with special needs into general education classes.

PL 94-142:
• free education
• IEPs
• equal ed. opp. for severe & profound
• least restrictive environment (mainstreaming)
• Ages 3-21 yrs!

PL 94-142 came about through the hard work of parents, advocacy groups, and professionals who were dissatisfied with the inadequate and inappropriate educational services provided to children with disabilities at that time. Prior to passage of PL 94-142, Congress recognized that more than half of the 8 million children with disabilities in the United States were not receiving an appropriate education, more than 1 million children with disabilities were entirely excluded from the educational system, and many families were forced to find and pay for services because of the inadequate services provided within the public education system (Ysseldyke & Algozzine, 1995).

Perhaps the most significant provision of PL 94-142 was that it mandated a *free appropriate public education* (FAPE) for all students with disabilities between the ages of 3 and 21 (Meyen, 1995). To receive federal funds, states had to comply with the mandates of the law, which included developing a plan of policies and procedures to put in place a FAPE and proper identification of students with disabilities. To ensure that students received a FAPE, schools had to develop an Individualized Education Program (IEP) for each student receiving special education services. The IEP was to serve as a blueprint to guarantee that the student's educational plan was appropriate for his or her needs.

In addition to having an IEP, PL 94-142 mandated that each student be educated in the *least restrictive environment* (LRE). Although the LRE varied for students depending on their individual needs, students with disabilities were expected to be educated with their peers without disabilities to the maximum extent appropriate. In the 1970s this generally took the form of instructional and social integration or *mainstreaming* of students with disabilities into the general education setting for a specific period of time during the day (e.g., lunch, recess). Later in the chapter we discuss other important principles or tenets of this law, which still guide our teaching practices for students with disabilities. By specifying educational practices and broadening the individuals that schools are responsible for serving, PL 94-142 has become the core of the legislative foundation for special education.

Amendments to PL 94-142

In 1983, amendments were made to PL 94-142 (PL 98-199), which established the Early Intervention Program for Infants and Toddlers with Disabilities. This program provided grants to states with early childhood grants to develop and offer early intervention services for families with children who have disabilities, from birth through age 2.

In 1986, PL 94-142 was amended again (PL 99-457) to include a new Preschool Grants for Children with Disabilities Program for children with disabilities ages 3 through 5 (USDE, 2000). To receive federal assistance, states now were required to provide FAPE for preschoolers with disabilities. The 1986 amendments also required that an *Individualized Family Service Plan* (IFSP) be developed for infants and toddlers with disabilities. The 1983 and 1986 amendments expanded services for this age group and established interagency collaborative arrangements. We will return to early childhood special education and the IFSP in Chapter 3.

*includes:
birth - 2 yrs
IFSP (IEP for family)*

Regular Education Initiative

In 1986 the Office of Special Education and Rehabilitative Services (OSERS) released a report entitled "Educating Children with Learning Problems: A Shared Responsibility" (Will, 1986). This report proposed a much stronger relationship between general and special education. It acknowledged the shortcomings of special education practices at that time and called for more integration of students with disabilities in general education.

That report had a significant effect on special education, the preparation of teachers, and the responsiveness of general education to the needs of students with disabilities. These changes led the way to the full-inclusion model that has emerged today with support of legislation as the contemporary model for the education of students with exceptional learning needs. As schools restructure to accommodate diverse learners, students with exceptional learning needs are but one of several groups of learners who bring to the classroom attributes that add to diversity. Their needs are no longer viewed as those of a separate set of learners but, instead, as contributors to the wide array of learner attributes to which teachers must respond in meeting the needs of all students in their classrooms. The shift is much more than a philosophical change, and it continues to evolve. It is the dominant model you will experience as you begin your teaching career in special education.

Individuals with Disabilities Education Act (IDEA)

In 1990 Congress reauthorized PL 94-142 and renamed it the Individuals with Disabilities Education Act (IDEA) (PL 101-476). IDEA expanded the range of children served to include those with autism and traumatic brain injury as individual categories, separate from emotional disturbance. IDEA also added a comprehensive definition of transition services for students 16 years and older, and definitions for "assistive technology device" and "assistive technology service."

Furthermore, IDEA expanded early education services for children ages 3–5 and defined transition services for infants and toddlers into early education. Particular attention was given to clarifying the language and achieving more acceptable terminology, such as substituting the term "disabilities" for "handicapped" in the title to emphasize the *individual* before his or her disability. When combined with Section 504 and ADA,

*PL 94-142 +
- autism ;
traumatic brain injury*

IDEA offered the most favorable public policy for ensuring equity to students with disabilities and their families, thereby adding significantly to the quality of life throughout the lifespan of people with disabilities.

The Language of Public Policy

In most fields of study, traditional terms take on different meanings over time and new terms are added to the nomenclature. That is especially true in special education, in which a series of terms, each with particular meanings and each serving to enhance communication, has evolved. These terms will be introduced in greater detail later. Nevertheless, in developing an overall perspective of special education and its evolution as a field of study, it is helpful from the start to understand the meaning of some general terms that are prevalent in public policy related to special education. These terms include *exceptional*, *handicapped*, *disability*, *categorical*, and *challenged*. As you continue your work with students and the public in general, you will be responsible for using appropriate terms and not using labels in a manner that is detrimental or stigmatizing to individuals with disabilities.

Exceptional/Handicapped

Includes gifted & talented

Exceptional refers to the wide range of children with handicapping conditions and special abilities who require instructional modifications and/or special education, including the gifted and the talented. *Handicapped* refers to a wide range of children with conditions requiring instructional modifications or special education, but not including the gifted and the talented. Currently, use of the term *handicapped* is discouraged because it refers to the person instead of the condition of having a handicap.

Disability/Handicap

Disability denotes a specific condition such as a heart ailment, loss of a limb, or paralysis. More precisely, the term refers to the inability to perform a certain function or the condition itself, not its impact on the person. *Handicap* describes the consequences of a disability. That is, a person becomes handicapped if he or she is limited functionally by a disability. Some individuals are able to function effectively in spite of a disability; others are not. Thus, a disability may become a

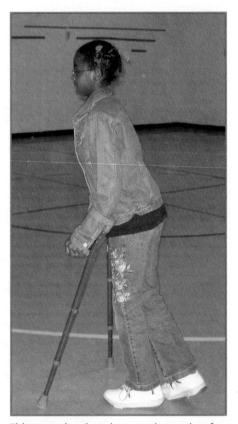

This exceptional student needs crutches for her disability but is still able to participate in all school activities, including physical education class.

handicap for some but not for others (Hallahan & Kauffman, 2003). For example, a hearing loss may result in a serious disability for some, whereas others may find ways to effectively compensate for their hearing loss.

Categorical/Noncategorical

Categorical refers to a specific type of exceptional child—for example, one with mental retardation, or deafness, or emotional disturbance. A type of exceptionality constitutes a category. When special education programs are organized to serve children by type of exceptionality, they often are referred to as *categorical programs*. By contrast, *noncategorical* refers to programs based on instructional needs rather than type of exceptionality. For example, children with different disabilities may have similar instructional needs in areas such as language, math, and reading. Thus, noncategorical programs emphasize common instructional needs rather than the cause of the need (disability). These programs sometimes are referred to as *interrelated*.

Challenged

Recent efforts to minimize the negative connotations of terms applied to students with disabilities have resulted in the preferential use of the term *challenged*. For example, a student with an orthopedic disability is said to be physically challenged. *Challenged* is supposed to convey an understanding of what a student with a disability is experiencing.

The Purpose and Definition of Special Education ■ ■ ■ ■ ■

Up to this point we have discussed public policy, federal legislation, and terminology without a clear connection of how this applies to children and youth with disabilities in educational settings. What is special education? What makes special education so special? Within IDEA, *special education* is defined as specially designed instruction, at no cost to the parents or guardians, to meet the unique needs of a child with a disability [20 U.S.C. 1400 § 602(25)]. The education should be individualized, provided in various settings, and designed to meet the unique needs of the student.

Under IDEA, a student is eligible for special education services if he or she has a disability *and*, because of the disability, the student has exceptional learning needs and would benefit educationally from specially designed instruction (Turnbull, Turnbull, Shank, & Smith, 2004). Thus, not all students with disabilities are eligible and/or need special education services. For example, a student could have a health impairment such as asthma but not require special education services because the health impairment does not affect his or her learning.

[handwritten margin note: What is Sp. Ed.? – defined – eligibility]

Types of Special Education Services ■ ■ ■ ■ ■

In addition to special education services, many students with disabilities require related services so they can access the specially designed instruction to meet their individual

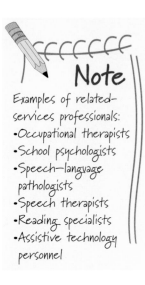

learning needs. Without these additional services, many students with disabilities would not benefit from special education services or could be placed in more restrictive environments. For example, occupational therapy might improve a student's fine-motor skills for writing, which would allow him or her a wider range of educational opportunities. Within IDEA, these additional services are referred to as *related services* and may be developmental, corrective, or supportive, and conducted either directly or indirectly [20 U.S.C. 1400 § 602(22)].

Direct services refer to the services provided directly to the student by specialists such as occupational therapists or speech therapists. A number of related-services professionals (itinerant teachers) are specially trained personnel, such as school psychologists, occupational therapists, and speech–language pathologists, who directly or indirectly provide services to students and their families. Depending on the nature and severity of their needs, students may receive services from a related-services professional daily or two to three times a week. Students also may receive support services such as transportation from home to school and/or adaptive physical education, as well as personnel for assistive technology. Not all students with disabilities receive or require related services to benefit from their special education.

Dominant Models of Service Delivery for Students With Exceptional Learning Needs

Another aspect that makes special education so special is that the instruction and placement are individualized for the student's specific needs. Thus, the specific instruction and types of services provided to the student wholly depend on the student's educational needs to enhance his or her educational performance (not on what is available to the student). Therefore, IDEA mandates that schools offer a variety or *continuum of services* and educational placements for students with disabilities [IDEA, 20 U.S.C. §1401(25)], ranging from the most inclusive to the most restrictive settings.

As mentioned, placement decisions for these students vary according to their exceptional learning needs and individual attributes. Furthermore, the level of restrictiveness of the placement is determined by requirements of the students' individual needs. Typically, the level of restrictiveness *increases* as students require additional instructional resources and services. We will briefly describe the most typical options for students with disabilities. Keep in mind that different school districts and even schools will vary in the types of service delivery models available to students, and the names also may have different meanings. It is important for you to understand the structure of service delivery in your local school district.

In addition to the continuum of placements, a number of professionals with different roles and responsibilities help to meet the instructional needs of the students with disabilities and provide them with support and related services. Within special education the teacher's primary role is to provide the student with instruction specific to the student's educational needs. Depending on the individual student and placement, a student with exceptional learning needs may receive instruction from multiple teachers or a combination of teachers. With the parents and students, the main roles and responsibilities of the teachers and related services personnel are to monitor and implement the student's IEP. We will return to the IEP and IEP meetings later in the chapter.

General Education Class/Classroom Teacher

The general education classroom is considered the least restrictive setting because the students' instructional needs are accommodated primarily in the general education classroom with peers who do not have disabilities. Today, full inclusion in the general education classroom is a philosophical preference of many parents and advocates of students with disabilities. Students in this placement may receive supplementary aids and services or related services within or outside the general education class as long as they spend at least 80% of the school day with their nondisabled peers in the general education setting.

If the student with a disability has a full-inclusion placement in the general education class, the student's main teacher is the general education classroom teacher. The student and teacher, however, may receive additional support from a *full-inclusion support teacher*, who acts as a consultant to, or co-teacher with, the general education teacher and can help resolve instructional or behavioral problems specific to individual students. This teacher also may develop curriculum, plan and monitor behavior modification programs, conduct assessments, and coordinate the IEP meetings with parents and school staff.

full - inclusion support teacher

Resource Specialist Program/Resource Specialist

In most schools a common alternative to the general education classroom is the *resource specialist program* (RSP). This is the second most common placement for students with learning disabilities, after the general education classroom (USDE, 2003). Students with disabilities in this placement receive special education and related services in the resource room for 21%–60% of the school day. The key element is not the

This student meets with her general education teacher and full-inclusion support teacher to chat about her academic and social needs in the classroom.

room but, rather, the role of the teacher and the way by which the teacher delivers instruction.

Generally, students attend the resource room for 1–2 hours each day, individually or in small groups, to receive more individualized instruction from a resource special-ist teacher. Sometimes the RSP teacher will "push in" his or her services and work with the student in the general education classroom. The goal is to improve the student's aca-demic performance so he or she can function effectively in the general education set-ting. The RSP teacher provides supplemental instruction and should not be regarded as the primary source of instruction.

Special Class/Special Education Teacher

Students placed in special classes, commonly referred to as a *special day class* (SDC), are those whose exceptional learning needs cannot be met in the general education set-ting with RSP services. Students in the SDC are self-contained—meaning that the other students in the class have similar learning or behavioral needs. These students receive special education and related services outside of the general education classroom for more than 60% of the school day, although they may be mainstreamed into the general education class for certain periods of the day or be pulled out for additional services.

More than 20% of students with exceptional needs are placed in this type of setting (Hallahan & Kauffman, 2003). In this placement the teacher is typically a certified spe-cial education teacher who has received specialized training in a K–12 certification/cre-dential program. The special education teacher is the primary source of instruction and is responsible for the students' entire curriculum across all content areas (e.g., reading, math, science, social studies). These classes tend to be smaller so the students can receive more individualized attention and instruction.

Separate School Facility   *Rutland Academy*

Students in a separate school facility receive special education and related services in a special day school for students with disabilities (private or public) for more than 50% of the school day. Placement in special day schools in the community is considered to be significantly more restrictive than the special day class in a neighborhood school.

Residential Facility

Settings in 24-hour-care residential facilities outside the home are considered the most restrictive. Students in these placements receive education in a public or private residen-tial facility for more than 50% of the school day.

Homebound/Hospital Setting   *Serves reg'l & sp. ed. students*

Funding jointly between sp. ed. & regular ed. sources

Some students with disabilities have orthopedic or other health-related problems that cause them to miss a lot of school time. To minimize interruptions to their education, a special teacher may be employed to provide instruction to the student at home or in a hospital setting. A major feature of these two placements is that the primary role of the special teacher is to coordinate instruction with the student's teacher(s) at the school site to help the student maintain progress and not fall too far behind.

Paraprofessionals

Paraprofessionals (also referred to as instructional assistants) may be a major resource to students with exceptional learning needs. Whether in general education classrooms or special day classes, paraprofessionals can provide meaningful support to students with a disability, as well as the other students in the class. Well-trained paraprofessionals can lead instruction in small groups and help to maintain behavior management plans. Still, the person who is primarily responsibility for the students' instruction is the classroom teacher!

Identifying Exceptional Children ■ ■ ■ ■ ■ ■

Because special educations programs historically have been the beneficiary of federal and state subsidies, eligibility requirements for receiving special education services have routinely been defined through federal and state legislation. Although this practice continues today, the criteria for eligibility are more focused on the educational needs of the learner and instructional options than the cause of their learning problems. Special attention also is given to developing definitions and eligibility criteria that minimize the probability that a child will be inappropriately placed in special education programs. This is an important focus of today's laws. The reason is that large numbers of students who have records of underachievement do not have a disability. Although they need instructional assistance, their needs may vary from those of students with disabilities. As a teacher, you will be expected to understand the eligibility requirements of your state that govern the assignment of students to you. It is also important to be sensitive to learner attributes suggesting that a student may be inappropriately identified as needing special education services.

As mentioned earlier, during the 1950s, students with special needs were grouped by disability or by age, and their educational needs were defined largely by their characteristics. Today the process of how we "define" exceptionality has shifted, based on how the child's needs match the features of special education programs. Thus, a child becomes "identified" as exceptional when he or she meets the criteria for special education services set by the state education agency. Unfortunately, one consequence of this approach is that children are referred to by labels such as "learning disabled" or "emotionally disturbed" to be eligible to receive special education services for a specific group of students.

Currently, IDEA recognizes 13 types of exceptionalities under which students aged 6–21 may be eligible to receive special education services [20 U.S.C. 1400 § 602(3)]. Although some characteristics and behaviors overlap across the groups, each type of exceptionality represents a discrete cluster of attributes. IDEA requires that these students receive a free and appropriate public education (FAPE). Although the names of the types of exceptionality vary slightly across the states, special education services are generally provided to students within these broad categories (USDE, 2003):

- specific learning disabilities
- speech or language impairments
- mental retardation
- emotional disturbance
- multiple disabilities

- hearing loss
- orthopedic impairments
- other health impairments
- visual impairments
- autism
- deaf–blindness
- traumatic brain injury
- developmental delay (applicable only to children ages 3 to 9)

Since 1975, when PL 94-142 was mandated, there has been a pattern of expanding the range of students eligible for special education. We can anticipate that this pattern will continue. As Congress reauthorizes IDEA every five to seven years, consideration will be routinely given to determine if any additional groups of children with exceptional learning needs should be receiving special education services. During your career as a teacher, you may see the definition of children with disabilities expanded.

Note

Much time is spent evaluating children, their skills, and their needs to ensure that they are not misidentified or inappropriately placed in special education programs.

Defining Students With Exceptional Learning Needs

Throughout the chapters of this book, we will discuss each of the following disability groups in more detail. The upcoming chapters will provide more detailed descriptions of the disability, characteristics of students, possible causes, and strategies for instruction and intervention. Here we will provide a brief introduction of how IDEA defines each disability. Keep in mind that definitions of disabilities have changed over the years as more becomes known about disability conditions. You can anticipate that the definition and/or eligibility criteria of the various disabilities will change during your teaching career.

Specific Learning Disabilities *largest group!*

Students with specific learning disabilities (LD) represent the largest group of students with disabilities, comprising half of all students served under IDEA. Students with LD have difficulty in one or more of the basic psychological processes involved in understanding or in using language, spoken or written, which may manifest itself in an imperfect ability to listen, think, speak, read, write, spell, or do mathematical calculations. In most cases the student has a severe discrepancy or gap between his or her potential (intelligence) and actual achievement. For example, a student may be the math whiz in her fourth-grade class but be able to read at only a first-grade level.

Speech or Language Impairments *2nd largest group*

Students with speech or language impairments (SLI) comprise the second largest group of students served under IDEA. These students have exceptional learning needs in the areas of language and communication skills (also called communication disorders). For example, a student with an SLI may have a stuttering problem or have difficulty receiving, understanding, organizing, and composing written or verbal ideas and information.

Mental Retardation

Students with mental retardation (MR) represent the third largest group of students served under IDEA. These students have exceptional learning needs in the areas of intelligence and adaptive behavior. For example, a student with mental retardation may have difficulty remembering multiplication facts or applying the values of money in a restaurant setting.

Emotional Disturbance

Students with emotional disturbances (ED) represent the fourth largest group of students served under IDEA. These students are a heterogeneous group with exceptional learning needs in the areas of social and emotional skills and behavior. Many of these students also have academic or learning problems. For example, a student with ED may display hostile behavior toward other students and/or withdraw from the classroom setting altogether.

Multiple Disabilities

Students with multiple disabilities have concomitant (a combination of) impairments and thus have two or more disabilities simultaneously. For example, a student may have mental retardation as well as a hearing loss. These students generally require extensive supports in a variety of need areas, such as adaptive skills and communication, which cannot be accommodated in special education programs solely for one of the impairments.

Hearing Loss

Students with hearing loss have exceptional learning needs in areas related to their use of hearing. These students have hearing loss, whether permanent or fluctuating, which adversely affect their educational performance. If the hearing loss is very severe, the student may be considered deaf. These students typically communicate orally, through sign language, or through a combination of the two.

Orthopedic Impairments

Students with orthopedic impairments, also referred to as *physical disabilities*, have exceptional learning needs in areas related to the movement and use of their hands, arms, legs, feet, or other body parts. This group represents a broad group of students whose orthopedic impairment, such as an amputation of the arm, adversely affects their educational performance. Students with orthopedic impairments are diverse, including, among many others, cerebral palsy, spina bifida, bone tuberculosis, and fractures or burns.

Other Health Impairments

Students with other health impairments include students with exceptional learning needs who have serious illnesses or medical conditions. Students in this group represent a wide range of health conditions that limit strength, vitality, or alertness enough to adversely affect their academic performance. Examples of health impairments include diabetes, epilepsy, heart condition, tuberculosis, rheumatic fever, nephritis, asthma, sickle cell anemia, hemophilia, lead poisoning, leukemia, and many others.

Visual Impairments

Students with visual impairments have exceptional learning needs related to their use of vision. Students in this group encompass a wide range, including those who have low vision, are partially seeing, are functionally blind, or are totally blind. For example, a student may have such a severe visual impairment that he or she learns to read using Braille rather than traditional text.

Autism

Students with autism have a specific developmental disability that falls within a broader group of disorders known as *pervasive developmental disorders* as used by the American Psychiatric Association. Students with autism have a wide range of characteristics and abilities, but they typically have exceptional learning needs in the areas of communication and social interaction. For example, a student with autism may prefer to interact with objects rather than people and may have limited communication and speech skills.

Deaf–Blindness

Students with deaf–blindness have exceptional learning needs related to their uses of hearing and vision. The term *deaf–blind* means concomitant hearing and visual impairments, the combination of which causes such severe communication and other developmental needs that the student cannot be accommodated in special education programs solely for deaf or blind children. For example, a child who is deaf–blind may need an individualized program that uses a sensory (touch) mode of communication.

Traumatic Brain Injury   *Not Ss born w/ impairments!*

Students with traumatic brain injury have experienced a brain injury as a result of an external physical force or an internal occurrence (e.g., stroke). This group of students includes those who have incurred open and closed brain injuries but not children who are born with brain injuries or injuries that result from birth trauma. Students with traumatic brain injury may share similar characteristics with students who have speech and language impairments, physical disabilities, health impairments, learning disabilities, mental retardation, or emotional disturbance (Appleton & Baldwin, 1998).

Developmental Delay   *Ss between 3-9 yrs only.*

Children with developmental delays are those between 3 and 9 years of age who have delays in one or more of the following areas of development: physical, cognitive, communicative, social or emotional, or adaptive. For example, a child with a developmental delay may be slightly behind his or her peers and have difficulty learning the letters of the alphabet or counting from 1 to 100. Because of their young age, it is hard to judge whether children with developmental delays are just "late bloomers" or will be eligible to receive special education services under a different type of exceptionality such as learning disabilities.

Incidence and Prevalence of Students With Exceptional Learning Needs

Each year, states are required to report to the Office of Special Education and Rehabilitation Services (OSERS) the number of children receiving special education services. These data then are included in the *Annual Report to Congress on the Implementation of the Individuals with Disabilities Education Act*. This is one way of keeping Congress informed and prepared to meet its legislative responsibilities in education. You will find this report to be a useful reference as you continue your studies in special education.

Definitions

The terms *prevalence* and *incidence* are commonly used synonymously to refer to the number of students served. *Prevalence* refers to the current number of exceptional children. *Incidence* refers to the number of children who at some time in their lives might be considered exceptional. Because incidence figures are harder to verify, we use prevalence data to infer incidence rates.

Prevalence by Age Group

In 2001, the number of infants and toddlers served under IDEA was 247,433 (USDE, 2003). This figure represents a 31% increase since 1998 and comprises 2.1% of the infants and toddlers in the United States. In 2001, 620,195 preschool children with disabilities ages 3 to 5 received services under IDEA. This represents a 47% increase from the preschool children served since 1991 and also comprises 5% of the total 3-to-5 age population in the United States. During this same period the number of students with exceptional learning needs ages 6–21 served under IDEA was 5.867 million (USDE, 2003). These students comprise of 11.5% of the general school enrollment for prekindergarten to the 12th grade. The prevalence of students with disabilities in all categories, however, has steadily increased in the last decade.

Prevalence Across Disability Groups

The prevalence of students with disabilities also varies across the disability groups and across the states. The distribution of prevalence, however, is heavily represented in four major types of disabilities: specific learning disabilities (50%), speech and language impairments (19%), mental retardation (11%), and emotional disturbance (8%). In fact, almost 88% of students aged 6–21 served under IDEA were classified under one of these groups in 2001–02 (USDE, 2003). Students of color and English Language Learners are overrepresented in these disability groups. We will return to overrepresentation of students from culturally and linguistically diverse backgrounds in chapter 2.

Prevalence Distribution

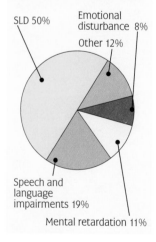

SLD 50%

Emotional disturbance 8%

Other 12%

Speech and language impairments 19%

Mental retardation 11%

Six Principles of Public Law 94-142 ■ ■ ■ ■ ■ ■

Over time, as a teacher, you will adopt principles based on your experience that will guide your teaching. You probably already hold certain beliefs on which many of your instructional practices will eventually be based. In contrast to general education, in which the curriculum and conditions that support classroom teachers are well established, the situation is different for special education teachers. Special education is still evolving and dependent on public policy to create the conditions essential to effective instruction.

We will discuss the six principles or tenets of PL 94-142 that make it possible for quality instruction to be provided to students with disabilities today. As a future special educator, you must understand the significance and implications of these tenet, as they are the foundation on which we base educational services for students with disabilities. These principles are (a) zero reject, (b) nondiscriminatory evaluation, (c) appropriate education, (d) least restrictive environment, (e) procedural due process, and (f) parent and student participation (Turnbull & Turnbull, 2000).

Zero Reject

important

Prior to 1975, access to public education was not a right for all children and youth. For years, local boards of education were allowed to ignore or resist parents' efforts to gain admission of their children with disabilities to the local schools. Thus, the first principle of PL 94-142 (and now IDEA) is *zero reject*. This principle basically forbids states and local school districts to exclude students with disabilities from educational programs. Thus, all students with disabilities between the ages of 3 and 21 have the right to full educational opportunities and a free appropriate public education.

The most important zero reject concept is that it ensures that all students with disabilities have *access* to education. This practice, the target of advocates for decades, brings equity to children with disabilities on a par with peers.

Nondiscriminatory Evaluation

Once students have gained access into the school system, the next step is to evaluate their capabilities and instructional needs accurately and fairly for eligibility purposes. Thus, the second principle is to provide each student with a *nondiscriminatory evaluation*. This refers to assessing the individual's abilities and needs in order to plan for an appropriate education based on each of his or her strengths, weaknesses, and exceptional learning needs.

Keep in mind that an education that is appropriate for one student may be totally inappropriate for another student even if they have the same type of disability. This reflects the complexity of teaching students with disabilities. There may be more variability among and within students with disabilities than among students who do not have disabilities.

Simply evaluating the student is not enough to fulfill this principle. States and local school districts must assess students in a manner that is both unbiased and nondiscriminatory. This part of the provision is necessary because of past discriminatory evaluation practices against students from diverse cultural backgrounds and students with physical or sensory disabilities. The intent of this principle is to ensure that the assessment is fair, and that students with disabilities are able to demonstrate, through the assessment, what they are able to do and not do.

This team of teachers meets with one of their students to discuss his IEP for the upcoming year.

Appropriate Education

Once the student has received a nondiscriminatory evaluation, the next step is to provide the student with an *appropriate education* based on results of the evaluation. This is the third principle. An appropriate education is one that is individually tailored and designed to fit each student with a disability, and one in which the student benefits from the instruction. Congress believes that the best way to achieve this principle is for states and local school districts to develop an IEP for each student with a disability aged 3 through 21. Infants and toddlers under the age of 3 must have an Individualized Family Services Plan (IFSP) to meet the requirements of an appropriate education.

The IEP and the IFSP are written documents developed by a team (usually members of the evaluation team) that must include the student's parents and a general education teacher (for the IEP). Essentially, the IEP states the student's educational goals and special education needs with regard to instruction, related services, and supplementary aids. Schools are required to review each student's IEP annually to see whether the student has achieved the set goals or if components in the IEP have to be revised (Meyen, 1995). Although the IEP is a useful tool to help guide instruction, many special education teachers feel burdened and overwhelmed with the amount of time and paperwork involved. We will discuss the IEP throughout the text.

Least Restrictive Environment (LRE)

The *least restrictive environment* (LRE) principle complements the appropriate education principle because two factors in providing students with disabilities an appropriate education are to ensure (1) that they have access to the general education curriculum, and (2) that they are being educated with students who do not have disabilities, to the maximum extent possible. These two provisions are at the core of the LRE principle. In essence, the law presumes that students with disabilities can receive effective instruction in the general education environment and that related services or supplementary aids should be provided in the general education classroom as well (whenever appropriate).

Future educators must keep in mind that special education is a *service* provided to students with disabilities, rather than a place where they are sent. Therefore, removing students from the general education setting should be seen as almost a last resort, used only if the severity of the student's disability or needs dictates it [20 U.S.C. 1400 § 612(5)]. In some cases, however, the LRE for a student with a disability may be in a special class or even a special school.

Procedural Due Process

If the parents/guardians of the students with disabilities believe the SEA and the LEA are not complying with the four principles just mentioned, they have the right to protest on behalf of their children. Thus, *procedural due process* constitutes the fifth principle. Many people perceive this principle as creating a litigious and adversarial atmosphere in special education, and sometimes it does. But the right granted to parents under procedural due process is more than just the right to take school districts to court. The goal is to make the best decision for the student, and parents have a right to influence this decision.

Two important components under procedural due process are the rules for *parental consent* and *procedural safeguards*. LEAs must obtain *informed parental consent* before they can evaluate or place any student into a special education program. This means that states and local school districts must present information to parents in a way they can comprehend it (e.g., in native language) and find it meaningful. Parents' consent also must be in writing, and they need to be informed that they can revoke their consent at any time during the evaluation process. To evaluate infants/toddlers for early intervention programs, service providers must obtain written parental consent before any evaluations are conducted or services provided.

Besides consent, parents must be given a copy of the procedural safeguards that are available to them. The notice of procedural safeguards is a written document explaining, in an understandable way, parents' rights and regulations under the law, including independent educational evaluations, access to school records, confidentiality of records, and complaints against the SEA or LEA. If parents do have a complaint, they are highly encouraged to resolve the dispute through mediation with an impartial third party. If the two parties cannot resolve their differences through mediation, the parents have the right to have a due process hearing with an impartial hearing officer. Despite the high cost of due process hearings, in terms of finances, emotions, and time, the parents' right to express discontent is valuable and necessary. The challenge is to get more disputes resolved through mediation and thereby prevent the high cost of hearings.

Parent and Student Participation

The sixth principle, *parent and student participation*, focuses on parents' right to be actively involved in their child's special education program. One way to reduce the number of disputes between parents and LEAs is to strengthen the role of parental participation in their child's education. This can be accomplished by providing parents with information regarding their child's progress, allowing them to express their concerns, and having them become full participants during discussions and decisions related to their child's educational program. In addition, parents have the right to access or challenge the content of their child's school records, through the Family Educational Rights and Privacy Act (FERPA). Parents also have the right to object to the release of certain information about their child, to protect family privacy.

As a future educator, a primary goal should be to make the parents of your students full partners in their child's education. With the LEA and parents working on the same side in the child's best interest, perhaps we can diffuse some of the adversarial nature of special education and invest the time, money, and energy spent in disputes back to the children that we serve.

1997 Reauthorization of the Individuals with Disabilities Education Act (IDEA)

When IDEA was reauthorized in 1997 (PL 105-17), Congress discovered that, although IDEA was successful in ensuring students with disabilities had *access* to a free appropriate public education, their progress in these programs was impeded by (a) "low expectations" concerning students with disabilities and special education programs, and (b) "an insufficient focus" on applying research-based methods of teaching and learning for those students [20 U.S.C. Sec 1400(c); Turnbull et al., 2002]. Congress realized that, through 20 years of research and experience, a lot more information had become known about students with disabilities and special education since the inception of PL 94-142. Many of these findings, such as having high expectations for students, were not being upheld for students receiving special education services.

Two important provisions included in IDEA '97 continue to have significant implications for current practitioners in special education and general education alike. IDEA '97 mandated that students with disabilities participate in the general curriculum and be included in district and statewide assessments and that states and districts develop and implement alternative assessment programs for students who cannot participate in the standard assessments (Goertz, McLaughlin, Roach, & Raber, 1999).

In addition, the performance of students with disabilities must be reported as part of the overall results for all students (Kampfer, Horvath, Kleinert, & Kearns, 2001). Simply putting a student with a disability in a general education classroom, however, does not guarantee that he or she will have access to the curriculum (Smith, 2004). To provide access to the general education curriculum, students will have to receive classroom accommodations and modifications that are individualized and tailored for their needs. We will return to this topic when we discuss instructional design and practices.

Passage of the No Child Left Behind Act of 2001 (NCLB) (PL 107-110) further increased the pressure on schools to raise the academic performance of all students on large-scale assessments (e.g., statewide assessments). NCLB requires states to implement statewide accountability systems for all students in public schools, based on state standards. This means that states are required to test annually all students in reading and mathematics (grades 3–8) and develop annual statewide progress objectives to ensure that all groups of students reach proficiency levels or better by the year 2013–2014. In addition, assessment results and state progress objectives must be disaggregated by income, race, ethnicity, disability, and English proficiency.

To include more students with disabilities in their large-scale assessments, many states now are allowing them to take the assessments with accommodations.

Note

NCLB was designed to do exactly what its name says: leave no child behind. That is, NCLB is meant to ensure academic success for all children, letting no child fall through the cracks.

Accommodations are changes in the presentation or mode of response of the testing materials and/or changes in the testing procedures (Koretz & Hamilton, 2000). The accommodations, however, should not change the construct of what is being measured (Thurlow, Ysseldyke, & Silverstein, 1995). Currently, the accommodations allowed for students with disabilities are grouped into four broad categories: (1) presentation/format, (2) response, (3) setting, and (4) timing/scheduling (Thurlow, 2000). In theory, providing students with accommodations on large-scale assessments can level the playing field because they ensure that the students' disabilities do not interfere with their abilities to demonstrate competency and that the assessment will accurately measure the students' knowledge and skills in a specific area (Johnson, Kimball, Olson–Brown, & Anderson, 2001). All of the states have developed written guidelines of their own regarding appropriate test accommodations for students with disabilities. Most of the states, however, recognize the importance of the IEP and leave the accommodations decision to the IEP teams (Thurlow, Elliot, & Ysseldyke, 1998).

The inconsistent and/or unsystematic use of accommodations may have serious implications for students with disabilities, especially if results of the assessments will be used to determine promotion, graduation, or even if a diploma or certificate of completion will be given. If these "high-stakes" decisions are being made, or if schools are being sanctioned based on the performance of the students with disabilities on large-scale assessments (e.g., statewide assessments), the differential allocation of accommodations might affect test results by benefiting certain students while disadvantaging others (O'Neill, 2001). As a future teacher, you will have to find out whether your state participates in *high-stakes assessment* and what accommodations are allowed for students with disabilities.

2004 Reauthorization of the Individuals with Disabilities Education Act

On December 3, 2004, Congress enacted the Individuals with Disabilities Education Improvement Act of 2004 (IDEA; Public Law 108-446). The statute makes significant changes to the Individuals with Disabilities Education Act of 1997 in several areas. One of the major components within IDEA 2004 is the requirement that all special education teachers be highly qualified. This is parallel to the teaching standard required by NCLB. Other major changes are related to the IEP, transition services, the evaluation process for students considered to have learning disabilities, and discipline policies. In the next section we highlight some of the major changes in these areas.

One of the most critical requirements found in the new IDEA is the addition of the definition of a highly qualified special education teacher. In order to be considered highly qualified, teachers must have (a) a bachelor's degree, (b) full state certification or licensure, and (c) subject-matter competency in the core areas (e.g., English, math, science) that they teach. In order to demonstrate competency, secondary teachers must have majored in the subject, have credits equivalent to a major, pass a state-developed test, receive an advanced certification from the state, or have a graduate degree in the subject. Current teachers can meet the highly qualified requirement by going through the High, Objective, Uniform State Standard of Evaluation (HOUSSE) process, which consists of a combination of teaching experience, professional development, and knowledge in the subject.

This definition applies only to public elementary and secondary school special education teachers and is consistent with the definition set by NCLB. The requirement does not apply to special education teachers who are only providing consultative services to other teachers who are highly qualified (e.g., general education teachers). Teachers who have students who are assessed based on alternate academic achievement standards must have subject-matter knowledge at the elementary level or above. As new teachers it is very important for you to inquire about how your state and/or district is implementing and monitoring the highly qualified requirement.

Other important changes in IDEA 2004 were made to the IEP, both in the content and the process of conducting IEP meetings. The intent of these changes is to reduce the amount of time special education teachers spend on IEP paperwork and/or in meetings. One of the changes is to remove the requirement to include benchmarks or short-term objectives (except for students who take alternate assessments) in the statement of annual measurable goals. However, a description of how the student is making progress toward the annual goals will be measured and periodically reported (e.g., through report cards) and must be included in the IEP. Another critical component that must be included in the student's IEP is a statement of any individual appropriate accommodations that he or she needs to participate in state- or districtwide assessments. If the IEP team determines that the student should take an alternate assessment, there needs to be statements as to why he or she cannot participate in the regular assessment and the specific alternate assessment that would be appropriate. Another change in the content of the IEP deals with transition services. In IDEA 1997, the requirements for transition services were included in the student's IEP beginning at age 14 or younger. Now the postsecondary goals and transition services must be included in the first IEP after the student turns 16. With regard to IEP meetings, IDEA 2004 allows for members of the team to submit their input in writing and be excused from attending the IEP meeting, as long as they have the written consent of the parents and the public agency. In addition, if the parent and the public agency agree not to hold an IEP meeting to make changes to the student's IEP (after the annual IEP), they can develop a written document to amend or modify the current IEP without holding an IEP meeting. The parent and public agency can also agree to use alternative ways to hold meetings and handle administrative matters such as through video conferencing or conference calls.

Another important change in IDEA 2004 is the way in which children suspected to have learning disabilities will be evaluated for special education services. In the past, these children were identified with a learning disability when there was a significant discrepancy present between their achievement and intellectual ability. There were many problems with this model, ranging from delayed interventions to the cost and time needed for the IQ testing. Thus, the reauthorized IDEA allows states not to reqire school districts to use the discrepancy model to determine the presence of learning disabilities. Instead, the preferred method, called the Response to Intervention model, is to examine whether the child responds to scientific, research-based interventions in general education. Given that there are a variety of alternative methods, it is important for you as a new teacher to be aware of the state and local procedures used to evaluate students with suspected learning disabilities.

Finally, IDEA 2004 makes substantial changes to the way in which students with disabilities are disciplined in the public school setting. One critical change is to the process of the manifestation determination. A *manifestation determination* is a process in which the IEP team determines whether or not the student's behavior that caused the disciplinary action that resulted in his or her removal from school for more than 10 days was directly related to his or her disability. The 2004 reauthorization puts the burden of proof on the parents to prove that the student's behavior was caused by or had a direct and substantial relationship to the disability or to prove that the behavior was a direct result of the district/school's failure to implement the IEP. Prior to this new mandate, the burden of proof was on the school district. IDEA 2004 also deletes the requirement for the team to consider whether the IEP, services, and placement were appropriate and appropriately implemented or if the child's disability impaired his or her ability to understand the impact and consequences of the behavior or the ability to control the behavior, unless it is specified in the IEP. As a new teacher, it is important for you to be aware of these changes so that you may properly inform parents who have children with emotional and/or behavioral needs about the discipline policies followed by your state and district.

Summary

There are few roles in education where the professional must possess an in-depth understanding of the laws that govern how children are served, but this is true for special education teachers. Resource people will be available to you, and detailed guidelines will be provided, but the expectation is that you understand eligibility requirements, the principles of IDEA, and your personal responsibilities as a special education teacher. This is in addition to your knowledge and skills in curriculum and instruction.

The reason for these additional requirements relates to the legislative history of how special education evolved. Without legislated public policies, the exceptional learning needs of children and youth most likely would not have been addressed in the public schools. Certainly, we would not have the special programs, knowledge base, and array of professionals committed to meeting the needs of these students had it not been for the advocacy of many groups to bring about the public policies that prevail today. This does not mean that the public policies governing the education of students with special needs have yielded the ultimate in education. Much remains to be learned about how best to meet their exceptional learning needs.

Throughout this book you will be provided an opportunity to add to your knowledge of the foundation that undergirds what is important to know as a beginning teacher. In many ways this is an added challenge. You must be a skilled teacher, and also must have broader knowledge of the public policies that contribute to the emerging practices in special education.

References

Appleton, R., & Baldwin, T. (1998). *Management of brain-injured children.* New York: Oxford University Press.

Gearheart, B. R. (1980). *Special education for the 80's.* St. Louis, MO: Mosby.

Goertz, M. E., McLaughlin, M. J., Roach, V., & Raber, S. M. (1999). What will it take? Including students with disabilities in standards-based education reform. In T. Parrish, J. Chambers, & S. Guarino (Eds.), *Funding special education: Yearbook of the American Education Finance Association* (pp. 40–61). Thousand Oaks, CA: Sage Publications.

Hallahan, D. P., & Kauffman, J. M. (2003). *Exceptional learners: Introduction to special education* (9th ed.). Boston: Allyn & Bacon.

Individuals with Disabilities Education Act Amendments of 1997. 20 U.S.C. Section 1400.

Johnson, E., Kimball, K., Brown, S. O., & Anderson, D. (2001). A statewide review of the use of accommodations in large-scale, high-stakes assessments. *Exceptional Children, 67*(2), 251–264.

Kampfer, S. H., Horvath, L., Kleinert, H. L., & Kearns, J. K. (2001). Teachers' perceptions of one state's alternate assessment: Implications for practice and preparation. *Exceptional Children, 67*(3), 361–374.

Koretz, D. & Hamilton, L. (2000). Assessment of students with disabilities in Kentucky: Inclusion, student performance, and validity. *Educational Evaluation and Policy Analysis, 22*(3), 255–272.

Meyen, E. L. (1995). Legislative and programmatic foundations of special education. In E.L. Meyen & T.M. Skrtic (Eds.), *Special education and student disability* (4th ed., pp. 35–95).

Murdick, N., Garten, B., & Crabtree, T. (2002). *Special education law.* Upper Saddle River, NJ: Prentice Hall.

O'Neill, P. T. (2001). Special education and high stakes testing for high school graduation: An analysis of current law and policy. *Journal of Law and Education, 30*(2), 185–222.

Smith, D. D. (2004). Introduction to special education: Teaching in an age of opportunity (5th ed.). Boston: Allyn & Bacon.

Thurlow, M. L. (2000). Standards-based reform and students with disabilities: Reflections on a decade of changes. *Focus on Exceptional Children, 33*(3), 1–16.

Thurlow, M. L., Elliot, J. L., & Ysseldyke, J. E. (1998). *Testing students with disabilities: Practical strategies for complying with district and state requirements.* Thousand Oaks, CA: Corwin.

Thurlow, M. L., Ysseldyke, J. E., & Silverstein, B. (1995). Testing accommodations for students with disabilities. *Remedial and Special Education, 16*(5), 260–270.

Turnbull, H. R., & Turnbull, A. P. (2000). *Free appropriate public education: The law & children with disabilities* (6th ed.). Denver: Love Publishing.

Turnbull, R., Turnbull, A., Shank, M., & Smith, S. (2002). *Exceptional lives: Special education in today's schools* (3d ed.). Upper Saddle River, NJ: Prentice Hall.

Turnbull, R., Turnbull, A., Shank, M., & Smith, S. (2004). *Exceptional lives: Special education in today's schools* (4th ed.). Upper Saddle River, NJ: Prentice Hall.

U.S. Department of Education. (2000). *To assure the free appropriate public education of all children with disabilities: Twenty-second annual report to Congress on the implementation of the Individuals with Disabilities Education Act.* Washington, DC: Author.

U.S. Department of Education. (2003). *To assure the free appropriate public education of all children with disabilities: Twenty-fifth annual report to Congress on the implementation of the Individuals with Disabilities Education Act.* Washington, DC: Author.

Will, M. C. (1986) Educating children with learning problems: A shared responsibility. *Exceptional Children, 52*(5), 411–415.

Wolfensberger, W. (1972). The principle of normalization. *Mental Retardation, 21*, 234–239.

Yell, M. L. (1998). *The law and special education.* Upper Saddle River, NJ: Prentice Hall.

Ysseldyke, J. E., & Algozzine, B. (1995). *Special education: A practical approach for teachers.* Boston: Houghton Mifflin.

Cultural, Linguistic, and Instructional Diversity

2

Yvonne N. Bui, Alicia Moore, & LaVonne Neal

ased on the 2000 U.S. Census, "We the People" means 282 million Americans (U.S. Census Bureau, 2004). Today's changing demographics suggest that the United States is becoming more culturally and linguistically diverse. In particular, increases in racial diversity and the number of children living in poverty are salient demographic trends that impact the U.S. educational system.

Demographic Trends

Unlike 50 years ago, when schools and classrooms were composed primarily of a homogeneous student population, today's schools and teachers are increasingly challenged with educating students from diverse cultural, linguistic, and economic backgrounds. At the same time, more students from culturally and linguistically diverse backgrounds are being identified with high-incidence disabilities such as learning disabilities, emotional disturbance, and speech and language impairment. As special educators, we are faced with the question, "What does this mean for schools, curriculum and instruction, and, finally our individual teaching practices?"

Cultural Diversity

As mentioned in chapter 1, the Supreme Court decision in the case of *Brown et al. v. Board of Education* in 1954 brought to the forefront of the American educational system the importance of preparing teachers to be able to teach culturally diverse children. Today, understanding how to teach children who are culturally and linguistically diverse continues to receive major emphasis as a result of the numerical and percentage growth of these student populations in our public schools. Because of immigration and higher fertility rates among people of color, it is expected that 50% of all students will be children of color by 2025, and 50% of Americans will be people of color by 2050 (see Table 2.1).

Moreover, racial lines are becoming more blurred. For the first time, the 2000 census allowed respondents to report themselves in multiple racial/ethnic categories. At least 40% of all Americans have had some racial mixing in the last three generations. As a special educator, this means that a large proportion of the students in your classroom or on your caseload will come from a variety of ethnic groups, possibly different from your own.

Children Living in Poverty

Another trend that affects education is the crucial need for teachers to understand the implications of poverty as another form of diversity within school settings. Over the past three decades, the number of American families living below the poverty line has increased dramatically, from 24.2 million in 1969 to 35.6 million in 1997 (Dalaker & Naifeh, 1998). Unfortunately, poverty has become a particular concern for children, as rates of *families* living in poverty have increased by 5% from 1973 (Fujiura & Yamaki, 2000).

| TABLE 2.1 Projected Population of the United States by Race and Hispanic Origin: 2000 to 2050 |||||||

(In thousands except as indicated. As of July 1. Resident population.)

Population or Percent and Race or Hispanic Origin	2000	2010	2020	2030	2040	2050
POPULATION						
TOTAL	282,125	308,936	335,805	363,584	391,946	419,854
White alone	228,548	244,995	260,629	275,731	289,690	302,626
Black alone	35,818	40,454	45,365	50,442	55,876	61,361
Asian Alone	10,684	14,241	17,988	22,580	27,992	33,430
All other races 1/	7,075	9,246	11,822	14,831	18,388	22,437
Hispanic (of any race)	35,622	47,756	59,756	73,055	87,585	102,560
White alone, not Hispanic	195,729	201,112	205,936	209,176	210,331	210,283
PERCENT OF TOTAL POPULATION						
TOTAL	100.0	100.0	100.0	100.0	100.0	100.0
White alone	81.0	79.3	77.6	75.8	73.9	72.1
Black alone	12.7	13.1	13.5	13.9	14.3	14.6
Asian Alone	3.8	4.6	5.4	6.2	7.1	8.0
All other races[1]	2.5	3.0	3.5	4.1	4.7	5.3
Hispanic (of any race)	12.6	15.5	17.8	20.1	22.3	24.4
White alone, not Hispanic	69.4	65.1	61.3	57.5	53.7	50.1

[1]Includes American Indian and Alaska Native alone, Native Hawaiian and Other Pacific Islander alone, and Two or More Races

Source: U.S. Census Bureau, 2004, "U.S. Interim Projections by Age, Sex, Race, and Hispanic Origin," <http://www.census.gov/ipc/www/usinterimproj/
Internet Release Date: March 18, 2004.

The following is a snapshot of the impact of poverty of children in the U.S. (National Center for Children in Poverty, 2004):

- *"Approximately 38% of American children under the age of 18 now live in "low-income" families (less than $28,500 for a family of three with one child)" (p. 1).*
- *"Some 16%—almost 12 million—of all U.S. children live in poverty (less than $14,255 for a family of three with one child)" (p. 1).*
- *"The child poverty rate is highest for African American (30%) and Hispanic American (29%) children. The poverty rate for Caucasian children is 13%" (p. 2).*

As these statistics indicate, children from culturally diverse backgrounds who live in geographically concentrated urban neighborhoods are most affected by poverty

(Dalaker & Naifeh, 1998; McLoyd, 1998). Families living in high-poverty communities (compared to their counterparts residing in more affluent neighborhoods) are disadvantaged by having reduced accessibility to jobs, high-quality private and public services, and informal social supports (McLoyd, 1998).

In addition, families that live in high-poverty neighborhoods have increased exposure to environmental stressors such as street violence, homelessness, illegal drugs, and negative role models (Duncan, 1991; Jargowsky, 1994; Shinn & Gillespie, 1994; Zigler, 1994). Numerous studies have also reported the significant adverse effects of poverty on children's cognitive and verbal skills development (Korenman, Miller, & Sjaastad, 1995; Liaw & Brooks–Gunn, 1994; Smith, Brooks-Gunn, & Klebenov, 1997).

Faced with these conditions, it is easy to feel helpless, give up, or blame the growing array of educational problems on students, their diverse culture and language, and family/socioeconomic background. As educators, however, we must find ways to support our students and help them succeed within the school system. It is important to get to know your students. What are their lives like outside of the classroom? By being aware of the students' lives, you will be able to link them to needed resources and become a more effective and caring educator.

> **Note**
>
> Having a diverse student population can create a classroom environment that fosters more enriched learning opportunities, both socially and academically for the students and the teacher.

Homogenous School Staff

As the student population in the United States continues to become more heterogeneous, the demographics of the school staff have become more homogenous (Santos, Fowler, Corso, & Bruns, 2000; Taylor, 2000). This incongruity between teachers' and students' cultural background, values, and behaviors can be a source of misunderstanding and influence teachers' reactions to students' culturally conditioned behaviors. Further, Moore (1997) concluded that teachers', of color as well as European American teachers' reactions to students', culturally conditioned behaviors affect students' self-concept. These misunderstandings also can lead to social failure for students from culturally diverse backgrounds (Moore, 1997; Neal, McCray, Webb-Johnson, & Bridges, 2003).

Getting to know your students involves first getting to know your own culture. By reflecting upon your own worldview, values, perspective, and biases (we all have them), you will be in a much better position to compare how your culture resembles, or is different from, your students' cultures. Keep in mind that there is no one "right" culture. This will help reduce the level of miscommunication and misunderstandings between you and your students.

Disproportionate Representation in Special Education

One major consequence of the incongruity between the personal and academic frames of reference of teachers and their students is a gap in understanding that may place the two groups at odds. Specifically, researchers have linked this gap to special education referrals and have identified cultural differences between students and teachers as a factor that may lead to a disproportionate representation of students who are culturally and/or linguistically diverse in special education programs.

Disproportionate representation refers to having a significantly higher or lower percentage of students who receive special education services than their percentage of the school population as a whole. Thus, disproportionality can refer to either "over" or "under" the level representative of the general population. Chinn and Hughes (1987) have suggested that disproportionality can be determined using the following formula: If more than 10% of any given student population is represented in the special education population, that student population is overrepresented in special education.

Students Served Under IDEA

The majority of students served under IDEA are served under the following four categories of disabilities (U.S. Department of Education, 2003) (see Table 2.2):

1. Specific learning disabilities
2. Speech or language impairments
3. Mental retardation
4. Emotional disturbance

Disproportionality Across Cultural Groups

Although the number of students receiving special education services has increased steadily across most disability categories in the past decade, African American, Hispanic, and Native American students tend to be overrepresented in programs for students with emotional disturbance, learning disabilities, mental retardation, and speech/language impairments, and underrepresented in gifted and talented placements. For example, although African American children and youth represent 17% of the school-age population, they represent 34.2% of all children receiving special education services for mild and moderate mental retardation and 27.3% of students in programs for emotional/behavior disorders (McCray, Webb-Johnson, & Neal, 2003). By contrast,

---

TABLE 2.2

Students Ages 6–21 Served Under IDEA in the 1991–92 and 2000–01 School Years

Category	1991–92	2000–01	Percent Change
Specific learning disabilities	2,247,004	2,887,217	28.5
Speech and language impairments	998,904	1,093,808	9.5
Mental retardation	553,262	612,978	10.8
Emotional disturbance	400,211	473,663	18.4
Multiple disabilities	98,408	122,559	24.5
Hearing impairments	60,727	70,767	16.5
Orthopedic impairments	51,389	73,057	42.2
Other health impairments	58,749	291,850	396.8
Visual impairments	24,083	25,975	7.9
Autism	5,415	78,749	1,354.3
Deaf–blindness	1,427	1,320	-7.5
Traumatic brain injury	245	14,844	5,958.8
Developmental delay	-	28,935	-
All disabilities	4,499,824	5,775,722	28.4

Source: U.S. Department of Education, 24th Annual Report to Congress.

the percentages of Caucasian students in most disability categories are all close to those for the IDEA student population as a whole.

To fully understand the impact of the disproportionate representation of students with cultural and linguistic diversity in special education programs, we must first recognize that this is not a new phenomenon; it has plagued special education for almost four decades. For instance, in 1968, Lloyd Dunn published an article calling attention to disproportionate representation by quoting statistics compiled by the U.S. Office of Education indicating that 60% to 80% of the children in special classes were minority children from impoverished homes. Dunn (1968) questioned the proliferation of special classes, which, he claimed, "raised serious educational and civil rights issues" (p. 7). He described his dissatisfaction with the referral process as follows:

> *I have loyally supported and promoted special classes for the educable mentally retarded for most of the last 20 years, but with growing disaffection. In my view, much of our past and present practices are morally and educationally wrong. We have been living at the mercy of general educators who have referred their problem children to us. And we have been generally ill prepared and ineffective in educating these children. (p. 5)*

In efforts to address this issue, each state has collected data on disproportionate representation since the reauthorization of IDEA in 1997. IDEA decrees that each state shall "provide for the collection and examination of data to determine if significant disproportionality based on race is occurring" (USDE, 2003, p. II-21) when identifying children with disabilities. In January 2002, the National Research Council (NRC) issued a report, *Minority Students in Special and Gifted Education*, that examined factors affecting both the disproportionate representation of minority students in special education and the underrepresentation of minority students in gifted and talented programs.

Multicultural Education

One way teachers and schools can respond to the growing diversity of students with disabilities is to provide multicultural education. This is a field of study and an emerging discipline whose major aim is to create equal educational opportunities for students from diverse racial, ethnic, social-class, and cultural groups. Multicultural education "arose out of the civil rights movement" (Banks, 1995, p. 391) and grew from the cultural pluralism model of the 1960s. Multicultural education was necessary to ensure that teachers received the resources they needed to develop appropriate instructional methods and provide culturally responsive curriculum materials and programs, and the tools to meet the needs of an emerging, diverse group of students.

A major goal of this approach is to mesh the cultural differences of teachers and students by providing a blueprint for teaching diverse students. One way is to utilize instructional strategies that meet students where they are and guide them to the desired outcomes. A goal of multicultural education is to

> *improve the academic success of students of color and preparing all youths for democratic citizenship in a pluralistic society. Students need to understand how multicultural issues shape the social, political, economic, and cultural fabric of the United States as well as how such issues fundamentally influence their personal lives. (Gay, 2003, p. 30)*

At the preliminary level, multicultural education consists of studying cultural elements such as the foods, dances, music, and artifacts from different ethnic groups and historical contributions (e.g., the work of Dr. Martin Luther King, Jr.). To infuse multicultural education to the next level, you can add to the mainstream curriculum a diverse book, unit, or course on diversity. At a more advanced level, changes are made to the basic assumptions of the curriculum that enable students to view concepts, issues, themes, and problems from several ethnic perspectives and points of view.

Since we know that teachers' perceptions of culture-related identities and their manifestations in the classroom are especially relevant to student achievement (Neal, McCray, Webb-Johnson, & Bridgest, 2003), we must take an active role in preparing ourselves now, and in the future, to teach children in ways that provide academic and behavioral avenues for success. African American students, for example, have been found to benefit from culturally responsive teaching that is theoretically grounded in research on teaching effectiveness (Gay, 2000; Irvine & Armento 2001; Ladson-Billings, 1994, 2001; Neal, Webb-Johnson, & McCray, 2003).

Consider the following example of culturally responsive teaching. Middle school students love music and they often want to spend most of their time discussing and studying only music that they know and like. Many music teachers are challenged by hip-hop music and question its place in the academic arena. However, culturally responsive models encourage exploring the poetry of African American artists such as Gil Scott-Heron, Nikki Giovanni, Tupac, India Arie, and Jill Scott. Further, social critique of the past and the present provides opportunities to redefine classical music to include the work of African American composers like Scott Joplin, Duke Ellington, and Quincy Jones. Interdisciplinary study is again important as a pathway to challenge and assist students in deep structural study of music contributions of many. This research asserts

Practicing with sight words on a daily basis can help linguistically diverse students with their reading and writing.

that culturally responsive teaching can be used to make connections between students and teachers who are culturally different. The challenge, however, lies in embracing culturally responsive teaching as a valid teacher practice.

Linguistic Diversity

In addition to cultural differences, a significant implication that demographic changes and immigration has for the public school system is the richness of different languages that students bring with them from their families and communities. Over the past 20 years, the number of 5- to 24-year-olds speaking a language other than English at home increased by 118% to 13.7 million in 1999 (NCES, 2004). In fact, English Language Learners (ELL) (i.e., students who come from homes where another language besides English is spoken) apparently are the fastest growing population in U.S. public schools (Pompa, 2000). In 1999–2000, more than 54% language-minority students were enrolled in public elementary and secondary schools. These students, however, were less likely than students who spoke only English at home to complete high school and more likely to come from low-income households (NCES, 2004).

Although approximately 350 languages are spoken in schools across the nation (Escamilla, 2000), eight languages comprise 85% of the linguistic diversity. These languages are: Spanish, Vietnamese, Hmong, Chinese (Cantonese), Cambodian, Korean, Laotian, and Navajo (Escamilla, 1999). With such a wide range of languages represented in the classroom, one has to wonder about the implications for educators and how we can address the language needs of all these children.

Don't worry. Becoming an effective educator does not mean you will have to learn 8 or 350 new languages! Depending on your geographical region, however, you likely will have students with disabilities in your classroom who do not speak English fluently or who come from households where English is not the primary language. Thus, you might have to adjust your own language so it is comprehensible to your students and access resources when necessary (e.g., arranging for an interpreter for IEP meetings, sending written notices in the parents' home language).

Difference Between Language Difference and Language Disorder

Addressing the needs of the ELL students is a central concern for special educators. First, we must be careful not to equate factors related to language *difference* with disorder or disability. These differential factors include students who are ELL, speak nonstandard dialects, have different communication styles, and/or come from oral cultures (Poplin & Phillips, 1993). As noted earlier, the combined effects of cultural and linguistic differences could be a major factor in the disproportionate referrals of students from these backgrounds for special education services and subsequent overrepresentation in special education settings. This is generally a result of the limited knowledge of school personnel about assessment and effective teaching practices for ELL students (Meese, 2001).

Educators often mistake language difference for language deviance (Flores, Cousin, & Diaz, 1991). As a result, ELL students frequently are misidentified with speech/language impairments or learning disabilities. IDEA mandates that students

Note

Some computer software programs and Web sites, such as www.freetranslation.com, offer simple translation services depending on your needs.

have the right to be assessed in their home language. If you do not speak the student's home language fluently, ask for an educational diagnostician or a school psychologist who is bilingual, or have an interpreter present for any formal assessments.

Relationship Between Language and Culture

Next we have to be careful not to overlook the close connection between a student's language and his or her family, community, and cultural identity. Many of the difficulties that ELL students face in the classroom can be attributed to teachers and other school personnel demeaning their language and cultural differences (Darder, 1991; Macedo, 1994). Thus, unfortunately, some educators still assume that students who are culturally or linguistically different from the mainstream will exhibit deficient academic achievement related to both language and behavior.

No matter what the child's cultural, linguistic, or socioeconomic background, we as educators must value, respect, and scaffold cultural and language *differences* rather than viewing them as deficits. By honoring students' cultural and linguistic differences in the classroom, we can be more effective in reducing their feelings of alienation toward the mainstream culture simply because the child is not forced to choose between the culture/language of his of her family and the culture/language at school.

Second-Language Acquisition

To support ELL students with disabilities in your classroom, you will have to understand how students acquire a second language (i.e., English). One of the best known models of second-language acquisition is Krashen's (1981) Monitor Model, which was proposed in the early 1980s.

Krashen's Monitor Model

The Monitor Model is based on five central hypotheses:

1. Acquisition
2. Natural order
3. Monitor
4. Comprehensible input
5. Affective filter

At the heart of the Monitor Model is the distinction between two linguistic systems—acquisition and learning (Krashen, 1981, 1982). Language acquisition occurs subconsciously as a result of participating in natural communication, whereas learning is the result of conscious or purposeful study of the formal properties of the language. For example, if you have ever studied a foreign language, think of acquisition as occurring when you travel to that country and immerse yourself in the language around you. Learning, on the other hand, would consist of taking a formal course where the grammar and vocabulary of the language are taught. This hypothesis is important as you want your students to *acquire* language so that they can use it on an automatic level.

The next hypothesis in the model is natural order, which indicates that learners follow a more or less consistent order in developing formal grammatical features (Ellis,

1986). For example, learners may first acquire nouns (e.g., *apples, pizza, car*), then verbs (e.g., *walks, talks, eats*), and then pronouns (e.g., *I, he, she*), to finally produce a complete sentence ("She eats apples"). Similarly, learners typically acquire the present tense first ("I have a car"), then the past tense ("I had a car"), and finally the future or more complicated tenses ("I will have a car"). Thus, in the classroom, it is best to start teaching ELL students with disabilities the easiest language concepts (e.g., nouns), followed by more difficult ones (e.g., prepositions).

In the monitoring hypothesis, monitoring is related to the *learning* rather than the acquisition of language. In fact, the items that are learned (e.g., formal rules) become part of what is known as the Monitor. The learner uses the Monitor to edit his or her language performance (see Figure 2.1). Teaching students the formal rules of language (e.g., phonology) is important because in some situations the Monitor can be maximally effective, such as when taking grammar tests, writing papers, or preparing speeches (Richard–Amato, 1996).

The next hypothesis states that acquisition of language occurs when the learner comprehends input that is slightly beyond his or her current level of competence. This concept is commonly referred to as "$i + 1$," where is the "i" represents *comprehensible input* at the learner's level and the "1" represents input slightly above the learner's current level. Therefore, to acquire language, in addition to being relevant and/or interesting, the input should approximate the student's $i + 1$. Thus, your classroom may be the optimal environment for the ELL student with a disability to understand or be understood, especially if you are supplying comprehensible input slightly above the student's level. At times, however, you might have to supplement your verbal input with visual cues.

Finally, the affective-filter hypothesis deals with how emotional factors such as attitude, motivation, and anxiety control the rate of developing a second language (Dulay & Burt, 1977). The affective filter is the device that controls how much input the learner receives and is converted into knowledge (Corder, 1967) (see Figure 2.2). Thus, the items that are acquired are those that must pass through the affective filter, which consists of a person's inhibitions, age, personality, motivation, self-confidence, and so on. For example, if a learner has high motivation and self-confidence with low anxiety,

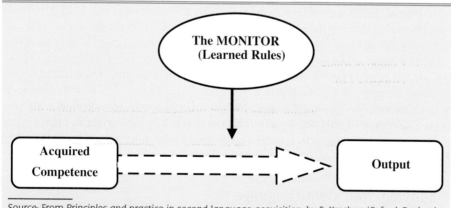

Source: From *Principles and practice in second language acquisition,* by S. Krashen (Oxford, England: Pergamon Press). Copyright © 1982.

FIGURE 2.1
Performance Model

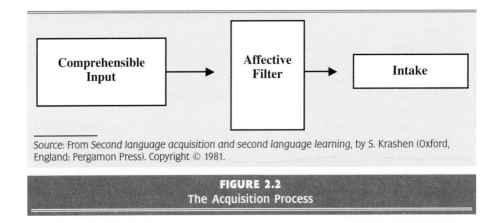

FIGURE 2.2
The Acquisition Process

his or her affective filter will be low and will allow for plenty of input to be received and converted to knowledge. As the teacher, you must create a classroom environment that keeps students' affective filters low so they are able to maximize the amount of learning that takes place.

Silent Period

In addition to keeping affective filters low, we must respect students' silent periods. There is a lag time, or silent period, between when learners begin to understand messages in a new language and when they are able to actually produce it (Asher, 1981; Krashen, 1985; Winitz, 1981). During this time, learners are taking in the language but may not feel confident enough to speak it. The length of the silent period varies depending on the individual learner and the learning environment, lasting from a couple of weeks to several months (Ervin–Tripp, 1974; Gibbons, 1985; Hakuta, 1974; Shannon, 1987).

Therefore, as a special educator, you should not expect your ELL students with disabilities to produce the second language as soon as they are able to comprehend some of it. Instead, this is a good time to provide comprehensible input that is slightly above the students' proficiency levels. Demands for early speech production will be futile and will cause students to increase their affective filters, considerably slowing their language acquisition (Dulay, Burt, & Krashen, 1982).

As this point in your training, understanding the theory of the Monitor Model is not as important as putting it into practice. When teaching ELL students with disabilities in your classroom, the keys are to respect students' silent periods, provide them with comprehensible input slightly above their level, and help reduce their affective filters by creating meaning-rich, supportive, and relaxed classroom atmospheres. Then, allow time for students' language production to emerge naturally.

Modifying Your Own Language

You also can support the ELL students with disabilities in your classroom by paying attention to your own language and communication and modifying it when appropriate. You can modify your language in several ways (Paul, 2001). First, you can reduce the rate of your speech. We often forget how quickly we speak, especially to other adults.

By slowing down a bit, we help students who have difficulty with receptive language and take longer to decode and process spoken messages.

Another modification is to repeat what you say more than once. This also helps students who have attention deficits or mild hearing impairments. These students sometimes ask repeatedly, "What? What did you say?" because they missed the gist of your message the first time (although you may think they are asking just to irritate you!).

Another useful modification is to speak clearly and highlight important words or word order with an exaggerated tone or a heightened vocal emphasis. This is particularly helpful for students who are learning phonology or grammar because it cues them to which words or phrases they should pay more attention.

Finally, make sure that your sentences are slightly longer than the students', that your sentences are grammatically correct, and that the vocabulary is accessible to the students. The students are looking to you as a language model, so your language must be appropriate and accurate. By modeling sentences that are slightly longer and more complex than theirs, you also are showing them how to extend their language skills to the next level.

Dialectal Variations

Some students from culturally and linguistic diverse backgrounds speak dialects different from the standard dialect typically used at school. This also may lead to overrepresentation in special education. Dialects are variations in the standard language rule system (e.g., English), and dialectal differences often are related to racial, ethnic, socioeconomic, situational or contextual, peer-group influenced, and first- or second-language learning factors (Owens, 1992). Most dialects spoken in the United States are variations of Standard English (SE) and share a common set of grammatical rules with SE. Although dialectal differences in SE are subtler than differences that stem from speaking another language, students who express themselves primarily through nonstandard dialects (e.g., Ebonics) are disadvantaged because SE is the major mode of instruction in the classroom. This is true particularly if school administrators and teachers consider the standard dialect as the *only* correct dialect, judging all variations as inferior or deficient.

Perceptions of Nonstandard Dialects

Teachers also may view students who speak a nonstandard dialect as less intelligent than students who speak Standard English. Even though society gives higher status to certain languages and dialects, all languages and dialects are *valid* rule systems and reflect differences rather than disorders or lower forms of language (Owens, 1992). Thus, to view students' languages or dialects as inferior is to view the students and their culture as inferior. As Delpit (1995) stated, "Children have a right to their own language, their own culture" (p. 37).

Difference Between Modeling and Correcting

Giving students the "right to their own language" does not imply that they should not be taught the forms of Standard English. Because SE is regarded with such high status in schools and workplaces, it would be an injustice not to teach it. Nevertheless, teachers must be careful with the approach and teaching methods they use. Teachers should model appropriate language and behavior rather than correct students' errors. For example, when students are reading aloud, teachers must avoid interrupting them to correct dialect-influenced pronunciations (e.g., "dis" instead of "this"). When teachers constantly overcorrect and interrupt students during reading, students have fewer opportunities to become fluent readers.

In addition, emphasizing the code and pronunciation of text takes away the energy students need to comprehend and make meaning from the text. Finally, constant correction while reading will most likely cause the student to raise his or her affective filter, resist reading, and possibly resent the teacher (Delpit, 1995).

Providing Opportunities for Practice

If correction is not effective, what can teachers do to help their students acquire the standard dialect form? Most students from culturally diverse backgrounds come to school with a *receptive* knowledge of Standard English, having heard it spoken on the radio, in cartoons and movies, and in the mainstream society. What teachers have to provide students is a *rationale* for learning the standard dialect (especially if they are older), as well as opportunities for them to use it in multiple contexts.

By providing a rationale (e.g., do well in school, get a job), students will come to understand that their teacher is trying to provide them with more tools to be successful learners and access the culture of power. This can be accomplished by discussing language with students and getting their input about which type of dialect is appropriate for different situations. When discussing languages or dialects with students, teachers should emphasize that students are *adding* another language form to their repertoire so they can code-switch (go back and forth between the two, depending on the social context), not diminishing what they bring into the classroom from home.

Once students understand the rationale for learning how to code-switch between the standard dialect and their own, teachers can incorporate several activities into the classroom curriculum to help them learn how and when to switch. For younger children, a good starting point is to discuss the ways in which television characters from different cultural groups speak. Many superheroes and cartoon characters speak explicit Standard English. Teachers also can bring in children's books written in dialects from different cultural groups or audiotaped stories narrated by individuals from various cultures. By being exposed to different language forms and dialects, students will discover that there is usually more than one way to say the same thing and that certain languages and language uses are more appropriate than others for specific situations. For example, students may use a more formal language inside the classroom than they would in the yard or in the cafeteria with their friends.

Older students can be asked to create bidialectal dictionaries of the nonstandard and standard forms of English. Together, the teacher and students can identify terms, words or phrases, or books that they would like to translate into Standard English. This also presents a good opportunity to incorporate some of the words or music (e.g., rap) from the students' culture. To give students opportunities to practice using Standard English, teachers can have them role-play situations (e.g., job interview), create puppet shows, and mimic newscasters. Incorporating drama techniques allows students the chance to become more familiar with the standard dialect without the threat of correction.

This student is practicing the use of standard English with his teacher by creating a puppet show that other students will later watch.

Inclusive Education

In addition to appreciating the richness that students from a variety of backgrounds bring to the classroom, teachers must embrace diversity in broader terms. In this context, diversity includes differences in ethnicity, race, language, gender, religion, and ability. Today, close to 6 million children and youth with disabilities receive special education services (USDE, 2003). This constitutes a significant number of children who need special services, modifications, or accommodations within their educational settings so they can be successful. A significant implication for general and special education teachers alike is the responsibility of schools to educate children with disabilities in general education classrooms. IDEA 2004 presents this charge as follows:

> To the maximum extent appropriate, children with disabilities, including children in public or private institutions or other care facilities, are educated with children who are not disabled, and special classes, separate schooling, or other removal of children with disabilities from the regular educational environment occurs only when the nature or severity of the disability of a child is such that the education in regular classes with the use of supplementary aids and services cannot be achieved satisfactorily. —20 U.S.C. 1412, Sec. 612 (a)(5)(A)

Difference Between Mainstreaming and Inclusion

As mentioned in chapter 1, the principle of the least restrictive environment (LRE) in Public Law 94-142 evolved into the practice of "mainstreaming" students with disabilities into general education settings. Mainstreaming typically involved sending a student with a disability from a segregated, special education homeroom class to a general education class for specified intervals during the school day. In mainstreaming, the student usually was expected to maintain the academic pace of the rest of the class without significant supplementary aids and services, or was integrated only during lunchtime or other nonacademic periods such as art, music, physical education, and the like. As the special education teacher, your responsibility will be to collaborate and work with other school staff members (e.g., general education teacher, paraprofessionals) to mainstream students with disabilities into general education settings to the maximum extent appropriate.

Under IDEA '97, integrating students with disabilities into the general education classroom further evolved into the philosophy and practice of *inclusion*. Inclusion may be defined as the practice of educating all students, regardless of their strengths or weaknesses, alongside their peers. It allows for the creation of learning communities in the LRE which, within inclusion, is designated to be the general education classroom. Although it is similar to the concept of mainstreaming, inclusion goes beyond the parameters of mainstreaming by offering opportunities for all children to be included in the educational and social aspects of their neighborhood schools and classrooms, not simply placed in the general education setting (Stainback & Stainback, 1990). Inclusion also provides for the necessary supplementary aids and services that allow the student to be successful in the general education classroom "to the maximum extent appropriate" (IDEA '97).

> *The fundamental principle of inclusive education is the valuing of diversity within the human community.... When inclusive education is fully embraced, we abandon the idea that children have to become "normal" in order to contribute to the world....We begin to look beyond typical ways of becoming valued members of the community, and in doing so, begin to realize the achievable goal of providing all children with an authentic sense of belonging. (Kunc, 1992, pp. 38–39)*

Neither the term *inclusion* nor the term *mainstreaming* has been defined specifically by IDEA, yet the implication for their importance to the field of special education is implicit in the wording of the law, which calls for inclusive educational opportunities. Both terms are based on philosophical beliefs that inclusion of students with disabilities in the general education classroom along with their nondisabled peers is an important goal that benefits all involved. This philosophical scaffold has laid the foundation for inclusion as a best-practice special education tenet—a scaffold that has been strengthened by position statements of national organizations such as the Division for Early Childhood (DEC) of the Council for Exceptional Children (CEC), the National Association for the Education of Young Children (NAEYC), the American Association on Mental Retardation (AAMR), and the National Association of the Deaf (NAD).

Yet, even with national position statements endorsing inclusive practices, inclusion continues to be a source of controversy. Specifically, this controversy is surrounded by misconceptions about its effects on children without disabilities, its demands on general education teachers, and disputes between proponents of full inclusion (full-time placement in the general education classroom) and those who favor partial inclusion (limited placement in the general education classroom).

Regardless of the position taken, school districts and teachers will continue to be held accountable for implementing practices that include students who have disabilities in the general education classroom with access to the general education curriculum. If a student with a disability is fully included in a general education classroom, the student's primary teacher is the general education teacher. The special education teacher (e.g., resource specialist, inclusion specialist), however, must collaborate or act as a consultant to the general education teacher with regard to modifying or adapting curriculum.

Nondiscriminatory Evaluation

Despite IDEA's mandate to remove children from the general education setting only as a last resort, the number of children referred for special education services and identified with disabilities has increased dramatically over the past decade. As mentioned in chapter 1, a nondiscriminatory evaluation is one of the requirements of IDEA. The purpose of the evaluation is to determine whether a student has a disability and if the student needs special education and/or related services.

Under IDEA, every student has the right to receive an evaluation (with the informed consent of the parent) that is fair, accurate, and free from cultural/racial bias prior to any initial placement for special education services or the provision of related services. Thus, as a future educator, you will have to understand the process of determining eligibility for special education services, especially as it relates to children and youth from culturally and linguistically diverse backgrounds, to prevent students from inappropriately being referred or being misidentified.

The following questions form a framework for understanding this process:

1. What is the responsibility of school personnel in implementing IDEA?
2. What process is followed when a parent or school representative suspects that a child has a disability?
3. What factors influence the teacher's opinion that the child may have special needs?

In the remainder of the chapter, we will look briefly at the components that make up the identification/evaluation process: screening, prereferral intervention, formal referral, evaluation, eligibility and, finally, individualized planning and placement.

Screening

For most students, the identification and evaluation process begins in the general education classroom. The first structured step in evaluation is *screening* (Turnbull, Turnbull, Shank, Smith, & Leal, 2002). Screening may be formally planned procedures that every student goes through, including vision and hearing tests or large-scale assessments related to academic skills administered by school or district staff. In addition, the teacher may use informal tests, skills inventories, criterion measures, or day-to-day observations. The results of screenings may serve as "red flags" to teachers and staff, alerting them to students with potential problems.

Note

Steps in the identification/evaluation process:
- Screening
- Prereferral intervention
- Formal referral
- Evaluation
- Eligibility
- Individualized planning and placement

The following are examples of questions that teachers should ask themselves before they proceed to the next step, prereferral intervention (Harry & Klingner, cited in Warger & Burnette, 2000):

1. Have hearing, vision, health, etc., factors been eliminated through primary screening?
2. Am I making judgments based my own beliefs about family values (e.g., child abuse, single parent family, parent(s) incarcerated) and on my perceptions about the community in which the child lives (e.g., drug-infested, high crime rate, low socioeconomic status)?
3. Are my instructional strategies and methods building on student strengths as a foundation for learning?
4. Do I feel pressured to refer this child because s/he may not be successful on state mandated assessments?
5. Have cultural or linguistic differences been assessed for possible effects on achievement?
6. Is my classroom instruction developmentally appropriate and culturally relevant?
7. Are my management techniques appropriate?
8. What are my perceptions and attitudes about the student based upon my own beliefs and/or biases?

Prereferral Team and Intervention Strategies

The second step in the nondiscriminatory evaluation is prereferral. This process consists of designing activities "to increase classroom teachers' capacity to instruct and manage

These teachers meet when necessary to discuss students who may need referrals for special education services.

difficult-to-teach students, thereby reducing unnecessary and inappropriate special education referrals—often 'brokered' by one or more support staff, such as a special educator or school psychologist" (ERIC Facility Extranet Entry, 1993). Schools typically take such a proactive approach to meeting students' needs through prereferral interventions conducted by the school's student assistance team (SAT).

Although the term used to designate the prereferral team varies from school to school, including child study team (CST), pupil assistance team (PAT), or some other designation, the team usually is made up of general education teachers, a bilingual educator, a special educator, special area educators (physical education, music, art, etc.), psychologists, speech and language pathologists, counselor(s), and an administrator. It is an informal and collaborative multidisciplinary team that reviews the difficulties a child experiences prior to making a formal referral for special education services.

Specifically, the team's purpose is to suggest classroom modifications or accommodations, or other prereferral intervention strategies such as a classroom management plan as a first line of classroom intervention. As the special education teacher, you may be asked to conduct observations of the student in his or her general education classroom and offer suggestions for accommodations or modifications that the teacher should implement and on which the teacher should subsequently collect data.

The SAT makes every effort to put into place accommodations or modifications that build on the child's strengths rather than the observed areas of challenge. For example, when a child has been identified as needing assistance, the teacher gathers data for the prereferral form that describe concerns to be reviewed by the SAT. Data elements reviewed include, but are not limited to, the following: observational data (collected by the teacher, parent, or other school representative), academic performance, behavioral data, known medical history, social/familial history, and work samples. The SAT uses the information on the prereferral form to discuss the following:

- The child's strengths, weaknesses, and interests
- The child's present level of performance (academic and behavioral)
- Previous accommodations and modifications attempted by the child's teacher
- Intervention strategies that may work, based upon current information
- Person(s) responsible for implementing the interventions

Formal Referral Process

If the general education teacher and the SAT have exhausted all of the prereferral interventions and the student still needs additional assistance, the next step is to initiate a formal referral for a nondiscriminatory evaluation (assessment) for special education services. A referral is the first formal step in the special education process. The referral form is a written statement that specifies the student's behavioral or academic difficulties and explains how these difficulties interfere with the student's learning. This form, typically available in the office of the counselor or other person responsible for special education administration at the school, is filled out by the teacher or whoever is concerned about the student's school performance and believes that the student might have a disability.

Evaluation

Before any evaluations or assessments are conducted, a member of the SAT must notify the student's parent/guardian (in writing in the native language or other principal mode of communication) of the proposed action and why an evaluation is proposed. Written parental consent must be obtained before the school district can conduct any initial evaluations. IDEA 2004 also ensures that the procedures and materials used for the evaluation and placement of children with disabilities are not racially or culturally discriminatory by setting forth the following requirements for Procedures for Evaluation and Determination of Eligibility (PEDE):

> *Each public agency shall ensure, at a minimum, that the following requirements are met:*
>
> *(a)(1) Tests and other evaluation materials used to assess a child under Part B of the Act—*
> *(i) Are selected and administered so as not to be discriminatory on a racial or cultural basis; and*
> *(ii) Are provided and administered in the child's native language or other mode of communication, unless it is clearly not feasible to do so; and*
> *(2) Materials and procedures used to assess a child with limited English proficiency are selected and administered to ensure that they measure the extent to which the child has a disability and needs special education, rather than measuring the child's English language skills.*
> *(b) A variety of assessment tools and strategies are used to gather relevant functional and developmental information about the child, including information provided by the parent, and information related to enabling the child to be involved in and progress in the general curriculum (or for a preschool child, to participate in appropriate activities), that may assist in determining—*
> *(1) Whether the child is a child with a disability under Sec. 300.7; and*
> *(2) The content of the child's IEP.*
> *—20 U.S.C. 1412, Sec. 300.532*

In addition, no single IQ test or other evaluation instrument may be used as the sole determinant of a disability or to determine the appropriate educational placement for a student. Instead, a variety of evaluation instruments must be used that specifically assess the areas of the student's educational difficulties. These instruments must be used to gather data on: (a) pertinent and practical information about the student (provided by the teacher, parent(s), and/or other school personnel); and (b) other related information that will assist in determining the student's educational needs within the general education classroom and will allow the student to benefit from the general education curriculum. As the special education teacher, you may be responsible for administering some of the achievement assessments, but only a trained school psychologist can conduct aptitude (IQ) tests.

Eligibility

Following the assessment and other evaluations, a multidisciplinary team (MDT) meeting is held to discuss the results and decide whether the child is eligible for special education and related services. This team may be referred to by various designations, including admission review dismissal (ARD) committee, multidisciplinary team (MDT), or student support team (SST). Regardless of the name of the team, IDEA 2004 specifies that the individualized education program team is a group of individuals composed of the following:

1. *The parents of the child with a disability*
2. *Not less than 1 regular education teacher of such child (if the child is, or may be, participating in the regular education environment)*
3. *Not less than 1 special education teacher, or where appropriate, not less than 1 special education provider of such child*
4. *A representative of the local educational agency who*
   - *is qualified to provide, or supervise the provision of, specifically designed instruction to meet the unique needs of children with disabilities;*
   - *is knowledgeable about the general education curriculum; and*
   - *is knowledgeable about the availability of resources of the LEA*
5. *An individual who can interpret the instructional implications of evaluation results*
6. *At the discretion of the parent or the agency, other individuals who have knowledge or special expertise regarding the child, including related services personnel as appropriate; and whenever appropriate, the child with a disability.*
—*20 U.S.C. 1412, Section 614(d)(1)(B)*

The team must determine whether the child meets the criteria to be considered a "child with a disability" and in need of special education and related services because of his or her disability. This decision is based upon information from a variety of sources, such as IQ and achievement tests; parent and teacher recommendations; developmental, physical, social, or cultural and linguistic information; and adaptive behavior. The decision to identify a student with a disability for special education services is serious and will greatly affect the student's education and life beyond school. Thus, it should consider all of the data, and it must be a *team* decision.

Individualized Planning and Placement

If the team agrees that the child (a) has a specific disability and (b) needs special education services because of the disability, the team develops an IEP. The team writes goals and objectives in the child's area(s) of need, along with modifications and adaptations designed to provide educational benefit to the student. Options for placement and services are also discussed, along with the identified LRE appropriate for the child. Further, the IEP lists any related services (e.g., speech therapy) the child needs. At times, the IEP and placement decisions take place at the same meeting. At other times, placement decisions are made at a separate meeting (usually called a placement meeting). The child will be placed in the general education classroom to receive services unless the IEP team determines that, even with supplementary aids and services, the child will not attain educational benefit.

As the special education teacher, you may be responsible for leading the initial IEP meeting and subsequent annual meetings and inviting all the parties involved (e.g., parents, administrator, general education teacher). Parents always must be notified of their due process rights, in writing, especially their right to disagree with any decisions regarding their child. Being prepared, organized, collaborative, and professional will produce positive and lasting outcomes for the students and families that you serve.

Summary

You are entering the profession of special education during an era when knowledge of cultural and linguistic differences among learners is more crucial than at any time in history. Diversity among learners has always been present in our public schools and in special education programs. But the demographics of the United States have changed dramatically in recent years, to such an extent that in some districts the majority of students are students of color. At the same time, diversity among teachers has remained largely unchanged.

The challenge for special education teachers is increased by the disproportionate representation of students from minority groups in programs for students with disabilities. In an attempt to avoid inappropriate referrals to and placements for special education services, IDEA requires nondiscriminatory assessment practices. Teacher education and staff development programs also are being improved to prepare general education teachers to teach in multicultural situations more effectively and reduce the number of inappropriate referrals for special education services. As a special education teacher, it will be incumbent upon you to develop the necessary skills and knowledge to be responsive to the cultural and linguistic diversity you may encounter in your classes.

References

Asher, J. J. (1981). Comprehension training. The evidence from laboratory and classroom studies. In H. Winitz (Ed.), *The comprehension approach to foreign language instruction* (pp. 187–222). Rowley, MA: Newbury House.

Banks, J. A. (1995). Multicultural education and curriculum. *Journal of Negro Education, 64*(4), 390–400.

Chinn, P. C., & Hughes, S. (1987). Representation of minority students in special education classes. *Remedial and Special Education, 8*(4), 41–46.

Corder, S. P. (1967). The significance of learners errors. *IRAL, 4,* 161–169.

Darder, A. (1991). *Culture and power in the classroom: A critical foundation for bicultural education.* Westport, CT: Bergin & Garvey.

Dalaker, J., & Naifeh, M. (1998). *Poverty in the United States: 1997.* Current Population Reports, Series P60–201. Bureau of the Census. Washington, DC: U.S. Government Printing Office.

Delpit, L. (1995). *Other people's children.* New York: The New Press.

Dulay, H., Burt, M., & Krashen, S. (1982). *Language two.* New York: Oxford University Press.

Dunbar, P. L. (1984). *Lyrics of lowly life: The poetry of Paul Laurence Dunbar.* Secaucus, NJ: Citadel Press.

Duncan, G. J. (1991). The economic environment of childhood. In A. Huston (Ed.), *Children in poverty: Child development and public policy* (pp. 23–50). New York: Cambridge University Press.

Dunn, L. (1968). Special education for the mildly retarded: Is much of it justifiable? *Exceptional Children, 35*(1), 5–22.

Ellis, R. (1986). *Understanding second language acquisition*. Oxford: Oxford University Press.

Ervin-Tripp, S. M. (1974). Is second language learning like the first? *TESOL Quarterly, 8*, 111–127.

ERIC Facility Extranet Site. Definition for *prereferral interventions*. Retrieved March 2004 from http://ericfacility.net/extra/newauth/thessearchresults.cfm

Escamilla, K. (1999b). The false dichotomy between ESL and transitional bilingual education programs: Issues that challenge all of us. *Educational Considerations, 26*(2), 1–6.

Escamilla, K. (2000, August). *Second language acquisition.* Presentation at the 2000 Bilingual Special Education Summer Institute, Golden, Colorado. Sponsored by the Bueno Center, University of Colorado.

Flores, B., Cousin, P. T., & Diaz, E. (1991). Transforming deficit myths and learning, language, and culture. *Language Arts, 68*, 369–379.

Fujiura, G. T., & Yamaki, K. (2000). Trends in demography of childhood poverty and disability. *Exceptional Children, 66*(2), 187–199.

Gartner, A., & Lipsky, D. D. (1997). *Inclusion and school reform: Transferring America's classrooms*. Baltimore: Paul H. Brookes.

Gay, G. (2000). *Culturally responsive teaching: Theory, research, & practice.* New York: Teachers College Press.

Gay, G. (December 2003/January 2004). The importance of multicultural education. *Educational Leadership, 61*(4), 30–35.

Gibbons, J. (1985). The silent period: An examination. *Language Learning, 35*, 255–267.

Hakuta, K. (1974). Prefabricated patterns and the emergence of structure in second language acquisition. *Language Learning, 24*, 287–298.

Individuals with Disabilities Education Act, 20 U.S.C. §§ 1400 et seq.; 34 C.F.R. §§ 300 et seq.

Irvine, J. J., & Armento, B. J. (2001). *Culturally responsive teaching: Lesson planning for elementary and middle grades*. Boston: McGraw–Hill.

Jargowsky, P. (1994). Ghetto poverty among Blacks in the 1980's. *Journal of Policy Analysis and Management, 13*, 288–310.

Korenman, S., Miller, J., & Sjaastad, J. (1995). Long-term poverty and child development in the United States: Results from the NLSY. *Children and Youth Services Review, 17*, 127–155.

Krashen, S. (1981). *Second language acquisition and second language learning*. Oxford, England: Pergamon Press.

Krashen, S. (1982). *Principles and practice in second language acquisition*. Oxford, England: Pergamon Press.

Krashen, S. (1985). *The input hypothesis: Issues and implications*. New York: Longman.

Kunc, M. (1992). The need to belong: Rediscovering Maslow's hierarchy of needs. In R. A. Villa, J. S. Thousand, W. Stainback, and S. Stainback (Eds.), *Restructuring for caring and effective education: An administrative guide to creating heterogeneous schools* (pp. 25–40). Baltimore: Paul H. Brookes.

Ladson-Billings, G. (1994). *The dreamkeepers: Successful teachers of African American children*. San Francisco: Jossey–Bass.

Ladson-Billings, G. (2001). *Crossing over to Canaan*. San Francisco: Jossey–Bass.

Liaw, F., & Brooks-Gunn, J. (1994). Cumulative familial risk and low-birthweight children's cognitive and behavioral development. *Journal of Clinical Child Psychology, 23*, 360–372.

Macedo, D. P. (1994). *Literacies of power: What Americans are not allowed to know*. Boulder, CO: Westview Press.

McCray, A. D., Webb-Johnson, G., & Neal, L. I. (2003). The disproportionality of African Americans in special education: An enduring threat to equality and opportunity. In C. C. Yeakey & R. D. Henderson (Eds.), *Surmounting all odds: Education, opportunity and society in the new millennium* (pp. 455–485). Greenwich, CT: Information Age Publishing, Inc.

McLoyd, V. C. (1998). Socioeconomic disadvantage and child development. *American Psychologist, 53*(2), 185–204.

Meese, R. L. (2001). *Teaching learners with mild disabilities* (2nd ed.). Belmont, CA: Wadsworth/Thomson Learning.

Moore, A. (1997). *African American teachers' decisions to refer: An exploration of the influences guiding special education student referral by African American early childhood teachers.* Unpublished doctoral dissertation, University of Texas at Austin.

National Center for Children in Poverty. (May 2004). http://www.nccp.org/pub_cpf04.html

National Center for Education Statistics. (2004). *Language minorities and their labor market indicators: Recent Trends.* Washington, DC: Klein, Bugarin, Beltranena, & McArthur.

National Research Council. (2002). *Minority students in special and gifted education* (Committee on Minority Representation in Special Education, Division of Behavioral and Social Sciences and Education, M. Suzanne Donovan and Christopher T. Cross, editors). Washington, DC: National Academy Press.

Neal, L. I., McCray, A. D., Webb-Johnson, G., & Bridges, S. T. (2003). The effects of African American movement styles on teachers' perceptions and reactions. *The Journal of Special Education, 37*(1), 49–57.

Neal, L. I., Webb-Johnson, G., & McCray, A. D. (2003, Spring). Movement matters: The need for culturally responsive teaching. *The Journal of the New England League of Middle Schools,* 28–33.

Owens, R. E. Jr. (1992). *Language development.* New York: Merrill/Macmillan.

Paul, R. (2001). *Language disorders from infancy from adolescence: Assessment and intervention* (2nd ed.). St. Louis, MO: Mosby.

Pompa, D. (2000, August). *Language development for the 21st century.* Presentation at the 2000 Bilingual Special Education Summer Institute, Golden, Colorado. Sponsored by the Bueno Center, University of Colorado.

Poplin, M., & Phillips, L. (1993). Sociocultural aspects of language and literacy: Issues facing educators of students with learning disabilities. *Learning Disability Quarterly, 16*(4), 245–255.

Richard-Amato, P. (1996). *Making it happen: Interaction in the second language classroom.* White Plains, NY: Addison–Wesley Publishing Group.

Santos, R. M., Fowler, S. A., Corso, R. M., & Bruns, D. A. (2000). Acceptance, acknowledgment, and adaptability: Selecting culturally and linguistically appropriate early childhood materials. *Teaching Exceptional Children, 32,* 14–22.

Shannon, S. M. (1987). *English in El Barrio: A sociolinguistic study of second language contact.* Unpublished doctoral dissertation, Stanford University.

Shinn, M., & Gillespie, C. (1994). The roles of housing and poverty in the origins of homelessness. *American Behavioral Scientist, 37,* 505–521.

Smith, J., Brooks-Gunn, J., & Klebenov, P. (1997). Consequences of living in poverty for young children's cognitive and verbal ability and early school achievement. In G. Duncan & J. Brooks-Gunn (Eds.), *Consequences of growing up poor* (pp. 132–189). New York: Russell Sage Foundation.

Stainback, W., & Stainback, S. (1990). *Support networks for inclusive schooling.* Baltimore: Paul H. Brookes.

Taylor, S. V. (2000). Multicultural is who we are: Literature as a reflection of ourselves. *Teaching Exceptional Children, 32,* 24-29.

Turnbull, H. R., Turnbull, A. P., Shank, M., Smith, S., & Leal, D. (2002). *Exceptional lives: Special education in today's schools* (3rd ed.). Upper Saddle River, NJ: Merrill Prentice Hall.

U.S. Census Bureau, Census 2000. http://www.census.gov/ipc/www/usinterimproj/

U.S. Department of Education. (2003). *Twenty-fifth annual report to Congress on the implementation of Individuals with Disabilities Act.* Washington, DC: U.S. Government Printing Office.

Warger, C., & Burnette, J. (2000). *Five strategies to reduce overrepresentation of culturally and linguistically diverse students in special education.* Arlington, VA: ERIC Clearinghouse on Disabilities and Gifted Education. (ERIC Document No. 447627)

Winitz, H. (1981). A reconsideration of comprehension and production in language training. In H. Winitz (Ed.), *The comprehension approach to foreign language instruction* (pp. 101–140). Rowley, MA: Newbury House.

Zigler, E. (1994). Reshaping early childhood intervention to be a more effective weapon against poverty. *American Journal of Community Psychology, 22,* 37–47.

Early Intervention and Secondary Transition: Family and Community Partnerships

3

Keith Storey & Jane Squires

uring the history of special education, we have learned much about how best to teach students with disabilities. Some of what we have learned is in the form of research-based practices, and this knowledge will be integrated throughout the book. Central to the lessons learned are four general principles that have found their way into public policy, and that transcend the full spectrum of individuals who, during their school years, become identified as students with exceptional learning need. These principles emphasize the following:

1. Early intervention
2. A smooth transition into meeting the demands of adult life as productive citizens
3. Community and agency involvement beyond the public schools to provide individuals with disabilities the knowledge, skills, behaviors, and motivations they need to achieve their potential as productive and contributing members of society
4. Family participation in the child's educational program

In many ways it is difficult to sort out the influence of communities and families. For example, we already have looked at the role that parents have played as advocates in bringing about changes in public policies and the responsiveness of communities as they strive to implement these policies.

As someone who has made a decision to study special education, you have already thought about your potential role. And you probably have reflected on how the needs of individuals with disabilities have benefited from the public policies that are now in place. At times you may have been disappointed with the nature of the services provided, but your intuition has helped you understand that, despite the challenges faced by some persons with disabilities, all citizens deserve quality of life and full citizenship in our society.

Early intervention and the transition to adult life represent two programmatic initiatives that have evolved as possibly the most significant contributors to ensuring that individuals with disabilities achieve the quality of life to which they are entitled. Early intervention and transition are discussed in Parts II and III. We are also including these topics here, as their significance warrants a more extensive discussion early in your study of children and youth with exceptional learning needs. This will help you prepare for the chapters focusing on the needs of students specific to disability groups and will be particularly useful as you reflect on your future role in special education and how early intervention and transition programs will benefit the students with whom you will be working.

Early Intervention: The Key to Optimal Outcomes ■ ■ ■ ■ ■

The birth of a child is usually anticipated with great excitement, joy—and some apprehension. What will she look like? Will he be fussy and cry all the time? Will she be "normal," with "all her fingers and toes," and able to play and learn like other children? Birth and the early years bring a time of rapid physical growth, as well as brain and cognitive development, providing the foundations for lifelong learning. If children are born with intact biological systems and are supported by a nurturing and responsive environment, they have the potential for optimal growth and development. Unfortunately, many children are exposed to a variety of risk factors that compromise their early growth and development. These risk factors can be divided into two categories:

1. *Biological risks factors*, including biological insult to the central nervous system such as being born prematurely or with a diagnosed medical disorder such as seizures
2. *Environmental risk factors*, including poverty, physical abuse and neglect, and parental drug and alcohol abuse

Often, these two types of risk—biological and environmental—overlap, such as in the example of Carmen, a mother who lives in poverty conditions, did not have access to prenatal care or healthy food and vitamins during pregnancy, and gave birth six weeks early, following a difficult labor, to a baby with a low birth weight, possible cognitive and language delays, and cerebral palsy.

The transactional model (Sameroff & Chandler, 1975; Sameroff & Feise, 2000; Sameroff, Seifer, Baldwin, & Baldwin, 1994) suggests that biological and environmental risks interact to determine developmental outcomes, and that an appropriate environment, as well as an intact biological and genetic makeup, contributes to maximal outcomes. In addition, development is a result of a series of ongoing interactions between the child and the environment. These transactions—the interactions between the child

CASE STUDY: TAN AND HIS FAMILY

Tan, the son of Carmen and James, is 3 years old. He has a huge smile, big brown eyes, and a healthy laugh. Excited with his new language skills, Tan constantly exclaims "duck!" "tuck!" (truck), as well as "Da," "Ma," and "Kee" (referring to Kareem, his younger brother). Tan has been walking for almost a year, but he is somewhat unsteady because of poor muscle control of his left foot from complications of cerebral palsy.

Tan attends Fox Point Preschool in a classroom of 15 children, where he is one of three children receiving early childhood special education services under the Individuals with Disabilities Education Act (IDEA). He participates in all preschool activities with his peers, including activity centers with writing and other fine-motor activities, drama, block play, snacks, and outdoor play.

An early childhood special education (ECSE) teacher, Therese, visits Fox Point two days a week to ensure that Tan and the other children with special needs are making progress toward the goals and objectives on their Individualized Family Service Plans (IFSPs). Therese leads selected activities, informally assesses Tan on his progress toward his motor, cognitive, and language goals, and advises his preschool teachers on how to integrate learning opportunities into the children's everyday activities. Carmen and James are thrilled with the progress that Tan has made in 3 years.

and his or her parents or caregivers—are the building blocks of early cognitive, motor, and social–emotional development.

The Risk Factors

The current economic conditions in the United States leave many young children without supportive, nurturing environments, and without parents who can attend to their developmental needs. Poverty is perhaps the greatest risk factor facing America's children, with one in six children living in poverty (Children's Defense Fund, 2004). Poverty contributes to premature births, poor health care, increased accidents, and a greater likelihood of exposure to tobacco, disease, violence, and environmental toxins such as lead (Halpern, 2000; Liptak, 1996). Indeed, half of all children with developmental delays come from impoverished environments, which is explained by this double jeopardy, the increased negative effects on development resulting from the interactions of biological and environmental risk factors (Garbarino & Ganzel, 2000; Sameroff & MacKenzie, 2003). Selected biological and environmental risk factors are listed in Table 3.1.

By intervening early, developmental outcomes can be maximized and children can achieve greater self-sufficiency and ability to attain vocational and life goals. The quality of transactions or interactions between the child and his or her environment can be maximized through early specialized instruction so the child receives adequate supports for growth and development.

Thus, the primary goal of early intervention and early childhood special education is to change children's developmental trajectories by remediating delays caused by developmental disabilities such as cerebral palsy, and to prevent secondary disabilities from developing (Sandall, McClean, & Smith, 2000). *Secondary disabilities* are additional difficulties a child experiences related to ineffective interventions for the primary disability. For example, a child who has cerebral palsy as her primary disability may have learning difficulties as well if her academic and learning needs are not met.

TABLE 3.1
Selected Biological and Environmental Risk Factors

Biological Factors	Environmental Factors
■ Low birth weight (1,500 grams or less)	■ Maternal age younger than 16 years
■ Small for gestational age	■ A parent with mental retardation or psychiatric disorder
■ Respiratory distress	■ Parental alcohol or substance abuse
■ Asphyxia	■ Lack of permanent housing
■ Neonatal seizures	■ Inadequate caregiving
■ Intracranial hemorrhage	■ History of abuse and neglect in parent(s) or sibling(s)
■ Central nervous system infection	■ Extreme poverty
■ Congenital infection	
■ Abnormal neurologic examination	
■ Maternal phenylketonuria (PKU)	
■ Human immunodeficiency virus (HIV) infection	
■ Prenatal exposure to illegal drugs	
■ Failure to thrive	

continuing case study of Tan

At 3 months of age, Tan began receiving physical therapy as part of his early intervention services. The physical therapist encouraged Tan to exercise his left foot and ankle so his muscles would remain flexible and strong. In addition, Carmen and James played muscle-strengthening games at home with their son and learned some massage techniques. Even though he could not put weight on his left leg until he was almost 18 months of age, a series of flexible braces allowed Tan to walk by age 2.

> **Note**
>
> Acronyms to remember:
> - IDEA = Individuals with Disabilities Education Act
> - EI = early intervention
> - ECSE = early childhood special education
> - IFSP = Individualized Family Service Plan

Early Intervention and Early Childhood Special Education

All states serve infants and toddlers with special needs and their families under Part C of IDEA. Services for children from birth to age 3 are called early intervention (EI) services and include educational, physical, speech and language, nutritional, and psychological services for infants, toddlers, and their families. Further, under IDEA for preschool children with developmental disabilities from age 3 until entry into public school, early childhood special education (ECSE) services are required. Because of the nature of early development and the tremendous impact a family has on the young developing child, the family is considered central to EI and ECSE services as discussed further below.

Assessment and Evaluation

Eligibility for EI and ECSE services, as well as the goals and objectives selected for children and families, are determined through individual assessment of the strengths and needs of the child and family. Part C specifies that the child's unique strengths and needs, as well as the services that are most appropriate for meeting those needs, are determined through assessment by qualified personnel such as a pediatrician or a psychologist. In addition, assessment is used to identify the family's resources, priorities, and concerns, and the supports and services necessary to enhance the family's capacity to support the child's development. The family assessment is voluntary. Families can decide whether they want to participate, and also the extent of their involvement.

Because of the difficulty of assessing very young children, play-based or activity-based assessments are recommended, in which children are observed and tested in natural environments such as their preschool classrooms (Petti, Frontczak, & Bricker, 2004). Assessments must be culturally appropriate, conducted in the family's native language, comprehensive, and multidisciplinary.

The Individualized Family Service Plan

The Individualized Family Service Plan (IFSP) is the centerpiece of early intervention services under IDEA. Based on appropriate assessment, the IFSP must include the infant's or toddler's strengths and needs in five areas: cognitive, motor, social or emotional, adaptive, and communication skills. A statement of the family's resources, priorities, and concerns related to enhancing the development of the infant or toddler is also required. Finally, the IFSP must outline proposed services for the child and family, along with specific goals and objectives and corresponding timelines. In addition to developmental and educational services for the child, services for the family can include nursing, social work, counseling, and service coordination.

With an emphasis on interdisciplinary services based on the family's resources and needs, EI services are designed to be family-centered and family-friendly. The family is to be an equal member of the IFSP team and can choose to participate in assessment and intervention as desired. Indeed, many states use the IFSP rather than the IEP for preschool ECSE children because of this emphasis on family-centered and family-directed services and supports.

Early Intervention Programs

Early intervention programs vary depending on the setting, community, needs of the family, and available resources. In the past, the "problem" was perceived to be within the child, so the primary goal was to change the child in order to "fix" the problem (Hanson, 1996). Today, most programs are family-centered, with a goal of assessing the child's and his or her family's strengths and weaknesses to build on their strengths and address their needs. To do so, an early intervention team typically is interdisciplinary and includes several professionals such as a social worker and physical, speech, and occupational therapists, as well as pediatricians and nurses.

The special education teacher often is expected to participate on the intervention team and provide input on academic curriculum and goals. For example, the team may need your input to develop goals for a child's functional skills (e.g., getting dressed, eating) and more complex skills (e.g., communication, playing). Thus, you may be called upon to gather information about the results of the child's multiple assessments, and get

Young children are often assessed in their homes in order to capture an accurate evaluation in a comfortable, family-focused environment.

to know the child's family and clarify your role and responsibilities as a member of the interdisciplinary team.

Effects of Disability on Family Members

A child with a disability can have an enormous impact on the entire family. That impact might result from the physical needs of an infant who cannot nurse or self-soothe and has round-the-clock health-care needs such as tube feedings. Or the impact might be more emotional, such as the shattering effect of a child born with cerebral palsy on the father's dreams of having a soccer or baseball star in the family.

---

continuing case study of Tan

James and Carmen were apprehensive when their family-practice doctor first recommended, at the 6-month well-baby check, that Tan might benefit from early intervention (EI) services. But after learning that the EI specialists would come to their home, that they would speak in Vietnamese if they preferred, and that services would be free, they consented to an initial assessment of Tan.

The physical therapist and the educator came to their apartment, talked with James and Carmen, and gave Tan some new toys to explore. Tan seemed to enjoy being around these new adults and didn't mind the gentle handling of the physical therapist. James and Carmen were excited to learn some ways to help Tan use his left leg more so he could roll over and begin crawling on the floor.

However, families and children are unique, and not all families have negative and burdensome reactions to the birth of a child with a disability. To the contrary, many families say that, in spite of increased physical and emotional demands, the birth of their child with a disability has enriched their lives. Regardless, levels of stress and anxiety are often magnified in new parents of children with developmental problems. In addition, families may need information on medical services, support groups, and community resources so they are able to meet the complex needs of a young child with a disability.

Parents as Partners

As mentioned, EI and ECSE services are designed to be family-centered and to view parents as equal partners in the education process. EI and ECSE services are intended to include families in all facets of assessment, curriculum planning, evaluation, and transition. Starting with the initial assessment of a child, parents are encouraged to participate in the process by completing screening questionnaires on their child's current skills (Squires, 1996) and to prioritize family and educational goals included on the IFSP (Bricker, 2004). By encouraging families to participate and to make decisions early on, they may be more likely to reinforce and expand upon the learning that takes place in the school environment. Finally, as a child moves from the school environment to postsecondary training and independent living, family members can assist the young adult in determining the supports and services he or she needs for successful community living.

Advocacy

Families are central to their child's education, whether the child has special needs and is served under IDEA or receives educational services in a general education classroom. Family advocacy was initially responsible for IDEA legislation passed in the mid-1970s, which guaranteed all children access to public education no matter how serious their disabilities. Similarly, families are central to the IFSP and IEP team and help determine placements and resources the child needs within community and educational settings. But the importance of their involvement does not stop there. As the child makes the transition from the public school environment, advocacy is just as important for helping the young adult receive the level of supports that he or she will need in work and living environments.

Students With Disabilities: Transition to Adult Life

Just as early intervention programs enhance the development of young children with disabilities, transition programs play a major role in preparing young adults with disabilities for productive citizenship. Both programs are applicable across disability groups and they are mandated by public policy. Transition programming can be tailored to the specific needs of individuals.

A successful transition to adult life (when the student leaves the K–12 school system) is probably *the* most important component of a student's education. If the transition process is not effective, students are more likely to end up unemployed, living in poverty, and having few educational opportunities (Blackorby & Wagner, 1996). Quality-of-life outcomes have generally been poor for individuals with disabilities, in part because of a poor transition to adult life. Students with disabilities must

On graduation day, this senior gets ready to pack up her locker, joining the workforce for the summer.

CASE STUDY: AETHELFLAED'S TRANSITION PLANNING

Aethelflaed is a student with a learning disability who is starting her final year of high school. She lives at home with her mom and three younger siblings. Aethelflaed would like to further her education and also wants to move into her own apartment. Thus, she will need income to support herself.

graduate from high school, and possibly college, with skills that will help them function as adults in employment, community, and residential environments.

Individual Transition Plan

When students receiving special education services turn 16, they are required to have an individual transition plan (ITP), which may be part of their IEP or a separate document. The ITP is intended to set goals for the transition process (e.g., "Evan will visit five job sites during the school year and interview the supervisor at each site regarding skills needed for three different jobs at the site"; "Anna will job-shadow workers at four different horse stables to gain experience regarding job duties at those sites").

Students with mild disabilities usually exit the K–12 school system at age 18. Some students with more severe disabilities continue to receive services from the school system while they are 18–22 years old. These services often are provided in off-campus transition programs where students receive instruction in employment, community, and residential skills.

continuing case study of Aethelflaed

Aethelflaed has met with her individual transition planning team since the end of her freshman year, and her future has been well planned. She has spent considerable time discussing her interests and goals with Mr. Szymusiak, her special education resource teacher, Ms. Ng, her school counselor, and Ms. Cervera, her vocational instructor.

Legal and Legislative Acts Affecting Adult Life

When students are in the K–12 system, they receive services primarily under IDEA. As adults (older than age 18), individuals' rights and services are often covered under the Americans with Disabilities Act (ADA), Section 504 of the Rehabilitation Act of 1973, Medicare (national insurance program for elderly people and eligible people with disabilities), Medicaid (payment for health-care services), and Vocational Rehabilitation (training and placement of people with disabilities in employment). A key issue for individuals with disabilities is accessibility into society. Accessibility can be physical accessibility (e.g., ramps into buildings), programmatic (e.g., sign language interpreter at meetings), or attitudinal (e.g., acceptance of people with disabilities by the general public).

Backlash Against Disability Rights

As a special educator, you must understand that discrimination against people with disabilities is rampant and cuts across all facets of people's lives (employment, housing, education, community access). The media and the general public do not see Ableism—the belief that it is better or superior not to have a disability than to have one, and that it is better to do things the way that nondisabled people do (Hehir, 2002)—as an important issue, or even acknowledge its existence. The lack of enforcement of the ADA and accessibility laws is based primarily on political and economic issues (Johnson, 2003). Politicians find it easy to *say* they support people with disabilities but do little to address their concerns. Similarly, businesses have a financial incentive to ignore ADA requirements because of the lack of damage awards, as well as more traditional negative attitudes:

> They accept that the city can inspect their electrical wiring to ensure that it "meets code" before they open for business. Yet they chafe if an individual wants an accommodation. Because, it seems, it is seen as "special for the handicapped," most of whom likely don't deserve it. (Johnson, 2003, p. 206)

If we are to make "them" the "us," disability rights (Fleischer & Zames, 2001; Shapiro, 1993) and disability culture (Longmore, 1995) are important, but political and economic variables will decide the issue. The parties we must educate and influence include the media that control the debate of these issues and the powers that ultimately make the decisions. Thus, students with disabilities must understand these issues, have individual skills such as self-advocacy to deal with specific instances they will face, and be involved in disability culture and political organizations.

Supports

All people need supports in life, whether for car repairs, financial planning, or academic advisement. None of us is completely independent. Students with disabilities may need supports beyond what is typical. For example, a student with a physical disability may need assistance taking a bath, getting dressed, and being positioned in a wheelchair.

Each student receives the support he or she needs to function *successfully* (which is not necessarily the same as independently) in each of the environments in which he or she lives (work, community, residential). In addition, we emphasize that different students may need different supports, and that disability labels (e.g., learning disability, orthopedic disability) do not indicate the type of support that an individual needs. Nevertheless, availability of services is often based upon disability labels rather than the student's individual needs.

For instance, a student with a developmental disability leaving the K–12 school system might qualify for a wide range of services, whereas a student with a learning disability leaving the school system might not qualify for any specific support services because of a lack of resources. The student with the developmental disability might qualify for vocational training or employment supported by a job coach. Supports could involve help for performing specific tasks and activities such as grocery shopping, being taught certain vocational skills such as mechanics, community and recreational activities, transportation, and so on. The supports may also come from family, friends,

Note

Because they will be faced with Ableism throughout their lives, students must be taught to be advocates for themselves. Teachers can help them understand the law, the issues at hand, and their power as individuals.

Aethelflaed's career choice is to work as an office assistant at a veterinary office. Her vocational instructor, Ms. Cervera, believes that this is a good choice as Aethelflaed has excellent social skills and is not easily flustered when things get hectic. Ms. Cervera knows, however, that Aethelflaed needs to improve her reading skills for tasks such as filing.

people in the community, and/or individuals who are not paid to provide support (e.g., natural supports).

Self-Determination

Self-determination refers to the right and capacity of people to control and direct their own lives, and involves goal setting, problem solving, decision making, and self-advocacy (Wehmeyer & Gragoudas, 2004). In the past decade, self-determination and teaching students with disabilities self-determination skills have become increasingly important in the transition process. Research has found that self-determination leads to more positive adult outcomes for students with disabilities (Weymeyer & Schwartz, 1997).

When learning and demonstrating self-determination, individuals with a disability move from a place where professionals make decisions for them to a place where people with disabilities themselves decide what they want to do with their lives, and professionals develop supports and services based upon those individual goals. Self-determination is mandated in IDEA and the Rehabilitation Act.

Person-Centered Planning

Closely related to self-determination, person-centered planning is a model of service delivery that involves empowering students with disabilities and their families to assert more control over their educational programs. Broadly speaking, this involves creating a vision for the person's future and then determining how that vision will be realized (Miner & Bates, 2002).

Self-Advocacy

Related to self-determination, as well as to assertiveness, is self-advocacy, which involves students' communicating about, and standing up for, their own interests, needs, and rights. As Chadsey and Sheldon (2002) noted, self-advocacy skills are critical in the

Aethelflaed's special education resource teacher, Mr. Szymusiak, has placed her in a support group at school, where she has been learning about dyslexia and self-advocacy and practicing the use of accommodations for her academic work.

successful transition from school to adult life. Merchant and Gajar (1997) have identified four key skills that students need for self-advocacy:

1. Understanding one's disability
2. Knowing one's rights under the law
3. Understanding and being able to express accommodations needed
4. Being able to communicate effectively

Employment

Whether people with disabilities should work, and, if so, where, is an issue that people with disabilities and their families, school systems, adult service systems, and governments have struggled with over the years (Storey, 2000; Wehman, 1998). The field faces unresolved questions such as whether people with disabilities are capable of working, whether they need to get "ready" to work, whether they should work in sheltered or in integrated environments, and the type of supports that are appropriate for workers with disabilities (Mank, 1994; Wehman & Kregel, 1995).

Sheltered environments are settings that serve only groups of individuals with disabilities and usually pay below-minimum wages for contract work such as stuffing envelopes. *Integrated environments* are regular jobs in the community alongside workers without disabilities, such as working in a fast-food restaurant. In this chapter we assume that students with disabilities should work in regular jobs, also known as *supported employment* or *competitive employment* placements such as being a teller at a bank or bagging groceries.

The Importance of Work

Working in integrated settings is important to individuals with disabilities for a number of reasons. First, it reflects that work is valued and that all people benefit from being productive and contributing members of society. This judgment has far-reaching effects. For instance, if a secondary teacher of students with disabilities does not believe it is important for her students to work while they are in school and after graduation, she is less likely to teach relevant employment skills and thus diminishes the chances of her students being employed after graduation.

Second, integrated work can be a powerful factor in changing attitudes and expectations toward people with disabilities. That is, if employers, co-workers, customers, and others see people with disabilities performing competently in regular jobs, people with disabilities are more likely to be seen as competent in their abilities and more likely to be accepted as equals.

Further, with good wages and good benefits, people with disabilities can avoid the poverty and dependency in which the vast majority of people with disabilities live. Unemployment rates for people with disabilities are much higher than for any other

---

continuing case study of Aethelflaed

To help her mom with the household bills, Aethelflaed has had several part-time jobs in high school, including clerical worker, grocery bagger, and stocker at a drugstore. None of the jobs led to more permanent positions with health benefits and enough money for her to live independently.

group and lead to dependency upon welfare, Supplemental Security Income, Medicare, Medicaid, and other government-assistance programs. Finally, along with economic independence comes political participation, which is how people with disabilities will ultimately influence and control the service delivery system (Longmore, 1995).

Employment Education for Students With Disabilities

It is never too early to start vocational instruction for students with disabilities. Vocational instruction or job training should be integrated into all components of the curriculum, and should occur throughout the school years, receiving increasing emphasis as the student gets older. For example, students need career exploration in which they research various careers, job development (e.g., internships) in which they work in a variety of jobs during high school, and job placement in which they are placed in a job they will keep (this should be part of the ITP process). Research indicates that perhaps the key factor in successful employment of students with disabilities is that they are placed in a job before they leave the public school system (Certo et al., 2003).

continuing case study of Aethelflaed

Ms. Cervera, Aethelflaed's vocational instructor, will make contacts with several local veterinary offices to obtain part-time jobs for Aethelflaed so the instructor can better assess the supports and/or modifications Aethelflaed will need. This will allow Ms. Cervera to provide instruction at school so the skills Aethelflaed is learning there will be meaningful in her future employment.

Postsecondary Education

Many students with disabilities want to further their education before they enter the world of work, by going to a vocational school, a community college, or a four-year university. These students often need support in those environments, in the form of accommodations and modifications, as well as information such as knowing what their rights are in a college setting. The supports usually are provided through a program such as the Disabled Students Program (Hunter & O'Brien, 2002). To ensure a smoother transition, students may be connected with these services while they are still in high school as part of the ITP process.

continuing case study of Aethelflaed

Ms. Ng, a member of Aethelflaed's ITP team, and her school counselor, has arranged for Aethelflaed to meet with the Disabled Student Services program at the local community college, where her diagnosis of dyslexia was confirmed, along with her eligibility for services and supports for her academic needs.

In the fall semester, Aethelflaed will begin taking an introductory biology course and an English course. As part of her services, Aethelflaed will be allowed to take tests in a quiet room in the Office for Disabled Students, and be given extended time to complete tests.

Note

Most colleges and universities are becoming more accommodating and accessible for students with disabilities, and some, including Gallaudet University for the deaf and hard of hearing in Washington, DC, were conceived to meet specific learning needs.

Living Environments

Everybody wants to live in a nice home that they can call their own, but adults with disabilities often have been forced to live in segregated settings such as institutions and nursing homes. Over the years, a variety of residential models and options have been developed for people with disabilities (Pancsofar, 1985) to enable them to live more independently. Thus, many students with disabilities leave their family homes after they exit the school system to live in a variety of environments.

Group Homes

Group homes are houses in the community where a group of people with disabilities live, usually supported by paid live-in staff. A counselor might live in the house to help residents with shopping, cooking, and balancing their checkbooks, for example. Although group homes provide better lifestyle outcomes than more segregated options such as institutions or nursing homes, many people who live there remain segregated from the community at large.

Supported Living

Supported living is broadly defined as individuals with disabilities living where and with whom they want, for as long as they want, with the ongoing supports needed to sustain that choice. Supported living sometimes involves a person living in his or her own house or apartment with a variety of supports based upon his or her needs (Davis, 2002). As one option, a caretaker could come in daily to assist with bathing and dressing, and to drive the individual to run simple errands. An emerging research base indicates that supported living is better than other options in terms of providing desirable lifestyle outcomes for individuals with disabilities (Carling, 1990).

Assisted Living

In an assisted living situation the individual with a disability might live with a roommate or two with a disability, with a roommate without a disability who provides support, in clustered apartments, or more independently, receiving some supports from an agency. In the latter case, the person from the support agency might come in once a week to deliver groceries or help pay bills.

Independent Living

In an independent living situation the individual with a disability does not receive any formal services or supports and is expected to perform all functions of daily living independently. As one example, a married couple, both with physical disabilities,

---

continuing case study of Aethelflaed

Although Aethelflaed wanted to be independent from her family, she did not feel comfortable living alone. Thus, the counselor at the Office of Disabled Student Services at the community college paired her up with two other students (without disabilities) who were looking for a third roommate to share their two-bedroom apartment across the street from the campus.

might rent an apartment in a building that has lowered kitchen counters and safety bars in the bathroom.

Recreational Services

Recreational services for students with disabilities have changed dramatically over the past 30 years, moving from being specialized and segregated services serving only students with disabilities to providing state-of-the-art services in inclusive settings with appropriate supports (Modell & Valdez, 2002; Schleien & Ray, 1997). An increasing research base indicates that services and supports in typical recreational settings might be the best way of achieving meaningful quality-of-life outcomes for individuals with disabilities and could replace more group and center-oriented services such as the Special Olympics (Datillo, 2002; Garcia & Menchetti, 2003; Storey, 2004). We will discuss two basic approaches to the inclusion of students with disabilities in community recreation: integration of generic recreation programs and zero exclusion.

Integration of Existing Generic Programs

In integrating the individual with a disability into an existing traditional, age-appropriate recreation program, an integration specialist or other professional identifies and ameliorates discrepancies between the skill requirements of the program and the individual's capabilities, and develops appropriate supports. An example of this type of program is to involve a student in an after-school aerobics group at a local health club (Halle, Gabler–Halle, & Bemben, 1989).

The advantages of integration in existing generic programs are as follows:

- Participation of people with disabilities in existing generic programs reflects the natural proportion to peers without disabilities.
- The program activities are age-appropriate and of high interest.
- Existing programs provide opportunities for extended natural peer interactions.

The disadvantages of integration of existing generic programs are as follows:

- Only a small number of participants with disabilities can be served at one time.
- Too much attention is often directed toward participants with disabilities.
- Participants with disabilities are not always welcome.
- The generic recreation staff may not be trained to work with people who have disabilities.

Zero Exclusion

In the zero exclusion approach, therapeutic recreation specialists and generic recreation program leaders collaborate to design programs that meet the needs of all participants, with or without disabilities. An example of this type of program is a Girl Scout program designed to serve students both with and without disabilities (Schleien, Green, & Heyne, 1993).

Advantages of zero exclusion are as follows:

- It allows the recreation needs of all individuals to be met.
- It promotes cooperation between therapeutic recreation staff members and generic recreation staff members.
- Participants with disabilities and their nondisabled peers have equal status.
- No one is excluded.

Disadvantages of zero inclusion are as follows (Schleien et al., 1993):

- Initial start-up costs may be high.
- Parents and people with disabilities who prefer segregated programs may fear that those programs will be eliminated.

Quality of Life

Quality of life is becoming one of the most important driving forces in human services (Schalock, 1990). After all, the most important outcome of the transition process is that students with disabilities attain a quality of life that is satisfying and that meets their needs after they leave the school setting. A quality-of-life approach tries to look at the person as a whole and determine if his or her life is satisfactory to the individual. This is important because often we look at individual components of individuals' lives (e.g., how much money they earn, where they live) without trying to put all the pieces together.

Defining Quality of Life

Quality of life is an elusive concept. Several global definitions have been proposed, but no operational definition or appropriate measures have been agreed upon (Lehman & Burns, 1990). For the general public, Campbell (1981) discusses 12 "life domains" as being components of quality of life:

1. Education
2. Marriage
3. Family life

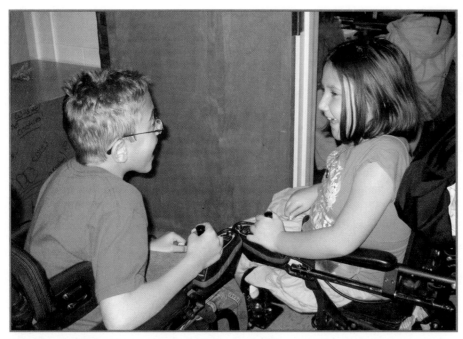

A quality education when young includes having positive social interactions, strong parental support, and challenging academics. This can help foster a high quality of life for adults with disabilities.

   4. Friendship
   5. Self
   6. Health
   7. Standard of living
   8. The country
   9. Neighborhood
10. Housing
11. Residence
12. Work

Schalock, Keith, Hoffman, and Karan (1989) have suggested that for persons with disabilities, quality of life combines environmental control, community involvement, and perception of personal change. Similarly, O'Connor (1983) noted that social relationships and social support (emotional, informational, and material aid) are critical in determining quality of life.

Determining What Quality of Life Means for Students With Disabilities

It is clear from the literature that the concept of quality of life focuses upon lifestyle outcomes and that, although objective measures are important (i.e., economic indicators), quality of life often must be measured subjectively from the unique perspective of each individual (Cheng, 1988). Thus, research often has found a poor correlation between objective indicators and subjective measures of life satisfaction (Hughes, Hwang, Kim, Eisenman, & Killian, 1995).

continuing case study of Aethelflaed

For the first month at the community college and working at the veterinarian's office, Aethelflaed was ready to quit school and work. She was homesick, felt overwhelmed with the coursework and, although she enjoyed her job, working 30 hours a week left her little time to rest, socialize, or do homework.

After her roommate suggested that she cut down her work to 20 hours a week and she joined a study group to help her with biology, Aethelflaed felt like she was able to juggle her responsibilities much better. She made it a routine to do homework and study in the evenings so she could visit her family and hang out with her new friends on weekends. Also, her employer recognized Aethelflaed's patience and love for working with animals and gave her more opportunities to work directly with the animals. For the first time in a long while, Aethelflaed felt happy.

Summary

In this chapter we introduced you to the effects of disability on individuals and family members across the life span from birth to postsecondary settings. As special education teachers, you will have to understand risk factors and how they affect the development of infants and toddlers with disabilities. Especially with young children, effective early intervention programs and services, involving the family and the parents, are essential. Thus, having knowledge of the components of the Individualized Family Service Plan and how to locate interdisciplinary resources are critical for teachers to help these children make a smooth transition from preschool to elementary programs.

Throughout their lives, children with disabilities will have to make many transitions—from preschool to elementary, elementary to secondary, and eventually to postsecondary environments. Perhaps the most problematic transition is from high school to postsecondary settings. Students with disabilities tend to have poorer outcomes than students without disabilities with regard to income, employment, higher education, and independent living. Thus, as special education teachers, you will be called upon to involve the student in his or her Individual Transition Plan and provide the needed supports with regard to career interests, employment, postsecondary education, recreation, and independent living. By supporting students within these primary areas of their lives, you can help them become productive and contributing members of our society and have the quality of their life that everyone deserves.

References

Blackorby, J., & Wagner, M. (1996). Longitudinal postschool outcomes of youth with disabilities: Findings from the national longitudinal transition study. *Exceptional Children, 62*(5), 399–413.

Bricker, D. (Ed.). (2004). *Assessment, evaluation, and programming system for infants and children: Volume 4. Curriculum for three to six years* (2d ed.). Baltimore: Paul Brookes.

Campbell, A. (1981). *The sense of well-being in America.* New York: McGraw–Hill.

Carling, P. J. (1990). Major mental illness, housing, and supports: The promise of community integration. *American Psychologist, 45*(8), 969–975.

Certo, N. J., Mautz, D., Pumpian, I., Sax, C., Smalley, K., Wade, H. A., Noves, D., Luecking, R., Weschler, J., & Batterman, N. (2003). A review and discussion of a model for seamless transition to adulthood. *Education and Training in Mental Retardation and Developmental Disabilities, 38,* 3–17.

Chadsey, J., & Sheldon, D. (2002). Social life. In K. Storey, P. Bates, & D. Hunter, (Eds.), *The road ahead: Transition to adult life for persons with disabilities* (pp. 137–155). St. Augustine, FL: Training Resource Network.

Cheng, S. (1988). Subjective quality of life in the planning and evaluation of programs. *Evaluation and Program Planning, 11,* 123–134.

Children's Defense Fund. (2004). *Children's mental health resource kit.* Retrieved January 15, 2004, from http://www.childrensdefense.org/mentalhealthresourcekit.php

Dattilo, J. (2002). *Leisure education program planning: A systematic approach* (2d ed.). State College, PA: Venture.

Davis, P. (2002). Supported living. In K. Storey, P. Bates, & D. Hunter (Eds.), *The road ahead: Transition to adult life for persons with disabilities* (pp. 173–188). St. Augustine, FL: Training Resource Network.

Fleischer, D. Z., & Zames, F. (2001). *The disability rights movement: From charity to confrontation.* Philadelphia: Temple University Press.

Garbarino, J., & Ganzel, B. (2000). The human ecology of early risk. In J. P. Shonkoff & S. J. Meisels (Eds.), *Handbook of early childhood intervention* (2d ed., pp. 76–93). New York: Cambridge University Press.

Garcia, L. A., & Menchetti, B. M. (2003). The adult lifestyles planning cycle: A continual process for planning personally satisfying adult lifestyles. In D. L. Ryndak & S. Alper (Eds.), *Curriculum and instruction for students with significant disabilities in inclusive settings* (pp. 277–306). Boston: Allyn & Bacon.

Halle, J. W., Gabler–Halle, D., & Bemben, D. A. (1989). Effects of a peer-mediated aerobic conditioning program on fitness measures with children who have moderate and severe disabilities. *Journal of the Association for Persons with Severe Handicaps, 14,* 33–47.

Halpern, R. (2000). Early intervention for low-income children and families. In J. P. Shonkoff & S. J. Meisels (Eds.), *Handbook of early childhood intervention* (2d ed., pp. 785–841). New York: Cambridge University Press.

Hanson, M. (1996). *Atypical infant development.* Austin, TX: Pro-Ed.

Hehir, T. (2002). Eliminating ableism in education. *Harvard Educational Review, 72,* 1–32.

Hughes, C., Hwang, B., Kim, J. H., Eisenman, L. T., & Killian, D. J. (1995). Quality of life in applied research: A review and analysis of empirical measures. *American Journal on Mental Retardation, 99,* 623–641.

Hunter, D., & O'Brien, L. E. (2002). Postsecondary education for students with disabilities. In K. Storey, P. Bates, & D. Hunter (Eds.), *The road ahead: Transition to adult life for persons with disabilities* (pp. 189–205). St. Augustine, FL: Training Resource Network.

Johnson, M. (2003). *Make them go away: Clint Eastwood, Christopher Reeve & the case against disability rights.* Louisville, KY: Advocado Press.

Lehman, A. F., & Burns, B. J. (1990). Severe mental illness in the community. In B. Spiker (Ed.), *Quality of life assessments in clinical trials* (pp. 357–366). New York: Raven Press.

Liptak, G. S. (1996). Pediatricians' role in caring for the developmentally disabled child. *Pediatrics in Review, 17*(6), 203–210.

Longmore, P. K. (1995). The second phase: From disability rights to disability culture. *The Disability Rag & Resource, 16*(5), 4–11.

Mank, D. M. (1994). The underachievement of supported employment: A call for reinvestment. *Journal of Disability Policy Studies, 5,* 1–24.

Merchant, D. J., & Gajar, A. (1997). A review of the literature on self-advocacy components in transition programs for students with learning disabilities. *Journal of Vocational Rehabilitation, 8,* 223–231.

Miner, C. A., & Bates, P. E. (2002). Person-centered transition planning: Creating lifestyles of community inclusion and autonomy. In K. Storey, P. Bates, & D. Hunter (Eds.), *The road ahead: Transition to adult life for persons with disabilities* (pp. 7–24). St. Augustine, FL: Training Resource Network.

Modell, S. J., & Valdez, L. A. (2002). Beyond bowling: Transition planning for students with disabilities. *Teaching Exceptional Children, 34,* 46–52.

O'Connor, G. (1983). Social support of mentally retarded persons. *Mental Retardation, 5,* 187–196.

Pancsofar, E. (1985). Community-based living facilities. In P. Wehman, A. Renzaglia, & P. Bates (Eds.), *Functional living skills for moderately and severely handicapped individuals* (pp. 23–44). Austin, TX: Pro-Ed.

Pretti-Frontczak, K., & Bricker, D. (2004). *An activity-based approach to early intervention* (3d ed.). Baltimore: Paul Brookes.

Sameroff, A., & Chandler, M. (1975). Reproductive risk and the continuum of caretaking casualty. In F. Horowitz (Ed*.), Review of child development research* (Vol. 4, pp. 187–244). Chicago: University of Chicago Press.

Sameroff, A., & Fiese, B. (2000). Transactional regulation: The development ecology of early intervention. In J. P. Shonkoff & S. J. Meisels (Eds.), *Handbook of early childhood intervention* (2nd ed., pp. 135–159). New York: Cambridge University Press.

Sameroff, A., & MacKenzie, M. J. (2003). A quarter-century of the transactional model: How have things changed? *Zero to Three, 24*(1), 14–22.

Sameroff, A., Seifer, R., Baldwin, A., & Baldwin, C. (1994). Stability of intelligence from preschool to adolescence: The influence of social and family risk factors. *Child Development, 64,* 80–97.

Sandall, S., McClean, M. E., & Smith, B. (2000). *DEC recommended practices in early intervention/early childhood special education.* Reston, VA: Council for Exceptional Children, Division for Early Childhood.

Schalock, R. L. (1990). *Quality of life: Perspectives and issues.* Washington, DC: American Association on Mental Retardation.

Schalock, R. L., Keith, K. D., Hoffman, K., & Karan, O. C. (1989). Quality of life: Its measurement and use. *Mental Retardation, 27,* 25–31.

Schleien, S. J., Green, F. P., & Heyne, L. A. (1993). Integrated community recreation. In M. E. Snell (Ed.), *Instruction of students with severe disabilities* (pp. 526–555). Columbus, OH: Merrill.

Schleien, S. J., & Ray, M. T. (1997). Leisure education for a quality transition to adulthood. *Journal of Vocational Rehabilitation, 8,* 155–169.

Shapiro, J. P. (1993). *No pity: People with disabilities forging a new civil rights movement.* New York: Times Books.

Squires, J. (1996). Parent-completed developmental questionnaires: A low-cost strategy for child-find and screening. *Infants and Young Children, 9*(1), 16–28.

Storey, K. (2000). Why employment in integrated settings for people with disabilities? *International Journal of Rehabilitation Research, 23*(2), 103–110.

Storey, K. (2004). The case against the Special Olympics. *Journal of Disability Policy Studies, 15,* 35–42.

Wehman, P. (1998). Work, unemployment and disability: Meeting the challenges. *Journal of Vocational Rehabilitation, 11,* 1–3.

Wehman, P., & Kregel, J. (1995). At the crossroads: Supported employment a decade later. *Journal of the Association for Persons with Severe Handicaps, 20,* 286–299.

Wehmeyer, M. L., & Gragoudas, S. (2004). Centers for independent living and transition-age youth: Empowerment and self-determination. *Journal of Vocational Rehabilitation, 20,* 53–58.

Weymeyer, M. L., & Schwartz, M. (1997). Self-determination and positive adult outcomes: A follow-up study of youth with mental retardation or learning disabilities. *Exceptional Children, 63,* 245–255.

STUDENTS WITH MILD TO MODERATE DISABILITIES (HIGH-INCIDENCE)

The chapters in Part I made frequent references to state and federal legislation designed to benefit students with disabilities and their families. This pattern of legislation has led to the evolvement of equal educational opportunity for students with disabilities. Those unfamiliar with public policy in education may wonder about the need to focus on legislating for a specific group of learners since a free public education has been the backbone of the public education system in this country since its beginning. However, despite this basic premise, in practice, large numbers of learners with special education needs have not been appropriately served in our public schools. Many learners with disabilities were not viewed by the schools as being educable. Consequently, schools did not admit them, or admitted them but did not serve them appropriately.

Legislation has changed that. When passing legislation for general education, legislators are now careful to ensure that the needs of all groups of learners are accommodated. While that has its advantages, it has also introduced some concerns. The No Child Left Behind Act of 2001 (NCLB) is one example. It is truly inclusive, but a careful look reveals some issues related to the effect that the inclusion of students with disabilities has on the overall performance level across a district. Specifically, it can bring into question the mandate of serving all students based on the perspective that achievement levels, when aggregated across a district, may be higher if the scores of students with disabilities are not included. Such controversies underscore how far we have yet to go in our society toward realizing true equal educational opportunities for all.

The passage of the federal mandate NCLB has changed how we teach in educational settings today. This legislation requires states to implement statewide accountability systems for all students in public schools based on state standards. For example, annual testing is mandated for all students in reading and mathematics (grades 3–8), and states must set annual statewide progress objectives aimed at ensuring that all groups of students, including students with disabilities, reach proficiency levels or better by 2013–2014. In addition, test scores are disaggregated by subgroups (e.g., ethnicity, disability, language learners) to ensure that these subgroups also make progress towards proficiency levels. Schools that do not make "adequate yearly progress" face a sequence of increasingly severe consequences set by the federal government.

NCLB and the 2004 Reauthorization of the Individuals with Disabilities Education Improvement Act (IDEA) also have serious implications for the roles, responsibilities, and expectations of the special education teacher. Both mandates require special education teachers to be "highly qualified" in core academic subjects (e.g., English, reading or language arts, mathematics, science, foreign language) that they teach. To be "highly qualified," a teacher is either (a) fully certified as a special education teacher, (b) has passed the state licensure exam, (c) is working towards full certification (with supervision) in an alternative certification program, and/or (d) has subject matter competency in every subject area that he or she teaches. These expectations are particularly difficult to meet for secondary teachers or teachers in rural areas who teach multiple subjects (e.g., math and English) in self-contained classes.

Additionally, as special education teachers find themselves more responsible for enhancing students' performance on statewide assessments, this impacts how they plan for instruction. Thus, in order for students with disabilities to reach proficiency levels on statewide assessments and high-stakes assessments, such as the high school exit exam, it is critical that they receive instruction in grade-level content in core subject areas. Although they continue to work towards the goals outlined on their individualized education programs (IEP), students with disabilities must also have access to the general education curriculum and the same academic content as students without disabilities.

As a beginning special education teacher, complying with the provisions of NCLB and IDEA 2004 can be very overwhelming and stressful on top of your other daily responsibilities: managing IEP paperwork, collaborating with other professionals, meeting with parents, conducting IEP meetings, and so on. Perhaps the most important task for you as a new teacher is to educate yourself about the policies and procedures of your state and local school district. This means communicating frequently with your school administrators as well as the district special education office and content specialist(s). You can also stay informed about changes in the law by joining professional organizations (e.g., Council for Exceptional Children) and/or attending professional development conferences and workshops. Although it is not necessary for you to be an expert on public policy, it is your responsibility to be aware of those aspects of the law that apply to the students and disability groups that you teach.

In this part of the book, we included chapters on four disability groups that are considered to be on the mild to moderate spectrum of disabilities: learning disabilities, emotional/behavior disorders, speech/language impairments and communication disorders, and physical and health disabilities. These four groups make up the majority population of students receiving special education services under IDEA. Thus, it is highly likely that as a special education teacher you will encounter students with mild to moderate disabilities in general and special education settings. We also included a chapter in this section on students who are gifted and talented.

Although the students in the disability groups are different from each other (both within and between disability categories), they share common behavioral traits, have comparable learning needs, and respond similarly to instructional practices. Thus, we have included a chapter that "bridges" topics that are applicable for many students with mild to moderate disabilities. This bridging chapter, chapter 9, complements the disability-specific chapters by focusing largely on instruction- and assessment-related topics.

In this chapter we discuss different forms of assessments and introduce you to research-based practices for reading, writing, and math. As we move toward an era of accountability in education, it is becoming more and more critical for new teachers to be able to implement teaching practices that are based on scientific evidence as well as make instructional decisions based on student data and outcomes. The intent of the chapter was not to teach you everything you need to know about teaching core content, but to give you a strong foundation in these subject areas and provide you with tools for how to adapt and modify them for your students with exceptional learning needs.

As a beginning teacher, there is much for you to know about students with exceptional learning needs. The knowledge base is extensive, as you must know the core content of the subjects, understand the instructional implications of learning and behavioral characteristics, and be familiar with research-based practices. All teachers will find the information in Part II to be helpful in their teaching roles. At the same time, the information is insufficient. It is merely a beginning on the way to becoming highly qualified. There is much more to learn. Some of this knowledge you will acquire elsewhere in your teacher education program, and your knowledge and skills will also be expanded through personal experience and professional development throughout your career.

Specific Learning Disabilities

4

Mary Brownell, Martha A. League,
& Seonjin Seo

Students with specific learning disabilities (SLD) comprise the largest population of students with identified disabilities. Because many students with SLD have normal to above-normal intellectual abilities, their learning disabilities often go unnoticed until they reach school age, when the demands of school begin to create difficulties for them, particularly in the area of literacy. Fortunately, for students with SLD and their families, researchers have acquired knowledge about the challenges that students with SLD face in school and how schools can best respond to those challenges. More than ever before, students with SLD can expect to have access to the same curriculum as their typically developing peers if special and general education teachers work together to use research-based methods, make accommodations and modifications, and incorporate the appropriate instructional technologies into their instruction.

The case study of a child with SLD in this chapter personalizes the struggles that these students and their parents face when confronting the demands of school. We begin by presenting definitions of SLD, then discuss the criteria for identifying SLD in schools and prevalence data, followed by possible causes of this disability. After suggesting some tools for assessment, we offer research-based educational interventions and strategies for improving the academic abilities of students with SLD and their access to the general education curriculum.

CASE STUDY: DEVIN

"Mom, I hate school and I'm not going back. I don't have any friends, and I'm stupid. I can't read like the other kids. I wish I could just disappear!"

Today began the same as many days begin for Devin—with tears and arguments. He awoke with a stomachache, did not want to go to school, and had to be cajoled by his mother to meet the bus at the end of his street. On the way, he intently focused on the bugs on the sidewalk and nearly missed his bus. After arriving at school, Devin sat with a few friends in the cafeteria but had difficulty following their conversation. He often inserted loud comments that were only marginally related to the topic at hand, causing irritated looks to be cast his way. These reactions drove Devin once again to the verge of tears, and he entered the second-grade classroom with his anger and confusion barely contained. He could not understand why he often felt out of step, and the resulting frustration was tangible.

Devin's success on the soccer field, along with his striking good looks, made him widely popular in first grade, but by second grade many of his friends were beginning to lose patience with him. Though he was anxious to be a part of his peer group, Devin often expressed his diminishing self-worth by being defiant in his classroom. He had become increasingly aware that most of his friends were beginning to read fluently while the task continued to frustrate him. Sometimes he approached reading with

(continued)

determination, particularly when his mother or his teacher, Ms. Watson, worked with him individually. Other times he barely contained his frustration and tore his papers or stubbornly refused to attempt any task that involved reading.

Devin had begun first grade as successful in math. He liked the concreteness of the counters and took pride in his ability to solve addition and subtraction problems rapidly. He liked group problem-solving activities, too. When his teacher read problems to the class, his hand was often the first to go up. His strong reasoning ability helped him discover solutions quickly, and his classmates respected him for his successes. Second-grade math, however, increasingly involved word problems that Devin was expected to read and solve on his own. His confusion and frustration at being unable to read many of the words rapidly gave way to anger as he began to experience failure in math as well as in reading.

Science class was consistently Devin's favorite part of the day. Ms. Watson had a strong interest in science and arranged many outdoor science activities for the class. Students investigated the habits of insects by observing them in their natural habitats and recording their findings with simple tallies or pictures. Devin's science journal drew admiration from his peers as his detailed drawings reflected his outstanding talent in art, his strong background knowledge in science, and his natural interest in the environment. Ms. Watson frequently used Devin's work as an example for others, which helped to bolster his dwindling self-esteem.

Devin's concerned parents met with Ms. Watson frequently. Her advice to wait for Devin to become ready to read seemed plausible in the fall but questionable by mid-year. His parents were unable to afford individual tutoring for Devin but thought they had to do something immediately. They faithfully heeded Ms. Watson's advice to continue to read to Devin daily, but that seemed not to result in increased achievement. They watched anxiously as their son fell further behind academically and became more defiant and difficult to handle at home. His frequent crying created a sense of urgency and a deep sense of helplessness in finding a solution to Devin's problems.

Even Ms. Watson began to worry that she did not have sufficient resources in the classroom to help Devin. She already had met with the multidisciplinary team for suggestions and followed through on those suggestions. She had placed Devin in small-group instruction for building phonics and oral reading fluency. While Devin was making small improvements, he still was having great difficulty learning to read. Ms. Watson started to realize that Devin was not one of those children who lag in reading but catch up later. He seemed to have genuine literacy problems that were going to require much more intervention. Ms. Watson asked herself, "Does Devin have a learning disability in reading? Should I talk to his parents about referring him for special education services?"

Who Are Students With Specific Learning Disabilities? *→ Hard to identify!* ■ ■ ■

Devin's success in mathematics and science and his lack of achievement in reading, despite exposure to good instruction, indicate that he may have a learning disability. Students with SLD typically exhibit an uneven academic profile, performing well in some areas and poorly in others. This suggests a discrepancy between intellectual ability and achievement in a specific academic area. The varied nature of their academic disabilities makes it difficult to differentiate students who have learning disabilities from those who do not. Consequently, educators, parents, and policymakers have engaged for decades in debate over how to best define and identify students with learning disabilities.

At a minimum, all states must develop identification criteria that operationalize the federal definition of learning disabilities. The IDEA '97 definition of learning disabilities originated with Public Law 94-142, the Education for All Handicapped Children Act, which states:

Dr. Samuel Kirk coined the term *learning disability* in 1963.

> Specific learning disabilities *means a disorder in one or more of the basic psychological processes involved in understanding or in using language, spoken or written, that may manifest itself in an imperfect ability to listen, think, speak, read, write, spell, or to do mathematical calculations, including conditions such as perceptual disabilities, brain injury, minimal brain dysfunction, dyslexia, and developmental aphasia. The term does not include learning problems that are primarily the result of visual, hearing, or motor disabilities, of mental retardation, of emotional disturbance, or of environmental, cultural, or economic disadvantage. (34 CRF§§300.7)*

Many professionals in the field have concerns about the federal definition of learning disabilities, considering portions of the definition to be outdated and potentially open to misinterpretation. Specifically, the term *minimal brain dysfunction* is seldom used in current literature and brain injury appears as a separate category under IDEA. Also, the definition implies that a learning disability cannot occur with other disorders, but this is not the case. Students can have a visual impairment and a learning disability concurrently, or exhibit an emotional disorder and have a learning disability. To respond to these concerns, the National Joint Committee on Learning Disabilities and the Learning Disabilities Association (NJCLD) has proposed this alternative definition:

> *Learning disabilities is a general term that refers to a heterogeneous group of disorders manifested by significant difficulties in the acquisition and use of listening, speaking, reading, writing, reasoning, or mathematical skills.*
>
> *These disorders are intrinsic to the individual, presumed to be due to central nervous system dysfunction, and may occur across the life span. Problems in self-regulatory behaviors, social perception, and social interaction may exist with learning disabilities but do not, by themselves, constitute a learning disability.*
>
> *Although learning disabilities may occur concomitantly with other disabilities (e.g., sensory impairment, mental retardation,*

> *serious emotional disturbance), or with extrinsic influences (such as cultural differences, insufficient or inappropriate instruction), they are not the result of those conditions or influences. (NJCLD, 1998, p. 187)*

Although the federal and NJCLD definitions are at some variance, they have significant similarities. Both definitions (a) assume *central nervous system dysfunction* as a potential cause; (b) describe academic areas that can be affected, including listening, speaking, reading, writing, and math; and (c) exclude learning problems attributable primarily to other conditions, such as mental retardation or cultural difference.

How Do States and Local Districts Define Specific Learning Disability?

While debates over the definition of learning disability continue, states and local districts are still responsible for finding ways to identify students for services. For Devin to receive special education services, he must be formally diagnosed as having a specific learning disability. Criteria to establish the presence of a learning disability are determined by individual states and local school districts but must meet the minimum criteria established in the IDEA '97 rules and regulations. Specifically, a multidisciplinary team may declare a student eligible for learning disability services if the following is true (Mercer, Jordan, Allsopp, & Mercer, 1996):

1. *A severe discrepancy exists.* The student does not achieve commensurate with his or her ability in one or more academic areas even after receiving appropriate instruction.
2. *Specific academic deficits versus pervasive deficits are identified.* A student must exhibit a severe discrepancy between ability and achievement in at least one of these areas: oral expression, listening comprehension, written expression, basic reading skills, reading comprehension, mathematics calculation, mathematics reasoning.
3. *Need is demonstrated.* The student's learning disability is significant enough that it requires more intensive instruction than students typically receive.
4. *Exclusion of other disabilities or conditions is established.* A student is not regarded as having a learning disability if his or her failure to achieve is the result of conditions specifically articulated in IDEA.

What Are the Academic and Social Characteristics of Students With SLD?

Students like Devin constitute a diverse group. The academic abilities of students with specific learning disabilities vary from one student to another, and the severity of their needs varies as well. For instance, some students have difficulty reading and writing, and others have trouble with math. Moreover, some students with mild learning disabilities can be included fully in the general education classroom with minimal support, whereas others have severe learning disabilities and require more intensive special education services. In addition, some students like Devin exhibit problems with social skills or behavior.

Academic Performance

Approximately 60% to 90% of students with SLD have language-related disabilities (Bender, 2001). Like Devin, many students first manifest SLD in their problems with learning to read. Most beginning reading problems result from deficient language skills, particularly the skills necessary for decoding words. *Phonological awareness*—the ability to blend sounds to form words and segment words into individual sounds—is usually responsible for these decoding difficulties (Blachman, 1995). A severe problem in learning to read, usually associated with weak decoding skills, is termed *dyslexia* (International Dyslexia Association, 2002).

Students with SLD have additional language-related problems that can affect either written or spoken language. Writing difficulties can be related to handwriting and spelling difficulties that interfere with the fluent production of text (Graham, Harris, & Larsen, 2001). Some students with SLD have considerable difficulty forming the letters in words, and their writing is often laborious and illegible. Other students have severe spelling problems related to their deficits in phonological awareness (these problems also may be related to difficulties with phonics and word recognition). Writing deficits can be tied to problems generating ideas, organizing those ideas, and using appropriate grammar, or *syntax*. The term typically used to describe writing-related disabilities is *dysgraphia.*

Some students with SLD have problems using language to communicate (Mercer & Pullen, 2005) in both receptive and expressive language. Specifically, they may have difficulty finding the right words to describe their ideas (*semantics*), using appropriate grammar (*syntax*), or understanding the rules of communication (*pragmatics*). They may have problems communicating their thoughts or following conversational rules such as turn-taking.

Reading is an important part of instruction for all students of any ages.

A smaller percentage of students with SLD have difficulties with math, termed *dyscalculia*. Students with math disabilities have trouble with calculation and/or solving word problems (Cawley, Parmar, Foley, Salmon, & Roy, 2001; Montague & Applegate, 1993). Difficulties with calculation seem to be related to committing basic facts (e.g., 3×8 or $5 + 7$) to memory. Word problem-solving challenges, by contrast, seem to be associated with reading problems or cognitive and metacognitive deficits.

Memory and Metacognitive Problems

The difficulty that students with SLD have in decoding and memorizing basic facts could be related to problems with short-term memory (Keeler & Swanson, 2001), or the ability to remember information, such as how a word is spelled, while performing other cognitive functions, such as generating text. Often, students with SLD display *metacognitive problems* (Wong, 1991) that could be related to their short-term memory deficits. They have difficulty organizing and prioritizing academic tasks and effectively using strategies to tackle those tasks. These problems can cause difficulty with comprehending text, organizing ideas for writing, and developing an approach to solving word problems.

Social and Emotional Problems

Just as students with SLD have distinctive learning characteristics, they also have social/behavioral characteristics. These students may be *hyperactive*—prone to display impulsive actions without thinking about social norms or consequences. They also tend to make poor decisions in social situations because they have difficulty interpreting others' feelings and emotions or do not understand the rules for communicating with others. Unfortunately, by choosing less socially acceptable behavior, these students often alienate their peers. About three-fourths of students with SLD receive social skill ratings lower than their peers (Kavale & Forness, 1996).

Repeated failure in school also leads to motivational problems. Sometimes students with learning disabilities come to believe that the effort they exert to succeed in a task matters little. Thus, they begin to feel a loss of control in school and are apt to give up easily when faced with difficult tasks.

What Causes Learning Disabilities?

Although learning disabilities are presumed to be the result of intrinsic factors (factors unique to the individual, as opposed to the environment), researchers still have insufficient information about what factors contribute to learning disabilities. They have hypothesized that SLD is the result of three factors (Alarcon, Knopik, & deFries, 2000; Frank, 2000; Muir, 2000; Smith, 2000):

1. Abnormal brain development
2. Genetics or hereditary factors
3. Teratogens

Medical technology provides some insights into the biological basis for dyslexia. Technological innovations, such as magnetic resonance imaging, have shown differences in the brain activity of individuals with dyslexia versus individuals without dyslexia (Shaywitz et al., 2002). Research on families also shows that severe reading disabilities, language disorders, and mathematics disabilities might be inherited. Parents of children with learning disabilities sometimes indicate that they struggled with the same academic subjects in school.

Finally, exposure to certain pollutants and chemicals during pregnancy or early development can contribute to learning disabilities. For example, prenatal exposure to environmental pollutants such as PCBs and mercury seem to correlate with a higher incidence of learning disabilities in children.

How Many School-Age Students Have Learning Disabilities?

Of the almost 6,000,000 students ages 6 to 21 receiving special education services, more than half are identified as having SLD (U.S. Department of Education, 2002). Boys are diagnosed with SLD two to six times more often than girls (Smith, 1994), and the reasons for their overidentification are unclear. Perhaps underlying biological factors are more likely to affect boys. Or, because boys are likely to develop language skills more slowly than girls, they are more likely to be identified as having an SLD.

Learning disability is also the fastest growing category of disability. In 1969, prior to passage of the EHA, only 120,000 students were identified as having SLD (Kirk, 1972). By comparison, in the 2000–01 school year approximately 2.9 million students were identified as having an SLD (U.S. Department of Education, 2002). Reasons for this increase are not clear. Some professionals believe that increased survival rates for preterm infants, more students living in poverty, and more students from culturally and linguistically diverse populations may be contributing to the increased prevalence. These students often are at risk to be overidentified for special education services. Increased understanding of underachievement in reading and greater pressure for students to succeed on state performance assessments also may prompt teachers and parents to refer more children for learning disabilities.

3 million kids SLD

More boys

Note

The process to determine whether or not a student has a learning disability must be extensive and thorough in order to prevent any misidentification.

LD is fastest growing group

How Are Students With Learning Disabilities Identified and Served in Special Education?

In school, when students with SLD first encounter expectations to acquire literacy or numeracy skills, teachers and parents begin to notice that something is wrong. They are puzzled as to why an otherwise normally developing child seems to have so much trouble acquiring certain academic skills. Sometimes, as in Devin's case, the child himself begins to notice that something is wrong. Children with SLD realize they are not learning to read, write, spell, or do math like their classmates. They become increasingly frustrated in their attempts to learn and may try to avoid assigned work, or worse, become defiant when asked to do certain tasks. Teachers and parents eventually become aware that a little extra academic help is not going to be sufficient. Something more dramatic has to happen to ensure that these students do not fall further and further behind.

At this point, the classroom teacher formally refers a student for evaluation for a specific learning disability. During the prereferral process the classroom teacher tries different strategies recommended by the multidisciplinary team, but those strategies are insufficient. In the case of Devin, Ms. Watson tried the beginning reading strategies, but Devin needed more than that. Thus, she contacted Devin's parents and discussed the possibility of referring him for a formal evaluation to determine if he had an SLD.

Determining the Presence of a Learning Disability

In most states, students qualify for a learning disability when their academic achievement is significantly discrepant from their intellectual ability or aptitude (Mercer et al., 1996). This discrepancy can be in one area of academic achievement or in several and, as indicated earlier, may not be the result of some other physical limitation, such as a vision deficit, or the lack of opportunity to learn. Prior to the referral process, Devin's teacher requested a vision and hearing screening and found that the results were normal. Because the team knows that Devin does not have a visual or hearing impairment that could be affecting his learning, they direct their initial efforts at determining if he has an aptitude–achievement discrepancy.

Formal Assessment

Aptitude–achievement discrepancies are determined using formal assessments (Mercer & Pullen, 2005)—typically a battery of tests that have been normed on the school-age population of students. These standardized tests provide information about how the average school-age child is performing, and what type of scores are considered average versus significantly below average. The average score is termed the *mean* and a *standard deviation* is used to define how far the student is from the mean. On most aptitude and achievement tests, the mean is 100 and the standard deviation is 15. These tests are used to identify students with SLD because they can provide information about how discrepant a student's performance is in comparison to same-age peers.

To determine a student's aptitude, the school psychologist selects a standardized intelligence test that is well recognized for its validity and reliability. The most commonly used test for determining eligibility for SLD services is the Wechsler Intelligence Scale for Children-III (WISC-III). This test has multiple subtests that yield two scale scores. One scale, the *performance scale*, measures a variety of abilities that are closely related to the skills needed to achieve in mathematics. For instance, on one subtest, students must use blocks to represent a design presented to them on paper. A second scale, the *verbal scale*, measures abilities related more closely to reading and written expression, such as vocabulary. The verbal and performance scale scores are combined to determine a full-scale score.

To determine current achievement levels, either the school psychologist or the special education teacher uses a comprehensive achievement test, standardized on the school-age population of students, to individually assess the student. One of the most widely used instruments for assessing academic achievement is the Woodcock–Johnson Psychoeducational Battery-III (WJ-III), Tests of Achievement, which provides information about the student's performance in reading, mathematics, and writing. Like the WISC-III, it has a mean of 100 and a standard deviation of 15. The advantage of these standardized scores is that they can be compared to scores obtained on aptitude tests. The multidisciplinary team can use these standardized scores to determine if a significant aptitude–achievement discrepancy is present and if that discrepancy is significant enough to declare a student eligible for special education services under the SLD category.

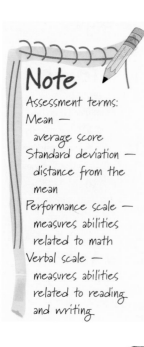

Note

Assessment terms:
Mean —
  average score
Standard deviation —
  distance from the
  mean
Performance scale —
  measures abilities
  related to math
Verbal scale —
  measures abilities
  related to reading
  and writing

Aptitude = WISC-III

Achievement = WJ-III

  ↰ looking for
discrepancies between
aptitude &
  achievement
    which might
  indicate
    SLD

States have different criteria for defining a severe aptitude–achievement discrepancy (Mercer & Pullen, 2005). In some states, students must exhibit a discrepancy that is more than one standard deviation from the mean. Thus, a child obtaining a full-scale score of 115 on the WISC-III and a score of 99 on the reading portion of the WJ-III would qualify for services because of the clear disability in reading. Other states have stricter criteria. For instance, some states require an achievement–aptitude discrepancy of 1.5 standard deviations (22 or 23 points) and others require a discrepancy of at least 2 standard deviations (30 points). The discrepancy in Devin's case was more than 40 points between the full-scale IQ score and the cluster score on the reading subtests of the WJ-III.

Because central nervous system dysfunction is presumed to be an underlying cause of SLD, the multidisciplinary team may collect assessment data about the student's processing abilities. For instance, the multidisciplinary team may administer the Comprehensive Test of Phonological Processing (CTOPP) to determine if the child has difficulty manipulating sounds—a processing deficit associated with dyslexia. This is a standardized test that allows the multidisciplinary team to determine how discrepant the student's phonological abilities are compared to those of his or her peers.

Informal Assessment

Although some students with disabilities do exhibit social difficulties and problems in adapting to specific situations or environments, traditionally the multidisciplinary team has not used formal assessments of adaptive or social behavior to identify difficulties in these areas. This situation is beginning to change, however, as more researchers develop social and adaptive assessments for students with SLD. More and more, educators are realizing that focusing solely on a discrepancy between aptitude and achievement does not provide a complete picture of the complex nature of learning disabilities.

Even though formal assessments help the team identify the academic areas in which the child needs assistance, they do not always provide the type of diagnostic information required to intervene successfully. Thus, the multidisciplinary team collects information from informal assessments to understand the student's behavior in the classroom and performance in the school curriculum. Informal assessments are not standardized and may involve observations in classrooms, a review of anecdotal records (e.g., discipline records, report cards), portfolio assessment or a review of student's class work, and curriculum-based assessments.

Informal assessments can provide more in-depth information about what a student can or cannot do in the curriculum or how he or she responds to certain activities and strategies in the classroom. In one type of curriculum-based assessment, oral fluency rates are calculated by counting the number of words the student reads correctly in 1 minute in selected reading passages. Reading passages are selected from different grade-level curricula to determine the type of reading materials a student can read independently versus with support. Another informal assessment might be used to analyze the student's writing samples for organization of ideas, vocabulary use, and other mechanical difficulties (e.g., problems with spelling, syntax, or the rules of punctuation and capitalization).

Ensuring an Appropriate IEP

Once a student is formally identified as having an SLD, the multidisciplinary team must determine the type of educational program and supports the student needs. The multidisciplinary team uses information collected from formal and informal assessments to determine appropriate goals and objectives for instruction and the instructional interventions and supports necessary to meet those goals and objectives.

When making decisions about appropriate instructional interventions and supports, the multidisciplinary team has to rely heavily on the research base on effective instruction for students with SLD and other struggling learners. The field of special education has amassed considerable knowledge about how to intervene with the academic problems of students with SLD, particularly in the areas of reading and writing. Professionals working with these students have an ethical responsibility to draw on that research base.

Research-Based Interventions and Best Practices

Without adequate intervention, Devin and other students with SLD will lag further and further behind their peers as they progress through school. The academic achievement gap between students with SLD and their peers without disabilities usually widens with each passing school year. By high school, students with disabilities are often functioning four or five years below grade level.

To minimize the achievement gap and ensure academic success for these students, instruction in the early years should be intensive, attempting to help students learn basic literacy, numeracy, and social skills. As students enter the upper elementary and secondary grades, however, the content demands increase and students may have to learn more sophisticated ways to acquire content despite their limited basic skills. We will describe the types of intensive interventions that students with SLD may require to maximize their academic potential.

Teacher-Directed Interventions in Reading

Like many students with SLD, Devin has problems with reading (Kavale & Reese, 1992). Thus, special education teachers working with students with SLD must have a well-developed knowledge base for teaching literacy to struggling learners. Because many students with SLD do not remember letters easily and have core deficits in phonological awareness and letter–sound relationships, carefully crafted beginning reading instruction is essential to their success. Instruction in the early years of school must incorporate systematic, explicit instruction in phonological awareness, decoding, and sight word recognition. Moreover, this instruction should be provided in small groups to ensure its intensity (Foorman & Torgesen, 2001).

Instruction in phonological awareness (PA) helps students develop an understanding of how words work: Words make up sentences, words are divided into syllables, and words are made up of individual sounds (Moats, 2000). Initially, PA instruction should involve sounds only, not letters. In kindergarten, however, teachers begin to combine phonics instruction with PA instruction. The primary goal of phonics instruction is to teach students to blend sounds to form words and help them recognize patterns in words. Phonics instruction combined with PA instruction and spelling instruction should go a long way in improving the word recognition skills of students with SLD (National Reading Panel [NRP], 2000).

To further assist students with SLD, teachers should simultaneously teach basic sight words that are not phonetically regular or irregular. In kindergarten, teachers can

This teacher gives individual instruction to a student as he reads his own work aloud.

focus on a few key words, such as *the* and *me*, to build students' sight-word vocabulary slowly. Good *decoding* skills and the ability to recognize frequently used words will help students with SLD develop basic literacy skills. Researchers have developed numerous classroom interventions and curricula that can be used to provide high-quality PA and phonics instruction.

Developing strong word-recognition skills is not the only necessary ingredient for successful reading. Teachers also must focus on developing *oral fluency* (the ability to easily read connected text), vocabulary, and comprehension. Because students with SLD struggle with basic literacy skills, they often read less, acquire less vocabulary, and have fewer opportunities to develop strategies for comprehending text.

In addition, the *cognitive and metacognitive problems* of some students with SLD cause difficulty in comprehending texts. Students with SLD need structured opportunities to read aloud daily, focusing on improving accuracy, speed, and *prosody* (NRP, 2000; Stahl, 2004). Moreover, special educators have to provide explicit, systematic instruction in vocabulary and comprehension (Gersten, Fuchs, Willams, & Baker, 2001). Vocabulary instruction should emphasize learning and using words that are likely to improve students' comprehension and writing. Comprehension instruction must actively teach students the processes that effective readers use while processing text.

As students get older, vocabulary and comprehension instruction that helps students learn to strategically define words and attack text becomes essential to successful content-area instruction. Although fewer research-based interventions are available for building fluency, vocabulary, and comprehension than for word recognition, some useful materials are available to teachers (for example, see "Big Ideas in Beginning Reading" at http://reading.uoregon.edu/index.php).

MCPS: use of Phonics & sign language!

→ Agree!

→ Often does not!

Teacher-Directed Interventions in Writing

Many students with SLD have deficits in written expression, which often reflect underlying phonological and *metacognitive* problems. Some students with SLD exhibit problems with handwriting and spelling that interfere so dramatically with production of text that the quality of their writing is impaired. In addition, these students sometimes have difficulty organizing, generating, and revising text.

Students who have problems with handwriting must receive careful instruction in letter formation that enables them

This student goes through the writing process, planning, generating, and editing his own text, while his teacher observes.

to develop fluency. Two of the handwriting curricula available to teachers are D'Nealian and Zaner–Bloser.

(handwritten margin notes: "Don't like D'Nealian!")

Poor spelling fluency also impairs students' abilities to transcribe their ideas into text, and many of these spelling difficulties are the result of underlying phonological and *orthographic* difficulties. Combining high-quality structured spelling instruction with systematic, explicit phonological awareness and phonics instruction can go a long way toward helping students with SLD become better spellers. In addition to being systematic and explicit, spelling instruction should be developmental in nature, focus on high-frequency sight words, teach students how to check and correct misspellings, and develop students' desire to spell correctly.

(handwritten margin notes: "Shouldn't strategies be useable outside of school? Yes!")

Instruction in written expression should teach students strategies for each component of the writing process: planning, generating, and editing text. Currently, many research-based strategies are available for teaching students each of these components. These strategies are appropriate for both narrative and expository text and can be used with elementary and secondary students. Some strategies, such as the *Sentence Writing Strategy* (Schumaker & Sheldon, 1985) and the *Paragraph Writing Strategy* (Schumaker & Lyeria, 1991), give specific instruction in early writing skills.

Teacher-Directed Interventions in Mathematics

The incidence of students with math disabilities is much smaller than the incidence of those with literacy problems. Yet, like students with disabilities in literacy, this population of students is diverse. Sometimes the students struggle to recall basic facts. Other times

Manipulatives can help instructors teach the concept of the base-ten system.

their difficulties are more conceptual in nature. Still other times, they have an underlying reading comprehension problem. Effective mathematics instruction, therefore, is predicated on determining the nature of the student's math disability.

Although less is known about the nature of effective mathematics instruction for students with SLD, research has revealed some effective interventions. Conceptual understanding can be improved by engaging students in instruction that progresses through concrete, semiconcrete, and abstract levels of understanding (Mercer & Pullan, 2005). Concrete instruction uses manipulatives, and semiconcrete instruction uses pictures, to help students understand concepts. For instance, students may use manipulatives to learn how addition or multiplication works. They also can use manipulatives to understand how place value operates in problems requiring regrouping. Fluency in basic facts can be improved by engaging students in repeated drill through peer-mediated and computer-assisted strategies.

Finally, students can be taught cognitive strategies for actively solving word problems. These strategies often teach students to comprehend word problems and determine how to represent them using number statements (e.g., John had 3 trucks of logs with 124 logs on each truck. How many logs was John hauling on the trucks? This problem can be represented as $3 \times 124 = 374$).

Behavioral and Social Interventions

Like many students with SLD, Devin has difficulty with social relationships and risks rejection from his peers. Further, his chronic frustration with academic tasks leads him to avoid these tasks, resulting in off-task or other inappropriate behaviors. The first step in helping these students achieve is to determine what contributes to their behavior problems. For instance, teachers must ask themselves if the students are off-task

Levione refers to this →

because they do not understand the directions, are trying to avoid the task, have trouble paying attention, or the task is too difficult. Answers to these questions dictate whether the teacher should provide more assistance with the task or teach students to *self-monitor* their time on task (Harris, Graham, Reid, McElroy, & Hamby, 1994; Harris, Reid, & Graham, 2004).

Students with SLD profit from the same strategies that help students with emotional and behavioral problems. These strategies include behavioral contracts, token economies, problem-solving strategies, and social-skills strategies. These and other strategies are discussed in chapter 5, on students with emotional and behavioral disorders.

Access to the General Education Curriculum and Settings

Since the reauthorization of IDEA in 1997, pressure has been building for access of students with SLD to the general education curriculum. Now, with the demands from No Child Left Behind and the 2004 reauthorized IDEA, state and local education agencies are under even more pressure to help students with SLD make adequate yearly progress in the general education curriculum. These requirements are pushing educators at all levels to consider what they can do to redesign the general education curriculum so students with disabilities can access it.

To meet this challenge, educators must be aware of the concepts of universal design for learning, accommodations, and modifications. *Universal design for learning* is a reconceptualization of the curriculum so it is accessible and appropriate for students with different learning profiles (Rose & Meyer, 2002). Using multimedia and various instructional strategies and approaches, teachers should be able to redesign the curriculum so all learners can access it.

In applying concepts of universal design, teachers and school professionals first must consider what goals they want all students to achieve. After determining curricular goals, they have to find ways to accommodate students in the curriculum or modify the curriculum so all students can reach these goals. *Accommodations* refer to any strategies that allow students with SLD to acquire the same concepts and skills as their typical peers. By contrast, *modifications* involve changing the curriculum so the learning expectations are realistic and individually appropriate. In the discussion that follows, we describe selected planning strategies, accommodations, and modifications that teachers might use to create a universally designed curriculum.

Planning Strategies

A few researchers have developed and tested planning routines that help teachers focus on what they want *all* students to accomplish versus what they want *some* students to accomplish. One of the best examples of these routines is the Unit Planning Pyramid (Schumm, Vaughn, & Leavell, 1994), which provides a classroom teacher with a structure of how to adjust a lesson to the diverse levels of student needs in the inclusive classroom.

Using the pyramid structure, the teacher prioritizes concepts of the content to be taught and then divides them into the three degrees of learning (the base, middle, and top levels). The base of the pyramid is composed of the fundamental concepts in the instructional unit ("What do I want *all* my students know?"). The middle part of the pyramid consists of the concepts that *most* students in that classroom are expected to acquire. The top of the pyramid represents more advanced and elaborated information about the targeted concepts in the lesson unit. By using the Unit Planning Pyramid, classroom teachers can plan different levels of objectives and content for mixed-ability groups and provide all students, including those with SLD, more accessible instruction. A form of the Unit Planning Pyramid is shown in Figure 4.1.

Planning routine helping to focus on what all Ss to accomplish.

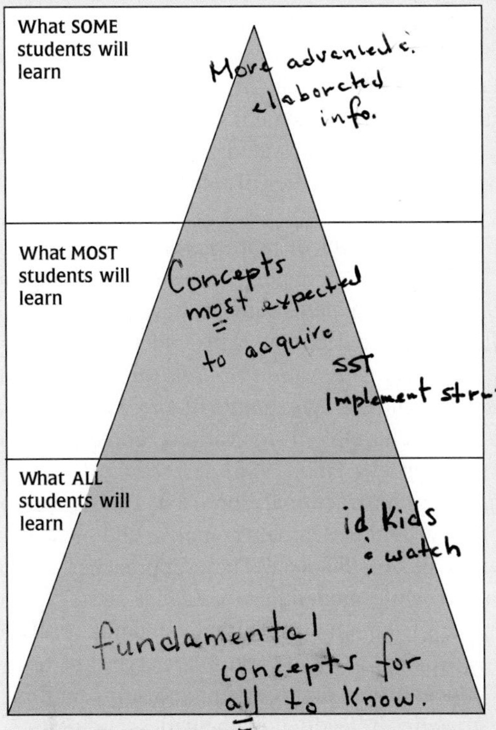
What SOME students will learn
More advanced & elaborated info.
What MOST students will learn
Concepts most expected to acquire
What ALL students will learn
id kids & watch
fundamental concepts for all to know.

Date: ______

Period: ______

Unit Title: ______

Materials/Resources: ______

SST
Implement strategies to help kids learn
Use continual assessment to monitor kids

Instructional Strategies: ______

Adaptation for Students With Disabilities: ______

In-Class Assignments/Homework: ______

Evaluations: ______

Source: From *Teaching exceptional, diverse, and at-risk students in the general education classroom* (2nd ed.), by S. Vaughn, C. S. Bos, & J. S. Schumm (Boston: Allyn & Bacon). Copyright © 1999. Used with permission.

FIGURE 4.1
Unit Planning Pyramid

Accommodation Strategies

Ways by which teachers can accommodate students with SLD to make curriculum more accessible to them include content-enhancement strategies, peer-mediated instruction, learning strategies, and assistive technology (Haager & Klingner, 2005).

1. *Content-enhancement strategies* provide teachers with a structure for organizing student learning that is more effective than traditional lecture instruction. These strategies include *advance organizers* and *graphic organizers* that enable students with SLD to acquire key concepts in the general education curriculum. An example of a research-based enhancement strategy is the *concept map* (Konopak, 1991; Martin, 1996), which helps students define a concept, such as democracy, by analyzing the characteristics of relevant examples and nonexamples.

2. *Peer-mediated strategies* draw on the strengths of more academically capable peers to help SLD students learn important content or learning strategies (Fuchs, Fuchs, & Mathes, 1997). Peer-mediated strategies have been used to help students memorize math facts, practice decoding skills, practice oral reading, and learn comprehension strategies. *Classwide Peer Tutoring*, developed by Charles Greenwood and his colleagues, is an example of a research-based, peer-mediated strategy that has been applied to various content areas (Delquadri, Greenwood, Whorton, Carta, & Hall, 1986).

3. *Learning strategies interventions* are instructional approaches designed to teach students with SLD and other struggling learners cognitive and metacognitive strategies (described earlier in this chapter). These approaches guide teachers in how to (a) think aloud while modeling a particular strategy, (b) engage students in guided practice of the strategy, (c) help students practice the strategy independently, and (d) adapt the strategy to other types of tasks and content areas. The special education research literature contains multiple examples of effective learning strategies in reading, mathematics, and writing.

This student works quietly with a math software program on the computer, which is a common mode of assistive technology.

4. *Assistive technology* refers to any item, equipment, or product that can be used to increase, maintain, or enhance the functional capabilities of students with SLD (Blackhurst, 1997). For instance, students with SLD who have difficulties in handwriting, spelling, or organization can use adaptive grips for pens/pencils, voice-recognition software that records students' orally generated text, and software that enhances students' organization, editing, and spelling during writing. Assistive technology offers students with SLD valuable opportunities to participate actively in general education curricular activities. Table 4.1 lists assistive technology devices for different school-related areas.

Modifications

Sometimes, planning for universal design requires that teachers adapt or modify curriculum materials and assignments or provide remedial instruction that enables students with SLD to acquire the skills and strategies necessary to successfully access the general education curriculum. Teachers can adapt or modify curriculum materials in a number of ways to achieve universal design. For instance, teachers providing instruction around a specific theme can use reading materials that vary in text difficulty but address the same concept. Further, teachers can create different assignments to address

TABLE 4.1
Assistive Technology Devices

Area	Low Tech → → → → → → → → → → → → High Tech
Reading	Predictable books → Changes in text size, spacing, color → Using pictures with texts → Single word scanners → Portable dictionary → Electronic books
Learning & Studying	Print or picture schedule → Highlight text → Small tape recorder for assignment or task → Electronic organizers → Software for organization → Handheld computers
Math	Enlarged worksheets → Calculators → Alternative keyboard → Math software
Writing & Handwriting	Pencils with adaptive grips → Adaptive papers (raised line or highlighted line) → Slantboard → Portable word processor → Voice recognition software → Talking calculator
Writing & Composition	Word cards or book → Pocket-sized electronic dictionary or thesaurus → Word processor with spell checker → Word processing software with writing support → Multimedia software
Communication	Communication boards with pictures → Voice output device with speech synthesis
Vision	Magnifier → Large print books → Screen readers/Text readers
Hearing	Signaling device → Captioning → Sound amplifier/Hearing aid
Position & Seating	Non-slip surface on chair, adapted/alternative chairs
Environment Control	Light switch extension

a learning goal that all students are required to achieve. The modified assignments may be designed to place fewer reading or writing demands on the student with an SLD.

Teachers also can group students for explicit instruction in skills or strategies that will support their learning in the content areas. This instruction may take place within the general education classroom or in a separate environment and should draw on the evidence-based practices in reading, writing, and mathematics discussed earlier. In addition to teacher-directed instruction, teachers can use computers to provide instruction, give extra practice in learning skills, or enhance curriculum. This is typically referred to as *computer-assisted instruction.*

The Role of Teacher Collaboration in Ensuring Access to the General Education Curriculum

Universal curriculum design and the accompanying accommodations and modifications can be achieved only when special and general education teachers have a clear sense of the goals they would like students to achieve. This planning requires careful collaboration. General and special education teachers can work together and share their expertise through various models of *teacher collaboration* (e.g., *teacher assistance teams*, *collaboration consultation* models, *peer collaboration* models, and *co-teaching*) (Cook & Friend, 1991).

During one or more phases of the instructional cycle—assessment, planning, instruction, evaluation—collaborative teachers draw on their unique expertise to optimize their educational services for all students, including those with SLD. General educators have a well-developed knowledge base about standard curriculum and subject matters, and special education teachers are well versed in identifying individual students' needs and learning characteristics, and in effective learning strategies, accommodations, and modifications (Pugach & Johnson, 2002). Through collaboration between the two groups, students with SLD are more likely to be successful in general education curriculum activities.

Summary

Students with SLD constitute the largest group of students served under IDEA. Approximately half of all students with identified disabilities have SLD. By definition, these students have some type of language processing deficit that interferes with their ability to listen, think, read, write, spell, or perform mathematical calculations. In most states, students with SLD are identified when a severe discrepancy between achievement and intellectual ability exists (that is, achievement in one or more academic areas is not commensurate with a student's intellectual ability) and the student's need in this area is sufficient to require more intensive instructional services than usually needed. Typically, formal assessments are used to identify students with SLD, whereas informal assessments or more classroom-based assessments are used to determine how best to teach such students.

What causes SLD is still a mystery, although researchers have some evidence that abnormal brain development, genetics or hereditary factors, and teratogens may be contributing factors. Despite the lack of confirmation and substantiation, educators have made considerable progress identifying educational innovations that enable students with SLD to grow academically. Research-based strategies in reading, writing, mathematics, and behavioral and social interventions, when properly implemented, can help students make tremendous progress. Additionally, more than ever before, educators know many strategies for modifying the general education curriculum and creating the type of accommodations that will enable students with SLD to acquire a knowledge base that will enable their success in college.

It is imperative that all prospective special educators become more knowledgeable about the information in this chapter, as our students with SLD depend on well-informed special educators to advocate for them and ensure their success. Currently, many students with SLD are not achieving as they should. Special and general education teachers who are knowledgeable about curriculum design, accommodations, modifications, and research-based intervention strategies can change this scenario. By working closely with parents and providing high-quality instruction in the general education curriculum, teachers can help many more students with SLD achieve successful outcomes.

References

Alarcon, M., Knopick, V. S., & DeFries, J. C. (2000). Covariation of mathematics achievement and general cognitive ability in twins. *Journal of School Psychology, 38,* 63–77.

Bender, W. N. (2001). *Learning disabilities: Characteristics, identification, and teaching strategies* (4th ed.). Boston: Allyn & Bacon.

Blachman, B. A. (1995, March). *Identifying the core linguistic deficits and the critical conditions for early intervention with children with reading disabilities.* Paper presented at annual meeting of the Learning Disabilities Association of America, Orlando, FL.

Blackhurst, A. E. (1997). Perspectives on technology in special education. *Teaching Exceptional Children, 29*(5), 41–48.

Cawley, J., Parmar, R., Foley, T. E., Salmon, S., & Roy, S. (2001). Arithmetic performance of students: Implications for standards and programming. *Exceptional Children, 67,* 311–328.

Cook, L., & Friend, M. (1991). Collaboration in special education: Coming of age in the 1990s. *Preventing School Failure, 35*(2), 24–27.

Delquadri, J., Greenwood, C. R., Whorton, D., Carta, J. J., & Hall, R. V. (1986). Classwide peer tutoring. *Exceptional Children, 52,* 535–542.

Foorman, B. R., & Torgesen, J. (2001). Critical elements of classroom and small group instruction that promote reading success in all children. *Learning Disabilities Research & Practice, 16,* 203–212.

Frank, Y. (2000). Learning disabilities: Classification, clinical features and treatment. In K. J. Palmer (Ed.), *Topics in pediatric psychiatry* (pp. 107–120). Kwai Chung, Hong Kong: Adis International Publications.

Fuchs, D., Fuchs, L. S., & Mathes, P. G. (1997). Peer-assisted learning strategies: Making classrooms more responsive to diversity. *American Educational Research Journal, 34,* 174–206.

Gersten, R., Fuchs, L. S., Williams, J. P., & Baker, S. (2001). Teaching reading comprehension strategies to students with learning disabilities: A review of the research. *Review of Educational Research, 71,* 279–320.

Graham, S., Harris, K., & Larsen, L. (2001). Prevention and intervention of writing difficulties for students with learning disabilities. *Learning Disabilities Research and Practice, 16,* 74–84.

Haager, D., & Klingner, J. K. (2005). *Differentiating instruction in inclusive classrooms: Special educator's guide.* Boston: Pearson Education.

Harris, K. R., Graham, S., Reid, R., McElroy, K., & Hamby, R. (1994). Self-monitoring of attention versus self-monitoring of performance: A cross-task comparison. *Learning Disability Quarterly, 17,* 121–139.

Harris, K. R., Reid, R., & Graham, S. (2004). Self-regulation among students with LD and ADHD. In B. Wong (Ed.), *Learning about learning disabilities* (3rd ed., pp. 167–195). Orlando, FL: Academic Press.

International Dyslexia Association. (2002, November 12). *What is dyslexia? Definition of dyslexia adopted by the IDA board of directors.* Retrieved December 8, 2003, from http://www.interdys.org/servlet/compose?section_id=5&page_id=95#What%20is%20 dyslexia

Kavale, K. A., & Forness, S. R. (1996). Social skill deficits and learning disabilities: A meta-analysis. *Journal of Learning Disabilities, 29,* 226–237.

Kavale, K. A., & Reese, J. H. (1992). The character of learning disabilities: An Iowa profile. *Learning Disability Quarterly, 15*(2), 74–94.

Keeler, M. L., & Swanson, H. L. (2001). Does strategy knowledge influence working memory in children with mathematical disabilities? *Journal of Learning Disabilities, 34,* 418–434.

Kirk, S. A. (1972). *Educating exceptional children* (2nd ed.). Boston: Houghton Mifflin.

Konopak, B. C. (1991). Teaching vocabulary to improve science learning. In C. M. Santa & D. E. Alvermann (Eds.), *Science learning: Processes and applications* (pp. 134–146). Newark, DE: International Reading Association.

Martin, D. J. (1996). *Elementary science methods: A constructivist approach.* Albany, NY: Delmar.

Mercer, C. D., Jordan, L., Allsopp, D. H., & Mercer, A. R. (1996). Learning disabilities definitions and criteria used by state education departments. *Learning Disability Quarterly, 19,* 217–232.

Mercer, C. D., & Pullen, P. (2005). *Students with learning disabilities* (6th ed.). Upper Saddle, NJ: Pearson Education.

Moats, L. C. (2000). *Speech to print: Language essentials for teachers.* Baltimore: Paul H. Brookes.

Montague, M., & Applegate, B. (1993). Middle school students' mathematical problem solving: An analysis of think-aloud protocols. *Learning Disability Quarterly, 16,* 19–30.

Muir, W. J. (2000). Genetics advances and learning disability. *British Journal of Psychiatry, 176,* 12–19.

National Joint Committee on Learning Disabilities. (1998). Operationalizing the NJCLD definition of learning disabilities for ongoing assessment in schools. *Learning Disability Quarterly, 24,* 186–193.

National Reading Panel. (2000). *Teaching children to read: An evidence-based assessment of the scientific research literature on reading and its implications for reading instruction.* Washington, DC: National Institute of Child Health and Human Development.

Pugach, M. C., & Johnson, L. J. (2002). *Collaborative practitioners, collaborative schools* (2nd ed.). Denver: Love Publishing.

Rose, D. H., & Meyer, A. (2002). *Teaching every student in the digital age: Universal Design for Learning.* Alexandria, VA: Association for Supervision and Curriculum Development.

Schumaker, J. B., & Lyeria, K. D. (1991). *The paragraph writing strategy.* Lawrence, KS: University of Kansas Center for Research on Learning.

Schumaker, J. B., & Sheldon, J. (1985). *The sentence writing strategy.* Lawrence, KS: University of Kansas Center for Research on Learning.

Schumm, J. S., Vaughn, S., & Leavell, A. G. (1994). Planning pyramid: A framework for planning for diverse students' needs during content area instruction. *Reading Teacher, 47,* 608–615.

Shaywitz, B. A., Shaywitz, S. E., Puch, K. R., Mencl, W. E., Fulbright, R. K., Skudlarkski, P., Constable, R. T., Marchione, K. E., Fletcher, J. M., Lyon, G. R., & Gore, J. C. (2002). Disruption of posterior brain systems for reading in children with developmental dyslexia. *Biological Psychiatry, 52,* 101–110.

Smith, C. R. (1994). *Learning disabilities: The interaction of learner, task and setting* (3rd ed.). Boston: Allyn & Bacon.

Smith, C. R. (2000). *Learning disabilities: The interaction of learner, task and setting* (5th ed.). Boston: Allyn & Bacon.

Stahl, S. A. (2004). What do we know about fluency? Findings of the National Reading Panel. In P. McCardle & V. Chhabra (Eds.), *The voice of evidence in reading research.* Baltimore: Paul H. Brookes.

Swanson, H. L. (1999). Reading research for students with LD: A meta-analysis of intervention outcomes. *Journal of Learning Disabilities, 32,* 504–532.

U.S. Department of Education. (2002). *Twenty-fourth annual report to Congress on the implementation of the Individuals with Disabilities Education Act.* Washington, DC: Author.

Wong, B. (1991). The relevance of metacognition to learning disabilities. In B. Wong (Ed.), *Learning about learning disabilities* (pp. 232–261). San Diego, CA: Academic Press.

Emotional/ Behavior Disorders

5

Stephen W. Smith &
T. Rowand Robinson

Students with emotional or behavioral disorders (EBD) present a significant challenge for education professionals. These students can exhibit behaviors that are so disruptive in the educational environment that they seriously impair their relationships with parents, peers, and teachers. To complicate matters, students with EBD are increasingly segregated, and they often fail in school (Kauffman, 2005). The problem is not restricted to their behavioral excesses or deficits. Adult responses to these students can worsen their behaviors. Because they are not responsive to typical management and discipline, students with EBD can be constantly difficult to manage, resulting in negative teacher actions and peer rejection.

Fortunately, teachers who become informed about students with EBD can have a significant influence on these students' lives. By learning about the complexities of

CASE STUDY: JASON

Jason is a sixth-grade boy who was referred for special education services when he entered the fourth grade. At that time, he often refused to complete classwork, was openly defiant with teachers and administrators, was verbally aggressive with classmates in various settings, and frequently disrupted classroom activities. In addition, Jason was falling behind in all of his subjects as a direct result of his behaviors. Teachers and administrators continuously tried to redirect and decrease his inappropriate behaviors. Over the course of the year, they collected data (e.g., anecdotal reports from teachers and staff, attendance and referral records, parent and teacher checklists, work samples) along with formal assessments. All showed a need for more extensive services than those provided in the general education setting without additional supports.

As a result, a multidisciplinary team developed an IEP that guided special education resources and supports to improve Jason's educational experience. Although his fifth-grade experience improved, Jason's sixth-grade year began with an increasing array of inappropriate behaviors that raised new concerns.

Currently, Jason is engaging in more troublesome aggressive behaviors that are disruptive wherever he goes in school. He came to school one day with a Mohawk haircut, and he tattooed his arm in several places with an ink pen. He often engages in verbal aggression toward other students and teachers and destroys property (e.g., throws a chair or book, kicks over tables or desks) when anyone asks him to start or complete his academic work.

Jason lives with his biological father and stepmother, who are both employed. Neither completed high school. There seems to be little support in the home for Jason to be successful in school. Jason's parents refuse to interact with his teachers or other school officials, fail to sign documents, and do not show up for scheduled meetings.

EBD as an educational diagnosis and ways to effectively manage the associated behaviors, teachers can ultimately help students become competent adults who develop positive personal relationships and contribute productively to the community.

In this chapter you will learn about defining EBD, characteristics of the disorder, and its complex causes. Also, you will learn how students with EBD are often served in schools and how they are identified for services. Finally, this chapter presents a brief overview of ways to effectively manage student behavior and provide access to the general education curriculum.

Definition of Emotional or Behavioral Disorders

The identification of emotional or behavioral disorders (EBD) in school-aged children and youth is a complicated and controversial matter, more so than other categorical areas in special education. Determining the exact nature of an EBD is inherently subjective, influenced by individual perceptions of human behavior within the realm of acceptable social norms and values. Although the concept that deviance is identified as being markedly different from what is socially acceptable seems easy to understand, the practice of identifying deviant behavior that merits special education services in schools is not so easy.

Basically, what defines a student with EBD is not the *type* of deviant or maladaptive behavior (e.g., impulsivity, aggression, truancy, social withdrawal, lying, noncompliance) but, rather, the degree to which the student exhibits the behavior (how much, how little, or how long). All students and adults are impulsive at times, are aggressive in some situations, or do not comply with others' requests. The difference is in individuals who are impulsive frequently, are verbally or physically aggressive toward others with little or no provocation, or who are so chronic in their noncompliance that their behavior interferes significantly with their ability to be successful in life's activities. Determining which students exhibit an EBD, as an educational diagnosis, involves determining what deviates significantly from the norm or the socially expected school behavior for children and youth.

Deviance, however, is as much a function of someone's reaction to the behavior as it is the behavior in and of itself. And no guideline, definition, or test clearly establishes at what point an individual's behavior or amount of behavior deviates from the group.

Further complicating the identification of deviant behavior is the multitude of factors that influence teachers, administrators, school psychologists, counselors, and parents who might make judgments about the existence of EBD in school-aged children and youth. Along with the sociological parameters of behavior (e.g., behaviors that violate cultural or social standards), an individual's tolerance for problem behavior, differences in the theoretical models from which professionals operate, and differences in terminology associated with emotional or behavioral problems all affect how a person views EBD (Coleman & Webber, 2002).

Professionals or parents who have a high tolerance for behaviors may consider a student as bothersome, perhaps described as "a handful" or as "having some issues." They might say, "John has some problems, but he's a good kid and we're working on it." Other adults do not tolerate certain behaviors as well. Of the same student, teachers might say, "He's out of control—terribly aggressive," or, "He's so much of a problem that I won't put up with it any more."

Differenting views of EBD

Professionals' training, beliefs, and ideas about behavior can influence how they think about deviance. The theoretical orientation from which a professional operates provides him or her a way to explain behavior, and it offers ways to effect behavioral change. Some teachers, administrators, school psychologists, mental health workers, and school counselors see behavior as the result of unconscious motivations or underlying mental problem or illness (the *psychoeducational* view). Others view an individual's behavior within a complex social system consisting of interactions with multiple individuals (e.g., school personnel, peers, service providers, family and community members), having a variety of roles in a variety of settings and situations (the *ecological* or *sociological* view), or believe that disordered behavior results from disease, chemical imbalance, hereditary influences, or injury (the *biological* or *medical* view).

Some professionals hold a behavioral orientation in which deviant behavior is viewed as a maladaptive learned response. These professionals focus on the relationship to various environmental stimuli that precede (an *antecedent*) or follow (a *consequence*) the behavior. Antecedents to behavior in the classroom could be teacher prompts, cues, questions, or demands, and consequences can be rewards or punishments.

Finally, the terminology used to label emotional or behavioral disorders may influence an individual's view of behavior. *Emotional disturbance* is the term used in IDEA. Yet, states have adopted other terminology such as *emotionally handicapped*, *emotionally disturbed*, *emotionally impaired*, or *behavioral disorders*. Professionals with a more medical or psychiatric orientation might consider children and youth with significant emotional or behavioral problems as having a *conduct disorder* or an *oppositional defiant disorder*. Professionals with a more psychological view may consider these children and youth as exhibiting *antisocial behavior* or being *socially maladjusted*.

In the professional field of special education, the preferred term is *emotional or behavioral disorder (EBD)*, a term intended to reduce the restrictiveness of other terminology and to include components of emotion and overt behavior, or both. The use of various terminology to label and define deviant behavior of school-aged children and youth leads to confusion, which contributes to difficulties in our understanding a phenomenon that is inherently difficult to understand, label, and, ultimately, to define.

Current Federal Definition

In the late 1950s, Eli Bower conducted a study in California to develop a screening device or process by which teachers could identify what he called *emotionally handicapped* children in public school classrooms (Bower, 1981). He hoped to devise an approach or measure that would be economical to use and score and would aid in identifying children at risk, with the goal of providing programming that would eliminate future problems. Bower's study encompassed 200 schools and approximately 5,000 students. He used five characteristics that are still used, with few changes, in the rules and regulations governing the implementation of IDEA.

Bower's definition, with extracts from the federal definition in bold, is as follows:

   (i)   *The term means a condition exhibiting one or more of the following characteristics over a long period of time and to a marked degree* **that adversely affects a child's educational performance:**

      (A) *An inability to learn which cannot be explained by intellectual, sensory, or health factors.*

> **Note**
>
> Professionals from varying schools of thought define the causes of EBD differently, depending on if they subscribe to a psychoeducational view, an ecological or sociological view, or a biological or medical view.

> **Note**
>
> The preferred term by professionals in the field—EBD—encompasses all of the following expressions:
> - Emotional disturbance
> - Emotionally handicapped
> - Emotionally disturbed
> - Emotionally impaired
> - Behavioral disorders
> - Conduct disorder
> - Oppositional defiant disorder
> - Antisocial behavior
> - Socially maladjusted

Federal Definition

> *(B) An inability to build or maintain satisfactory interpersonal relationships with peers and teachers.*
> *(C) Inappropriate types of behavior and feelings under normal circumstances.*
> *(D) A general pervasive mood of unhappiness or depression.*
> *(E) A tendency to develop physical symptoms or fears associated with personal or school problems.*
>
> *(ii)* **The term includes schizophrenia. The term does not apply to children who are socially maladjusted, unless it is determined that they have an emotional disturbance.**

Problems With the Federal Definition of ED

Bower's original definition is particularly strong in its delineation of five dimensions of behavior, one of which is specific to school and the learning process. What makes it difficult to use as a definition is the judgment required to determine "over a long period of time" and "to a marked degree." Certainly, there could be much disagreement over what a long time might be and the degree to which behavior would have to be exhibited to be considered a disorder. No doubt there is difficulty as well in using the characteristics to identify an emotional disturbance.

Including the statement "that adversely affects a child's educational performance" complicates Bower's definition. The definition offers little guidance as to what *educational* means. Does *educational* have a strictly academic focus or does it denote a broader interpretation of the academic, social, physical, and emotional components of schooling? Considering the first characteristic, which refers to an inability to learn, this statement also could be redundant.

Finally, intense confusion was created with the addition of section ii. Because schizophrenia is a clinical disorder of intense magnitude, a child or youth with that diagnosis clearly would exhibit one or more of the five characteristics. Even more puzzling is "socially maladjusted." To specifically exclude children and youth who are socially maladjusted is illogical and nonsensical, especially with regard to characteristic B. Bower's original definition has some enduring features that have existed for decades, but there have been attempts to better define EBD.

An Emerging Definition

(handwritten: Desired changes to Fed. definition)

As a result of dissatisfaction with the current definition of EBD, the National Mental Health and Special Education Coalition, composed of national organizations in the fields of special education, mental health and related services, along with state organizations and parent groups, began work in the early 1980s to petition Congress to adopt an alternative definition. Although this effort was unsuccessful, this alternative definition is, perhaps, an improvement:

> *1. The term emotional or behavioral disorder means a disability characterized by behavioral or emotional responses in school programs so different from appropriate age, culture, or ethnic norms that they adversely affect educational performance, including academic, social, vocational or personal skills, and which:*
>
> *(a) is more than a temporary, expected response to stressful events in the environment;*

> (b) is consistently exhibited in two different settings, at least one of which is school related; and
>
> (c) persists despite individualized interventions within the education program, unless, in the judgment of the team, the child's or youth's history indicates that such interventions would not be effective.
>
> 2. This category may include children or youth with schizophrenic disorders, affective disorders, anxiety disorders, or other sustained disturbances of conduct or adjustment when they adversely affect educational performance in accordance with section 1. (Forness & Knitzer, 1992, p. 13)

Given what we know about the elusiveness of conceptualizing and defining EBD, the field of special education will continue to struggle with providing more accuracy, precision, detail, and, most important, consensus about EBD. By understanding the difficulty of conceptualizing and defining EBD, teachers and other school professionals may be better equipped to ask questions, discuss and reflect, and demand well-informed decisions about students who may be eligible for special education services in an EBD program.

Characteristics of EBD

The characteristics of EBD can be discussed according to the areas of (a) intellectual functioning and academic achievement and (b) behavioral characteristics.

Intellectual Functioning and Academic Achievement

Students who are placed in special education programs for EBD have IQs in the low average range, although some with scores below 70 are often considered mentally retarded and those in the upper range might be considered gifted (Cullinan, 2002). In any case, most students with EBD in the low average range experience academic difficulties. These students typically display off-task behavior in the classroom, lack motivation to complete tasks, and may get further and further behind in their academic performance as they get older.

Interestingly, researchers have shown that 30%–40% of students who exhibit EBD also have learning disabilities (Fessler, Rosenberg, & Rosenberg, 1991). Students who are placed in EBD programs might have academic deficits in all areas, with serious deficits in math and reading (Bos, Coleman, & Vaughn, 2002), and are more likely to fail to complete homework when compared with similar peers in general education classrooms (Bryan & Nelson, 1994).

(Intellectual:)
- *low – average IQ*
- *off task behavior*
- *lack motivation to complete tasks*
- *many w/ LDs*

Behavioral Characteristics

What comes to mind most readily about students with EBD is their persistent and noxious acting-out behaviors such as fighting, teasing, arguing, and engaging in tantrums. Most people would agree that these behaviors are displayed openly (overt) and are not easily concealed from the view of others. Often unrecognized, however, are student

(Behavioral)
- *persistent & noxious acting out*
- *fears / phobias*
- *withdrawl*

behaviors such as withdrawal, sad affect, and excessive fears and phobias that are more covert or concealed from plain view.

Internalizing Behaviors

When asked to identify students who have significant behavior problems, teachers and other professionals often miss those who have internalizing or *intrapersonal* behavior problems. This is because students with internalizing disorders typically do not display classroom discipline problems and, thus, are not noticed as frequently as those with externalizing problems. Teachers and others in contact with students who have internalizing problems might say, "She seems like such a nice girl, very quiet. She never gives me any trouble, but she seems really depressed all the time," or "He doesn't seem to have any friends and always plays by himself at recess."

Internalizing problems can take the form of childhood depression, anxiety, fears and phobias, and obsessive–compulsive disorder. These problems can affect students' socialization with peers and adults, academic success, and overall development.

Externalizing Behaviors

Externalizing or overt behaviors are more *interpersonal* than internalizing disorders and, therefore, teachers and others professionals can more readily identify them. These behaviors typically are of the acting-out and noncompliant type sometimes described as "aggressive" and are associated with continual negative interactions with authority figures at school and in the community.

Teachers and others in contact with students who have externalizing problems might say: "I don't know what I'm going to do—he's bouncing off the walls"; "She gets so verbally aggressive at the slightest request that she even threw her book across the classroom once"; "He can't stay in his seat for even a minute, and the other kids don't want anything to do with him."

Externalizing behavior problems such as defiance or aggression may become part of an escalating spiral of conflict within the family and peer group, and in marital relationships. Because aggressive and other overt undesired behaviors frequently elicit negative responses, these behaviors can limit future opportunities for positive interactions and contribute to a persistent pattern of hostility and negative social status (Walker, Colvin, & Ramsey, 1995).

Students who exhibit externalizing maladaptive behavior often become caught up in a negative spiral of peer rejection and continued aggression and disruption (Dodge & Feldman, 1990). Their peers, who continuously look elsewhere for companionship and positive social interactions, might overlook their more positive social responses because these students have been labeled as aggressive and, thus, to be avoided. Because these students act out in disturbing and aversive ways (e.g., verbal aggression, disruption of class activities, generally "displeasing" behavior), they tend to elicit negative counter-responses from peers, which contributes to further aggression or withdrawal.

At times, peers unintentionally reinforce a student's aggressive behavior by attending to it or by complying with the aggressor's demands (Bierman, Greenberg, & CPPRG, 1996). Unfortunately, students who exhibit aggressive, antisocial behaviors tend to associate with peers who exhibit similar behaviors, thereby perpetuating their aggressive behavior and increasing their rejection by nonaggressive peers. In the case of students who exhibit more covert maladaptive behaviors, their depression, anxiety, or fears and phobias may elicit social rejection because of associated behaviors that can contribute to withdrawal from positive and lasting social relationships.

Note

Students with intrapersonal behavior disorders internalize their problems—such as depression, anxiety, and fear—and are often overlooked by educators. Students with interpersonal behavior disorders externalize their problems—such as aggression, acting out, and noncompliance—and often cause negative interactions with their peers and authority figures.

(Internal)

- Hard to notice these characteristics

- depression
- anxiety
- fear / phobia
- OCD

(External) "overt"

- acting out
- noncompliant
- aggressive

Causes and Prevalence   ■ ■ ■ ■ ■

(Causes?)
* Difficult to pinpoint!

Causes of EBD can be classified in a number of ways, which affects the prevalence figures.

Biological, Environmental, and School Factors

Identifying the causes of EBD is complex and intertwined with a variety of factors, making it difficult to find one factor alone to explain a significant behavioral problem. Coie et al. (1993) believe that many risk factors can contribute to maladaptive behavior. These include *perinatal* complications, *neurochemical* imbalances, or *sensory* disabilities. Addditional causal factors, the authors point out, might be low intelligence, reading disabilities, and social incompetence, along with impoverished environments, family mental illness, abuse, neglect, and family conflict and disorganization. Combined with peer rejection, social isolation, academic failure, school dropout, and unemployment, EBD clearly can be influenced by biological, social, cultural, and academic factors (Kauffman, 2005). These risk factors likely work together, to varying degrees, at different times in a student's life with a variety of outcomes.

Prevalence

For teachers and community and hospital-based mental health professionals, the prevalence of significant emotional or behavioral disorders in the general population is of little consequence. Yet, prevalence figures help school districts, community agencies, hospitals, and local and state governments establish the need for intervention programs and estimate the amount of funding necessary. Further, the regulations in IDEA require annual reports about the numbers served so the federal government, states, and local school districts can provide special education programs for children and youth. Thus, prevalence of significant behavior problems in the general population and in special education facilitates the work of therapeutic programs and provides a basis from which to adequately staff and equip programs.

Prevalence of Mental Disorders ✶ ✶

It is believed that between 5% and 20% of children and youth have some type of mental disorder (Cullinan, 2002). These students meet the criteria for a clinical psychiatric diagnosis such as anxiety disorder, major depression, bipolar disorder, schizophrenia, oppositional defiant disorder, conduct disorder, or an eating disorder. The behavior of these children and youth is described as severe, pervasive, and chronic, and they often have difficulty meeting the behavioral, emotional, and social demands of daily living. Many children and youth who exhibit these problems are referred for special education services.

Prevalence of EBD

A modest estimate of the school population served in special education programs for EBD is about 1%, or about 473,000 students (U.S. Department of Education, 2002). A more reasonable estimate by teachers and other adults is that 3%–6% of a school population could benefit from placement in EBD programs (Kauffman, 2005). Understanding the subjective nature of identifying EBD, it is not surprising to see such discrepant figures, indicating that students with EBD are underidentified and, thus, are

Big discrepancy between # teachers/schools report : estimate by US Dept. of Ed.

Why?

underserved. Boys outnumber girls in EBD programs, perhaps because behaviors that boys typically exhibit are more likely to be considered conduct disorders.

Assessment and Evaluation for Special Education and Related Services

Assessment and evaluation of students with EBD to obtain special education services has a number of goals. The main purpose is to ensure appropriate screening, identification, and placement of students. Evaluation can result in knowledge about a student's academic and social strengths and weaknesses, including information about a student's family and community life, that may necessitate additional related services such as speech, physical or occupational therapies, psychological counseling, or social work (Braaten & Kauffman, 2000).

With this information, a multidisciplinary team consisting of education professionals, parents, and the student, if appropriate, must determine whether a student should be identified or classified to receive special education services. If so, they should use the gathered information to design appropriate and individualized educational programming documented in a student's IEP. But before a student is referred for special education services for significant emotional or behavior problems, prereferral strategies—strategies designed to prevent student referral for special education—need to be documented.

Prereferral Strategies

Before formal referral, prereferral efforts must be documented and indicate that the student is failing to respond positively to reasonable accommodations (Kauffman, 2005).

Prereferral strategies represent attempts to prevent formal referral and placement of students in special education programs through systematic and collaborative efforts. Prereferral also is designed to help teachers when they are faced with student problems requiring immediate attention (Noll, Kamps, & Seaborn, 1993). On

This teacher evaluates her student to assess his progress and development.

a routine basis, teachers employ prereferral strategies such as moving a disruptive student to the front of the classroom to monitor the student's behavior more closely, increasing contact with the home, or relying on support from other professionals, such as the school counselor.

Teachers must try & document intervention stratgies before meking sp. ed. referral request

As an example, Ms. Olsen has been having difficulty with Reginald, a second-grader who has shown increasing noncompliance, verbal aggression toward other students, and chronic temper tantrums when asked to complete his work. After using multiple behavior management strategies in the classroom, conferring with an assortment of school professionals, and meeting with Reginald's mother, his behavior did not improve. As a result, Ms. Olsen, along with the special education teacher, school counselor, school psychologist, and behavioral specialist, formed a *prereferral team* and problem-solved about Reginald's behaviors. They then developed specific action plans to enable Reginald to be successful in the general education environment.

Referral Processes

If prereferral strategies fail to yield the necessary supports for success, special education referral procedures become necessary. Referral for placement in special education because of a suspected EBD includes all of the typical evaluation procedures, such as measures of intelligence and achievement, but also might include assessment of social competence and peer relations through interviews, self-reports, anecdotal reports, direct behavioral observations, and behavior rating scales.

Assessment Processes

Numerous strategies should be used to ensure appropriate screening, identification, and placement of students with behavioral problems in special education (Lloyd, Kauffman, Landrum, & Roe, 1991). Academic and behavioral assessments are both necessary to completely depict the strengths and deficits of students suspected of having EBD. After initiating formal referral for assessment, the multidisciplinary team conducts nondiscriminatory, norm-referenced intelligence and achievement tests. If warranted, the team also might include developmental, motor, and/or adaptive behavior tests. For students with suspected EBD, direct observation (a method of recording specific behaviors typically conducted by someone other than the teacher) and the use of behavior rating scales ensure that the assessment is based on numerous informational sources (i.e., people and behavioral instruments).

1. Initiation of formal request for assessment

2. Multi-team conducts nondiscriminatory, norm-ref. IQ & achievement tests & observation using behavior rating scale.

3. Eligibility determined after assessments & collection of data.

4. Placement

5. Functional Behavioral Assessment is mandated by IDEA

Behavior rating scales that help to assess the extent of emotional or behavior problems include the Systematic Screening for Behavior Disorders Scale (Walker & Severson, 1992), Scale for Assessing Emotional Disturbance (Epstein & Cullinan, 1998), and the Social Skills Rating System (Gresham & Elliott, 1990). For example, the Child Behavior Checklist contains items that describe a broad range of behavior problems and social competencies, and it includes forms for parents, teachers, and the students themselves to fill out (Achenbach, 1991). The purpose of completing behavior rating scales is to describe the variety of behavioral characteristics of students with significant behavior problems compared to their age and grade-level peers. As such, behavior rating scales help to ensure proper identification and the design and implementation of appropriate interventions.

As part of the assessment process, multidisciplinary team members must assess the effect of a student's behaviors on peers, teachers, and family members, and also assess the effect of the teacher's behaviors. Because a teacher's interactions with the student may make the student's behavioral problems worse, observations of teacher and student interaction can significantly influence classification, placement, and treatment recommendations.

Eligibility and Placement

After academic and behavioral information is collected, students suspected of having EBD become eligible for services if they exhibit behavioral problems as specified in IDEA over a long period of time and to a marked degree, and if their educational performance is affected. At the same time the multidisciplinary team makes an eligibility decision, it considers the need for related services (e.g., counseling, social services). Various placement options are available for students requiring special education and related services. These range along a continuum from least restrictive (general education class with supports) to most restrictive (hospital or homebound instruction). Other possible placements might be general class placement with some programming in a special education resource room, a separate special education class for students with EBD for most of the school day, a separate school for students with EBD, or a residential setting. The multidisciplinary team has to decide what setting is in the best interest of the student and what programming best meets his or her academic and social needs.

Placement options

Functional Behavioral Assessment

After a student is determined to be eligible for special education services and is provided placement and programming, IDEA mandates that a *functional behavioral assessment* (FBA) be conducted for those whose behaviors either cause a change in

Headphones can keep children focused and prevent them from being distracted.

school placement or constitute a continued chronic pattern of misbehavior. FBA is a process whereby professionals try to identify the purpose of a behavior (e.g., to escape a teacher's demand to complete work or to get social reinforcement from peers for inappropriate behavior). This type of assessment includes environmental factors such as desk location, classmate behavior, difficulty of assigned work, distractions such as activities and noise levels outside the classroom, and time of day the behaviors are most likely to occur.

FBA is a multifaceted approach that focuses on the function or purpose—the *why*—of the behavior in relation to the environment, or *context*, in which it occurs. An FBA is conducted so appropriate interventions can be identified and implemented for a student to achieve the same or a similar goal (e.g., to gain something or to escape) by engaging in socially acceptable behaviors. In short, by using FBA, professionals can identify factors or causes that contribute to inappropriate behaviors and, from that information, design programs that result in academic and social success for individuals with EBD.

Research-Based Interventions and Best Practices

Interventions for students with EBD can be discussed as academic, EBD, schoolwide and classroom, and group and individual management systems.

Academic Interventions

The emphasis on behavioral issues can be a disservice to students in that it sometimes works to the detriment of academic instruction. Teachers often create inflexible external controls to manage student behavior and social learning that result in the neglect of academic instruction (Walker et al., 1998). The difficulty for teachers is that emotional and behavioral interventions should be implemented throughout a school day and across settings (e.g., classroom, playground, cafeteria, hallway), yet state and national performance standards demand academic accountability (e.g., No Child Left Behind Act).

Thus, it is equally important to address behavioral excesses and deficits and to continue building academic strengths at the same time. When the academic focus is less for students with EBD, it can put them at further disadvantage because they lose skills that, over time, become increasingly difficult to regain.

EBD Interventions

The main goals of a behavior management system include preventing misbehavior, redirecting misbehavior positively, and promoting trust among students, teachers, and other educational professionals. Effective behavior management systems should be perceived as fair by students, be supported by parents, and, as much as possible, be easy to use. Behavior management strategies must address the multiple, complex emotional and behavioral needs of students with EBD.

In addition to school-related problems, students placed in EBD programs often are experiencing crises in the home and community environments (e.g., strained family relationships, substance abuse, illegal activities). Thus, no single agency can meet all of the needs of these students, resulting in a strong need for interagency collaboration and coordination. Nonetheless, school clearly plays an integral function in their educational and social development.

Schoolwide and Classroom Interventions

School personnel sometimes have been reactive rather than proactive in managing student behavior by using punishment (e.g., time-out, in-school suspension) if a student breaks the rules, hoping that aversive methods will prevent their repeated mistakes. Fortunately, educators are now creating positive learning climates and providing proactive support for all students. Being proactive allows educators to spend quality time planning and teaching academics, as well as dealing effectively with critical behavior issues.

Schoolwide Positive Behavioral Support

Researchers are continuously validating the use of schoolwide *positive behavioral supports* (PBS) for students with chronically challenging behaviors (see, e.g., Leedy, Bates, & Safran, 2004). PBS is an approach whereby systematic change of the student's environment (e.g., school, classroom) creates an atmosphere in which appropriate behavioral choices are encouraged, taught, and valued. Schoolwide PBS encourages change in schedules, routines, and procedures, as well as in the way in which education professionals view discipline (Colvin, Kameenui, & Sugai, 1993).

PBS consists of three interrelated goals:

1. Establish systems that create positive behavioral norms.
2. Facilitate positive social and learning interactions among students and staff.
3. Encourage the selection of research-based interventions and programs that fit specific environments.

Specifically, PBS encourages defining and teaching behavioral expectations to all students, acknowledging the occurrence of expected behaviors through a rewards system, proactively correcting behavioral errors, and establishing a representative schoolwide team to make data-based decisions and report progress to all school personnel.

Conflict Resolution

Instituting conflict resolution (CR) programs can be a proactive schoolwide effort to manage social conflicts in a constructive rather than a destructive manner. Smith and Daunic (2002) identified two basic forms of school-based conflict resolution programs:

1. Schoolwide conflict resolution curricula
2. Peer mediation

Curriculum-based programs are designed to be preventive by teaching students about conflict, understanding and managing anger, and effective communication. Conflict resolution curricula also can focus on empathy training, stress management, conflict styles, bias awareness, negotiation, and large-group problem solving. Conflict resolution actively teaches students to address conflict with others by concentrating on developing skills to produce a win–win outcome for all involved.

Note
The term proactive means setting up a positive learning environment and rewarding good behavior, whereas reactive means punishing a student for breaking the rules.

1. PBS
2. Conflict resolution
3. Positive Classrooms

A formal intervention of CR, *peer mediation* (PM) allows students (i.e., peer mediators and disputants) to engage in formal negotiation in a safe setting. The peer mediators are students who receive specific, intensive training in mediation. In PM conferences, disputants sit face-to-face in the company of a trained peer mediator and present their viewpoints in a supportive environment. During PM, the problem between disputants is defined, solutions are delineated, and the potential outcomes are evaluated (Robinson, Daunic, & Smith, 2000).

Designing Positive Classrooms

Managing disruptive behavior in the classroom can consume a teacher's instructional time and emotional energy and distract other students from their learning opportunities. A daily priority for teachers should be to create a positive classroom climate by proactively instructing students in classroom procedures and behaviors. Arranging a room to maximize instruction can decrease student noise and disruption, improve the level and quality of student interactions, and increase the percentage of time that students spend on academic tasks.

Other areas for careful consideration in any teacher's classroom include the classroom schedule, daily routines and procedures, and classroom rules. A carefully thought-out classroom schedule provides a predictable classroom structure and organization for all class activities and school events. The purpose of classroom routines and procedures (e.g., using the restroom and water fountain, sending work home, entering the classroom, working independently) is to systemize everyday, commonplace tasks so students can accomplish them with minimal teacher assistance. Effective classroom routines and procedures enable the creation and maintenance of appropriate behavior patterns throughout the school day.

According to Hardman and Smith (1999), a basic and fundamental classroom component is to establish rules or develop a social contract between teacher and students. If students are to live up to classroom expectations, they need to know exactly what the rules of behavior are. Establishing classroom rules has to be a collaborative exercise in which students and teachers discuss the expected behaviors. All too often, teachers are quick to point out what happens when students don't follow the rules, yet they forget positive consequences for following the rules.

When students abide by rules established collaboratively, they can receive positive attention from adults and peers, have friends, receive good grades, and generally get what they want. Following rules will help students form positive habits, resulting in a safe and caring classroom community in which students interact appropriately and succeed academically.

Group and Individual Management Systems

Schoolwide programs that seek to address behavior for all students, along with careful attention to classroom design to promote a positive learning environment, are fundamental to managing student behavior. Although they are necessary, these programs may not be sufficient, especially for students who exhibit EBD, who might benefit from more intensive group and individualized behavior management measures such as social skills training, use of reinforcement and punishment, and self-regulation strategies.

Social Skills Training

Smith and Travis (2001) argue that changing challenging behavior is not successful until the social situation of individuals is changed so they are no longer segregated or isolated from peers and have greater opportunities for developing positive social relationships. Quality of life will improve for students with EBD when they exhibit social skills valued by the community in new and novel situations over time.

From movie: "A Child is waiting"

Social skills are a set of behaviors needed to meet social demands and consist of guidelines and rules for making decisions about their use. Specific social skills involve general nonverbal behaviors (e.g., using appropriate body language, avoiding others' personal space, attending to personal hygiene), giving specific verbal compliments (e.g., "Thank you for letting me play!" "I really appreciate your help"), and employing specific nonverbal behaviors (e.g., eye contact, firm handshake).

What's more, students need to perceive social situations accurately, select the best social skill to use in a given situation, perform a number of social-skill steps, and translate these into appropriate words and actions. Students then must create a "flowing" social interaction, monitor and adjust their performances, and continue to motivate themselves.

A number of social skill curricula are available, one of which is *Skillstreaming* (Goldstein & McGinnis, 1997). *Skillstreaming* consists of nine steps that teach individual skills, such as starting a conversation, giving a compliment, apologizing, expressing feelings, and responding to teasing. Other skills include dealing with being left out or accused of something, standing up for your rights, and dealing with group pressure.

Reinforcement and Punishment

Generally, teachers use reinforcement to increase socially desirable behaviors and punishment to reduce behaviors that are considered undesirable. In adult life, receiving a paycheck (i.e., reinforcement) increases or maintains the behavior of going to work and producing a desired output. Conversely, receiving a traffic ticket (i.e., punishment) typically results in

Rewards are a good way to keep students motivated and encourage them to work hard.

a decrease in speeding. What must be remembered most about reinforcement and punishment is that they are *effects* on behavior (e.g., Tanisha stays in her seat because the teacher praises her behavior). Reinforcement increases behavior, and punishment decreases it.

Positive reinforcement is so named because it is a reward that is pleasing to a student after he or she has exhibited an appropriate behavior. Reinforcers can be of four types:

1. *Tangibles/edibles* (e.g., small toys, school supplies, posters, gummy bears)
2. *Contingent activities* (e.g., playing board games, using art materials, listening to music)
3. *Social reinforcement* (e.g., giving a high-five, clapping, giving a thumbs-up; saying "Great job!" "Wow—keep up the good work!" "I'm so proud of you!")
4. *Token reinforcement* (e.g., points, stars on a chart that are exchangeable for some object or activity the student values; candy and other "junk foods" as edibles may not be appropriate for some students, so every teacher should think carefully about using them)

Punishment is only one way to decrease behavior. Typically, teachers use reprimands, response cost, time-out, and overcorrection:

1. *Reprimands* consist of verbal scolding or correction designed to discourage inappropriate behavior (e.g.,"Stop it, Michael!" "Ramona, you know you're not supposed to be out of your seat!").
2. *Response cost* means removing something the student has or expects to have, such as points or privileges.
3. *Time-out* might consist of sending a student back to his or her desk because of inappropriate behavior during group work, sending a student into the hallway or to another teacher, or sending a student to the principal's office.
4. *Overcorrection* could mean a teacher having a student clean up the mess he created after kicking over the trashcan and then cleaning up the entire classroom floor. Or a teacher using overcorrection could ask a student to sit back down in her seat, then practice getting in line calmly and orderly a few times.

Punishment should be a teacher's last resort to decrease unwanted behaviors from happening in the classroom. Many more positive techniques are available to help students decrease socially undesirable behaviors and replace them with more socially appropriate ones.

Self-Regulation Strategies

Self-regulation strategies consist of self-management and *cognitive–behavioral interventions* (see Polsgrove & Smith, 2004). Self-management strategies, including self-assessment, self-monitoring, and self-reinforcement, are recommended for students who are manipulative or oppositional when they are confronted. These strategies are particularly appropriate for facilitating the success of students who are mainstreamed, and they represent an important component in reducing or fading teacher participation in controlling a student's behavior.

A key principle underlying self-management strategies is that the student takes responsibility for his or her behavior and begins to internalize the processes that will enable success when external systems are unavailable. Professionals must prepare students to eventually act appropriately as a result of using internal rather than external mechanisms. Self-management strategies should be implemented when a student is aware of, and is motivated to change, a behavior. Otherwise, substantive change is unlikely to occur.

Cognitive–behavioral interventions utilize verbal self-regulation, the use of language as an internal control over rational thought that impacts the development of overt behavior. In its simplest form, verbal self-regulation has been described as talking to oneself to guide problem solving or some other behavior (Smith, 2002). Problem solving incorporates teaching students a "how-to-think" framework, rather than "what-to-think" instruction from a teacher, for students to use when modifying their behavior.

Access to the General Education Curriculum and Settings

IDEA 2004 specifies that a student's IEP has to include the program modifications or supports necessary to attain annual goals, to be involved and progress in the general education curriculum, and to participate, as much as possible, with their typical peers. Students with EBD, however, have difficulty accessing the general education curriculum and participating with typical peers because they often are placed in the most restrictive programs, such as self-contained classrooms or day school settings far removed from general education environments (Kauffman, 2005).

Solutions are few as to how students with EBD can access and, especially, progress in the general education curriculum while at the same time benefit from a program that meets their educational needs. What is needed are formal and informal school and district policies, procedures, and supports that allow administrators, general and special education teachers, parents, related-service personnel, and students themselves to address individual learning in a rigorous curriculum aligned with high standards.

Even though the challenges for teachers of students with EBD are many, they can reap rewards. When a student, after many meetings, comprehensive planning, and intensive instruction, keeps his temper in check during a social conflict, or decides on a constructive rather than a destructive solution to a problem with another student, the teacher's rewards are great. Armed with information about EBD and a clear understanding of the nuances of student behavior, teachers can demonstrate academic, social, and emotional success with the students who demand the most and who deserve the best.

Summary

As a special education teacher you will likely have students in your class who have emotional or behavioral disorders (EBD). While their behavioral characteristics may vary, you can anticipate that they will need considerable support. For students with EBD, the challenge is generally directly related to helping them manage their own behavior so that they are able to apply their academic skills in meeting their school-related achievement goals. Students with EBD may require instructional strategies designed specifically to assist them in focusing on their academic work. They may also be disruptive and their behavior distract their classmates.

Thus, of all the students with exceptional learning problems, these students may require more skills and knowledge on your part to ensure that their instruction is appropriate (both in academic and behavior areas) and that they maximally benefit from the instruction. You will need to understand the assessment data that will be shared by the school psychologist and mental health professionals as well as the insights of the child's parents. Much of this information will be focused on behaviors and contributors to behavior, whereas with other students with exceptional learning problems the emphasis is more on academic performance and cognitive difficulties.

References

Achenbach, T. M. (1991). *Manual for the Child Behavior Checklist/4–18 and 1991 profile.* Burlington: University of Vermont, Department of Psychiatry.

Bierman, K. L., Greenberg, M. T., & the Conduct Problems Prevention Research Group (CPPRG). (1996). Social skills training in the Fast Track Program. In R. D. Peters & R. J. McMahon (Eds.), *Preventing childhood disorders, substance abuse, and delinquency* (pp. 65–89). Thousand Oaks, CA: Sage Publications, Inc.

Bos, C. S., Coleman, M., & Vaughn, S. (2002). Reading and students with EBD: What do we know and recommend? In K. L. Lane, F. M. Gresham, & T. E. O'Shaughnessy (Eds.), *Interventions for children with or at risk for emotional and behavioral disorders* (pp. 87–103). Boston: Allyn & Bacon.

Bower, E. M. (1981). *Early identification of emotionally handicapped children in school* (3rd ed.). Springfield, IL: Charles C. Thomas.

Braaten, S. R., & Kauffman, J. M. (2000). *Making placement decisions: Constructing appropriately restrictive environments for students with emotional and behavioral disorders.* Champaign, IL: Research Press.

Bryan, T., & Nelson, C. (1994). Doing homework: Perspectives of elementary and junior high school students. *Journal of Learning Disabilities, 27,* 488–499.

Coie, J. D., Watt, N. F., West, S. G., Hawkins, J. D., Asarnow, J. R., Markham, H. J., et al. (1993). The science of prevention: A conceptual framework and some directions for a national research program. *American Psychologist, 48*(10), 1013–1022.

Coleman, M. C., & Webber, J. (2002). *Emotional and behavioral disorders: Theory and practice.* Boston: Allyn & Bacon.

Colvin, G., Kameenui, E. J., & Sugai, G. (1993). Reconceptualizing behavior management and school-wide discipline in general education. *Education and Treatment of Children, 16,* 361–381.

Cullinan, D. (2002). *Students with emotional and behavior disorders: An introduction for teachers and other helping professionals.* Upper Saddle River, NJ: Pearson.

Dodge, K. A., & Feldman, E. (1990). Issues in social cognition and sociometric status. In S. R. Asher & J. D. Coie (Eds.), *Peer rejection in childhood* (pp. 119–155). Cambridge: Cambridge University Press.

Epstein, M. H., & Cullinan, D. (1998). *Scale for Assessing Emotional Disturbance.* Austin, TX: Pro-Ed.

Fessler, M. A., Rosenberg, M. S., & Rosenberg, L. A. (1991). Concomitant learning disabilities and learning problems among students with behavioral/emotional disorders. *Behavioral Disorders, 16,* 97–106.

Forness, S. R., & Knitzer, J. (1992). A new proposed definition and terminology to replace "serious emotional disturbance" in Individuals with Disabilities Education Act. *School Psychology Review, 21,* 12–20.

Goldstein, A. P., & McGinnis, E. (1997). *Skillstreaming the adolescent.* Champaign, IL: Research Press.

Gresham, F. M., & Elliott, S. N. (1990). *Social Skills Rating System.* Circle Pines, MN: American Guidance Service.

Hardman, E., & Smith, S. W. (1999). Promoting positive interaction in the classroom. *Intervention in School and Clinic, 34,* 178–180.

Individuals with Disabilities Education Improvement Act of 2004. 20 U.S.C. § 1400.

Kauffman, J. M. (2005). *Characteristics of emotional and behavioral disorders of children and youth.* Upper Saddle River, NJ: Pearson.

Leedy, A., Bates, P., & Safran, S. P. (2004). Bridging the research-to-practice gap: Improving hallway behavior using positive behavioral supports. *Behavioral Disorders, 29,* 130–139.

Lloyd, J. W., Kauffman, J. M., Landrum, T. J., & Roe, D. L. (1991). Why do teachers refer pupils for special education? An analysis of referral records. *Exceptionality, 2,* 115–126.

Noll, M. B., Kamps, D., & Seaborn, C. F. (1993). Prereferral intervention for students with emotional or behavioral disorders: Use of a behavioral consultation model. *Journal of Emotional and Behavioral Disorders, 1,* 203–214.

Polsgrove, L., & Smith, S. W. (2004). Informed practice in teaching self-control to children with emotional and behavioral disorders. In R. B. Rutherford, M. Quinn, & S. R. Mathur (Eds.), *Handbook of research in emotional and behavioral disorders* (pp. 399–425). New York: Guilford.

Robinson, T. R., Daunic, A. P., & Smith, S. W. (2000). The social validity of peer mediation according to middle school students. *Middle School Journal, 31*(5), 23–29.

Smith, S. W. (2002, August). *Applying cognitive–behavioral techniques to social skills instruction.* Arlington, VA: ERIC Clearinghouse on Disabilities and Gifted Education. (ERIC Digest No. E630)

Smith, S. W., & Daunic, A. P. (2002). Using conflict resolution and peer mediation to support positive behavior. In R. Algozzine & P. Kay (Eds.), *Preventing problem behaviors: Handbook of successful prevention strategies* (pp. 142–161). Thousand Oaks, CA: Corwin Press.

Smith, S. W., & Travis, P. C. (2001). Conducting social competence research: Considering conceptual frameworks, *Behavioral Disorders, 26,* 360–369.

U.S. Department of Education. (2002). *Twenty-fourth annual report to Congress on the implementation of the Individuals with Disabilities Education Act.* Washington, DC: Author.

Walker, H. M., Colvin, G., & Ramsey, E. (1995). *Antisocial behavior in school: Strategies and best practices.* Pacific Grove, CA: Brooks/Cole Publishing.

Walker, H. M., & Severson, H. H. (1992*). Systematic Screening for Behavior Disorders (SSBD): A multiple gating procedure.* Longmont, CO: Sopris West.

Walker, H. M., Forness, S. R., Kauffman, J. M., Epstein, M. H., Gresham, F. M., Nelson, C. M., et al. (1998). Macro–social validation: Referencing outcomes in behavioral disorders to societal issues and problems. *Behavioral Disorders, 24,* 7–18.

Speech/language Impairments and Communication Disorders

Cindy H. T. Lian

Federal regulations governing the Education for All Handicapped Children Act of 1975 (EHA) and the Individuals with Disabilities Education Act of 1990 (IDEA) permit delivery of speech and language services to children in two ways:

1. Those for whom the communication disorder is determined to be a primary disability can be so classified and served under *special education*.

2. Those whose speech and language problems are secondary to another condition can be served on the basis of the primary disability and then receive speech and language habilitation as a *related service*.

In the 2000–01 school year, children between the ages of 6 and 21 who received services for speech and/or language impairments represented 18.9% (1,093,808) of all children with disabilities served in public schools under IDEA Part B. This was the second largest category of disability served, and the estimate did not include children whose speech and/or language problems were secondary to another primary condition (U.S. Department of Education, 2002).

As more and more students with speech and language disorders participate in the general curriculum under inclusion plans, teachers can expect to work in consultation with a speech–language pathologist (SLP) who enters their classroom instead of pulling out students for special services. In this chapter you will learn about various speech and language impairments and their impact on learning, understand how students are identified and served, and gain an overview of ways to collaborate with an SLP to better serve students with special needs.

CASE STUDY: LISA

Shortly after she entered kindergarten at age 5, Lisa, now 9, was identified as having a specific language impairment. Her speech was said to be unintelligible and her language delayed. Although she spoke six-word utterances and used both plural and tense markers correctly, she had few words to express her needs or feelings, and she did not use appropriate openings to initiate conversations. Instead, she struck others when she was thwarted, demanded attention by pulling or grabbing, and was perceived by teachers as aggressive toward peers and adults. In the course of her first school year, she kicked her teacher and other students, threw books, and ran out of the classroom frequently when she was asked to complete tasks.

She was retained in first grade because she did not label common objects; describe spatial, causal, or temporal relationships; or follow directions for small-group or independent work. During her repeated year in first grade, her work refusals increased to the point at which an evaluation team recommended half-day placement in a learning center, where management systems brought Lisa's behavior under classroom control. By the end of sec-

(continued)

continuing case study of Lisa

ond grade, Lisa had made virtually no progress in the district's adopted phonics-based reading series, but a management system helped her follow directions and complete some assigned tasks in the general education classroom.

By third grade, using an alternative reading series based on a word-family approach instead of phonics, Lisa had developed a basic sight vocabulary of more than 100 words so she could read connected text and join a reading group. Her peers in the reading group constituted her first successful social contacts, and social-skills lessons helped her interact with peers using appropriate words. With intensive speech therapy she reduced her consonant omissions and substitutions and became more willing to talk instead of kicking or hitting when she was frustrated. Concept-building lessons took place in small-group sessions delivered three times a week in her general third-grade classroom.

Lisa's communicative-competence problems centered on limited vocabulary and social language skills. The team monitoring her individualized program tied improvements in her speech intelligibility and comprehension of meaning directly to gains in her classroom task and social behavior.

As she begins to demonstrate academic progress, Lisa's status remains well below expectations based on her current nonverbal intellectual functioning, but she now is expected to make regular gains toward age-appropriate use of language. Lisa's case shows the relationship between acting-out behavior and lack of appropriate speech and language to communicate with others.

Communication and Language Concepts

Communication is a physical, interactive, cognitive, and social process in which a message is conveyed from one person to another, shown in Figure 6.1. Face-to-face communication occurs through speech sounds accompanied by intonation, stress, and pauses; gestures; facial expression; eye contact; posture; and physical distance between participating parties.

The content of speech is *language,* a symbol system agreed upon by a community and used for interactive communication, storage, and retrieval of concepts, and other noncommunicative functions such as reasoning and rehearsal of motor behaviors. For some groups speech is replaced by a visual–gestural system such as *American Sign Language,* which has no written counterpart.

Communication also can occur without a language system of any kind, spoken or manual. This type of *nonverbal communication* is evidenced when children who know no English enter an American school and play readily with classmates using signs and pantomime. Even though nonverbal systems are a form of communication, they are not considered in this chapter.

Given the ever-increasing cultural and linguistic diversity occuring in this country, the importance of avoiding inappropriate identification and placements cannot be

Signing *turtle*

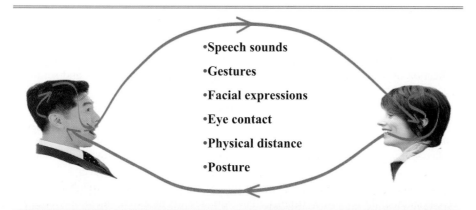

- •Speech sounds
- •Gestures
- •Facial expressions
- •Eye contact
- •Physical distance
- •Posture

FIGURE 6.1
Face-to-Face Communication: A Physical, Interactive, Cognitive, and
Social Process Whereby a Message Is Conveyed From One Person to Another

understated. As you continue reading, the discussion regarding linguistic diversity, dialects, English Language Learners (ELL) and Second Language Acquisition in chapter 2 should be at the forefront of your thoughts.

Communication Disorders, Delays, and Differences

Acknowledging the need to distinguish between disorder, delay, or difference, the following definitions are offered (bold added):

> A ***communication disorder*** is an impairment in the ability to send, receive, process and comprehend verbal, nonverbal, and graphic symbol systems. A communication disorder may be evident in the process of hearing, language, or speech; may be developmental or acquired; and may range in severity from mild to profound. A communication disorder may result in a primary disability or may be secondary to other disabilities. (ASHA, 1993, p. 40)
>
> A ***communication delay*** exists when the rate of acquisition of language or speech skills is slower than expected according to developmental norms; however, the sequence of development is following a predicted order. (Nicolosi, 1989)
>
> A ***communication difference*** is a variation of a symbol system used by a group of individuals that reflects and is determined by shared regional, social, or cultural/ethnic factors. A regional, social, cultural, or ethinic variation of a symbol system is not considered a disorder of speech or language. (ASHA, 1993, p. 41)

Learners who demonstrate a delay or disorder rather than a difference may have both speech and language impairments in various combinations. Speech problems may involve articulation (the way sounds are produced), fluency (speech rate and rhythm), or voice (speech pitch, volume and quality). Language problems, as organized in Figure 6.2, might involve syntactic structure (organization of phrases and clauses), morphology (use of prefixes and suffixes to build words), phonology (rules for combining sounds into words), semantic content (concepts and vocabulary), or pragmatics (the application of semantics, syntactics, and morphology to varied listeners and settings) (Lahey, 1988; Leahy, 1989).

Although they are separated for discussion purposes, these conditions are unlikely to occur in isolation. When problems are identified in a specific subsystem, the relationship of that impaired component to the whole communication system—and to the whole communicating person—is what is important. Generally, an individual's communicative competence—capacity for using speech and language to receive, analyze, organize, and store information; to share information with others through a cultural value system; and to adjust to listener characteristics—is assessed. Put simply, the relevant question is: How does this breakdown interfere with other aspects of the individual's academic, linguistic, and social development?

Speech Disorders

For purposes of this chapter, speech disorders are categorized in the areas of articulation, fluency, and voice.

Articulation Disorders

The term *articulation* refers to the management of tongue and lip movements to form specific sounds in association with teeth and other articulators. The related term *phonology* concerns the patterns of sound that make a difference in meaning between words such as *pin* and *pen,* and the rules that govern the combination of sounds. An

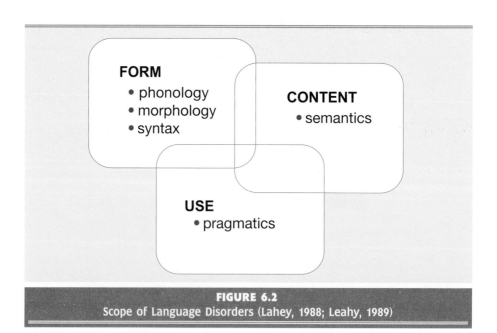

FIGURE 6.2
Scope of Language Disorders (Lahey, 1988; Leahy, 1989)

articulation or phonological disorder is "the atypical production of speech sounds characterized by substitutions, omissions, additions, or distortions that may interfere with intelligibility" (ASHA, 1993, p. 40).

According to McReynolds (1988), normally developing children of preschool ages may substitute (/t/ for /k/ in *kitten),* add (suhleep for *sleep),* omit (buh for *bus),* or make other less frequent changes in speech sounds. Mastery of consonant sounds begins about age 2. Between 6 and 8 years of age, most children master speech sound production spontaneously.

Among children who have learning disabilities, mental retardation, and behavior disorders, their articulation problems and lack of phonological awareness persist into school age. Articulation disorders are a typical characteristic of children and youth with cerebral palsy and those with cleft palate. For a larger number of learners, however, articulation problems are not explained readily.

Learning problems associated with articulation errors center on beginning reading and spelling. A curriculum that offers beginning reading instruction using a phonics approach puts at a disadvantage students who misperceive individual phonemes, cannot reproduce them on demand, and fail to blend separate sounds into words they can recognize as part of their oral vocabulary. If, however, beginning reading is presented as a total language experience, integrating listening and speaking with reading and writing, less emphasis is placed on the sound system, which minimizes the effects of articulation problems or lack of phonological awareness.

Spelling depends on word recognition skills. Students cannot spell words they do not recognize. Breakdowns in discriminating and producing individual sounds affect both reading and writing of phonetically regular words. Of course, many English words are not phonetically predictable. Learning irregular sight vocabulary by a whole-word method may not be affected by articulation errors unless the beginning reader is unwilling to pronounce words orally because of self-consciousness about substitutions or distortions.

Children who are unintelligible are readily referred. Behavioral indicators of referral for articulation evaluation include pronunciations appropriate for chronologically younger children. For example, the common substitution of /w/ for /r/ and /l/ is worth treating because this could lead peers to ostracize a third-grader as using baby talk, and being treated as younger may lead children to adopt social patterns appropriate for earlier developmental stages.

Fluency Disorders

> *A fluency disorder is an interruption in the flow of speaking characterized by atypical rate, rhythm, and repetitions in sounds, syllables, words and phrases. This may be accompanied by excessive tension, struggle behavior, and secondary mannerism. (ASHA, 1993, p. 40)*

During the preschool years, all normally developing children demonstrate some degree of nonfluency in the form of word and phrase repetitions or revisions to correct false starts. This differs from early stuttering, which includes word and phrase repetitions at higher frequencies, in that it includes sound and syllable repetitions and sound prolongations. More severe stuttering is often associated with secondary facial or motor mannerisms, such as spasms, in efforts to avoid or hide prolonged disruptions in speech.

Note

Students who stutter are often reassured to know that many well-known people have also had problems with stuttering—people such as Marilyn Monroe, Sir Isaac Newton, James Earl Jones, and Lewis Carroll.

According to Wall (1988), "Children are likely to be diagnosed as stutterers if they exhibit sound and syllable repetitions that contain a minimum of two or three repetitions per unit or if their dysfluencies last for 2 seconds or longer" (p. 629).

The incidence of childhood stuttering is highest between ages 2 and 4. While the ratio of boys to girls is approximately equal, girls are more likely to exprience unassisted recovery, usually within the first one to two years after stuttering is first noted. The ratio of boys to girls who persist in stuttering increases to approximately 3 to 1 (Zebrowski, 2003). While unassisted recovery does occur, approximately 20%–25% of children will continue to stutter (Curlee, 1999).

Learning problems emerging from dysfluency center on reluctance to engage in verbal interactions. Those whose speech is dysfluent may develop poor self-esteem and become so reluctant to talk that in the early years they fail to engage in the interactive process of attempting patterns for feedback. That lack of experience with early language deprives them of natural opportunities to gain the specific language information that listening adults typically provide. Later, in school, students who stutter tend to avoid group discussions, oral reports, and volunteering to answer questions from the teacher. Limited opportunities for oral rehearsal of content in classroom groups translate into problems in organizing written responses when similar content appears on tests.

Voice Disorders

> *A voice disorder is characterized by the abnormal production and/or absence of vocal quality, pitch, loudness, resonance, or duration, which is appropriate for an individual's age and/or sex. (ASHA, 1993, p. 40)*

Childhood vocal disturbance may be attributable to structural problems, neurological disorders ranging from vocal fold paralysis to spasticity, vocal abuse such as screaming, or functional causes related to psychoneurosis or faulty learning (Wilson, 1987). Reported occurrence of "hoarseness" ranges from 6% to 23% of school-aged children (Faust, 2003).

Voice problems carry few implications for specific learning or social behavior, but they may indicate medical or psychological conditions that should be investigated. For example, hoarseness secondary to a cold or ear infection may recur several times over a winter or might last up to three weeks. If hoarseness persists longer, however, a referral for medical evaluation is in order because a chronic hoarse voice signals a potentially serious medical condition.

Language Disorders

> *A language disorder is the impaired comprehension and/or use of spoken, written, and/or other symbol systems. The disorder may involve the form (phonology, morphology, syntax), content (semantics), and/or function (pragmatics) of language in communication in any combination. (ASHA, 1993, p. 40)*

Specific language impairment (SLI) is a significant deficit in linguistic functioning that does not appear to be accompanied by deficits in hearing, intelligence, or motor functioning (Shames, Wiig, & Secord, 1998). Most children with severe language difficulties are identified before they start school; however, many are not identified until they start formal education (Laing, Law, Levin, & Logan, 2002).

The overall prevalence of SLI during preschool and early school years is estimated to be between 2% and 8%, with greater prevalence in boys than girls (National Institute on Deafness and Other Communication Disorders, 2002). Students with SLI often present a combination of delays or disorders in the following categories:

- Phonology (rules for combining sounds into words)
- Syntactic structure (organization of phrases and clauses)
- Morphology (use of prefixes and suffixes to build words)
- Semantic content (concepts and vocabulary)
- Pragmatics

Phonology

A *phonological disorder* is an impaired comprehension of the sound system of a language and the rules that govern the sound combinations. Children with phonological disorders have trouble producing speech sounds of their language for their expected age. Although the term is often used interchangeably with *articulation disorder,* a phonological disorder emphasizes the language that governs the sound combinations whereas an articulation disorder emphasizes the motor activity of producing the speech sound (Bleile, 1995).

For 80% of children with phonological disorders, the disorders are sufficiently severe to require clinical treatment (Gierut, 1998). There is an observed relationship between early phonological disorders and subsequent reading, writing, spelling, and mathematical abilities. Children with phonological disorders often require other types of remedial services, and 50% to 70% exhibit general academic difficulty through grade 12 (Gierut, 1998).

Syntactic Structure

Organizing principles used to form phrases and clauses comprise the syntactic system of any language. In English, word order is the major factor. Thus, children have to learn to sequence patterns. For example, "The dog bit the boy" and "The boy bit the dog" have entirely different meanings. Because syntactic patterns are few, they can be mastered early in normal development, usually by 6 years of age (Johnston, 1988).

In addition to resequencing, behavioral indicators of syntactic breakdowns may be omissions or failures to match sentence parts. Thus, a child may delete part of a verb phrase and say, "He running" instead of "He is running." Other children use a pronoun form without matching it to the referent for gender, case, or number, saying, for example, "Him go they house" when identifying a picture of a girl walking into a home. Or they may violate the order of specific word types, as in reversing the position of the verb in a question ("What time lunch is?") or not stating multiple modifiers conventionally ("The green big second ball").

Learning problems arise from syntactic disorders because they disrupt comprehension of both subject matter content and oral directions in classrooms. According to Laughton and Hasenstab (1986), the inability to grasp complex structures using "who" and "which," or subordinating terms such as "because" or "if," leads to misunderstandings, and learners are so preoccupied with trying to grasp what is happening procedurally in class that they do not take in information. When the students then attempt production, their utterances are limited to syntactic structures that may lead to crossed messages. Finally, students who do not form questions conventionally cannot ask for the help they need to clarify instructions or lesson content.

Morphology

A *morpheme* is the smallest unit of meaning in any language. A word always consists of at least one morpheme but contains more than one if the word is plural (book/s), has a past-tense marker (test/ed), or contains a prefix (pre/test) or suffix (learn/ing). The study of and application of these word parts to add meanings to base words is called *morphology*.

This student works on word order and sequence after reading a new story with his class.

Up to about age 5, children follow a relatively predictable order of acquisition of inflectional markers for number, tense, possession, and so forth. They often omit such markers, however, during stages when they are trying to consolidate several syntactic features simultaneously. Normally developing preschool children overgeneralize markers, as in "We goed home"—which indicates that the speaker has internalized the rule for regular past tense. By school entry, they typically have corrected omissions such as "We play yesterday" and redundant markers such as "two shoeses." If such a pattern persists, it may indicate a problem, but some children do not master irregular verb forms such as *buy/bought* until age 10 or so.

Failing to build words conventionally with morphemes seldom interferes with meaning in English as much as do errors in word order. Because listeners usually can understand intended meaning even if children misapply a number marker, the learning implications are relatively minor. Still, children may be penalized socially for nonstandard use of plural or tense markers.

Semantic Content

The *semantic system* is concerned with meaning, both broadly in terms of schema or concepts about how the world works, and narrowly, reflected in the number and types of vocabulary words an individual can use. Learning the semantic system of a language permits children to map the reality they perceive through their senses and to talk about objects and relationships when these are not available physically to their senses.

Children do not use words as adults do. Semantic acquisition is a process of discovering features until learners' meanings approach those of adults. In the process, children can both overextend and underextend meanings. For example, they may call all furry pets with four legs and a tail "dog" or, conversely, call any dog "a Frisky" if that is the name of their family dog.

They tend to learn first the most general features of a word class, and later the more specific or restricted features that distinguish one example from another. Because they learn new words and additional concepts throughout a lifetime, learners never can be said to have mastered the semantic content of a language. For school-age learners, vocabulary norms on standardized tests can estimate whether progress fits with that of a large census-based sample of representative children of the same age.

Indicators for vocabulary problems usually are of two types:

1. Children simply have not learned the names of commonly seen objects, places, or persons; their vocabulary is inadequate to describe their experience.
2. Children cannot recall known labels on demand; learners who have a word-retrieval problem cannot produce the label "book" if a teacher asks, "What is this?" but can point to the correct object if told, "Point to the book."

More serious vocabulary problems are associated with failure to organize incoming information into concepts or schema about the world. This might be indicated by gross misuse of relational terms, for example, so that a child uses "before" when she means "after," or a child says "to" when he intends "from." These small words that hold sentences together—called *function words*—require more abstract learning than the labels associated with tangible objects (nouns), actions (verbs), or attributes (adjectives and adverbs).

Because learning problems that arise from inadequate vocabulary pervade all instruction, the learners lack basic foundation tools. Word-retrieval problems interfere with oral lessons and also with early oral reading because the child cannot pronounce even a recognized word.

Researchers on reading emphasize that stored concepts (schemas) must combine with the text on a printed page to allow readers to construct meaning (Lipson & Wixson, 1986). New information in the reading passage becomes incorporated into what readers already knew. Inadequate schema prevent reading comprehension. Children who lack basic classification systems for organizing incoming information are not prepared to gain from reading. If the concepts of "same" and "different" are not established, for example, a passage classifying objects on this basis in a third-grade science text remains meaningless.

Pragmatics

Pragmatics is the term designating sets of competencies that is concerned with the appropriateness for audience and setting in relation to

- the way speech and language are delivered—with facial expressions, eye contact, physical distance, and so forth;
- whether the speaker distinguishes shared prior information from new information in selecting vocabulary and syntax, and

Regardless of a student's verbal ability, facial expressions enhance communication so that messages are clearly received.

■ whether the speaker judges the interaction usefully in terms of taking turns, repairing misunderstandings, maintaining a mutual topic, and generally grasping the needs and intentions of the other party.

Pragmatic applications both precede and supersede other language learning. They precede other language learning because infants of 6 months or so develop social communication systems by eye contact, gesture, turn-taking, and topic maintenance before the spoken words appear half a year later. Preverbal infants can readily express requests, refusals, greetings, and numerous other functions. Pragmatic systems supersede other language systems because articulation, fluency, voice, syntax, semantics, and morphology have to function together in appropriate interaction with another speaker/listener before communication can be said to occur.

Behavioral indicators that pragmatic competencies are inadequate may be overt, as when a student grabs others to gain attention instead of calling their names, says "He hit me" without identifying who "he" is, or rudely insists on introducing a new topic into a small group engaged in mutually satisfying discussion. An example of a more subtle indicator is a child's standing too close to another person while talking.

A common complaint by teachers is that some students miss the indirect request to stop talking when the teacher says, "It's getting noisy in here." Other typical reports from teachers of students with disabilities include asking personal questions, initiating conversations in disruptive ways, and missing jokes or sarcasm.

The learning implications of breakdowns in pragmatics are serious. Many referrals to special education based on classroom disruptions arise from lack of pragmatic skills, as when students talk out or interrupt other speakers. A high proportion of learners' frustration with instruction can be traced to their inability to read nonverbal signals, follow indirect commands, or know when a question would be in order. Students who cannot judge the interpersonal and setting contexts so they can adjust according to the status of the listener and the demands of the situation are at a disadvantage in dealing with others. In short, pragmatic disorders disrupt basic interpersonal human relationships.

Asessment and Evaluation for Special Education and Related Services ▪ ▪ ▪ ▪ ▪ ▪

Many children and youth show long-standing limitations in speech or language abilities, yet simply fall at the low end of the distribution of speech and language skills. These students are not necessarily considered to have a specific disability (Leonard, 1991). Also, children whose language acquisition is slower than that of their brothers, sisters, or neighbors tend to be identified early by the family and referred for appropriate preschool intervention.

Learners with mild hearing loss and those who develop some language but follow an atypical sequence and fail to master certain concepts or linguistic patterns are more difficult to identify. Many language problems do not become apparent until the youngsters begin academic instruction.

Screening

Usually, hearing is screened first because speech and language depend on intact sensory function. If a student does not hear a narrow volume range across the pitches at which speech is heard, a complete audiometric test by an audiologist is warranted. Speech and language screening by an SLP may consist of short versions of standardized or nonstandardized tests and review of developmental and medical history, as well as informal conversation and observations. Screening data are used to compare language data with motor and social developmental milestones.

Screening results are used to determine

1. whether referred individuals demonstrate the minimum discrepancies that would permit schools to serve them under federal and state regulations, and
2. which speech and language systems require a closer look through more comprehensive assessment.

Prereferral interventions or accommodations also may be recommended by an SLP to determine if program modification, supports, or supplementary aids and services are sufficient to address the identified problem in the general education environment.

Referral

If prereferral intervention is not successful, a referral may be intiated by the SLP, teacher, parent or any other service provider. The referral is a request for assessment of a student with suspected special education needs, which requires written consent from the parent/guardian in accordance with federal mandates, state regulations and guidelines, and local policy and procedures.

> **Note**
>
> Order of assessment and evaluation:
> - Hearing screening
> - Speech and language screening
> - Preferral interventions and accommodations, if necessary
> - Referral
> - Assessment
> - Intervention planning

Assessment and Intervention Planning

The SLP's role on the multidisciplinary assessment team is to conduct a thorough and balanced speech, language, or communication assessment using measures that are free of cultural and linguistic bias, are age-appropriate, describe the child's differences when compared to peers, describe the student's specific communication abilities and difficulties, elicit optimal evidence of the student's communication competence, and describe real communication tasks (ASHA, 2002).

SLPs follow their state's and local educational agency's eligibility criteria, severity classifications, recommended amount of service, and service delivery options. But to qualify for speech and language services as a primary disability, students in most states, in addition to other test results, must demonstrate a discrepancy between current intelligence quotient (IQ) and speech or language test scores that compare a testee with a large census-matched national group of the same age. Evidence for combinations of speech and language problems secondary to other disabilities is weighed on a case-by-case basis when the comprehensive evaluation is completed by a multidisciplinary school team.

Teams adjust the comprehensive assessment batteries to meet presenting problems. To support an intervention, speech and language evaluation must describe deviations from expected limits in detail, document how regularly they occur, and estimate their severity. A balanced assessment may involve the following (ASHA, 2000):

1. A detailed student history collected via observation and interviews with parents/staff/student and a review of medical and family history, communication development, social–emotional development, academic achievement, primary language, and the like.
2. Checklists and developmental scales to obtain a large amount of information in an organized or categorized form to note the presence or absence of specific communication behaviors.
3. Curriculum-based assessment to measure a student's language intervention needs and progress (Nelson, 1998). An example is an information reading inventory that could be analyzed collaboratively by the SLP and the classroom teacher.
4. Dynamic assessment to provide information regarding how well a student can perform after receiving assistance.
5. Portfolio assessment that includes reviewing a collection of products such as student writing samples, comparisons of language samples in connected speech, dictations, video/audio recordings and transcriptions. Depending on the caseloads, clinicians often utilize a language sample of 100 words or more, transcribed and scored.
6. Observation/anecdotal records collected in natural settings such as classrooms, the cafeteria, halls, and recreation areas, to make a distinction between language disorder and language difference. Two advantages of observation over testing are

   (a) the opportunity to collect data without the bias inherent in test instruments, and
   (b) the chance to note whether referred students engage in code-switching by, for example, using more formal language with teachers than with peers.

   Natural settings allow a speaker from a minority culture to select usages from the language repertoire and demonstrate strengths that some tests may not reveal.

7. Standardized assessment information to compare a student's current performance with that of peers. Although all aspects of speech, language, and communication are interrelated, specific standardized tests are used to measure specific skills such as articulation, phonology, fluency, voice/resonance, language comprehension and production (syntax, semantics, morphology, phonology, pramatics), discourse organization, following directions, and so on.

An SLP also considers the student's attentional behaviors, cognitive factors that may be associated with congenital or acquired conditions, hearing loss or deafness, social–emotional factors, or other health factors. Of utmost importance is to consider cultural and/or linguistic diversity and whether students have limited English proficiency.

Research-/Theory-Driven Intervention and Best Practices

An outcome of comprehensive assessment is the identification of a student's communication strengths and needs, complete with prognostic indicators. A student's preferred communication modality, interests, and academic strengths and needs also are identified. This information guides the recommendations and interventions. In addition, the SLP's theoretical views on how disorders are organized affects the selection of intervention procedures and priorities. McReynolds (1988) suggests three theories that attempt to account for articulation problems:

1. *The phonologic disorders model* holds that rule-governed error patterns arise from learners' attempts to simplify adult forms they cannot reproduce.
2. *The perceptual–motor theory* proposes that articulation is a matter of cognitive and motor planning.
3. *The discrimination model* explains articulation problems as the inability to distinguish one speech sound from another; experts disagree on whether discrimination is based on production or vice versa.

An SLP who views articulation as based on phonologic rules develops interventions differently from one who is committed to perceptual–motor or discrimination training. Similarly, when language intervention is planned, an SLP who believes in following the sequence of normal acquisition for language therapy develops objectives differently from SLPs who follow other theoretical models.

Some practitioners choose to start with language structures that appear first developmentally in children without disabilities. Others select first the targets that are considered easier to teach because they are less complex, or those most amenable to patterns or rules. Still others make decisions based on social considerations, selecting to work first, for example, on speech features that help a speaker sound age-appropriate, or on pragmatic language competencies to help a student become better accepted by adults and peers.

> *Recommendations regarding the nature (direct or indirect), type (individual or group) and location of service delivery (SLP resource room, classroom, home or community) are based on the need to provide free, appropriate public education for each student*

in the least-restrictive environment and consistent with the student's individual needs as documented on the IEP. (ASHA, 2000, p. 272)

Table 6.1 presents options provided by ASHA (2000, p. 273). As the needs of students change, these options will need to be reevaluated. It is not intended that one service delivery model be used exclusively. For all models, there must be time in the schedule for collaboration and consultation with general educators, special educators, parents, and other service providers.

Access to General Education Curriculum and Settings

The focus of access to general education should first be on prevention, beginning in preschool. General and special education teachers should collaborate in utilizing the existing research and knowledge in curriculum modifications to meet the needs of students with speech and language delays and disorders.

Prevention

Researchers have repeatedly demonstrated a strong link between children's reading and writing skills and their competence in oral language (Achilles, Yates, & Freese, 1991; Canady & Krantz, 1996). As outlined in IDEA 2004, an expanded focus for SLPs is the prevention of speech–language disorders through inservice training and consultation with teachers, parents, and other professionals.

SLPs' knowledge of intervention techniques for phonological delays and disorders can be applied in planning and supporting phonological awareness programs in the preschool and elementary grades (Catts, 1991). This help with reading and writing difficulties can be extended throughout the school years (Catts & Kahmi, 1999). In addition, SLPs can use their knowledge of pragmatics to consult and improve social–emotional communication skills through staff and parent training, as well as lesson demonstration and model techniques of problem solving, social communication, and emotional expressive skills.

Suggestions for Teachers of Children With Speech–Language Disorders/Delays

Regardless of the nature or extent of a communication disability, learners are likely to remain the responsibility of the general education teacher, who must modify instruction for varied disabilities in the general classroom. Special education and general education teachers can work together in promoting a child's speech and language communication.

Teachers can foster expressive speech and language skills by

- focusing on speech content (avoid calling attention to the manner of expression);
- validating the comunication that the students use;
- responding to the intelligible parts of a message;
- providing extra time for the child to respond;
- suggesting that children express themselves through gestures/pantomines (e.g., raising a hand for a true statement versus a false statement);

TABLE 6.1 Service Delivery Options	
Delivery Option	**Description**
Monitor	The speech–language pathologist sees the student for a specified amount of time per grading period to monitor or "check" on the student's speech and language skills. Often this model immediately precedes dismissal.
Collaborative Consultation	The speech–language pathologist, regular and/or special education teacher(s), and parents/families work together to facilitate a student's communication and learning in educational environments. This is an indirect model in which the speech–language pathologist does not provide direct service to the student.
Classroom-Based	This model is also known as integrated services, curriculum-based, transdisciplinary, interdisciplinary, or inclusive programming. There is an emphasis on the speech–language pathologist providing direct services to students within the classroom and other natural environments. Team teaching by the speech–language pathologist and the regular and/or special education teacher(s) is frequent with this model.
Pullout	Services are provided to students individually and/or in small groups within the speech–language resource room setting. Some speech–language pathologists may prefer to provide individual or small group services within the physical space of the classroom.
Self-Contained Program	The speech–language pathologist is the classroom teacher responsible for providing both academic/curriculum instruction and speech–language remediation.
Community-Based	Communication services are provided to students within the home or community setting. Goals and objectives focus primarily on functional communication skills.
Combination	The speech–language pathologist provides two or more service delivery options (e.g., provides individual or small group treatment on a pullout basis twice a week to develop skills or preteach concepts and also works with the student within the classroom).

- providing opportunities for children to select a one-word answer from a choice of two;
- providing opportunities for a child to answer earlier rather than later when questions are posed to an entire group;
- treating all students with courtesy as a model for students.

Teachers can foster receptive language skills by

- limiting directions to no more than two steps (avoid multiple directions);
- giving essential information in short utterances (keep the sentence subject close to verb);
- avoiding indirect comments, either/or statements;
- showing (demonstrating) rather than telling.

An example of an approach that combines listening, speaking, reading, and writing activities within integrated lessons is the *whole-language approach*. Designs for integrated literacy instruction, as presented by Weaver (1994), for example, combine discrete lessons into a coherent program for learners and a more realistic instructional task for teachers. Listening, oral discussion, reading, spelling, composing, and handwriting activities can be based on content-free scripts and a common vocabulary across tasks. Whole-language programs contrast with separate basal reading series and spelling or handwriting workbooks based on different vocabularies, which require students to shift their focus and content between tasks.

Whether instruction in language arts is traditionally separate or holistic, general educators typically promote generalization of new speech and language competencies to the classroom. They can ask the SLP and the special educator which competencies

This teacher is conducting a small-group whole-language lesson, focusing on listening and reading comprehension strategies.

are being emphasized in a given week so they will be able to reinforce those competencies. For example, students working on relational concepts of *behind, between, above, below,* and so forth, could be asked to follow an arithmetic workbook lesson with a 1-minute session in which they point to specific numerals located *behind*, *between*, *above*, or *below* others on a workbook page. Brief extra lessons like this in inclusive classrooms are powerful when provided with regularity to reinforce more structured lessons delivered by the SLP or special educator.

Technology Applications

The goals of using *augmentative or alternative communication* (AAC) devices are to enhance (augment) and/or replace (alternative) conventional forms for expression when needed. The system should supplement any gestural, spoken and/or written communication abilities (ASHA, 2002). In describing some early technology for AAC systems, Russel (1984) distinguished unaided systems requiring no hardware—visual gestural sign systems, fingerspelling, and pantomime—from aided systems that rely on electronic hardware, usually a computer,

Features of technology systems differ across vocabulary selection, symbol types, means of indication, and overall complexity of steps necessary to use the aid. Outputs vary from a visual display employing pictures or printed words to auditory messages conveyed in a synthesized voice. Systems can be activated by motions ranging from head movement to manual push buttons. Slower systems use scanning and selection of predetermined choices; faster ones are personalized, using most frequently needed items.

An augmentative communication device

Here is an example of an adaptation for computer-based, augmented, literacy instruction, as this student uses a microphone for speech-to-writing techniques.

Some students with language or visual disorders are *print-impaired* (Wolverton, Beukelman, Haynes, & Sesow, 1992). They may benefit from specific adaptations for computer-based, augmented, literacy instruction. Students who need help with reading text can use text-management systems that read aloud, using speech-synthesis technology, some of which simultaneously highlight printed text to provide sound–print associations. Computers can, of course, modify print size and letter shapes to make stored text accessible to those with visual impairments. Students can vary text color or intensify contrast between print and background. Those who cannot handwrite may use word processors that provide auditory feedback. As typed words are spoken aloud, the students gain help with monitoring grammatical and spelling patterns of the text they are producing.

Programs to enhance writing speed and provide spelling assistance include those that allow the user to enter frequently occurring words, phrases, sentences, or paragraphs so they can be retrieved and used again by inserting a brief alphabetic code. Some of these systems provide tables of words used most recently by an individual, who then can select by an initial consonant or a number code that transfers a selected word to a document in progress.

In all of these systems, the goal is to increase independent reading and writing. Many individuals using augmentative and alternative devices need extra time to complete academic work. To increase their productivity and reduce fatigue, teachers can adapt formats of written work so the students have to write less and, instead, insert a few critical words to show how well they have mastered the concept.

Summary

Speech–language pathologists, special educators, and professional colleagues in the general curriculum use a variety of interventions derived from different theories and models. These professions are united in their view of interweaving speech and language instruction with academic subject matter and competencies.

Language systems are interdependent during the school years. Oral language provides concepts, schemas about the world, vocabulary, sentence structure, and social conventions that form the basis for literacy. Two prerequisites for literacy are

1. the ability to use semantic, syntactic, or morphological cues to recognize print phrases or clauses; and
2. the ability to call up stored concepts about how the world operates, which emerges either during normal development or must be assisted by intervention teams.

When literacy becomes established, reading and writing progress begins to reinforce understandings of the sound, form, and meaning systems of oral language so that all communication systems benefit when learners profit from literacy instruction.

Assessment, specific interventions, modifications of demands or learning conditions, and monitoring of growth in communication requires integrated efforts by families, audiologists or hearing conservationists, and teams of speech–language pathologists, general curriculum, special education, and reading teachers, all working in cooperation with administrators who set school hiring priorities and organize delivery systems.

References   ■ ■ ■ ■ ■ ■

Achilles, J., Yates, R. R., & Freese, H. N. (1991). Perspectives from the field: Collaborative consultation in the speech and language program of the Dallas independent school district. *Language, Speech, and Hearing Services in Schools, 22,* 154–155.

American Speech–Language–Hearing Association. (1993). Definitions of communication disorders and variations. *Asha, 35* (Suppl. 10), 40–41.

American Speech–Language–Hearing Association. (2000). *Guidelines for the roles and responsibilities of school-based speech–language pathologist.* Rockville, MD: Author.

American Speech–Language–Hearing Association. (2002). Augmentative and alternative communication: Knowledge and skills for service delivery. *ASHA Supplement, 22,* 97–106.

Bleile, K. (1995). *Manual of articulation and phonological disorders.* San Diego, CA: Singular Publishing Group.

Canady, C. J., & Krantz, S. G. (1996). Reading and communication: A comparison of proficient and less proficient fourth-grade readers' opinion. *Language, Speech, and Hearing Services in Schools, 27,* 231–237.

Catts, H. W. (1991). Early identification of reading disorders. *Topics in Language Disorders, 12,* 1–16.

Catts, H. W., & Kahmi, A. G. (1999). *Language and reading disabilities.* Needham Heights, MA: Allyn & Bacon.

Curlee, R. F. (1999). *Stuttering and related disorders of fluency* (2nd ed.). New York: Thieme.

Faust, R. A. (2003, January/February). Childhood voice disorders: Ambulatory evaluation and operative diagnosis. *Clinical Pediatrics, 42,* 1–9.

Gierut, J. A. (1998, February). Treatment efficacy: Functional phonological disorders in children. *Journal of Speech, Language, and Hearing Research, 41,* S85–S100.

Johnston, J. R. (1988). Specific language disorders in the child. In N. J. Lass, L. V. McReynolds, J. L. Northern, & D. E. Yoder (Eds.), *Handbook of speech–language pathology and audiology* (pp. 685–715). Toronto: B. C. Decker.

Kamhi, A. (1987). Metalinguistic abilities in language-impaired children. *Topics in Language Disorders, 7,* 1–12.

Lahey, M. (1988). *Language disorders and language development.* New York: Macmillan.

Leahy, M. M. (1989). *Disorders of communication: The science of intervention.* New York: Taylor & Francis.

Laing, G. J., Law, J., Levin, A., & Logan, S. (2002, November 16). Evaluation of a structured test and a parent led method for screening for speech and language problems: Prospective population based study. *British Medical Journal, 325,* 1152–1156.

Laughton, J., & Hasenstab, M. S. (1986). *The language learning process.* Rockville, MD: Aspen.

Leonard, L. (1991). Specific language impairment as a clinical category. *Language, Speech and Hearing Services in Schools, 22,* 66–68.

Lipson, M. Y., & Wixson, K. K. (1986). Reading disability research: An interactionist perspective. *Review of Educational Research, 56,* 111–136.

McReynolds, L. V. (1988). Articulation disorders of unknown etiology. In N. J. Lass, L. V. McReynolds, J. L. Northern, & D. E. Yoder (Eds.), *Handbook of speech–language pathology and audiology* (pp. 419–441). Toronto: B. C. Decker.

National Institute on Deafness and Other Communication Disorders. (2002, December 12). *Statistics and human communication.* Retrieved March 14, 2005, from http://www.nidcd.nih.gov/index.asp>

Nelson, N. W. (1998). *Child language disorders in context.* Needham Heights, MA: Allyn & Bacon.

Nelson, N. W. (1989). Curriculum-based language assessment and intervention. *Language, Speech and Hearing Services in Schools, 20,* 170–184.

Nicolosi, L., Harryman, E., & Kresheck, J. (1989). *Terminology of communication disorders: Speech–language–hearing.* Baltimore: Williams & Wilkins.

Russel, M. (1984). Assessment and intervention issues with the nonspeaking child. *Exceptional Children, 51,* 64–71.

Shames, G. H., Wiig, E. H., & Secord, W. A. (1998). *Human communication disorders: An introduction* (5th ed.). Boston: Allyn & Bacon.

Snyder, L. (1984). Developmental language disorder: Elementary school age. In A. Holland (Ed.), *Language disorders in children* (pp. 129–158). San Diego, CA: College Hill Press.

U.S. Department of Education. (2002). *To ensure the free appropriate public education of all Americans: Twenty-fourth annual report to Congress on the implementation of the Individuals with Disabilities Education Act.* Retrieved March 14, 2005, <http://www.ed.gov/about/reports/annual/osep/2002/index.html

Wall, M. J. (1988). Dysfluency in the child. In N. J. Lass, L. V. McReynolds, J. L. Northern, & D. E. Yoder (Eds.), *Handbook of speech–language pathology and audiology* (pp. 622–639). Toronto: B. C. Decker.

Weaver, C. (1994). *Reading process and practice: From socio-psycholinguistics to whole language* (2nd ed.). Portsmouth, NH: Heinemann.

Wilson, D. (1987). *Voice problems of children* (3d ed.). Baltimore: Williams & Wilkins.

Wolverton, R. D., Beukelman, D. R., Haynes, M. S., & Sesow, D. (1992). Strategies in augmented literacy using microcomputer-based approaches. *Seminars in Speech and Language, 13,* 154–157.

Zebrowski, P. M. (2003, July). Developmental stuttering. *Pediatric Annals, 32*(7), 453–458.

Physical and
Health Disabilities

7

Donna Lehr

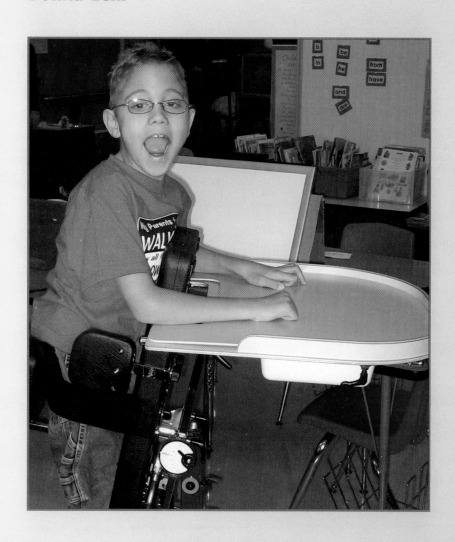

Students with physical and health disabilities are considered to be those students whose primary disabilities are due to orthopedic impairments, health impairments, and traumatic brain injuries and who require specialized adaptations to their instruction. This chapter is designed to increase your understanding of

1. who is included in this population of students;
2. the characteristics of student with physical and health disabilities;
3. etiology of the disabilities;
4. the focus of educational assessment design to identify needed educational interventions and supports;
5. the nature of educational and related service supports provided; and
6. methods for ensuring progress in the general education curriculum.

CASE STUDIES

A considerable range of differences exists in this population of students. No one case study could serve as an illustration of a "typical" student with physical and health disabilities, so three are provided. Consider both the differences and the similarities of the needs of the students described in the following cases studies.

***

Cassie

Cassie was born after a normal pregnancy and delivery, but early on, her mother noticed that she did not meet some of the motor developmental milestones that other infants her age were demonstrating. More specifically, by 3 months of age, Cassie did not lift her head when lying on her stomach, she seemed stiff when she was picked up, and she seemed to move around less than other children. She also had difficulty with nursing.

During routine well-baby checks, Cassie's mom reported her observations to the pediatrician. After several months of observation and assessment, Cassie was diagnosed with cerebral palsy, spastic quadriplegic type.

Now age 9, Cassie uses a wheelchair for locomotion and is looking forward to learning how to use a joystick to steer her soon-to-arrive power chair. Only those who are very familiar with her understand her speech, so Cassie uses multiple modes of communication, including talking, using a voice output communication device, and using a computer with an adapted keyboard to select pictures and words to write simple sentences.

Cassie has continued to have difficulty with eating and had a g-tube (gastrostomy feeding tube) surgically placed into her stomach so she could receive sufficient nutrition. Presently, she is tube-fed lunch while at school.

***

(continued)

continuing case studies

Ben

Ben's parents referred to Ben lovingly as their little "whirling dervish." At first he seemed to be just a very active little boy. Born after a normal pregnancy and delivery, he reached all the developmental milestones consistent with the books his parents were reading and with the children with whom he played at the park. But he did seem to be a lot more active; he was difficult to keep tabs on at the playground, and he showed no fear. His parents noted that he seemed to prefer to run around in the playground rather than join the games the other children were playing, and when friends came over to play, there were frequent squabbles.

When Ben went to kindergarten, the school personnel were concerned. Ben demonstrated a higher level of activity than the other students in his class. At the same, he had difficulty learning the skills his classmates were learning.

The evaluation team members, including his parents, were uncertain if Ben's difficulties stemmed from his inability to sit long enough to learn or because of another type of disability, such as a learning disability. Diagnostic testing in the school setting revealed that his IQ was in the normal range but that he did have some difficulty processing information.

During the same time that the school team was conducting an educational evaluation of Ben, his parents took him to a pediatrician who specialized in children with attention deficit/hyperactivity disorders (AD/HD). The doctor determined that Ben did have AD/HD and prescribed Ritalin for him. Once on medication, Ben seemed to do better at attending to schoolwork. The team also implemented a plan to aid him in developing early literacy and interacting with other students.

***

Albert

Albert is a 19-year-old student attending a public high school in a suburban community near a major city. Last year, Al attended an exclusive private school, where he was on the honor roll and a star player on the school's award-winning soccer team. In the middle of the school year, he was struck by a school bus while riding his bike. He was wearing a helmet, but it was not fastened under his chin. Albert sustained a closed head injury and was hospitalized for 6 months, first in intensive care and then in a rehabilitation hospital, where he received intensive occupational, physical, and speech therapy.

He has regained his ability to speak, but with some difficulty in articulation. He continues to have severe paralysis on his right side and some loss of function on his left side. He has to use a cane for support while walking and has difficulty regulating his impulses and emotions and organizing himself to do tasks.

Definitions

Three different categories of disabilities are used to describe students who have physical and health disabilities. These categories are identified within IDEA as "orthopedic impairments," "other health impairments," and "traumatic brain injury."

Orthopedic Impairments

The term *orthopedic impairment* refers to

> *a severe orthopedic impairment that adversely affects a child's educational performance. The term includes impairments caused by congenital anomaly (e.g., clubfoot, absence of some member, etc.), impairments caused by disease (e.g., poliomyelitis, bone tuberculosis, etc.), and impairments from other causes (e.g., cerebral palsy, amputations, and fractures or burns that cause contractures). —§300.7 20 U.S.C. 1401(3)(A) and (B); 1401(26)*

Other Health Impairments

IDEA defines the population of students with health impairments in the following way:

> *Other health impairment means having limited strength, vitality or alertness, including a heightened alertness to environmental stimuli, that results in limited alertness with respect to the educational environment, that—*
>
> *(i) Is due to chronic or acute health problems such as asthma, attention deficit disorder or attention deficit hyperactivity disorder, diabetes, epilepsy, a heart condition, hemophilia, lead poisoning, leukemia, nephritis, rheumatic fever, and sickle cell anemia; and*
> *(ii) Adversely affects a child's educational performance. —§300.7 20 U.S.C. 1401(3)(A) and (B); 1401(26)*

Traumatic Brain Injury

The third category of disabilities often included in descriptions of students with physical disabilities and other health impairments is traumatic brain injury. Traumatic brain injury is also a specific category of disability defined in IDEA, as follows.

> *Traumatic brain injury means an acquired injury to the brain caused by an external physical force, resulting in total or partial functional disability or psychosocial impairment, or both, that adversely affects a child's educational performance. The term applies to open or closed head injuries resulting in impairments in one or more areas, such as cognition; language; memory; attention; reasoning; abstract thinking; judgment; problem-solving; sensory, perceptual, and motor abilities; psychosocial behavior; physical functions; information processing; and speech. The term*

does not apply to brain injuries that are congenital or degenera-
tive, or to brain injuries induced by birth trauma.
—*§300.7 20 U.S.C. 1401(3)(A) and (B); 1401(26)*

Although these descriptions may have been somewhat helpful in understanding the general categories used to describe students who have physical and health disabilities, they are probably too brief to enable you to truly understand the nature of the disabilities. This chapter is intended to add to your understanding of this population of students and their needs.

Characteristics of Physical and Health Disabilities

If you think back about each of the students introduced at the beginning of the chapter, you can see that the first student, Cassie, is likely to be identified under IDEA as a student with an orthopedic impairment; the second student, Ben, as a student with a health impairment; and the third student, Albert, as a student with a traumatic brain injury. You may have noticed that all three students have one thing in common: Their conditions affect their ability to learn or to access learning opportunities. Beyond that, a few general statements can be made about these students and others identified as having these types of disabilities.

One student with a physical disability may have a primary need for accessible entrances to the building and rooms. Another student might have a need for adjustment in the curriculum to compensate for intermittent absences from school for surgeries to correct congenital malformations or for recurring illness. Still another student (e.g., Cassie) might need support to learn how to use a specialized communication system. Yet another may need constant monitoring of breathing and intermittent suctioning to maintain clear airways.

Some students need all of the services mentioned, and others need services and supports not described. Sometimes, in addition to physical and health-care needs, students have disabilities that affect their ability to learn, as is the case with both Cassie and Ben.

The diversity in the population of students with physical and health disabilities makes a general discussion of their academic, social, and emotional characteristics difficult. Few generalizations can be made. These students differ in the cause of their disabilities, age of onset, and so on, and also in their learning abilities and their social and emotional development. Characteristics unique to *some* students as a result of their physical and health disabilities relate to academic and social/emotional adjustment.

Academic Development

The academic performance of some students with physical and health disabilities is affected by co-existing cognitive disabilities. Other students' academic performance is affected by limitations in their opportunities to learn. Learning is enhanced for all students

1. through exposure to a rich variety of experiences at home, in school, and in the community;

Note

Physical and health disabilities can affect a student's accessibility to the natural environment (stairs may be difficult or impossible to maneuver), the curriculum (doctors' appointments can keep a student out of school), and everyday functions that other students may take for granted (fine- and gross-motor skills can make writing and playing ball difficult).

2. by regular attendance at school;
3. through participation in instructional activities provided in classroom settings;
4. though the ability to attend to formal instruction; and
5. through the ability to learn informally or incidentally through interactions with a variety of people.

Students with physical and health-care disabilities often have fewer of these opportunities and may have frequent interruptions. Their disabilities might result in fewer trips to museums, less time for informal play in the park, fewer invitations to play at friends' homes, fewer trips to visit other cities, and so on.

Opportunities to learn through reading—reading that takes you places you cannot get to—also may be more limited for some students. Merely picking up a book or a magazine, flipping through it or reading it carefully, is something many students cannot do independently. The book must be placed in an adaptive holder so the student can see it, or the student might need a page turner (human or mechanical) to turn the pages. Someone else must arrange the access. Independent opportunities for incidental learning are restricted.

Some students have extended absences from school because of periods of acute illness, repeated surgeries, or ongoing medical treatments. Others have short but frequent absences from school as a result of recurring illnesses or numerous medical appointments. Although schools are responsible for providing in-hospital or in-home instruction for students with disabilities who are physically unable to attend school-based programs, there are often periods, during acute illnesses, when students simply are unavailable for learning. Students with limited stamina are unable to handle the length of a typical school day and require periods of rest during the day and/or a shortened school day, again limiting their opportunities to learn. Some students with impaired mobility lose precious instructional time during the school day because they need more time to get from place to place.

The ability to *attend* to instruction is also sometimes a challenge for students with physical and health disabilities. Oversensitivity to environmental stimuli, as is often the case with students who have AD/HD, makes focus and concentration difficult. Students such as Ben report that it feels like they miss things as their mind races from thought to thought. Students with epilepsy who have absence seizures (see page 157) may miss instructional opportunities for brief periods throughout the day. Under these circumstances, even the most intellectually competent students have difficulty keeping up with their nondisabled peers. Delays in developing academic skills and suppressed scores on standardized achievement tests are understandable. Therefore, teaching compensatory skills for these interferences becomes a goal of the special education support for these students.

Social and Emotional Development

An additional challenge affecting students with physical and health disabilities is in their social and emotional development. They must learn to adjust to their disability. Consider the challenges that students such as Albert face, returning to school after serious accidents in which they sustained traumatic brain injury. These students have to learn to deal with the loss of prior function and perhaps the loss of a group of friends who no longer are sure how to interact with this person whom they now perceive as being very different from the one they knew previously.

The ability of individuals to adjust to their disability is affected by the nature of the disability and the reaction of their family, friends, and society in general. Some students face considerable discrimination because of the type of disorder or disease they have. For example, some students with HIV have been barred from school, and others have experienced extreme physical and social isolation within the school. The physical and health disability interferes with typical social interactions and, consequently, their development of social skills and emotional health.

Augmentative and alternative communication (AAC) methods used by students with physical disabilities can interfere with peer

These boys enjoy recess time with their classmates on the school's accessible playground.

interactions, which are critical to social and emotional development. Some students with physical and health disabilities spend considerably more time with adults (parents, physicians, therapists, etc.) than with nondisabled children their same age, again serving as a barrier to the typical process of social and emotional development.

It is important to point out that many students with physical and health disabilities overcome the challenges facing them academically, socially, and emotionally. They are able to do this when the needed medical, educational, related services, and family supports are provided. Some of these services and supports are discussed later in this chapter.

Causes/Prevalence

The three categories of physical and health disabilities identified in IDEA— orthopedic impairments, other health impairments, and traumatic brain injury—encompass a number of different conditions that affect students. Their causes are prevalence are discussed next.

Orthopedic Impairments

Among the most common types of orthopedic impairments in students receiving special education are cerebral palsy and spina bifida.

Cerebral Palsy (CP)

Cerebral palsy (CP) is a nonprogressive disorder of the central nervous system that interferes with a child's ability to control movement or posture. Researchers have identified many different causes of cerebral palsy, but often the cause is unknown (Pellegrino, 1997).

Possible causes include genetic disorders, teratogens, intrauterine infections, premature birth, and asphyxia. Cerebral palsy is diagnosed in approximately 1 in 500 live births (Winter, Autry, Boyle, & Yeargin-Allsopp, 2002).

No medical tests (blood test, X-ray, ultrasound, etc.) are available to determine if an individual has CP. Only after observing differences in the posture or movement of young children, when compared to that of typically developing children, can further evaluations of motor development be accomplished to confirm the diagnosis of CP. In children who are mildly affected by CP, differences in posture or development may not be evident until the child is a year old or later. In children with severe impairments, the absence of expected developmental milestones and increased muscle tone, as seen in the case study of Cassie, increases the likelihood of earlier diagnosis.

Various types of motor impairments may be evident in individuals with cerebral palsy. These types are distinguished by the parts of the body affected and the ways in which the muscle tone is affected and are categorized as follows:

1. *Monoplasia, di, tri,* and *quadri plegia* refers to involvement of one, two, three, or four limbs.
2. *Hemiplegia* refers to involvement of one side of the body.
3. *Parapalegia* refers to involvement of the lower part of the body.

As a result of damage to the area of the brain responsible for coordinating movement and posture, the muscles of individuals with cerebral palsy receive faulty information regarding the amount of tension their muscles should have. If a student has too much muscle tension, it is called *hypertonicity*, general tightness in the muscles resulting in contractures that further limit movement. By contrast, individuals with *hypotonicity* have too little muscle tone. They can appear "floppy" and have difficulty with things like closing their lips around a bottle or a spoon, holding a pencil firmly, or sustaining trunk control.

Some individuals with CP have fluctuating muscle tone. Their muscle tone changes from too much to too little in different parts of their body, over the course of seconds, hours, times of day, or based on the nature of the activity. *Athetosis* or *dyskinesis* causes jerky movements of the limbs of individuals with this type of CP. *Ataxia* often results in the person walking with an unsteady gait, because of a lack of balance and control of the trunk and limbs. It is often marked by tremors that interfere with hand control.

Though not always the case, some individuals with cerebral palsy have additional disabilities. For some, whatever caused damage to the part of the brain associated with motor coordination also affected the part of the brain responsible to learning and memory. As a result, some individuals with CP have mental retardation or learning disabilities, others have associated vision and hearing impairments, and yet others have multiple disabilities.

Spina Bifida

Another type of physical disability present in school-age students is spina bifida, a neural tube defect that occurs during early fetal development and results in the spine not completely closing around the spinal cord. Consequently, the nerves of the spinal cord are subject to insult and injury, which may result in paralysis from the point of the opening on down.

1. The mildest type of spina bifida, *occulta*, is noted by a small patch of fat or a tuft of hair on the lower back; the child may not have any damage to the spinal cord.
2. In others, the opening is more pronounced and a membrane covers the opening. While the symptoms of this type, *meningocele,* may be less severe, surgery is required to cover the thin membrane to prevent infections that could further damage the nervous system.
3. In the most severe type of spina bifida, *myelomeningocele*, babies are born with a sac on their back with parts of the spinal cord visible and protruding into the sac.

Damage to the spinal cord results in varying degrees of paralysis from the point of the sac downward. The paralysis and loss of sensation result in difficulty with walking and in controlling bowel and bladder functions.

Spina bifida occurred in 20 of 100,000 live births in 2001 (Mathews, Honein, & Erickson, 2001). Although the precise cause of neural tube defects remains unknown, research has shown a 20% decrease in the incidence of neural tube defects in infants born to women whose diets were supplemented with 0.4 mg of folic acid prior to conception (Mersereau et al., 2004). Research continues into the hypothesized genetic, environmental, and nutritional causes of this disorder.

Other Health Impairments

The category of "other health impairment" includes students with chronic conditions that affect their strength, vitality, or alertness and interferes with their ability to learn. A few of the many conditions of students who may be categorized as having other health impairments are described here.

Attention Deficit/ Hyperactivity Disorder (AD/HD)

AD/HD is probably the most talked about and most controversial disorder of students in today's schools. Although there have always been children identified as having difficulty with attention and high levels of activity, the number of children (and adults) labeled as having AD/HD has increased dramatically. Approximately 3% to 7% of children in the United States are estimated to have AD/HD (American Psychiatric Association, 2000).

Playing games outdoors can be a great way for all students to expend their extra energy and get some fresh air.

> **Note**
>
> Physical therapy can be a very integral part of the daily lives of children with orthopedic impairments.

Although a great deal of research continues to be conducted about AD/HD, little is known about its cause. There is a presumption of brain differences, but there is no conclusive scientific evidence of brain injury or structural difference in most individuals with the diagnosis (U.S. Department of Education, 2003).

No definitive medical tests are available to determine the presence of AD/HD in children or adults. The criteria listed in the *Diagnostic and Statistical Manual–IV TR* of the American Psychiatric Association (2000) typically are used as a guide to diagnose this disorder. These criteria include behavioral characteristics in the general categories of inattention and hyperactivity/impulsivity. The behaviors must be inconsistent with the child's age, have been demonstrated prior to the age of 7, and have persisted for a minimum of 6 months.

Students identified as having AD/HD are described as (a) having difficulty with sustained attention, (b) being hyperactive and impulsive, or (c) having both challenges. Not all students who meet the American Psychiatric Association criteria for AD/HD are eligible for special education services. As with all "other health impairments," students are eligible only if the disability affects their learning. Some students with AD/HD do not require specialized instruction but receive accommodations such as extended time or an environment free of distraction for test-taking. Others are eligible because they have accompanying disabilities (for example, learning disabilities) and qualify for services within that category of disabilities (U.S. Department of Education, 1999).

Epilepsy

Epilepsy is a condition of repeated seizures caused by the irregular discharge of electrical energy within the brain. In some cases, a known insult or injury to the brain can be identified as precipitating the seizures, but more often the cause is unknown (National Institute of Neurological Disorders and Stroke, 2004).

Seizures are manifested differently in different individuals, but the two general categories of seizure disorders are *partial* and *generalized*. In partial seizures, the irregular discharge of activity begins in one specific part of the brain, in contrast to generalized seizures, which result from a discharge throughout the cortex. Partial seizures are further characterized as *simple* or *complex*.

Outward signs of simple partial seizures include jerking of an arm or a leg, facial twitching, changes in facial color, and rapid heartbeat. Complex partial seizures typically begin with a brief loss of consciousness marked by a blank stare, followed by blinking, twitching, or repeated lip smacking. Generalized seizures include *tonic–clonic seizures* (previously known as grand mal seizures), characterized by a loss of consciousness, convulsions, and post-seizure lethargy. When individuals demonstrate another type of generalized seizure called an *absence seizure*, they appear to be daydreaming or staring blankly off in space for a few seconds.

For most students with epilepsy, medication is an effective treatment that decreases or, for some, eliminates seizure activity. For others, for whom medication alone is ineffective, a ketogenic diet rich in fat and low in carbohydrates may result in a reduction of seizure activity. When medication and/or diet do not work, surgery may be conducted to remove the part of the brain found to have lesions causing the seizures. For others, the vagus nerve stimulator, a battery-powered device, may be surgically implanted in the chest. The wires in the device connect with the vagus nerve at the base of the neck, and the device helps to maintain a steady rate of electrical activity (much like a pacemaker does for the heart), thereby reducing the spikes that are manifested as seizures (National Institute on Neurological Disorders and Stroke, 2004).

No one treatment works for all students with epilepsy and, for some, none of the aforementioned treatments effectively reduces seizure activity. Additional concerns to school personnel are the side effects of medications, including sleepiness and lethargy.

Asthma

Asthma is a chronic lung disease in which individuals have serious reactions to allergens and irritants in the environment, sometimes associated with changes in seasons, weather, stress, and physical activity. An estimated 5 million children under the age of 18 have asthma, making it the most common childhood disease (Asthma and Allergy Foundation of America, 2004). Characteristics of asthma are restricted breathing and periodic episodes of wheezing and coughing as the respiratory system reacts to the environmental conditions. Treatment for asthma includes modifying the environment to decrease the irritants and administering medication to minimize reaction to the pollutants.

Diabetes

Diabetes is a metabolic disorder that affects 12% of children under the age of 18 (National Center for Health Statistics, 2002). Typically, children have Type 1 diabetes, a condition in which the body either does not produce sufficient insulin or uses insulin ineffectively. Too little insulin produces a number of symptoms, including extreme thirst, frequent urination, increased appetite, weight loss, blurred vision, and general fatigue. If untreated, diabetes can lead to blindness, loss of limbs, kidney failure, and heart disease.

Type 2 diabetes traditionally has been a disease of overweight adults; however, this type of diabetes is increasingly being diagnosed in children who are overweight. Children with Type 2 diabetes show many of the same symptoms associated with Type 1 diabetes, along with frequent infections and slow-healing wounds. Treatment for both types includes medication and dietary control.

HIV/AIDS

The human immunodeficiency virus (HIV) is transmitted to children through transfusions of infected blood, or from their HIV-positive mothers in utero, or through breast-feeding. Some children who are HIV-positive remain symptom-free. Other children eventually develop acquired immunodeficiency syndrome (AIDS), which is characterized by a weakened immune system and the loss of the ability to fight off infections and other diseases.

Considerable progress has been made in the United States in decreasing the initial transmission of the virus to children, and medications have slowed progression of the disease considerably, resulting in infected children remaining symptom-free for a longer time. When children do become symptomatic, however, particularly if this happens early, the disease takes a different course than in adults. The developing brains of children seem more susceptible to the infection, and often children with AIDS develop neurological conditions that cause them to lose previously acquired developmental milestones and to develop motor challenges similar to those of children with cerebral palsy.

HIV/AIDS continues to be a medical condition that elicits considerable fear. In the early 1980s, when the first cases of pediatric AIDS emerged and HIV-positive children attempted to attend school, they were denied access to school buildings. Since that time, much has been learned about how the virus is transmitted and the steps to decrease the risks of transmission. Now we know that the virus is not transmitted through casual contact, such as in schools, and that good hygienic practices with all students (universal precautions) (Centers for Disease Control, 1988) in schools make school attendance of students with HIV appropriate and safe for the students themselves and for others in their presence. The American Academy of Pediatrics (2000) has developed clear policy guidelines regarding school attendance of students with HIV.

Traumatic Brain Injury

Traumatic brain injury (TBI) is caused by a physical insult to the head that causes damage to one or more parts of the brain. While the skull serves the function of protecting the brain, the delicate nerves in the brain can become damaged as a result of automobile and bicycle accidents, gunshot wounds, and abuse (shaken baby syndrome). The resulting damage can affect the way the nerves in the brain relay information regarding moving, thinking, and feeling. The U.S. Department of Education (2002) reported that 14,844 students with traumatic brain injury received special education services during the 2000–01 school year.

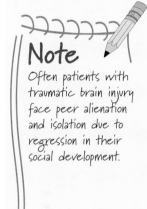

Note

Often patients with traumatic brain injury face peer alienation and isolation due to regression in their social development.

Head injuries are described by type of injury (open or closed), the level of severity (mild, moderate, and severe), and the kind of injury that results. The word *open* is used when the skull is penetrated by something and the piercing object (e.g., a bullet or a sharp object, including a bone skull fragment) enters the brain tissue. A *closed* injury occurs when the head is hit sharply or violently and damage results from the brain hitting against the skull, as in shaken baby syndrome.

The brain damage resulting from the trauma can lead to significant changes in all areas of functioning. It can affect memory, speech, vision, and executive functioning, which includes selective attention, organization, impulse control, and organization—all critical for learning.

Assessment and Evaluation for Special Education and Related Services ■ ■ ■ ■ ■ ■

Assessment and evaluation must take into account needed supports and services as well as the students' social and emotional adjustment.

Needed Supports and Services

Typically, the first step in accessing special education services for individual students is a diagnostic evaluation to determine if the student indeed has a disability and, if so, what type (category) best describes the primary disability. Most children and youth with physical and health disabilities were diagnosed by medical personnel prior to their referral for special education. Consequently, the focus of assessment in school shifts from determination of eligibility to identification of the necessary supports and services.

Albert, for example, had been attending private school prior to the accident in which he sustained traumatic brain injury. Because that school did not serve students with severe disabilities, he entered a school in his local public school district after his stay in the rehabilitation facility with a clear diagnosis of traumatic brain injury.

While in rehab, thorough evaluations were conducted of Albert's motor and cognitive functioning. That information was provided to the receiving school district, and subsequent assessments focused on questions of physical access, safe care, specific educational needs, identification of goals and objectives, intervention approaches, assistive technology needs, and the process of collaborative planning to implement and evaluate his educational and related-services supports.

Many students with physical and health disabilities require nursing support beyond that provided to the general education population (e.g., Cassie, who must be tube-fed). Prior to these students attending school, a careful assessment of their routine health-care and emergency needs must be conducted to ensure their safety. Often, a careful individualized health-care plan is developed based on assessment of the students' needs.

The specific physical and health disabilities often result in an ongoing need for assessment (and intervention) of the students' motor and communication development and support needs. The first step in developing programs to meet their needs is to conduct specialized assessments of their fine- and gross-motor functioning and their communication skills. Many students with physical and health disabilities need specialized adaptive equipment and assistive technology supports so they can benefit from special education. This should be emphasized within the assessment process.

Even though comprehensive assessments of these areas of functioning might have been conducted for students such as Albert after his traumatic brain injury, school-based therapists must conduct additional assessment of functioning relative to the school environment to determine appropriate goals, objectives, and interventions that will maximize access to instruction while at school.

Social and Emotional Adjustment

Assessment of students' social and emotional adjustment also must be conducted so necessary supports can be provided. Because acceptance by peers (and other individuals within the school) often affects students' adjustment to their disabilities, an assessment of the peers' needs for information is also beneficial.

Research-Based Interventions and Best Practices

The multiple and complex needs of students with physical and health disabilities require that professionals from a variety of disciplines work collaboratively with the students and their families to identify solutions unique to each student's needs. As with all students identified as having special educational needs, decisions must be made regarding what and how to teach to meet the students' individual needs.

For this population of students, some additional emphases are necessary. The team must develop, implement, and evaluate carefully written plans to ensure safe care and physical access. As mentioned, the instructional needs of students with physical and health disabilities vary greatly. Consequently, readers are referred to other chapters in this book to learn about curricular considerations for the population of students who have accompanying learning disabilities, mental retardation, communication disorders, and sensory impairments.

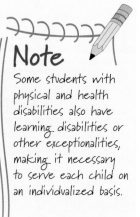

Note

Some students with physical and health disabilities also have learning disabilities or other exceptionalities, making it necessary to serve each child on an individualized basis.

Safe Care

Many students with physical and health disabilities require careful attention to routine care as well as highly specialized health care while at school. Because of these students' increased care-providing needs, along with their increased vulnerability resulting from compromised immune systems, contagious and infectious diseases, and/or weakened respiratory systems, the first step in ensuring their safe care is careful attention to hygienic procedures.

Common childhood diseases such as chicken pox and the flu, while minor inconveniences for some students, can be life-threatening for student who have complex health-care needs. Experts consider proper hand washing to be a key to decreasing the risks for transmitting these diseases. This routine procedure, sometimes taken for granted, is credited as being the single most important factor in minimizing the transmission of infectious diseases. Beyond careful hand washing, hygienic care-providing procedures have to be followed for diaper changing, toileting, and generally for sanitizing items and surfaces that have come into contact with blood and bodily fluids (toys, diaper-changing surfaces, food-handling items, etc.)

It is further recommended that universal precautions be taken with all students. The term *universal precautions* (Center for Disease Control, 1988) refers to the use of hygienic care-providing practices for all individuals, not just those known to have infectious diseases. This ensures safe care for all and respects the privacy of individuals with infectious diseases who may want to—and have the right to—keep their diagnosis confidential. This may be especially important for students with HIV, who continue to experience discrimination when their status is known to others.

Many students with physical and health disabilities must receive medication while they are at school. Schools have to follow state and district guidelines regarding administration of medication, which typically address who can administer the medication and permissions necessary before the medication can be administered. Although some students can be administered their medication on a routine, scheduled basis, other students—for example, those with asthma—require plans that are sufficiently flexible to permit administration on an as-needed basis.

Often, only first aid is required when a student has a seizure, but at other times (e.g., when the seizure is prolonged), emergency care must be provided. Other students—for example, those with diabetes—must have ongoing monitoring of glucose levels and injections to regulate the levels as necessary. Still other students require highly specialized health care, including tube feeding, tracheostomy care, ventilator monitoring, and clean intermittent catheterization, which requires administration by specially trained individuals. For these students, experts recommend the development of comprehensive Individualized Health Care Plans (IHCPs), which become a part of the students' IEPs and describe the health-care procedure(s) needed, the schedule for administering the procedures, who is responsible for administering the procedures, the nature of the training to ensure competent delivery of care, and signs indicating the need for emergency care (Lehr, Greene, & Powers, 2003). An excellent resource for designing IHCPs is Porter, Haynie, Bierle, Caldwell, and Palfrey's book *Children and Youth Assisted by Medical Technology in Educational Settings: Guidelines for Care* (1997).

Physical Access

Even though federal accessibility laws require that new school buildings and buildings undergoing renovations meet accessibility standards, many school buildings still are

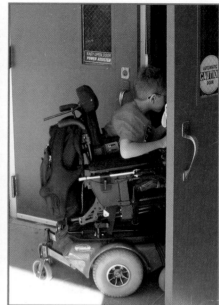

This building is accessible for all students, due to its automatic doors and ramps.

inaccessible to individuals with mobility impairments. Students must have accommodations to allow them physical access into school buildings (accessible routes with curb-cuts, ramps, and railings) and access to locations within the school building. In addition, toileting facilities, drinking fountains, and playground areas might have to be modified.

Proper positioning, transferring, and handling are critical to the provision of education to some students with physical and health disabilities. Proper positioning of students with physical disabilities minimizes the risks for further impairment, improves circulation, facilitates movement, and enhances their availability for learning. Physical and occupational therapists work closely with teachers in selecting and using appropriate equipment to support the students while they are sitting, standing, and walking, and they develop therapeutic interventions to maximize the students' motor functioning.

Programs demonstrating "best practices" for students with physical and health disabilities carefully evaluate students' need for assistive technology for environmental control, instructional access, communication, and mobility. Careful evaluation can lead to selection of "low-tech" devices such as pencil grips and rings on zippers to improve physical manipulation and/or "high-tech" devices such as sophisticated computer communication systems with specialized switches as substitutes for a computer mouse, adapted or alternatives to keyboards, and software that permits speech-to-text or text-to-speech conversions.

An increasing array of assistive technology is available, and the team must make thoughtful decisions regarding choice of technology to facilitate functioning for specific students while at the same time maximizing normalization of function. For example, a computer and a piece of cardboard can both be used to display two items from which a nonverbal student can communicate a preferred item. An advantage of the low-tech board is that it can be made available wherever in the room the student is located, not just where the child must be in his or her wheelchair in front of the computer. Thus, the low-tech cardboard communication board creates more natural conditions for communication (Lehr, Greene, & Powers, 2003).

Instructional Priorities

The goal for all students is independence. Vital to the independence of students with physical and health disabilities is the development of skills to provide or direct the management of their own care. Students with diabetes must learn to monitor their own glucose levels; students with asthma must learn to recognize triggers, signs of distress, and how to administer their own medication. Students who require catheterization can learn to self-catheterize. Students with tracheostomies who require suctioning to maintain clear airways can be taught to signal to a care provider when they wish to receive suctioning.

Learning to schedule their own doctors' appointments, have their prescriptions filled, and prepare questions for their physicians are just some of the important skills to be taught to increase the independence of these students. Instructional priorities for students with AD/HD and traumatic brain injury also focus on management—self-management or self-control. For these students, important instructional priorities include learning (a) to control impulsive behavior, (b) to organize themselves to accomplish tasks, (c) to understand necessary supports to facilitate their own learning, (d) time-management techniques, and (e) self-advocacy skills. Effective strategies to support student learning and increase independence include specific instruction and monitoring their the use of assignment notebooks, calendars, and checklists (U.S. Department of Education, 2004). (More information about these approaches may be found in chapter 4, which deals with students with learning disabilities.)

This teacher escorts her students to art class while the line leader controls her own movements and operates her walking device independently.

Collaboration

The medical, education, therapeutic, social, and emotional needs of students with physical and health disabilities are complex. Many of these students see a large number of professionals in and out of the school (e.g., general pediatricians, medical specialists, nurses, counselors, teachers, occupational, physical, and speech therapists, paraprofessionals, bus drivers) and are supported by many family members and friends.

No one individual, working alone, can design, implement, and evaluate an effective individualized program for a student with a physical or health disability. Essential to these students' success is frequent sharing of information about student needs, the effectiveness of interventions, and changes in students' educational, health care, and social/emotional status. Opportunities to exchange information and ideas, while always a challenge to arrange, are essential to ensure these students' safety and progress as learners.

Access to the General Education Curriculum and Settings

Access to general education involves proper placement, including any necessary accommodations. Also important is what has been termed "attitudinal access."

Placement

Historically, many students with physical and health disabilities did not have access to general education settings. In the past, many of these students did not live past either the newborn period or the period of critical medical need (Lehr & Noonan, 1989). Now, however, as a result of improvements in medical technology, many children are surviving that critical period of intensive care. Many with ongoing needs for medical technology support benefit from portable equipment such as suctioning machines and ventilators. In addition, because of the movement toward normalization and deinstitutionalization, children and youth who survive are no longer educated exclusively in hospitals, at home, or in segregated schools (Lehr & Noonan, 1989).

Students with physical and health disabilities are being educated in general education schools and classes in increasing numbers. Still, some students require a level of health care that results in teams deciding on placements in more restrictive environments. This sometimes stems from the lack of availability of school nurses, which leads to the clustering of students for care and education or the provision of education in home settings.

Accommodations

Most students with physical and health disabilities require a range of accommodations to enable their access to, and success in, the general education curriculum. At the most basic level, school buildings must be accessible. Additional examples of accommodations are adjustments in the curriculum to compensate for absences; extended time to pass from class to class; low-tech and high-tech assistive technology to enable environmental control, instructional access, communication, and mobility; extended time to complete in-class tests and other assignments; and distraction-free settings for instruction and testing. Each of these factors increases access to, and progress in, the general education curriculum for students with physical and health disabilities.

"Attitudinal Access"

One additional barrier that must be addressed to ensure access to the general education curriculum and settings for students with physical and health disabilities is "attitudinal access." Arranging for physical access and providing accommodations are relatively easy. More difficult to address are the attitudes of students and school personnel to ensure that students are accepted as equal members in the school community.

At times, students with HIV have encountered significant discrimination arising from concern about their transmitting the disease and the stigma associated with the etiology of the disease. Concern about the fragility of students who have been described as "medically fragile" and the costs of providing supportive services to these students have been attitudinal barriers to their access to general education settings. Some are afraid the students will simply "break," and some resent the high cost of providing education and related services for these students. Lack of understanding of how to communicate with students who use augmentative and alternative communication systems further contributes to the social segregation of students within general education classes and schools.

A great deal of progress has been made in ensuring access for students with physical and health disabilities in the general education curriculum and settings. The hard work of teams of professional and families to develop knowledge and skills in students and their peers has resulted in many students with physical and health disabilities enjoying full citizenship in their schools.

Summary

The population of students who have physical and health disabilities has unique needs that must be addressed to ensure the right to receive an appropriate education in the least restrictive environment. Their needs for safe environments, specialized health care, physical access, and specialized transportation require that individualized plans be developed to meet these related-service needs and ensure the students' health and safety.

In addition, unique aspects of these students' IEPs are the need to schedule adjustments to absences resulting from illnesses and corrective surgeries as well as specific goals and objectives designed to increase students' participation in and management of their own physical and health care. Finally, information and training of other school personnel and peers are vital to increase students' participation in the mainstream of school life.

References

Asthma and Allergy Foundation of America. (n.d.). *Asthma facts and figures*. Retrieved June 25, 2004, from http://www.aafa.org/templ/display.cfm?id=29

American Academy of Pediatrics, Committee on Pediatric AIDS. (2000). Education of children with human immunodeficiency virus infection. *Pediatrics, 105*(6), 1358–1360.

American Psychiatric Association. (2000). *Diagnostic and statistical manual of mental disorders* (4th ed., text revision). Washington, DC: Author.

Centers for Disease Control. (1988). Perspectives in disease prevention and health promotion update: Universal precautions for prevention of transmission of human immunodeficiency virus, hepatitis b virus, and other bloodborne pathogens in healthcare settings. *Morbidity and Mortality Weekly Report, 37*(24), 377–382.

National Center for Health Statistics, Center for Disease Control. (2002). *Summary of health statistics for U.S. children: National health interview survey, 2002*. Retrieved June 24, 2004, from www.cdc.gov/nchs.

Lehr, D. H., Greene, J., & Powers, S. (2003). Managing the needs of students with physical and health challenges in inclusive settings. In D. Ryndak & S. Alper (Eds.), *Inclusion and curriculum for students with significant disabilities* (pp. 432–447). Boston: Allyn & Bacon.

Lehr, D. H., & Noonan, M. (1989). Issues in the education of students with complex health care needs. In F. Brown & D. Lehr (Eds.), *Persons with profound disabilities: Issues and practices* (pp. 139–158). Baltimore: Paul H. Brookes Publishing Co.

Matthews, T. J., Honein, M. A., & Erickson, J. D. (2002). Spina bifida and anencephaly prevalence—United States, 1991–2001. *Morbidity and Mortality Weekly Report, 51*(13), 9–11.

Mersereau, P., Kilker, K., Carter, H. Fassett, E. Williams, J., Flores, A., et al. (2004). Spina bifida and anencephaly before and after folic acid mandate—United States, 1995–1996 and 1999–2000. *Morbidity and Mortality Weekly Report, 53*(17), 362–365.

National Institute on Neurological Disorders and Stroke. (2004). *Seizures and epilepsy: Hope through research*. Retrieved June 30, 2004, from http://www.ninds.nih.gov/health_and _medical/pubs/seizures_and_epilepsy_htr.htm.

Pellegrino, L. (1997). Cerebral palsy. In M. Batshaw (Ed.), *Children with disabilities* (4th ed., pp. 499–528). Baltimore: Paul H. Brookes Publishing.

Porter, S., Haynie, M., Bierle, T., Caldwell, T., & Palfrey, J. (Eds.). (1997). *Children and youth assisted by medical technology in educational settings: Guidelines for care* (2nd ed.). Baltimore: Paul H. Brookes Publishing.

U.S. Department of Education, Office of Special Education and Rehabilitative Services, Office of Special Education Programs. (2003). *Identifying and treating attention deficit hyperactivity disorder: A resource for school and home*. Washington, DC: Author.

U.S. Department of Education, Office of Special Education and Rehabilitative Services, Office of Special Education Programs. (2004) *Teaching children with attention deficit hyperactivity disorder: Instructional strategies and practices* Washington, DC: OSEP.

U.S. Department of Education. (1999). *Children with ADD/ADH—Topic brief*. Retrieved July 4, 2004, from http://www.ed.gov/policy/speced/leg/idea/brief6.html

U.S. Department of Education. (2002). *Twenty-fourth annual report to Congress on the implementation of the Individuals with Disabilities Education Act*. Washington, DC: U.S. Government Printing Office.

Winter, S., Autry, A., Boyle, C., & Yeargin-Allsopp, M. (2002). Trends in the prevalence of cerebral palsy in a population-based study. *Pediatrics, 110,* 1220–1225.

Gifted and Talented

8

Kimberley Chandler

In 1971, a comprehensive national survey known as the *Marland Report* (Marland, 1972) indicated that only a small percentage of students thought to be gifted were receiving any special services. As a result of that report, the first federal definition of giftedness was adopted and the Office of Gifted and Talented (OGT) was established. In a review of state definitions of the terms *gifted* and *giftedness*, Stephens and Karnes (2000) found widespread differences across the nation and within states. For purposes of this book, the definition of *gifted learner* is one that evolved from language in the Jacob K. Javits Gifted and Talented Students Education Act and the U.S. Department of Education's 1994 report *National Excellence: A Case for Developing America's Talent*, which describes gifted learners as

> *children and youth with outstanding talent [who] perform or show the potential for performing at remarkably high levels of accomplishment when compared with others of their age, experience, or environment.*
>
> *These children and youth exhibit high performance capability in intellectual, creative, and/or artistic areas, possess an unusual leadership capacity, or excel in specific academic fields. They require services or activities not ordinarily provided by the schools.*
>
> *Outstanding talents are present in children and youth from all cultural groups, across all economic strata, and in all areas of human endeavor. (p. 26)*

Related Definitions

The following terminology is applied to the population of gifted and talented students.

Gifted and talented student: one identified for special programming based on local or state criteria.

G/T: the abbreviated term used in many programs to refer to gifted and talented students.

Differentiated curricula: "modified courses of study designed to make the schools more responsive to the educational needs of ... exceptional learners" (Borland, 1989, p. 171).

Acceleration: a curricular approach often used with G/T students, based on "...deciding that competence rather than age should be the criterion for determining when an individual obtains access to particular curricula or academic experiences" (Benbow, 1998, p. 281).

Enrichment: a curricular approach commonly used with G/T students that involves modifying the curriculum to provide greater depth and breadth than typically is provided through the standard curriculum (Davis & Rimm, 1998).

CASE STUDY: CANDACE

Scene: A parent–teacher conference, September 15, 3:oo p.m.:

Second-grade teacher, Ms. McGowan:

Candace is working far beyond the level of any of the other second-graders in my classroom. I have given her the second-grade end-of-the-book math test, and she missed only one problem. For language arts, I determined her instructional reading level to be sixth grade. I'm trying my best to differentiate and provide for her needs, but I'm not equipped to do this.

Candace's mother, Mrs. Bridge:

I know the school personnel are working hard to meet Candace's needs, but I think the second-grade placement is limiting for her. As much as I like you, Ms. McGowan, I'm aware that you have 24 other second-graders in your class. The best you can do is to give Candace some extra enrichment sheets here and there when time allows.

G/T resource teacher, Miss Lingerfelt:

Technically, Candace hasn't been formally identified as gifted, because she is only in second grade. I work mainly at another building, so my time here is limited and I don't usually serve students in the primary grades or students who haven't been identified. I do have some extra time on Monday afternoons. Maybe I could work with Candace in math and language arts to provide some extra enrichment activities. Knowing Candace, though, I don't think an extra hour a week will really be the answer to meeting her needs.

Principal, Mr. Cooper:

Candace is a delightful student and certainly does outstanding work. I think we need to be realistic about what any one teacher can do to provide services to her. Miss Lingerfelt, are any other options available through the gifted education program?

Miss Lingerfelt:

I'll check with my supervisor and get back to you as soon as possible.

Candace's mother:

I want to throw out an idea that I've been exploring in reading some articles about gifted education. Much of the literature in gifted education seems to support acceleration. What is the school district's policy on that?

Principal:

There is no policy, per se, other than that we try to meet students' needs. If acceleration would help to meet a child's needs, that option could be explored.

(continued)

continuing case study of Candace

Guidance counselor, Mr. Worley:

I would be concerned about putting a second-grade student in a class with older students, in terms of her social–emotional well-being.

G/T resource teacher, Miss Lingerfelt:

I've heard of reports to the contrary. The research seems to indicate that if a child's academic needs are met, the social–emotional piece should not be a primary concern.

***

The concerns raised in this case study are indicative of some of the issues that may arise when dealing with gifted students in the school setting. Identification, the provision of services, philosophies, and logistical considerations are just a few of the challenges that educators face when trying to serve gifted students.

Characteristics of Gifted and Talented Students

Teachers working with gifted students have to understand the unique characteristics of these students and how to adapt curriculum and instruction to meet their needs.

Characteristics of the disability can be considered in terms of academic/cognitive traits, as well as emotional/affective characteristics.

Academic/Cognitive Characteristics

The academic/cognitive needs of gifted students and related curricular implications are summarized in Table 8.1.

Emotional/Affective Characteristics

Among the emotional characteristics associated with gifted students are

- perfectionism,
- intensity, and
- heightened sensitivity.

At times these characteristics become a barrier for gifted students in the way they manage their academic and personal lives. Although most gifted programs attempt to include components that address the emotional needs of students, the guidance and counseling services catering to their needs are often inadequate. Some general suggestions for addressing the emotional needs of gifted students are as follows:

- Be aware of the child's temperament.
- Provide role models of risk taking and coping with mistakes.

Note

Some people expect students who are gifted and talent to behave more maturely than their classmates because of their academic successes; however, just because children are intellectually gifted does not mean that their emotional needs surpass that of their age or their peers'.

> **TABLE 8.1**
> Characteristics of Gifted Learners and Related Curriculum Implications

Characteristics	Curriculum Implications
Reads well and widely	■ Individualize a reading program that diagnoses reading level and prescribes reading material based on that level ■ Form a literary group of similar students for discussion ■ Develop critical reading skills ■ Focus on analysis and interpretation in reading material
Has a large vocabulary	■ Introduce a foreign language ■ Focus on building vocabulary ■ Develop word relationship skills (antonyms, homophones, etc.)
Has a good memory for things heard or read	■ Present ideas on a topic to the class ■ Prepare a skit or play for production ■ Build in "trivial pursuit" activities
Is curious and asks probing questions	■ Develop an understanding of the scientific method ■ Focus on observation skills
Is an independent worker and has lots of initiative	■ Focus on independent project work ■ Teach organizational skills and study skills
Has a long attention span	■ Assign long-term work ■ Introduce complex topics for reading, discussion, and project work
Has complex thoughts and ideas	■ Work on critical thinking skills (analysis, synthesis, evaluation) ■ Develop writing skills
Is widely informed about many topics	■ Stimulate broad reading patterns ■ Develop special units of study that address current interests
Shows good judgment and logic	■ Organize a field trip for the class ■ Prepare a parent night ■ Teach formal logic
Understands relationships and comprehends meanings	■ Provide multidisciplinary experiences ■ Structure activities that require students to work across fields on special group/individual projects
Produces original or unusual products or ideas	■ Practice skills of fluency, flexibility, elaboration, and originality ■ Work on specific product development

Source: From *Comprehensive Curriculum for Gifted Learners* (pp. 158–159), by J. VanTassel-Baska, J. Feldhusen, K. Seeley, G. Wheatley, L. Silverman, & W. Foster (Boston: Allyn & Bacon). Copyright © 1988 by Allyn & Bacon. Reprinted by permission.

- Praise the *child*, not his or her accomplishments.
- Encourage empathy.
- Foster discussions related to perfectionism, and being "different."
- Don't confuse intellect with ability in all areas.
- Listen for feeling and content in discussions.
- Provide opportunities for interaction with peers of similar abilities.
- Allow for individual differences.
- Foster the use of problem solving, decision making, and prioritizing in social arenas.
- Model appropriate social interaction.
- Stay alert to stressors (e.g., peer pressure, competing expectations).

Concomitant Traits

Gifted students have *concomitant traits*— traits that exist concurrently—that are important for teachers to understand. Usually, one of these traits is considered positive and the other is seen as negative. Teachers have to be aware of what may be a negative manifestation of a positive characteristic. Table 8.2 gives some examples of concomitant traits in the areas of cognitive, leadership, and motivation.

TABLE 8.2 **Concomitant Traits**	
Positive	Negative
Cognitive	
Rapidly grasps facts and concepts	Dislikes routines and drills
Supports thinking with logical explanations	Has difficulty accepting the illogical
Is a keen and alert observer	Is overly particular about the details of others' ideas
Comprehends abstract concepts	Omits details in the communication of his or her own ideas
Critically evaluates others' ideas	Is intolerant of others' opinions
Leadership	
Has a sense of justice and fair play	Has unrealistic expectations of others
Is self-confident	Is perceived as cocky
Is able to plan, direct, and evaluate activities	Dominates others
Motivation	
Perseveres with an idea or task until completion	Is perceived as stubborn, willful, or uncooperative
Pursues topics of interest for self-fulfillment	Is bored with the pace of classroom work or imposed group work
Enjoys the challenge of difficult activities	Sets unrealistic goals because of high ambition
Demonstrates independence in thought	Is unresponsive to external direction and action

Prevalence and Identification

There is no nationwide system of identification of students for gifted programs. School districts typically identify from 3% to 12% of their student population for gifted programs. This percentage and the criteria for identifying students vary from state to state and within a state depending upon district and state policies, funding available, and district philosophy.

A major concern in the field of gifted education is identification and programming for underserved populations (examples: low socioeconomic status, students with learning disabilities, English Language Learners). It is believed that traditional measures (standardized ability and achievement tests) may be biased and unfair for these populations. Alternative assessments (performance-based; nonverbal ability tests) have been implemented to address this problem. In addition, much teacher and administrator training has been used to facilitate the appropriate identification of underserved populations.

Note

In order to avoid the bias that can be found in traditional standardized tests, alternative assessments are often used, such as portfolio assessment, observation, performance-based tests, and nonverbal ability tests.

Assessment and Evaluation for Special Education and Related Services

In some states, gifted education falls under the aegis of special education. In these situations, regulations and funding formulas provide a legal basis for gifted education programming. Individualized education plans (IEPs) are required for gifted students in those states. Where gifted education is not part of special education, it may fall under another umbrella, such as curriculum and instruction. In many states it exists as a category by itself. The advantage of being part of special education is the force of the law and all its protections, including the IEP. In states where gifted education is not part of special education, the degree of compliance with local and state regulations varies widely.

Most program policies require the use of multiple criteria for identifying gifted students. These instruments may include

- ability tests (standardized tests, such as the Cognitive Abilities Test);
- achievement tests (standardized tests, such as the Iowa Test of Basic Skills);
- behavioral checklists and narratives completed by parents;
- behavioral checklists and narratives completed by teachers;
- portfolios of student work;
- course grades; and
- interviews.

Research-Based Interventions and Best Practices

In 1996, a task force of the National Association for Gifted Children (NAGC) was established to determine the feasibility of developing programming standards for gifted education. Membership on the task force included representatives from higher education, state-level gifted administration, local-level gifted administration, and parent groups.

The *NAGC Pre-K–Grade 12 Gifted Program Standards* were published as the culmination of the group's work (Landrum & Shaklee, 1998). The document stated that

"Gifted education services must include curricular and instructional opportunities directed to the unique needs of the gifted learner" (p. 5). The *Standards* included seven essential criteria for gifted education programming:

1. Program design
2. Program administration and management
3. Socioemotional guidance and counseling
4. Student identification
5. Curriculum and instruction
6. Professional development
7. Program evaluation

For each criterion, guiding principles formed the basis for each standard. The guiding principles for program design are as follows (Landrum & Shaklee, 1998):

1. Rather than any single gifted program, a continuum of programming services must exist for gifted learners.
2. Gifted education must be adequately funded.
3. Gifted education programming must evolve from a comprehensive and sound base.
4. Gifted education programming services must be an integral part of the general education school day.
5. Flexible groupings of students must be developed to facilitate differentiated instruction and curriculum.

In a follow-up report, Landrum, Callahan, and Shaklee (2001) stated that these represent "standards consistently cited across sources as critical to program success" (p. ix).

Students receive enriched instruction and advanced assignments in general education classrooms as part of their gifted education programming.

Programming

Borland (1989) defined programs for the gifted as an "acknowledgement by a school or school district that there are gifted students in the system, that these students have special educational needs, and that educators have an obligation to address these needs within the curriculum" (pp. 44–45). He noted that the mere existence of a program does not guarantee that it will be of high quality. In many school districts, the state education agency seeks compliance regarding the regulations but does not have the authority or adequate personnel to monitor the quality of gifted programs.

Shaklee (2001) noted that "the belief that any type of gifted programming is 'better than nothing at all' is often held out of fear or reluctance for change to improve inadequate gifted education services" (p. 1).

Policies specific to adapting and adding to the nature and operations of the general education program are necessary for gifted education. To give structure to education for G/T students, Davis and Rimm (1998) suggested four core components of gifted program planning:

1. Program philosophy and goals
2. Definition and identification
3. Instruction
4. Evaluation/modification

Related to those four components are 15 areas of concern:

- Needs assessment
- Personnel and staff education
- Philosophy, rationale, goals, objectives, and a written program plan
- Types of gifts and talents to be provided for and estimated enrollment
- Identification methods and specific criteria
- Specific criteria for identifying underserved populations
- Staff responsibilities
- Support services
- Acceleration and enrichment plans
- Organizational and administrative design
- Transportation needs
- Community resources
- Training and workshops
- Budgetary considerations
- Program evaluation

The authors noted that these areas of concern are not sequential and vary in their importance.

Coleman and Cross (2001) characterized programming for gifted students as being divided into three dimensions:

1. Curriculum
2. Instructional strategies
3. Administrative arrangements

While cognizant that school districts are typically attuned to the administrative arrangements, they emphasized the need to see these dimensions as intertwined. When school district gifted program plans are translated at the local level, the administrative component often becomes the focus of the gifted program coordinator's job, and the curriculum and instructional strategies are given varying emphasis, depending on time, financial resources, and the interest of the personnel.

Grouping

In each service option model, ability grouping is involved in determining which students will be allowed to participate. *Ability grouping* is a practice in which school personnel utilize test scores and school records to assign children in the same grade to classes that differ substantially in characteristics affecting learning (Kulik & Kulik, 1997). In a meta-analytic review of grouping programs, Kulik and Kulik (1992) delineated the following five distinct instructional programs that were used for separating students by ability:

1. Accelerated classes
2. Multilevel classes
3. Within-class cluster grouping
4. Cross-grade programs
5. Enrichment classes

Major characteristics of each grouping program include the following (Kulik & Kulik, 1992):

■ *Accelerated classes*: Students with high academic aptitude receive instruction that allows them to proceed through their schooling at a more rapid rate than what is customary. According to Gallagher and Gallagher (1994), acceleration has as its two primary purposes (a) to place students with advanced ability and achievement in courses with similar students to provide adequate challenge, and (b) to reduce the amount of time a student spends in the educational system.

■ *Multilevel classes*: Students in the same grade are divided into groups on the basis of ability; the groups are instructed in different classrooms for the entire day or for one subject.

■ *Within-class cluster grouping*: The teacher forms ability groups within the classroom and provides appropriate instruction based on the students' abilities.

■ *Cross-grade programs*: Students from several grades are grouped according to their abilities and are taught the given subject in separate classrooms without regard to their regular grade placement.

■ *Enrichment classes*: Children identified as having high aptitudes are given richer educational experiences than what is provided in the general curriculum.

Feldhusen and Moon (1992) advocated flexible grouping practices as most beneficial to gifted students. To maintain or increase the academic achievement of these students, they found that students should be grouped according to ability and achievement levels and also that the groups should involve an element of fluidity so the students could move to different levels as their progress indicated. Too often, the authors noted, schools adopt new grouping practices without sufficient regard to the impact on gifted and high-ability students.

Westberg and Archambault (1997) conducted a multi-site case study in which they reviewed differentiation practices geared to the needs of high-ability students. For their study they observed in classrooms and interviewed students, teachers, parents, and administrators. They also examined documents, such as policy statements, faculty meeting notes, administrative memos, curriculum guides, and enrichment materials. They found that flexible grouping practices were essential, along with a commitment from teachers and administrators to provide the best possible circumstances for the students. Rather than focusing solely on the effects of the grouping practices, their research determined that teacher practices and attitudes are crucial in providing appropriate instruction for gifted learners.

Omdal (1997) used a case-study format to review the grouping practices for gifted students in an elementary school in a small seacoast town in New England. He observed a fourth-grade class in which the teacher used a variety of options in grouping for instruction. Although the teacher frequently used ability grouping for mathematics and reading, she emphasized the need for flexibility and fluidity within the groups. At times, whole-class instruction was utilized for introducing new concepts, and she also used cooperative learning groups, small-group mini-lessons, and individual contracts to meet students' individual needs.

Jones and Southern (1992) studied the grouping practices of 56 rural and 47 urban school districts in Ohio. Their study, quantitative in nature, utilized a questionnaire with a Likert scale. They found that most urban school systems used ability grouping in their general education programs at both the elementary and secondary levels, but fewer rural districts used grouping at either level. The reasons given for utilizing ability grouping included

- program/teacher orientation (easier scheduling and teacher planning),
- student-oriented issues (meeting individual needs), and
- tradition (past history).

At both the elementary and secondary levels, gifted program coordinators seemed to consider ability grouping as a necessary practice to meet the needs of highly able students.

In her case study of a New England elementary school's services for the gifted, Leppien (1997) found that a variety of grouping practices were effective in meeting the needs of the students. Reading groups were flexible; sometimes the students were grouped according to ability and sometimes according to interest. Although math lessons were taught in a whole-group format, pull-out enrichment classes allowed for differentiation. In Leppien's study, the need for flexibility in grouping, rather than reliance on a single method, was most important.

In an article reviewing program practices in gifted education. Shore and Delcourt (1996) categorized practices as

- uniquely appropriate for gifted learners,
- needing additional research to be considered uniquely appropriate for gifted children,
- effective with gifted students but applicable to all students, and
- lacking evidence as being uniquely appropriate for gifted learners.

Grouping practices, particularly ability grouping of some sort, received strong support in the literature as being uniquely appropriate for gifted learners.

Curriculum

Curriculum is "that reconstruction of knowledge and experience, systematically developed under the auspices of the school (or university), to enable the learner to increase his or her control of knowledge and experience" (Tanner & Tanner, as cited in Borland, 1989, p. 175). It includes planned student goals, outcomes, activities, strategies, resources, and assessment mechanisms (VanTassel-Baska, 2002). The key point to be emphasized is that G/T children require higher expectation levels for performance.

According to VanTassel-Baska, "The basis for all differentiation in the curriculum for gifted students should emerge from the differences in their characteristics and needs as reflected in formal test data and careful observation of performance behaviors (VanTassel-Baska, 1994, p. 54). Differentiation of curriculum for gifted learners must include acceleration, complexity, depth, challenge, and creativity (VanTassel-Baska, 2000). In some cases, this may require that differentiated learner outcomes be developed to challenge students appropriately

In other situations, teachers of the gifted need assistance in developing appropriate learning experiences and in streamlining the standard curriculum. This assistance may come in the form of a district plan for creating differentiated curriculum. Ideally, "the written curriculum needs to reinforce the expectation of academic responsiveness and help teachers in the difficult task of responsive teaching" (Tomlinson & Allan, 2000, p. 90).

Tomlinson (2001) echoed the importance of responsiveness to learner needs and delineated the elements of curriculum that could be differentiated as

1. content,
2. process, and
3. products.

Many of the elements of a defensible differentiated curriculum for gifted learners found in the current literature of the field are recommended practices, which, according to Shore's (1988) definition, are suggestions based on the scholarly work of theorists but not necessarily based on empirical research.

Borland (1989) noted that, although defining defensible curricula for the gifted is influenced by an individual's philosophy regarding the appropriate education of these learners, the key to defensibility is demonstrating the relationship between the students' exceptionalities and the features that make the curriculum differentiated. He believed that the minimum requirements for a curriculum for gifted learners must include

1. agreement regarding what gifted students should learn beyond the core curriculum,
2. a scope and sequence to frame the knowledge and resulting instructional design, and
3. systematic and intentional alignment with the core curriculum.

Once a framework has been established based upon these requirements, the curriculum should feature

- an emphasis on thinking processes,
- meaningful content,
- independent study, and
- accelerative options.

Note

Differentiation of the curriculum is an effective way to allow students who are gifted to foster their creativity, explore their boundaries, and self-direct their learning experiences.

In her discussion of appropriately differentiated curriculum, VanTassel-Baska (1994) first emphasized the following three distinguishing characteristics of gifted learners:

1. Their ability to learn at faster rates than their peers
2. Their ability to find and solve problems
3. Their ability to understand abstractions and make connections

She noted that these learner characteristics must be considered and can be addressed through modifications of the content model, the process/product model, and the epistemological model to create a differentiated curriculum; these models include many of the features that Borland considered essential.

Maker (1982) explicated the common elements found in definitions of differentiated curriculum conceptualized by numerous authors:

1. The basis for differentiation is the unique characteristics of gifted learners.
2. The curriculum includes concepts of greater complexity or higher levels of abstraction.
3. There is an emphasis on the development of advanced thinking skills.
4. Materials or logistical arrangements facilitate student growth.

With a focus on learner needs as the driving force, Maker's list of characteristics of a differentiated curriculum includes the need for sophisticated content, an emphasis on higher-level thinking skills, development of quality products, and opportunities for independent study.

Maker and Nielson (1995) acknowledged the difficulty of defining qualitatively different curricula in operational terms, particularly given the lack of research comparing the effectiveness of various approaches. In a field that emphasizes the need for qualitatively differentiated curricula, the paucity of research about the effectiveness of various curriculum interventions and models has sometimes been a barrier to the advancement of various initiatives. To bridge the gap between general education and gifted education, practitioners must see and understand the student gains that can result from using a qualitatively different curriculum and the related instructional strategies.

Modifications

To meet the needs of gifted students effectively, some modification in the usual school setting is necessary. This may include opportunities for grade-level and/or content acceleration, enrichment experiences provided through a pull-out model, direct instruction in problem-solving skills, and participation in student competitions (Gallagher, 1994). In the case of pull-out programs, Gallagher deemed coordination of instructional experiences as essential for achieving integration within the total instructional program. Thus, the modifications should be designed so they are

1. reflections of local goals,
2. sequential and continuous,
3. indicative of a match between the assessment of student potential and options provided,
4. integrated into the total school program, and
5. provided continuously instead of intermittently.

Some curriculum modifications for gifted students are integrated into the daily classroom routine in order to meet students' social needs as well as academic needs.

Modifications for gifted/talented students found throughout the literature may be categorized as relating to

1. content,
2. process,
3. product,
4. learning environment, and
5. affective concerns.

When making modifications to meet the needs of gifted learners, it is important to consider the curriculum, instruction, and assessment components. Each component should be determined based on the needs of the students.

Access to the General Education Curriculum and Settings

"In response to socio-political demands, education has embarked on a course of school reform that affects organizational and curricular structures for all students" (VanTassel-Baska, 1992, p. 68). For gifted education specifically, a trend has emerged in which the role of teachers of the gifted is being redefined. They frequently are working with teachers in the general classroom, where they demonstrate lessons and help plan instruction for gifted students.

In a call to individuals and professional organizations in the field of gifted education, Gallagher (2000) indicated a need for gifted students to have a minimum of three hours of direct contact per week with a specialist and five hours per week with a support person in the general education classroom. He noted that the role of the support person would include "consultation with the classroom teacher, direct work with cluster groups within the classroom, resource room activities, and individual work with extremely gifted students" (p. 10).

Kirschenbaum, Armstrong, and Landrum (1999) outlined the following initiatives in the educational reform movement that they perceived as having the most detrimental impact on the education of gifted children:

1. The elimination of ability grouping
2. The development of the middle school model
3. The inclusion movement

In their view, for gifted education to survive, services for gifted children must be redesigned so they complement general education practices rather than conflict with them. They proposed a model of gifted education programming in which collaboration and consultation with general education are key elements in developing integrated services rather than separate ones.

Landrum (2000) described resource collaboration and consultation as a service delivery strategy that may be promising for the transition of gifted education from being a separate and segregated entity to one that is integrated more fully with the total school program. In an evaluation of the Catalyst Program in the Charlotte-Mecklenburg Schools' Program for the Gifted, Landrum found that collaboration and consultation "was an effective service delivery strategy for providing differentiated education to gifted learners, had positive spill-over effects for the entire school, led to a redefined role of the gifted education specialist, and initiated an articulation of the nature of the consulting process when applied to gifted education" (Landrum, 2000, p. 2).

Increasingly, emphasis is being placed on the use of technology with these learners—primarily, the use of computers and related technologies. In most cases, gifted students are served in the general education classroom for most of the instructional day. This creates a situation that may be challenging to the classroom teacher in terms of managing the wide range of learner needs in the heterogeneous setting. Thus, differentiation training, with an emphasis on classroom management, is crucial.

> **Note**
>
> Teachers need to remember that students who are gifted have special needs. Although their requirements may differ from those of students with other exceptionalities, these students and their unique educational needs should not be overlooked.

Summary

Gifted learners are defined as students with outstanding talent who perform or show the potential for performing at exceptionally high levels of accomplishment in the areas of intellect, creativity, and artistic ability; students who possess an uncommon leadership aptitude; and students who excel in specific academic disciplines, when compared with others of the same age, experience, or environment.

Teachers working with gifted students must understand the unique characteristics of gifted students and how to adapt curriculum and instruction to meet their needs. Characteristics can be considered in terms of academic/cognitive traits, such as high reading ability and large vocabulary, as well as emotional/affective traits, such as perfectionism and heightened sensitivity. Some gifted students have concomitant traits, and teachers need to be aware of what may be a negative manifestation of a positive characteristic. Although most gifted programs attempt to address the emotional needs of gifted students, the guidance and counseling services catering to their needs are often inadequate.

In some states, gifted education falls under the aegis of special education, and in others, it falls under another umbrella or exists as a category by itself. Most school districts have gifted programs, but many need to include core components or address areas of concern. Only a small percentage of students thought to be gifted receive special services. There is no nationwide system of identification of gifted students, with the percentage and the criteria varying from state to state and within states. A major concern in the field is identification and programming for underserved populations, as traditional measures may be biased and alternative assessments need to be implemented. Most gifted program policies require the use of multiple criteria for identifying gifted students, using instruments such as ability tests, behavioral checklists, and portfolios of student work.

Research has been done on the most effective way to group gifted learners. Much of the research points to ability grouping, which includes accelerated classes and cross-grade programs. Flexible grouping practices have been emphasized as being beneficial.

Curriculum differentiation and modification are important topics in gifted education. Characteristics of a differentiated curriculum include the need for sophisticated content and an emphasis on higher-level thinking skills. Modifications may include enrichment experiences provided through a pull-out model and participation in student competitions.

There are some initiatives in the educational reform movement that are perceived as having a detrimental impact on the education of gifted children. Collaboration and consultation of gifted education programming with general education are key elements in developing integrated services. The role of gifted teachers is being redefined, and training is crucial.

References

Benbow, C. M. (1998). Acceleration as a method for meeting the academic needs of intellectually talented children. In J. VanTassel-Baska (Ed.), *Excellence in educating gifted and talented learners* (pp. 279–294). Denver: Love Publishing .

Borland, J. H. (1989). *Planning and implementing programs for the gifted.* New York: Teachers College Press.

Coleman, L. J., & Cross, T. L. (2001). *Being gifted in school: An introduction to development, guidance, and teaching.* Waco, TX: Prufrock Press.

Davis, G. A., & Rimm, S. B. (1998). *Education of the gifted and talented* (4th ed.). Boston: Allyn & Bacon.

Feldhusen, J. F., & Moon, S. M. (1992). Grouping gifted students: Issues and concerns. *Gifted Child Quarterly, 36,* 63–67.

Gallagher, J. J. (1994). Current and historical thinking on education for gifted and talented students. In P. Ross (Ed.), *National excellence: A book of readings.* Washington, DC: U.S. Department of Education.

Gallagher, J. J. (2000). Unthinkable thoughts: Education of gifted students. *Gifted Child Quarterly, 44,* 5–12.

Gallagher, J. J., & Gallagher, S. A. (1994). *Teaching the gifted child* (4th ed.). Boston: Allyn & Bacon.

Jones, E. D., & Southern, W. T. (1992). Programming, grouping, and acceleration in rural school districts: A survey of attitudes and practices. *Gifted Child Quarterly, 36,* 112–117.

Kirschenbaum, R. J., Armstrong, D. C., & Landrum, M. S. (1999). Resource consultation model in gifted education to support talent development in today's inclusive schools. *Gifted Child Quarterly, 43,* 39–47.

Kulik, J. A., & Kulik, C. C. (1992). Meta-analytic findings on grouping programs. *Gifted Child Quarterly, 36,* 73–77.

Kulik, J. A., & Kulik, C. C. (1997). Ability grouping. In N. Colangelo & G. A. Davis (Eds.), *Handbook of gifted education* (pp. 230–242). Boston: Allyn & Bacon.

Landrum, M. S. (2000). *An evaluation of the Catalyst Program: Consultation and collaboration in gifted education.* Unpublished manuscript.

Landrum, M. S., & Shaklee, B. (Eds.). (1998). *Pre-K–Grade 12 gifted program standards.* Washington, DC: National Association for Gifted Children.

Landrum, M. S., Callahan, C. M., & Shaklee, B. D. (Eds.). (2001). *Aiming for excellence: Annotations to the NAGC pre-K–grade 12 gifted program standards.* Waco, TX: Prufrock Press.

Leppien, J. H. (1997). Successful practices at Forest Hills School: A collective response in meeting the individual needs of gifted and talented students. In K. L. Westberg & F. X. Archambault (Eds.), *Profiles of successful practices for high ability students in elementary classrooms* (pp. 43–69). Storrs, CT: National Research Center on the Gifted and Talented.

Maker, C. J. (1982). *Curriculum development for the gifted.* Rockville, MD: Aspen Systems Corp.

Marland, S. P. (1972). *Education of the gifted and talented: Vol. 1. Report to the Congress of the United States by the U.S. Commissioner of Education.* Washington, DC: U.S. Government Printing Office.

Omdal, S. N. (1997). Successful practices at Salisbury Elementary School. In K. L. Westberg & F. X. Archambault (Eds.), *Profiles of successful practices for high ability students in elementary classrooms* (pp. 43–69). Storrs, CT: National Research Center on the Gifted and Talented.

Shaklee, B. D. (2001). Program design. In M. S. Landrum, C. M. Callahan, & B. D. Shaklee (Eds.), *Aiming for excellence: Annotations to the NAGC Pre-K–Grade 12 gifted program standards* (pp. 1–14). Waco, TX: Prufrock Press.

Shore, B. (1988). *Recommended practices in the education and upbringing of the gifted: A progress report on an assessment of knowledge base.* Indianapolis: Indiana Department of Education, Office of Gifted and Talented Education.

Shore, B. M., & Delcourt, M.A.B. (1996). Effective curricular and program practices in gifted education and the interface with general education. *Journal for the Education of the Gifted, 20,* 138–154.

Stephens, K. R., & Karnes, F. A. (2000). State definitions for the gifted and talented revisited. *Exceptional Children, 66,* 219–238.

Tomlinson, C. A. (2001). *How to differentiate instruction in mixed-ability classrooms.* Alexandria, VA: Association for Supervision and Curriculum Development.

Tomlinson, C. A., & Allan, S. D. (2000). *Leadership for differentiating schools and classrooms.* Alexandria, VA: Association for Supervision and Curriculum Development.

U.S. Department of Education (USDOE). (1993). *National excellence: A case for developing America's talent.* Washington, DC: Author.

VanTassel-Baska, J. (2003). Content-based curriculum for high-ability learners: An introduction. In J. VanTassel-Baska & C. A. Little (Eds.), *Content-based curriculum for high-ability learners* (pp. 1–23). Waco, TX: Prufrock Press.

VanTassel-Baska, J. (1992). *Planning effective curriculum for gifted learners.* Denver: Love Publishing.

VanTassel-Baska, J. (1994). *Comprehensive curriculum for gifted learners* (2nd ed.). Boston: Allyn & Bacon.

VanTassel-Baska, J. (2002). *Curriculum planning and instructional design for gifted learners.* Denver: Love Publishing.

VanTassel-Baska, J., Bass, G., Ries, R., Poland, D., & Avery, L. D. (1998). A national study of science curriculum effectiveness with high ability students. *Gifted Child Quarterly, 42,* 200–211.

Westberg, K. L., & Archambault, F. X. (1997). A multi-site case study of successful classroom practices for high ability students. *Gifted Child Quarterly, 41,* 42–51.

Mild to Moderate Disabilities Instructional Perspectives

Yvonne N. Bui & Edward L. Meyen

Students with mild/moderate disabilities are a heterogeneous group, encompassing students with learning disabilities, emotional/behavioral disorders, speech and language impairments, and in some cases students with mild mental retardation and/or autistic spectrum disorders. You may hear these disability groups described as *high-incidence*, as they represent the majority of students receiving special education services under the 2004 Individuals with Disabilities Education Improvement Act (IDEA).

Not surprisingly, these students have a variety of academic, behavioral, and social–emotional needs that at times interact and affect each other. For example, a student with a learning disability (SLD) may display aggressive behavior because of the frustration he feels at reading three grades below his grade level. A student with a speech impediment may become withdrawn and have low self-esteem because peers tease her.

Thus, as a special education teacher you must get to know your students, their individual strengths and weaknesses, their families, and life circumstances, as this information will help you plan appropriate instruction and interventions. Collaborating with general education teachers, paraeducators, and related-services personnel also will be critical because the majority of these students receive a portion of their educational program in the general education setting. Despite having a variety of needs, these students have many learner attributes in common and respond similarly to academic and behavioral interventions.

To help plan for this diverse group of students, this chapter introduces you to a variety of instructional methods and strategies for assessment, literacy instruction, and mathematics instruction—the areas in which most beginning teachers feel challenged. Keep in mind that this is not a methods text. You will complete courses in teaching methods in your teacher education programs. As you learn about students with disabilities, however, the information in this chapter will add to your repertoire of teaching skills and your knowledge base about the instructional needs of students with disabilities.

Assessment

With passage of the No Child Left Behind Act of 2001 (NCLB), the role of assessment in American schools has taken on increased importance. Schools are required to administer standards-based statewide assessments in reading and math to all students in grades 3–8 and in one grade at the secondary level. There are no exemptions for students with disabilities. Students with mild to moderate disabilities are allowed accommodations to enhance their test-taking abilities, but they must take the same standards-based tests as all other students. The intent of NCLB is to improve students' academic performance and to hold schools accountable for their achievement. Schools' failure to demonstrate Adequate Yearly Progress for two consecutive years can result in serious federal corrective actions (USDE, 2002).

Because the focus is on the performance of students at the school level, the school's performance is affected when students with disabilities do poorly on statewide assessments. Thus, as a special education teacher, you must familiarize yourself with the state's grade-level content standards so you can integrate appropriate experiences into

Note

Reminder: No Child Left Behind is a federal law intended to ensure that all children reach challenging standards in reading and math and to close the academic achievement gap by race and class. NCLB is a landmark in education reform designed to improve student achievement and change the culture of America's schools via accountability of results, emphasizing what works for students based on scientific research, expanded parental options, and expanded local control and flexibility.

187

your instructional program and thereby enhance the performance of your students. In some states, the assessments are considered "high-stakes" and decisions about promotion and graduation are based solely on the students' performance. For example, to earn a high school diploma, students may have to pass a high school exit exam.

Clearly, assessment is a central part of our educational system today. Thus, conducting assessments will be an important part of your job as a special education teacher. There are many different kinds of assessments, of which the assessments required for NCLB are just one form. In addition to large-scale assessments such as these, you may become part of the evaluation team that assesses students' achievement levels to determine their eligibility for special education services. For the purposes of developing classroom instruction, large-scale assessments may not yield enough information about the students' specific academic needs for you to develop goals for the IEP. You will have to conduct standardized and informal assessments with your students to measure their educational needs and develop appropriate instruction.

Standardized Assessments

Standardized assessments constitute a group of formal tests that typically are conducted by psychologists, education specialists, or special education teachers in one-to-one testing sessions. Standardized assessments have set guidelines and standard directions for administration and scoring that must be adhered to for the results to be valid. One benefit of using standardized assessments is that they are *norm-referenced*. This means that you can compare your student's performance on the test (through standard scores) against that of his or her peers at the same grade/age level. For example, the results of a standardized assessment may indicate that the student is performing two years below what is expected for his or her age group. Typically, these tests are used to make decisions about whether a student qualifies to receive special education services and to measure annual progress toward IEP goals.

Standardized achievement tests are designed to measure students' academic progress in a specific area, such as reading, or across the curriculum in several areas such as reading, writing, spelling, and math. Many different standardized achievement tests are available in all curriculum areas. You will have to find out which achievement tests are preferred and available within your school district. Some commonly used tests for school-aged children are the Peabody Individual Achievement Test Revised (PIAT-R) (Markwaldt, 1989), the Woodcock Johnson III (McGrew & Woodcock, 2001), the Kaufman Test of Educational Achievement (K-TEA) (Kaufman & Kaufman, 1985), and the Wide Range Achievement Test (WRAT) (Wilkinson, 1993).

Standardized tests give you a broad sense of the student's academic performance but typically not enough information about how to develop instruction that specifically targets his or her strengths and needs. Although standardized tests are based on grade level and content standards, they may not be a direct measure of the student's learning in the classroom. Furthermore, some standardized tests are biased against students whose native language is not Standard English. Thus, to provide appropriate instruction, you must conduct ongoing nonstandardized or informal assessments with your students.

Informal Assessments

Unlike standardized assessments, most informal assessments do not compare a student's performance to that of his or her peers. Instead, most informal assessments are *criterion-referenced*. A criterion-referenced test compares the student's performance against a set criterion on a given skill in a specific area such as reading, math, or even behavior (Fahey, 2000; Ysseldyke & Algozzine, 1995). The criterion can be based on an IEP goal, a lesson objective from the curriculum, or a standard from a commercial test (Overton, 2003). From the criterion, you can determine how far the student has progressed toward mastery. For example, on a math test with 50 questions, if Shelly answers 45 (90%) of the questions accurately, she is considered at the *advanced* level. If she answers 40 (80%) of the questions accurately, she is at the *proficient* level, and so on.

Each criterion-referenced test has its own criteria for what constitutes mastery, and in some cases the classroom teacher sets the criteria. Criterion-referenced assessments represent a good way to measure and report students' progress on their IEP goals and benchmarks, as well as evaluating learning in the classroom. Examples of criterion-referenced tests are the Brigance Diagnostic Inventory of Basic Skills (Brigance, 1977) for elementary students and the Brigance Diagnostic Inventory of Essential Skills (Brigance, 1981) for secondary students.

The many benefits of informal assessments (Overton, 2003) include

- the special education teacher can administer these assessments individually or as a whole group in the natural setting of the classroom;
- teachers may design their own criterion-referenced tests;
- *curriculum-based assessments* are tied directly to the curriculum, to provide an accurate measure of the student's progress;
- the teacher can set the criteria for the required level of mastery and adjust instruction as needed.

For example, before teaching a social studies unit on mythology, you could create a curriculum-based assessment (pretest) to determine students' prior knowledge about specific concepts (e.g., Greek myths) that will be covered in the unit. This will help to inform you of the students' needs and background knowledge so you can adjust the level and pace of instruction accordingly. Then, after the unit is completed, you can administer a curriculum-based assessment (posttest) covering the same concepts to measure the extent to which students learned and retained the information taught. This will help you determine if students reached mastery and are ready to move on to the next unit or if some students need more practice or intensive instruction. We will discuss more specific informal assessments later in the chapter.

Authentic Assessments

Concerns about test bias, group norm issues, and linguistic and cultural differences have led to the search for more authentic assessments as alternatives to traditional and standardized assessments. *Authentic assessments* comprise a group of informal assessments that you can use to gain a more holistic depiction of a student's learning in the classroom. Among the many different types of authentic assessments are observations, checklists, student interviews, rating scales, informal reading inventories, rubrics, and portfolio assessments. Two goals of authentic assessment (Lavadenz, 1996) are

1. to complement and enhance traditional assessment, and
2. to inform instructional practices for students who historically have received negative and differential school treatment.

Note

Authentic assessments:
- Observations
- Checklists
- Interviews
- Rating scales
- IRIs
- Rubrics
- Portfolio assessments

Authentic assessments provide teachers with qualitative or descriptive information about students' skills and abilities and can be helpful in assessing students' academic performance in the classroom because they can be integrated into daily instruction.

Some authentic assessments are based on teacher *observations* or interactions with the student. For example, a teacher could list targeted behaviors on a *checklist* to rate and monitor a student's progress with a new behavior management plan over time (see Figure 9.1 for a sample checklist). If you want to find out which strategies students are using to solve complex math problems, conducting an informal *interview* would be appropriate.

By using a *rating scale*, the teacher can measure whether a student has a skill and the extent to which the student has demonstrated that skill or knowledge. For example, when assessing a student's level of English proficiency, a holistic rating scale requires the rater to give a single impression of the student's performance, such as beginning, intermediate, or advanced (Richard-Amato, 1996).

One authentic assessment of students' reading skills is through an *informal reading inventory* (IRI). The student reads aloud a selected passage (100 words) at his instructional level while the teacher listens and notes the types of errors he makes. For example, you could observe that the student has difficulty using the first letter of the word to "sound out" an unfamiliar word, or the student frequently skips over unknown words rather than using contextual cues to help decode the word. After conducting the IRI, the teacher evaluates the pattern of errors the student makes in order to develop a reading plan to reduce the frequency and type of errors (Lavadenz, 1996).

Other types of authentic assessments are based on the student's work samples (e.g., writing samples, projects) (Overton, 2003). A *rubric* involves assigning the student a number that corresponds to a description of performance level. For example, the quality of students' writing samples can be scored on a 6-point scale. A score of 2 indicates a poorly developed essay that has organizational, syntactical, and mechanical errors. At the other end of the scale, a score of 6 is given to an essay that is highly developed in all those areas.

Perhaps the most comprehensive and popular form of authentic assessments is *portfolio assessment*. Portfolios are individual collections of students' work compiled over time. The key to establishing an effective portfolio is to use it as a formative evaluation—a collection that grows and evolves along with the student's learning. The portfolio might contain, for example, exemplary pieces of work, works in progress, teacher's observations and performance checklists, writing samples, tests, reading logs, informal reading inventories, oral samples recorded on tape, journal entries, and so on. The contents of the portfolio also may be used for placement and eligibility purposes, to measure achievement levels, and to provide ongoing feedback to students, their parents, and other teachers over time (Richard-Amato, 1996).

Planning for Curriculum and Instruction

Most students with mild/moderate disabilities receive their education in inclusive settings. The instruction likely will be couched in the context of accessing the general education curriculum. This means that at times the students will need classroom accommodations or be engaged in instructional activities that are different from those of their grade-level peers who do not have exceptional learning needs.

Today's Date: _____

This progress report is for: _____

E = **Excellent**: Was able to work productively and cooperatively with teachers and
         peers during academics and transitions
O = **Okay**: Needed teacher support to stay focused on academics and to help with
         transitions or peer interactions
D = **Difficult**: Was unable to focus or be redirected by the teacher to work on
         academics independently or with peers

8:50 – 10:25
_____ I was respectful of my teacher and other adults.
_____ I was cooperative and had a good attitude with peers.
_____ I stayed focused on my work during independent activities and group activities.
_____ I followed directions.
_____ I solved conflicts without arguments or escalation.
_____ I completed all my assignments in a timely manner.

Recess 10:25 – 10:40

10:40 – 12:15
_____ I was respectful of my teacher and other adults.
_____ I was cooperative and had a good attitude with peers.
_____ I stayed focused on my work during independent activities and group activities.
_____ I followed directions.
_____ I solved conflicts without arguments or escalation.
_____ I completed all my assignments in a timely manner.

Lunch 12:15 – 1:00

1:00 – 2:40
_____ I was respectful of my teacher and other adults.
_____ I was cooperative and had a good attitude with peers.
_____ I stayed focused on my work during independent activities and group activities.
_____ I followed directions.
_____ I solved conflicts without arguments or escalation.
_____ I completed all my assignments in a timely manner.

Comments: _____

Teacher's signature: _____

Parent's signature: _____

Source: Fagan, Y. (2004). Daily Progress Report, San Francisco, California.

FIGURE 9.1
Daily Progress Report

Their level of achievement also may not be as high as their peers'. But academic expectations for students with disabilities should follow a similar curriculum pattern to that of their nondisabled peers (e.g., grade-level standards). Thus, as the teacher, you will have to call upon your understanding of the students' learning attributes to develop instructional strategies and appropriate methods that align with the general education curriculum.

This may be most challenging in the curricular areas of reading and writing because the majority of students with mild to moderate disabilities have difficulty in these skill areas, and competency in literacy is basic to their later success in life. Literacy also is critical to success in other curriculum areas such as mathematics, science, and social studies. The following discussion on reading, writing, and mathematics instruction will give you a broad overview of instructional content and teaching activities. As you progress in your teacher education program, you will receive more opportunities to develop your instructional skills and develop a comprehensive teaching program.

Components of a Balanced Reading Program

In pursuit of a healthy and happy life, we strive for balance—to find the balance between work and play, exercise and diet, carbohydrates and protein. Similarly, developing an effective reading program for students with disabilities is about finding the proper balance between what to teach, the instructional methods used, and how much time to devote to each area. The ability to develop and implement a balanced approach to reading instruction is essential to be an effective special education teacher.

Reading is an area of difficulty for many students with disabilities. Actually, literacy problems constitute the most common reasons for referrals for special education services (Reschly, 1992). Thus, in this section we provide an overview of the five most important components of a balanced reading program: phonemic awareness, phonics, fluency, vocabulary, and comprehension strategies (NICHD, 2000). In addition, we will suggest instruction and informal assessments for elementary and secondary students. To provide a balanced reading program, significant time and attention must be devoted to all facets of reading instruction, and how much time you spend teaching certain skills will depend on the students' needs and ability levels.

Personal reading time is an important part of literacy instruction.

Most of us learned to read without even realizing that we could read independently. With some basic instruction in the alphabet, letter sounds, and opportunities to read and listen to stories, we learned the patterns, rules, and exceptions of our first language and applied them to written text. For many students with disabilities, however, reading is perhaps one of the most mysterious and difficult skills they will encounter. If you can read street signs, newspapers, magazines, and entire books effortlessly without having to stop to sound out the words, it is hard to imagine the level of frustration and feelings of helplessness of students with reading disabilities. Or if you had to stop after every three sentences to make sure you understood the content, you might understand why a student might want to stop trying and quit after the first page.

The research indicates that, unlike learning how to speak, reading is not considered a "natural" process (Lyon, 1998), and many students with disabilities do not learn how to read by being read to or by simply reading more. Instead, these students need *explicit, systematic*, and *direct instruction* of phonemic awareness, letter–sound correspondence (phonics), sight-word recognition and fluency, a developing vocabulary, and comprehension strategies to become independent readers (NICHD, 2000).

Phonemic Awareness

Phonological awareness is the knowledge that language can be broken down into smaller segments and involves skills such as breaking sentences into words, words into syllables, syllables into sounds, and recognizing and producing rhyming words. A subset of phonological awareness, *phonemic awareness* emphasizes the identification and manipulation of phonemes in spoken words.

A *phoneme* is the smallest unit of speech sound. For example, the word *she* has two phonemes, /sh/ and /e/. English has approximately 44 phonemes—26 consonant sounds and 18 vowel sounds. Phonemic awareness is a necessary condition for students to read and spell (Moats, 2005), as it helps them connect sounds to letters and letter patterns. Teaching phonemic awareness to students across a range of grade and age levels significantly improves their reading ability (NRP, 2000).

One of the most challenging phonemic awareness tasks is the ability to manipulate or work with individual phonemes in spoken words (Adams, 1990). Manipulating phonemes includes tasks such as matching, isolating, blending, segmenting, deleting, and substituting phonemes. As mentioned, these skills do not occur naturally for students with disabilities and therefore have to be explicitly taught and learned.

As an auditory (listening) skill, phonemic awareness typically does not involve showing students actual letters until they have mastered the concepts. Phonemic awareness activities should be fun and game-like so students will be encouraged to experiment with the language (Yopp, 1992). In *sound matching*, students are asked to identify the beginning sound of actual objects (e.g., sun, soap, car) and asked to point to the pictures that begin with the /s/ sound. In another activity, the teacher says two words (e.g., *bear* and *bottle*) and asks the students if these words begin with the same sound. Or the students could be asked to name two words that begin with the /m/ sound (e.g., *man, mom*). A more difficult task would be to have the students match phonemes that appear in the middle of words. For example, "Is there an /a/ sound in 'mat'?" A related activity would be for students to find the "odd word out." For example, students would be asked to identify which word starts with a different sound: *bear, bug, man, bat*?

More difficult phonemic awareness skills involve isolating, blending, and segmenting phonemes. In *isolating sounds*, students are asked to listen to a word and identify

Note

A <u>phoneme</u> is the smallest unit of speech sound (such as /k/ and /i/), and a <u>morpheme</u> is the smallest unit of meaning (including prefixes, roots, and suffixes).

the beginning, middle, or end sounds. For example, "What sound do you hear at the beginning of 'nose'? What sound do you hear at the end of 'mat'?" Students also should be taught to count phonemes in words by stretching out spoken words. For example, you might ask, "How many sounds do you hear in the word mmm … aaa … nnn? That's right—there are three: /m/, /a/, /n/."

Next, students must be taught how to *blend* sounds to make words. Blending prepares them to read or "sound out" unknown words by putting sounds together. One oral activity would be for the teacher to say slowly the isolated sounds in a word and then have the students blend the sounds and say the word quickly. For example, say to the students, "I'm going to say the sounds really slow, and then I want you to put them together and say the word fast. Ssss—aaa—t." (The students say "sat.")

A more challenging but related skill is for students to orally *segment* words or break words into their separate sounds. The ability to segment words contributes to accurate spelling and writing. To teach students how to segment sounds in words, begin by having them isolate and say the first sound in words: "Who can tell me what the beginning sound in 'fan' is? Yes, it is /f/. Now I'm going to say the word slowly and I want you to tap your finger every time the sound changes: fff … aaa … nnn … Good. there were three sounds in 'fan.' Say the word slowly, and let's see if you can tell me which three sounds you heard.… Right, /f/, /a/, /n/." When they hear the sounds like the ones shown in Figure 9.2, the students could push coins and, later, letters into boxes instead of tapping (Elkonin, 1973).

The most difficult phonemic tasks are *deletion* and *substitution* because they involve phonemes at the word level. *Phoneme deletion* requires that students remove individual or blended sounds from words or identify remaining words once a phoneme(s) has been deleted. For example: "What word would be left if the /s/ sound were taken away from 'sat'?" …What sound is left when we take away the /sh/ sound in 'ship'?"

In *phoneme substitution*, students have to be able to add or substitute one phoneme for another to make a new word. One activity would be to have a "sound of the day," such as /p/, and have the class pronounce the names of all the students in the class but substitute that beginning sound (e.g., Paria, Pan, Polie).

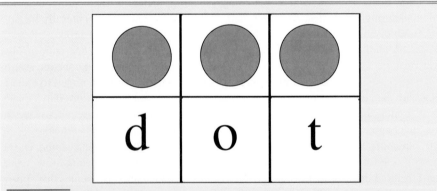

Source: From "U.S.S.R." by D. B. Elkonin, in *Comparative reading* (pp. 551–580), by I. Downing (Ed.) (New York: Macmillan). Copyright © 1973.

FIGURE 9.2
Sound Boxes

Phonics

In contrast to phonemic awareness, which is primarily an auditory skill, *phonics* requires students to understand and use letter–sound correspondence to read or decode written words. Although phonemic awareness and phonics are separate skills, phonological awareness instruction combined with phonics instruction enhances early spelling and accelerates the rate at which children learn to read new words in text (Blachman, Tangel, & Ball, 2004). In phonics instruction, students must be taught that each phoneme or phoneme blend corresponds with a grapheme (letter or letter combination) (Moats, 2005).

Keep in mind that many letter names bear little resemblance to the sound of that letter when it is pronounced. For example, in the word *dodge* the /j/ sound corresponds to the letter combination "dge." Thus, teaching and learning phonological skills is not as simple as it seems. That is why explicit teaching of the letter–sound correspondences for students with disabilities is so important. *Explicit* means that the students are told the sounds that individual letter or letter combinations make; the students should not have to guess or discover the sounds (CDE, 1999).

The following five principles of explicit instruction (Rosenshine & Stevens, 1984) should be applied to most instruction for students with disabilities:

1. Provide direct teacher instruction of the skill or strategy.
2. Model the strategy in controlled materials.
3. Provide guided practice in application of the skill.
4. Monitor students and give corrective feedback.
5. Allow for independent student practice of the skill.

Examples for each of the above are as follows:

1. Write the letter "m" on the board and say, "This letter says 'mmmmm.'"
2. "When I put my finger on the letter 'm,' I will say and hold its sound. Listen… mmmm."
3. "Next I want you to practice the sound that 'm' makes with me— /mmmmm/."
4. "Now I'm going around the room, and when I point to you, I want you to say the sound that 'm' makes."
5. "You are going to look for the letter 'm' on this page. Every time you see the letter 'm,' I want you to point to it and say the sound it makes."

Notice that only one letter–sound correspondence is taught at a time, and students are given guided and independent opportunities to practice what they have learned.

In addition to being explicit, phonics instruction for students with disabilities should be *systematic*. This means that instruction has a sequenced order that builds on previous instruction and students' prior knowledge. To make this process easier and more successful, letter sounds should be taught in a certain order (Carnine, Silbert, & Kameenui, 1997). The sounds of more useful letters are introduced before less useful letters. The letter sounds for "a" and "m" should be taught first because they are more useful and easy to pronounce. Starting with easy-to-pronounce letters makes initial-sound tasks more accessible for instructionally naïve students. The letter sounds for j, y, x, q, and z are taught at the end of the sequence because they are not as common as some of the other letters.

After students have a sense of letter sounds, they should learn how to blend the sounds to read words. Similar to learning letter sounds, there is a preferred order to introduce new words. For example, word types should be taught according to their relative difficulty, from easy to more difficult. The first word type that should be introduced is the vowel–consonant (VC) and consonant–vowel–consonant (CVC) words that begin with continuous sounds (e.g., *am, map*). The teacher continues to extend the student's knowledge and introduces new word types that build on the previous types of words.

During phonics instruction, the use of controlled materials or decodable text is essential. *Decodable text* refers to reading materials that use the letter sounds and words the students have learned already (with a few known sight words) (CDE, 1999). Because decodable text does not build on comprehension skills or teach new vocabulary, these activities should be combined and balanced with language-rich activities in which students are exposed to authentic literature.

For secondary students, a critical part of phonics instruction is decoding multisyllabic words using phonics generalization rules. The six types of syllable patterns are

1. closed,
2. open,
3. vowel–consonant–silent e (vce),
4. r-controlled vowels (v–r),
5. vowel team, and
6. consonant–le (cle).

Below are descriptions of the first three, along with brief explanations of how to divide the syllables and decode them when reading.

- In a closed syllable pattern (VC/CVC) in either a word or a syllable, a single vowel letter is followed by a consonant letter, digraph, or blend. This type of syllable pattern usually represents a short vowel sound such as in *am, mat, mask, math*. For multisyllabic words (CVCCVC), divide the syllables between the two consonants ("blan-ket, hap-py, bot-tle, rab-bit").
- In an open-syllable pattern (CV), if there is one vowel letter in a word or syllable and it comes at the end of the word or syllable, it usually represents the long vowel sound *(he, she, go, my, cry)*. For multisyllabic words (VCV), divide the syllables before or after the consonant ("ro-bot, rob-in, po-ny, po-ta-to").
- In a vce pattern in one-syllable words containing two vowel letters, the first vowel letter represents a long vowel sound, and the final *e* is silent, such as in *make, like, hope, flute, rotate*. There are exceptions to this rule for words that end in *v*, such as "have" and "love."

Sight-Word Recognition and Fluency

Because so many words in English (e.g., *friend, cousin, autumn*) do not follow phonics rules, students with disabilities need to recognize common or irregular sight words with automaticity in addition to having decoding or "word attack" skills. *Automaticity* refers to the ability to identify words quickly, accurately, and effortlessly at the word level. Automatic word recognition involves explicitly teaching students high-frequency words as well as specific spelling patterns such as onset-rimes or word families (e.g., *sat, mat, hat, pat, fat, flat, splat*) and syllable patterns. Research indicates that repeated exposure to high-frequency words enables students to store the orthographic (spelling) representation of the words in their memory (Ehri, 1995).

These students practice their word attack skills and fluency while their teacher guides and observes.

Moreover, to be proficient readers, students with disabilities must read with *fluency*. Many teachers and students believe that fluency pertains just to reading quickly because most fluency assessments are timed. Fluency, however, involves rate and accurate word recognition as well as appropriate prosodic features such as rhythm, intonation, and phrasing (Hook & Jones, 2004). Teachers should read aloud to students so they have a model of what fluent reading sounds like. The repeated reading method (Samuels, 1979) has been found to be an effective intervention to increase students' rates of speed and accuracy and to develop fluency (Mercer, Campbell, Miller, Mercer, & Lane, 2000). This method involves having students read and reread a passage (with a partner or the whole class) until he or she reads with fluency and comprehension.

Reading fluency and comprehension have a strong connection. If students were to spend all of their time and energy decoding words at the phoneme level (only to find the word is irregular), this would negatively affect their ability to comprehend and enjoy the text (Lyon, 1995; Torgesen, Rashotte, & Alexander, 2001).

"Even mild difficulties in word identification can pull attention away from the underlying meaning, reduce the speed of reading, and create the need to reread selections to grasp the meaning" (Hook & Jones, 2004, p. 16). Thus, it is important for teachers to build students' fluency and word recognition skills so they can devote more cognitive attention to the meaning of the text.

Vocabulary and Comprehension

For many students, especially in the early elementary grades, intensive and direct teaching of phonemic awareness, sound–symbol relationships, word recognition, and reading fluency are the most important reading skills to learn. As students move into upper elementary and secondary grades (4–12), however, attention and instruction must be devoted to developing students' *vocabulary* and *reading comprehension* skills so they can construct meaning from text. These two skills are complementary because it is impossible to comprehend text without understanding the vocabulary within the text.

This is also a critical period in the student's reading development because grade-level text and assessments become more demanding and challenging. After fourth grade, most reading tests are tests of comprehension (Lyon, 2005). Students are required to read longer and more complex sentences, read longer passages with fluency, recognize thousands of new words "by sight" and know the meanings of the words, improve their conceptual thinking and reasoning skills, and use a variety of reading comprehension strategies (Torgesen, 2005). This means that teachers will have to provide students with explicit and systematic instruction in language skills, thinking skills, background knowledge, vocabulary, and comprehension strategies such as recognizing narrative and expository text structures, identifying the main idea, summarizing, outlining, drawing logical inferences, and using reference materials.

Vocabulary Instruction

Vocabulary is particularly difficult for students with mild/moderate disabilities because these students typically have smaller sight-word vocabularies than their peers without disabilities. They may struggle with accessing words during thinking, speaking, or writing; establishing relationships between ideas and concepts; and using known information to determine missing information (make inferences). As the students progress through school, vocabulary knowledge is also important in developing figurative language forms such as metaphors and humor.

One strategy to increase students' vocabulary is to explicitly teach new vocabulary words. According to Beck, McKeown, and Kucan (2002), the best way to teach students new vocabulary words is to

1. first select the right words to teach—words that extend students' language skills,
2. then develop child-friendly definitions for the word,
3. engage students in interesting and playful activities in which they can access and use the words in multiple contexts, and
4. devote more time during the day for explicit vocabulary instruction.

Building students' vocabulary can also be accomplished through *morphology*. A *morpheme* is the smallest unit of meaning. Morphological instruction consists of explicit and systemic instruction in prefixes, suffixes, compound words, inflectional endings (-s, -es, -ed, -ing), and Latin/Greek root words. For example, by teaching the root word *-spec* (to look), students can generate related words such as *inspect, spectator, speculate, spectacle, respect, specter, inspector, circumspect,* and so on. This type of instruction improves students' vocabulary as well as spelling skills as they learn to see relationships between words.

Another strategy to help students increase their vocabulary is to create *semantic maps,* visual representations or graphic organizers of the relationship between a central concept/topic and meaningful links to other related words. For example, if the class is working on a unit about habitats, the semantic map could classify different types of animals according to where they spend most of their time (see Figure 9.3 for a semantic

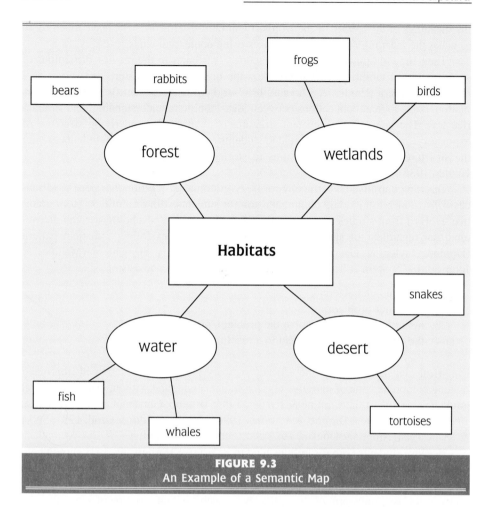

FIGURE 9.3
An Example of a Semantic Map

map). As another example, the students could be asked to create a semantic map or "word web" around a concept such as "freedom" when studying the Civil War. This is an excellent tool to activate their background knowledge as well as generate new vocabulary.

Semantic maps can be developed individually or in cooperative groups. Older students can create semantic maps around more complex ideas such as cause–effect relationships. The goal of semantic mapping is to provide students with a strategy to organize, integrate, and visualize information, as well as to help with word retrieval during discussion of new information.

Reading Comprehension Instruction ▪ ▪ ▪ ▪ ▪

As students are faced with more complex reading material, the academic demands placed on them switch from decoding and learning to read to comprehension and reading to learn (Gardill & Jitendra, 1999). Students' successful comprehension of text depends on many factors: accurate decoding, fluency, vocabulary and background knowledge, and comprehension strategies. To comprehend what is read, students must be able to decode approximately 95% of words in text (instructional level) and know the meanings of 90%–95% of the words (Lyon, 2005). This does not leave much room to guess the meaning of words and phrases using contextual clues.

Their limited knowledge of text structure contributes to the reading difficulties of students with disabilities. *Text structure* is the organizational feature that serves as a frame or a pattern (Englert & Thomas, 1987) to help readers identify important information, make logical connections between ideas, facilitate understanding, and summarize text. The goal of teaching text structure is to make the underlying structure of expository and narrative text apparent to students rather than expect the students to infer the structure from multiple exposures to stories and informational text (Carnine & Kinder, 1985).

Teaching narrative text structure, or story-grammar instruction, has been used successfully to increase reading comprehension for students with disabilities. Story grammar evolved from studies by anthropologists and cognitive psychologists who discovered that regardless of age or culture, retellings of stories follow a distinct pattern (Dimino, Taylor, & Gersten, 1995). In its simplest form, the pattern (Mandler & Johnson, 1977; Stein & Trabasso, 1982; Thorndyke, 1977) consists of

1. the main character,
2. his or her problem,
3. his or her attempts to solve the problem, and
4. the chain of events that lead to a resolution.

Empirical evidence supports the efficacy of story grammar instruction in improving reading comprehension of narrative text for students with and without disabilities at all grade levels (Bui, 2002; Carnine & Kinder, 1985; Dimino, Gersten, Carnine, & Blake, 1990; Gurney, Gersten, Dimino, & Carnine, 1990; Idol, 1987; Idol & Croll, 1987; Short & Ryan, 1984; Singer & Donlan, 1982).

Because students with disabilities tend to be passive learners, teachers should help them activate their brains before they read. In one suggested activity, students tap into their prior or background knowledge about the story before reading it. This can be done orally as a class brainstorm or through a "word web," which is a type of semantic map where students brainstorm related words and/or examples. Word webs are critical in making connections between students' prior knowledge and new vocabulary words or concepts they will encounter in the text. Students also should be encouraged to make and write down their predictions about what will happen in the story. After they have read the story, they go back to their predictions to see if the predictions were or were not correct. During reading, students have to be taught how to monitor their own comprehension and to use repair strategies such as rereading when comprehension fails.

Finally, the students should answer comprehension questions, fill out a *story map* (see Figure 9.4 for a sample story map), or write/say a retelling of the story after reading it, to ensure that they understood the story. When asking questions, the questions should be organized in sequence and include both *literal* (factual) questions to which students can find the answers in the text and *inferential* questions, which are more difficult to answer because this involves "reading between the lines" or using background knowledge.

For expository text, instruction on how to find the main ideas in text has been highly effective for students with disabilities (Jitendra, Hoppes, & Xin, 2000). In her study, Longo (2001) taught students to find the main idea by following four steps:

1. Ask yourself: What does the author say about this topic?

Name: _____ School: _____ Date: _____

Setting
Time: _____

Place: _____

Characters
Main: _____

_____

_____

Supporting: _____

_____

_____

Problem
_____

_____

_____

_____

Main Events
1. _____
2. _____
3. _____
4. _____
5. _____

Resolution / Outcome
_____

_____

_____

Look Deeper: Read between the lines—what's the lesson in the story?
_____

_____

_____

FIGURE 9.4
Story Map

2. Read the first paragraph. It often states the main idea.
3. Skim the rest of the selection to check what the author is saying about the topic in each paragraph.
4. Write a sentence that states the author's most important idea.

Other effective comprehension strategies for expository text include summarizing strategies (Simons, 1991) and having students create visual aids such as maps, pictures, and graphs to represent the main ideas and details as well as relationships between ideas (Rakes, Rakes, & Smith, 1995).

Informal Reading Assessments

An important component of a balanced reading program is assessment. Many informal assessments can be used for formative purposes to enable individualized reading instruction for your students. For phonemic awareness and phonics, the Abecedarian Reading Assessment (Wren & Watts, 2002) assesses early reading with six major subtests:

1. Letter knowledge
2. Phonological awareness (rhyme and phoneme identity)
3. Phoneme awareness (first and last sounds and phoneme segmentation)
4. Alphabetic principle
5. Vocabulary (production, synonyms and antonyms)
6. Decoding (fluency, regular words, irregular words)

The Consortium on Reading Excellence's CORE also has a comprehensive assessment for phonics and phoneme segmentation. Finally, the Yopp–Singer Test of Phoneme Segmentation assesses students' ability to segment words into phonemes.

Having a student read aloud while conducting an informal reading assessment is a good way to gauge student progress.

To assess word recognition, the San Diego Quick Assessment (Pray & Ramon, 1969) is a graded word list that can be used to assess students' decoding ability. Similarly, the Dolch Basic Sight word list of 220 high-frequency words (Dolch, 1948) can be used to assess students' word recognition skills.

Fluency typically is measured by the number of words correct per minute (WCPM). One way to measure fluency is to conduct an informal reading inventory for 1 to 3 minutes. Choose a passage that is unfamiliar to the student but at his or her instructional level (90%–100% accurate word recognition). Note the student's errors as well as rhythm, pace, and intonation. After 3 minutes, subtract the number of errors from the total words read. To calculate words correct per minute, divide that number by the number of minutes of reading. For example, if the student read 100 words in 3 minutes but missed seven words, her WCPM would be 93 ÷ 3 = 31.

Reading comprehension can be assessed in several ways, two of which are the following:

1. Ask reading comprehension questions at the end of the story or passage (both literal and inferential), consisting of "who, what, when, where, and why" questions based on the story grammar.
2. Ask the student to retell the story in his or her own words. This can be done either verbally or in written format. During the retelling, note if the student includes the main parts of the story, retells the story in sequence with a beginning, middle, and end, and adds information that was not in the story.

Many commercial reading programs have reading assessments as part of the curriculum. Table 9.1 contains a list of these programs.

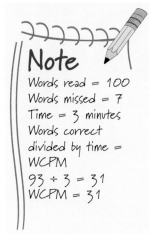

Note

Words read = 100
Words missed = 7
Time = 3 minutes
Words correct
divided by time =
WCPM
93 ÷ 3 = 31
WCPM = 31

Writing Instruction

Although less so than in reading, special education researchers have made an effort to design and validate writing instruction for elementary and secondary students with disabilities. The goals of these interventions have been to improve the students' written language by providing them with a broad repertoire of writing strategies. The research-based writing interventions for students with disabilities that have emerged in the professional literature can be grouped into four broad categories: prewriting planning instruction, text-structure instruction, writing strategies instruction, and a process approach to writing instruction.

Prewriting Planning Instruction

The first component of a comprehensive writing program is to teach students how to plan before they write. Before they actually start to write, students need to be taught how to set goals, generate ideas, and organize their ideas The prewriting planning process also involves developing some sort of written or visual plan (e.g., outline, story web, graphic organizer). Students with disabilities typically utilize an approach to writing that minimizes the role of prewriting planning (Graham & Harris, 1997). They tend to convert writing tasks to "telling what they know" with little regard to establishing goals, organizing text, and meeting the reader's needs (McCutchen, 1988). By contrast, skilled writers use planning processes in their approach to writing (Graham & Harris, 1996).

TABLE 9.1	
Commercial Reading Programs & Texts	
Reading Is FAME	This is a research-based, developmental reading program for adolescents who are reading below grade level. Designed specifically for high schools, it takes students through the different developmental stages of reading.
Wilson Language Training	This program trains teachers to provide direct, systematic, and multisensory instruction that allows students to trust English as a reliable language system and enables them to become fluent, independent readers.
Slingerland Institute for Literacy	The Slingerland Institute for Literacy is a teacher-training organization that provides training for teachers in the Slingerland Multisensory Approach. The Slingerland Approach is an adaptation for classroom use of the Orton-Gillingham method. This structured, sequential, simultaneous, multisensory teaching approach is designed to help students with dyslexia with speaking, reading, writing, and spelling.
Strategic Instruction Model	Content Enhancement Series and Learning Strategies Curriculum are research-based interventions for adolescents with learning disabilities, developed at the University of Kansas Center for Research on Learning.
SRA Direct Instruction	Reading Mastery and Corrective Reading are research-based reading, language arts, and math programs for students K–12.
The Lindamood Phonemic Sequencing® (LiPS®) Program	Formerly called the ADD [Auditory Discrimination in Depth] Program, LiPS® successfully stimulates phonemic awareness. Individuals become aware of the mouth actions that produce speech sounds, and this awareness becomes the means of verifying sounds within words and enables individuals to become self-correcting in reading, spelling, and speech.
Read Naturally	For over 14 years, Read Naturally has been the pioneer in improving fluency. The Read Naturally program combines three research-proven strategies to develop the reading fluency of students receiving special education services, English learners, and mainstream students.
Great Leaps	The Great Leaps program is divided into three major areas: (1) phonics—developing and mastering essential sight–sound relationships and/or sound awareness skills; (2) sight phrases—mastering sight words while developing and improving focusing skills; and (3) reading fluency—using age-appropriate stories specifically designed to build reading fluency, reading motivation, and proper intonation.
Peer Assisted Learning Strategies (PALS)	PALS Reading and PALS Math enable classroom teachers to accommodate diverse learners and to help a large proportion of these students achieve success. PALS Reading and PALS Math have been approved by the U.S. Department of Education's Program Effectiveness Panel for inclusion in the National Diffusion Network on effective educational practices.

Several research-based practices incorporate a planning technique into writing instruction for students with disabilities. In the Self-Regulated Strategy Development (SRSD) model (Harris & Graham, 1996), students are instructed to set goals, brainstorm ideas, sequence their ideas, and organize their writing (De La Paz, 1999; Troia, Graham & Harris, 1999). The intervention includes the use of acronyms and mnemonics to help students with the planning process.

Text Structure Instruction

The second component of a comprehensive writing program is to teach students the underlying text structures in different writing genres. *Text structure* refers to the organizational features that serve as a frame or pattern that helps readers to identify important information and logical connections between ideas (Seidenberg, 1989). For example, within expository text, students are taught the different structures, which include description, sequence, enumeration, problem–solution, classification, illustration, procedural description, and compare/contrast (Meyer & Rice, 1984; Weaver & Kintsch, 1991). Students with disabilities generally do not focus on text structures while reading and writing (Seidenberg, 1989), and their writing frequently lacks even the most basic story parts such as character and goals (Barenbaum, Newcomer, & Nodine, 1987).

Text-structure instruction typically has been used to increase reading comprehension. Some researchers, however (e.g., Englert, Raphael, Anderson, Anthony, & Stevens, 1991; Graham & Harris, 1989; Wong, 1997), have utilized text structure to improve the writing performance of students with LD. For writing narrative text (e.g., stories), students should be taught how to plan and write the different story parts:

1. Setting (location, time)
2. Characters (main and supporting)
3. Main events
4. Problem
5. Solution
6. Reaction

Writing Strategies Instruction

The third component of the comprehensive writing program is to teach students strategies for written expression. Students with disabilities tend to be less skilled writers than students without disabilities (Graham & Harris, 1997). The writing difficulties faced by students with disabilities fall in areas such as

- focusing on one topic (Englert & Thomas, 1987; Graham & Harris, 1989);
- organizing their writing and using organizational strategies (Englert, Raphael, Fear, & Anderson, 1988; Graves, Montague, & Wong, 1990);
- mastering basic writing skills such as spelling, sentence formation, capitalization, and handwriting (Graham, 1997; Graham, Harris, MacArthur, & Schwartz, 1991);
- writing complete and complicated sentences (Kline, Schumaker, & Deshler, 1991; Schmidt, Deshler, Schumaker, & Alley, 1989); and
- using effective revising and editing techniques (MacArthur, Graham, & Schwartz, 1991; Schumaker et al., 1982).

As a result, the essays written by students with disabilities have been consistently judged to be of poorer quality than those written by students without disabilities (Graham & Harris, 1989). Thus, they need explicit instruction on basic mechanical skills, how to write complete sentences, how to organize their ideas in paragraphs and essays, and how to edit and revise their writing.

As part of the Strategic Instruction Model curriculum (Deshler & Schumaker, 1986), four learning strategies were designed to teach written expression skills to adolescents with learning disabilities. The written expression strategies include

1. Sentence Writing Strategy (Schumaker & Sheldon, 1998);
2. Paragraph Writing Strategy (Schumaker & Lyerla, 1991);
3. Theme Writing Strategy (Schumaker, 2002); and
4. Error Monitoring Strategy (Schumaker, Nolan, & Deshler, 1985).

Together, these strategies teach students how to write simple and complex sentences, expository paragraphs, essays containing several connected paragraphs, and also to monitor and correct their basic writing errors (e.g., spelling, punctuation). Several studies (e.g., Kline et al., 1991; Schmidt et al., 1989; Schumaker et al., 1982) have been conducted to validate learning strategies instruction for students with disabilities.

Process Approach to Writing Instruction

While students are being taught explicit strategies for *how* to write, they must also be taught that writing is a *process* (Clippard & Nicaise, 1998). The literature indicates that students with disabilities typically lack general knowledge about the writing process (Englert et al., 1988; Graham, Schwartz, & MacArthur, 1993). A process approach to writing instruction focuses on giving students opportunities to immerse themselves in

This student demonstrates part of the writing process by sharing his work with his teacher and a peer.

the writing process at their own pace (Calkins, 1985). This type of instruction includes features such as the following (Atwell, 1985; Clippard & Nicaise, 1998; Goodman & Wilde, 1996; MacArthur, Graham, Schwartz, & Schafer, 1995):

- A community of writers is established in the classroom.
- Students are engaged in authentic writing tasks.
- Opportunities for social discourse and individual interactions are created between teachers and students.
- Students share their work with audiences of peers.
- A predictable structure helps to guide students through the writing process (e.g., planning, drafting, revising, publishing).

The process approach to writing instruction is based on the premise that if students are engaged in authentic writing tasks (e.g., they follow their own interests), the quality of their writing will improve (Bechtel, 1985).

The efficacy of a sole or integrated process approach to writing instruction such as a Writer's Workshop for students with disabilities remains uncertain (Clippard & Nicaise, 1998; Danoff et al., 1993; MacArthur et al., 1995). Although they seem to have benefitted from this type of writing instruction, students with disabilities still struggled with the basic mechanics of writing after this type of intervention. Nevertheless, students should understand the process approach to writing instruction because writing standards require that students write for a variety of purposes and audiences, and a process approach to writing seems to be appropriate to help meet this standard. In addition, students need to be taught the Six Traits of Writing—ideas, voice, conventions, organization, word choice, and sentence fluency (Northwest Regional Educational Laboratory, 2001)—as large-scale writing assessments typically measure students' writing proficiency based on these traits.

Mathematics Instruction

In addition to reading and writing difficulties, many students with mild to moderate disabilities have math disabilities (i.e., dyscalculia) and/or math difficulties. In a national study of 1,724 students with LD, 50% were identified as having weaknesses in mathematics (Bryant, Bryant, & Hammill, 2000). Even though difficulty with math has been recognized as a type of disability for more than 20 years, it has received considerably less attention and research than reading disabilities (Fuchs, Fuchs, & Prentice, 2004). This is unfortunate because, given the rapid changes in technology and increased work demands in math- and science-related industries, proficiency in math is critical for students to demonstrate during and after school.

Student Characteristics

Students with math disabilities or difficulties face quite a challenge in meeting national and state grade-level math standards. Mathematics competency requires students to go beyond simply computing (add, subtract, divide, multiply) or manipulating numbers. In addition to knowing math facts and basic procedures, students must have higher-order reasoning and problem-solving skills, as well as the ability to explain their thought processes. This is especially problematic for students with disabilities because they

This teacher uses popsicle sticks to help the student with number sense.

generally perform two grade levels below students without disabilities (Wagner, 1995), and adolescents with LD typically perform at the fifth-grade level (Cawley & Miller, 1989) in math.

Further, the majority of secondary students with disabilities do not take higher-level mathematics courses such as geometry or algebra, in which they would learn and practice these skills. This may have long-lasting negative effects for these students, as it could hinder their chances to pursue postsecondary education and/or limit their future career choices.

In addition to difficulty with computing basic math facts automatically, students with LD and ED tend to have academic and behavior characteristics related to their disabilities that affect their higher-order math competency (Maccini & Gagnon, 2002). These include

- difficulties with representing word problems and problem solving (Maccini & Ruhl, 2000; Montague & Applegate, 1993);
- difficulty paying attention to important aspects of tasks (Kauffman, 2001);
- deficits using metacognitive strategies (Bricklin & Gallico, 1984; Gallico, Burns, & Grob, 1991); and
- deficits with working memory (Keeler & Swanson, 2001).

Research suggests that word problems are the most challenging for students with LD across elementary and secondary grades. Difficulty with multi-step problems and math language and failure to check their work for mistakes are also common (Bryant et al., 2000). Moreover, students with ED may have difficulty concentrating for long periods of time and often give up rather than persevere when they are frustrated (Bos & Vaughn, 1994).

Math Standards

In response to the growing demands for a technologically savvy workforce, current reform efforts focus on addressing problem-solving and reasoning skills rather than retaining basic math skills. This effort is represented in the National Council of Teachers of Mathematics (NCTM) Standards, which focus on conceptual understanding of mathematics rather than basic computation skills (Maccini & Gagnon, 2002).

The first five standards present goals in the following content areas: numbers and operations, algebra, geometry, measurement, and data analysis and probability. The next five standards are goals for the processes of problem solving, reasoning and proof, connections, communication, and representation. Because many states have used the NCTM standards to develop their own math content standards (Blank & Dalkilic, 1992) and statewide assessments, teachers have to be familiar with both national and state standards in planning mathematics instruction for students.

Research-Based Practices

Given the difficulties that students with mild to moderate disabilities face with traditional mathematics curriculum, research efforts are increasing to validate "best practices" or interventions to enhance and improve elementary and secondary students' mathematical performance and abilities. The three interventions highlighted here are peer tutoring, mathematics word problems, and an algebra problem-solving strategy.

Peer Tutoring

Peer tutoring has been shown to be an effective intervention for mathematics instruction at both the elementary and the secondary levels. In peer tutoring, students with and

Peer tutoring and PALS instruction can be useful for other subject areas as well, including reading and writing.

without disabilities are paired as tutor and tutee with grade-level peers and/or younger students. Several studies have shown that secondary students with disabilities tutoring low-achieving students without disabilities and/or younger students with disabilities increased the mathematics achievement for both the tutor and the tutee (Maher, 1984; Melberg, 1980; Roach, Paolucci-Whitcomb, Meyers, & Duncan, 1983; Singh, 1982).

The Peer-Assisted Learning Strategies (PALS) intervention is one form of peer tutoring, based on classwide peer tutoring developed by researchers at Juniper Gardens (University of Kansas) (Delquardi, Greenwood, Whorton, Carta, & Hall, 1986). PALS has been found to be highly effective for improving both math computation and math concepts/applications for elementary students in grades 2–6 with and without disabilities (Fuchs, Fuchs, Hamlett, Phillips, & Bentz, 1994; Fuchs, Fuchs, Hamlett, et al., 1997; Fuchs, Fuchs, Phillips, Hamlett, & Karns, 1995) and math computation for secondary students (Calhoon & Fuchs, 2003). Results from high school student surveys indicated that the students enjoyed working with a partner and believed that PALS "helped them improve and work harder in math" (Calhoon & Fuchs, p. 241).

In PALS, students work in pairs and tutor each other as they practice individualized math skills. During a typical PALS session, the teacher assigns students to be partners based on their individual needs and behaviors. After students are paired up, they are given roles of tutor "coach" and tutee "player" and a problem sheet divided into four equal parts. The sheet should be related to the students' deficit skill area in math. During the first part, the "coach" models, verbalizes, and guides the "player" by asking the statements and questions provided on the worksheet. The "coach" also corrects the "player" if he or she provides an incorrect response and offers additional help. The coaching portion lasts about 15–20 minutes.

After the initial coaching, the "player" works independently on the next set of problems on the worksheet. During this practice time, the player explains his or her work to the "coach" so the coach can make corrections and/or provide additional help if needed. The practice session lasts 5–10 minutes. Then the partners reverse their roles and repeat the first two steps to ensure that each student gets a chance to be both a coach and a player.

PALS should be used as a supplement, not an alternative, to the traditional math curriculum (two to four times a week, 25–35 minutes per session), as it gives students more opportunities to practice skills at their own level. This is crucial for students with disabilities. Tutoring pairs should be changed every two weeks.

As an additional motivator or incentive, students can earn tangible reinforcers (e.g., points, prizes, rewards) for cooperating and engaging in on-task behaviors during the PALS sessions. This was more effective with elementary students than with secondary students.

Mathematics Word Problems

As mentioned, solving mathematics word problems is one of the most difficult tasks for students with disabilities—one that students try to avoid at all costs. Part of the difficulty with word problems is that they involve reading, and perhaps unknown vocabulary or math terms. Even if students can read the problem or have the problem read to them, other challenging aspects are

- understanding what the problem is asking (looking for known and unknown factors),

- setting up the problem correctly,
- choosing the correct mathematical operation to use, and then
- solving the problem accurately.

The research indicates that using schema-based strategy instruction has been effective in improving the solving-problem abilities of students with LD, ED, and mild mental retardation and low- and normally achieving students across the grade levels in both general and special education classrooms (e.g., Jitendra, DiPipi, & Grasso, 2001; Jitendra, DiPipi, & Perron-Jones, 2002; Xin & Jitendra, 1999). Schema-based strategy instruction consists of teaching students to represent a word problem graphically into a schema or diagram. This is different from having students draw a picture of the problem because specific diagrams coincide with different types of word problems. Once students have represented the information of the problem in the structured diagram, they can identify the relevant information needed to solve the problem.

This strategy has three main steps:

1. Students must learn how to identify the type of word problem.
2. After they have identified the type of word problem, students are taught how to translate the problem from words into a graphical representation (i.e., structured diagram).
3. Students are taught how to choose the appropriate mathematical operation (e.g., subtract, multiply), apply the operation, and solve the problem.

To know which structure diagram to use, students must be taught how to recognize the unique features of different types of word problems: change, group, and compare. Each type of word problem is like a mini story problem. In the *change* type of problem, the problem starts with a specific quantity. The quantity is then changed because of some event, and the problem ends with a new quantity.

For example, Maria baked 36 chocolate chip cookies (beginning). She gave 12 cookies to her neighbor (change). She has 24 cookies left (end). See Figure 9.5 for the change diagram (Jitendra, 2004).

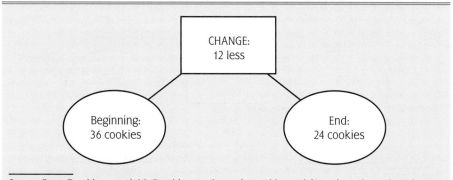

Source: From *Teaching tutorial 3: Teaching mathematics problem solving using schema-based strategy instruction*, by A. K. Jitendra (Reston, VA: Council for Exceptional Children, Division of Learning Disabilities). Copyright © 2004. Used by permission.

FIGURE 9.5
Change Diagram

In the *group* problem, the problem consists of two or more quantities that are added together or taken apart to create one quantity. For example, Ms. Fayer's fifth-grade class had a bake sale to raise money for a planned camping trip. They earned $10.40 on Monday (part), $5.28 on Tuesday (part), and $7.45 on Wednesday (part). Altogether they earned $23.13 for their camping trip (whole). Figure 9.6 presents the group diagram (Jitendra, 2004).

Finally, in the *compare* problem, the problem includes two or more quantities and a comparative statement about the relationship between the quantities. For example, Angie is 8 years old (referent). Her oldest brother Sean is twice as old as she is (difference). Sean is 16 years old (compared). See Figure 9.7 for the compare diagram (Jitendra, 2004).

The researchers suggest that when using schema-based strategy instruction, it is best to teach explicitly one type of problem at a time until the students have mastered

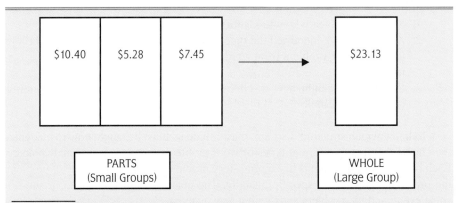

Source: From *Teaching tutorial 3: Teaching mathematics problem solving using schema-based strategy instruction,* by A. K. Jitendra (Reston, VA: Council for Exceptional Children, Division of Learning Disabilities). Copyright © 2004. Used by permission.

FIGURE 9.6
Group Diagram

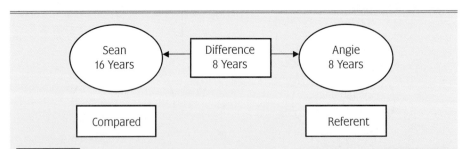

Source: From *Teaching tutorial 3: Teaching mathematics problem solving using schema-based strategy instruction,* by A. K. Jitendra (Reston, VA: Council for Exceptional Children, Division of Learning Disabilities). Copyright © 2004. Used by permission.

FIGURE 9.7
Compare Diagram

each one consistently. Practice problems used for instruction should not include unknown information, as this may confuse the students. In addition, students may need to create note cards or posters of the different strategy steps as reminders for themselves. Finally, teachers should provide students with the structured diagrams until they learn how to create them independently.

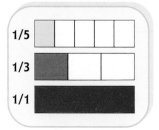

Fraction bars are a good example of concrete manipulatives.

Algebra Problem Solving

Teaching students to solve algebraic problems is challenging because it requires students to use abstract thinking, higher-order math reasoning, and problem-solving skills. Students with LD struggle with higher-level math such as algebra because it requires them to (a) master basic skills and understand terminology, (b) represent problems, (c) solve problems, and (d) use self-monitoring strategies (Hutchinson, 1987; Mayer, 1985). Components of effective algebra interventions include

- teaching first-letter mnemonic strategies (Miller & Mercer, 1993; Scruggs & Mastropieri, 1989),
- incorporating feedback strategies during lessons (Maccini & Ruhl, 2000),
- using concrete objects and manipulatives (Huntington, 1994; Mayer, 1985), and
- utilizing a gradual teaching sequence (Maccini & Ruhl, 2000).

STAR is a basic algebra problem-solving strategy (Maccini, 1998) that incorporates many of the instructional components suggested in the literature. It is a first-letter mnemonic representing steps that students can use to remember a problem-solving strategy (p. 470):

Search the word problem
Translate the words into an equation in picture form
Answer the problem
Review the solution

In addition to the first-letter cues, the strategy utilizes a gradual teaching sequence in which students apply the steps in different phases: concrete, semi-concrete, and abstract. This allows students to learn the algebraic concepts using concrete manipulatives before they are expected to apply the strategy to abstract problems.

For example, for the second step, "Translate the words into an equation," in the concrete phase students use manipulatives (e.g. algebra tiles) to represent the picture form of the equation. In the semi-concrete phase of this step, students stop using manipulatives and instead draw a picture to represent the problem. In the abstract phase, students write an algebraic equation to represent the problem. Students apply the last two steps of the STAR strategy (Answer and Review) only in the abstract phase (see Figure 9.8 for detailed strategy steps).

In their study, Maccini and Ruhl (2000) reported that secondary students with LD were able to learn and apply the STAR strategy, which increased their mathematical performance in representing and solving basic algebraic word problems.

Summary

Students with mild to moderate disabilities represent the largest segment of students defined by IDEA as eligible for special education services and related services. Within

Concrete (C) Application

1. Search the word problem.
   a) Read the problem carefully.
   b) Ask yourself questions: "What facts do I know?" and "What do I need to find?"
   c) Write down facts.

2. Translate the words into an equation in picture form.
   a) Choose a variable.
   b) Identify the operation(s).
   c) Represent the picture using manipulatives.

Semi-Concrete (S) Application

1. Search the word problem.
   a) Read the problem carefully.
   b) Ask yourself questions: "What facts do I know?" and "What do I need to find?"
   c) Write down facts.

2. Translate the words into an equation in picture form.
   a) Choose a variable.
   b) Identify the operation(s).
   c) Draw a picture of the representation.

Abstract (A) Application

1. Search the word problem.
   a) Read the problem carefully.
   b) Ask yourself questions: "What facts do I know?" and "What do I need to find?"
   c) Write down facts.

2. Translate the words into an equation in picture form.
   a) Choose a variable.
   b) Identify the operation(s).
   c) Write an algebraic equation.

3. Answer the problem.

4. Review the solution.
   a) Reread the problem.
   b) Ask the question "Does the answer make sense? Why?"
   c) Check answer.

Source: From "Effects of a graduated instructional sequence on the algebraic subtraction of integers by secondary students with learning disabilities," by P. Maccini & K. L. Ruhl, 2000, *Education and Treatment of Children, 23*(4), 465–489.

FIGURE 9.8
STAR Strategy at Each Application Level

this broad group are students with emotional disturbances (often called emotional/ behavioral disorders), speech and language impairments, learning disabilities, mild mental retardation, and/or autistic spectrum disorders. Together these students are referred to in many policies as high incidence. However, this does not mean that they necessarily share common attributes as each experiences particular instructional needs. What they do have in common is participation in the general education curriculum and having to respond to state and national policies driven by legislation such as the No Child Left Behind Act of 2001. This translates into academic expectations and the need to ensure that they are afforded opportunities to experience instruction appropriate to their needs and aligned with state and national curriculum standards. In this bridging chapter the focus has been on complementing the content presented in individual chapters on disability groups for students with mild to moderate disabilities by introducing a context for beginning teachers to consider as they develop their repertoire of pedagogical skills in the areas of reading, writing, and math. Particular attention has been given to those skills that tend to generalize across disability groups and that can contribute to enhancing the achievement of these students. The underlying premise of this chapter is that these students possess the potential to be successful in the general education curriculum and that there is an emerging knowledge base of research-based practices that offer beginning teachers direction as they prepare for their instructional responsibility in meeting the educational needs of their students.

References

Adams, M. A. (1990). *Beginning to read: Thinking and learning about print.* Cambridge, MA: MIT.

Atwell, N. (1985). How we learned to write. *Learning, 13,* 51–53.

Barenbaum, E., Newcomer, P., & Nodine, B. (1987). Children's ability to write stories as a function of variation in task, age, and development level. *Learning Disability Quarterly, 7,* 175–188.

Bechtel, J. (1985). *Improving writing and learning: A handbook for teachers in every class.* Boston: Allyn & Bacon.

Beck, I. L., McKeown, M. G., & Kucan, L. (2002). *Bringing words to life.* New York: Guilford Press.

Blachman, B. A., Tangel, D. M., & Ball, E. W. (2004, Spring). Combining phonological awareness and word recognition instruction. *Perspectives, 24*(2), 12–14.

Blank, R., & Dalkilic, M. (1992). *State policies on science and mathematics education.* Washington, DC: State Education Assessment Center, Council of Chief State School Officers. (ERIC Document Reproduction Service No. ED 350 163)

Bos, C. S., & Vaughn, S. (1994). *Strategies for teaching students with learning and behavior problems* (3rd ed.). Boston: Allyn & Bacon.

Bricklin, P. M., & Gallico, R. (1984). Learning disabilities and emotional disturbance: Critical issues in definition, assessment, and service delivery. *Learning Disabilities, 3,* 141–156.

Brigance, A. H. (1977). *Brigance Diagnostic Inventory of Basic Skills.* North Billerica, MA: Curriculum Associates.

Brigance, A. H. (1981) *Brigance Diagnostic Inventory of Essential Skills.* North Billerica, MA: Curriculum Associates.

Bryant, D. P., Bryant, B. R., & Hammill, D. D. (2000). Characteristic behaviors of students with LD who have teacher-identified math weaknesses. *Journal of Learning Disabilities, 33*(2), 168–177, 199.

Bui, Y. N. (2002, Summer). Using story-grammar instruction and picture books to increase reading comprehension. *Academic Exchange Quarterly,* 128–139.

Calhoon, M. B., & Fuchs, L. S. (2003). The effects of peer-assisted learning strategies and curriculum-based measurement on the mathematics performance of secondary students with disabilities. *Remedial and Special Education, 24*(4), 235–245.

Calkins, L. M. (1985, Fall). I am one who writes. New approaches to children's writing. *American Educator,* 26–44.

Carnine, D., & Kinder, B. D. (1985). Teaching low-performing students to apply generative and schema strategies to narrative and expository material. *Remedial and Special Education, 6*(1), 20–30.

Carnine, D. W., Silbert, J., & Kameenui, E. J. (1997). *Direct instruction reading* (3rd ed.). Upper Saddle River, NJ: Prentice Hall.

Cawley, J. F., & Miller, J. H. (1989). Cross sectional comparisons of the mathematical performance of children with learning disabilities: Are we on the right track toward comprehensive programming? *Journal of Learning Disabilities, 23,* 250–254, 259.

California Department of Education (CDE). (1999). *The California reading initiative and special education in California: Critical ideas focusing on meaningful reform.* Sacramento: California Special Education Reading Task Force, California State Board of Education.

Clippard, D., & Nicaise, M. (1998). Efficacy of writers' workshop for students with significant writing deficits. *Journal of Research on Childhood Education, 13*(1), 7–25.

De La Paz, S. (1999). Self-regulated strategy instruction in regular education settings: Improving outcomes for students with and without learning disabilities. *Learning Disabilities Research & Practice, 14*(2), 92–106.

Delquardi, J., Greenwood, C. R., Whorton, D., Carta, J. J., & Hall, R. V. (1986). Classwide peer tutoring. *Exceptional Children, 52,* 535–542.

Deshler, D. D., & Schumaker, J. B. (1986). Learning strategies: An instructional alternative for low-achieving adolescents. *Exceptional Children, 52,* 583–590.

Dimino, J. A., Gersten, R., Carnine, D., & Blake, G. (1990). Story grammar: An approach for promoting at risk secondary students' comprehension of literature. *Elementary School Journal, 91*(1), 19–32.

Dimino, J. A., Taylor, R. M., & Gersten, R. M. (1995). Synthesis of the research on story grammar as a means to increase comprehension. *Reading & Writing Quarterly: Overcoming Learning Difficulties, 11*(1), 53–72.

Dolch, E. W. (1948). *Problems in reading.* Champaign, IL: Garrard Press.

Ehri, L. C. (1995). Phases of development in learning to read words by sight. *Journal of Research in Reading, 18,* 116–125.

Elkonin, D. B. (1973). U.S.S.R. In I. Downing (Ed.), *Comparative reading* (pp. 551–580). New York: Macmillan.

Englert, C. S., Raphael, T. E., Anderson, L. M., Gregg, S. L., & Anthony, H. M. (1989). Exposition: Reading, writing, and the metacognitive knowledge of learning disabled students. *Learning Disabilities Research, 5*(1), 5–24.

Englert, C. S., Raphael, T. E., Fear, K. L., & Anderson, L. M. (1988). Students' metacognitive knowledge about how to write informational texts. *Learning Disability Quarterly, 11,* 18–46.

Englert, C. S., & Thomas, C. C. (1987). Sensitivity to text structure in reading and writing: A comparison of learning disabled and nonhandicapped students. *Learning Disability Quarterly, 10,* 93–105.

Fahey, K. R. (2000). The development of oral language. In K. R. Fahey & D. K. Reid (Eds.), *Language development, differences, and disorders* (pp. 79–133). Austin, TX: Pro-Ed.

Fuchs, L. S., Fuchs, D., & Prentice, K. (2004). Responsiveness to mathematical problem-solving instruction: Comparing students at risk of mathematics disability with and without risk of reading disability. *Journal of Learning Disabilities, 37*(4), 293–306.

Fuchs, L., Fuchs, D., Hamlett, C. L., Phillips, N. B., & Bentz, J. (1994). Classwide curriculum-based measurement: Helping general educators meet the challenge of student diversity. *Exceptional Children, 60,* 518–537.

Fuchs, L., Fuchs, D., Phillips, N. B., Hamlett, C. L., & Karns, K. (1995). Acquisition and transfer effects of classwide peer-assisted learning strategies in mathematics for students with varying learning histories. *School Psychology Review, 24,* 604–620.

Gallico, R., Burns, T. J., & Grob, S. C. (1991). *Emotional and behavioral problems in children with learning disabilities.* San Diego, CA: Singular.

Gardill, C., & Jitendra, A. K. (1999). Advanced story map instruction: Effects on the reading comprehension of students with learning disabilities. *Journal of Special Education, 33*(1), 2–17.

Goodman, Y. M., & Wilde, S. (1996). *Notes from a kidwatcher: Selected writings of Yetta M. Goodman.* Portsmouth, NH: Heinemann.

Graham, S. (1997). Executive control in the revising of students with learning and writing difficulties. *Journal of Educational Psychology, 89,* 223–234.

Graham, S., & Harris, K. (1989). Components analysis of cognitive strategy instruction: Effects on learning disabled students' compositions and self-efficacy. *Journal of Educational Psychology, 81*, 353–361.

Graham, S., & Harris, K. R. (1996). Self-regulation and strategy instruction for children who find writing and learning challenging. In M. Levy & S. Ransdell (Eds.), *The science of writing: Theories, methods, individual differences, and applications* (pp. 347–360). Mahwah, NJ: Erlbaum.

Graham, S., & Harris, K. R. (1997). Self-regulation and writing: Where do we go from here? *Contemporary Educational Psychology, 22*, 102–114.

Graham, S., Harris, K. R., MacArthur, C. A., & Schwartz, S. (1991). Writing and writing instruction for students with learning disabilities: Review of a research program. *Learning Disability Quarterly, 14*, 89–114.

Graham, S., Schwartz, S. S., & MacArthur, C. A. (1993). Knowledge of writing and the composing process, attitude towards writing, and self-efficacy for students with and without learning disabilities. *Journal of Learning Disabilities, 26*, 237–249.

Graves, A., Montague, M., & Wong, Y. (1990). The effects of procedural facilitation on story composition of learning disabled students. *Learning Disabilities Research, 5*, 88–93.

Gurney, D., Gersten, R., Dimino, J. A., & Carnine, D. (1990). Story grammar: Effective literature instruction for learning disabled high school students. *Journal of Learning Disabilities, 23*, 335–342.

Harris, K. R., & Graham, S. (1996). *Making the writing process work: Strategies for composition and self-regulation.* Cambridge, MA: Brookline.

Hook, P. E., & Jones, S. D. (2004). The importance of automaticity and fluency for efficient reading comprehension. *Perspectives, 24*(2), 16–21.

Huntington, D. J. (1994). Instruction in concrete, semi-concrete, and abstract representation as an aid to the solution of relationship problems by adolescents with learning disabilities (Doctoral dissertation, University of Georgia, 1994). *Dissertation Abstracts International, 56*(2), 512.

Hutchinson, N. L. (1987). Strategies for teaching learning disabled adolescents algebraic problems. *Reading, Writing, and Learning Disabilities, 3*, 63–74.

Idol, L. (1987). Group story mapping: A comprehension strategy for both skilled and unskilled readers. *Journal of Learning Disabilities, 20*, 196–205.

Idol, L., & Croll, V. J. (1987). Story-mapping training as a means of improving reading comprehension. *Learning Disability Quarterly, 10*, 214–229.

Jitendra, A. K. (2004). *Teaching tutorial 3: Teaching mathematics problem solving using schema-based strategy instruction.* Reston, VA: Council for Exceptional Children, Division for Learning Disabilities.

Jitendra, A. K., DiPipi, C. M., & Grasso, E. (2001). The role of the graphic representational technique on the mathematical problem solving performance of fourth graders: An exploratory study. *Australian Journal of Special Education, 25*, 17–33.

Jitendra, A. K., DiPipi, C. M., & Perron-Jones, N. (2002). An exploratory study of word problem-solving instruction for middle school students with learning disabilities: An emphasis on conceptual and procedural understanding. *Journal of Special Education, 36*, 23–38.

Jitendra, A. K., Hoppes, M. K., & Xin, Y. P. (2000). Enhancing main idea comprehension for students with learning problems: The role of a summarization strategy and self-monitoring instruction. *Journal of Special Education, 34*(3), 127–139.

Kauffman, J. M. (2001). *Characteristics of emotional and behavioral disorders of children and youth* (7th ed.). Upper Saddle River, NJ: Simon and Schuster.

Kaufman, A. S., & Kaufman, N. L. (1985). *Kaufman Test of Educational Achievement.* Circle Pines, MN: American Guidance Service.

Keeler, M. L., & Swanson, H. L. (2001). Does strategy knowledge influence working memory in children with mathematical disabilities? *Journal of Learning Disabilities, 34*, 18–34.

Kline, F. M., Schumaker, J. B., & Deshler, D. D. (1991). Development and validation of feedback routines for instructing students with learning disabilities. *Learning Disability Quarterly, 14*(3), 191–207.

Lavadenz, M. (1996). Authentic assessment: Toward equitable assessment of language minority students. *New Schools, New Communities, 12*(2), 31–35.

Longo, A. M. (2001, Spring). Using writing and study skills to improve the reading comprehension of at-risk adolescents. *Perspectives.* Baltimore: International Dylexia Association.

Lyon, G. R. (1995). Towards a definition of dyslexia. *Annals of Dyslexia, 45,* 3–27.

Lyon, G. R. (1998). Why reading is not a natural process. *Educational Leadership, 55*(6), 14–18.

Lyon, G. R. (2005, March). *Why scientific research must guide reading instruction: Fads, philosophies, and untested assumptions about reading instruction really do harm children.* Presentation at CORE Leadership Conference, Oakland, CA.

MacArthur, C. A., Graham, S., & Schwartz, S. S. (1991). Knowledge of revision and revising behavior among learning disabled students. *Learning Disability Quarterly, 14,* 61–73.

MacArthur, C. A., Graham, S., Schwartz, S. S., & Schafer, W. D. (1995). Evaluation of a writing instruction model that integrated a process approach, strategy instruction, and word processing. *Learning Disability Quarterly, 18,* 278–291.

Maccini, P. (1998). *Effects of an instructional strategy incorporating concrete problem representation on the introductory algebra performance of secondary students with learning disabilities.* Unpublished dissertation, Pennsylvania State University, University Park.

Maccini, P., & Gagnon, J. C. (2002). Perceptions and application of NCTM standards by special and general education teachers. *Exceptional Children, 68*(3), 325–344.

Maccini, P., & Ruhl, K. L. (2000). Effects of a graduated instructional sequence on the algebraic subtraction of integers by secondary students with learning disabilities. *Education and Treatment of Children, 23*(4), 465–489.

Maher, C. A. (1984). Handicapped adolescents as cross-age tutors: Program description and evaluation. *Exceptional Children, 51,* 56–63.

Mandler, J. M., & Johnson, N. S. (1977). Remembrance of things parsed: Story structure and recall. *Cognitive Psychology, 9,* 111–151.

Markwaldt, E. C. (1989). *Peabody Individual Achievement Test-Revised.* Circle Pines, MN: American Guidance Service.

Mayer, R. E. (1985). The elusive search for teachable aspects of problem solving. In J. A. Glover & R. R. Ronning (Eds.), *Historical foundations of educational psychology* (pp. 327–347). New York: Plenum.

McCutchen, D. (1988). "Functional automaticity" in children's writing. *Written Communication, 5,* 306–324.

McGrew, K. S., & Woodcock, R. W. (2001). Technical manual. *Woodcock–Johnson III.* Itasca, IL: Riverside Publishing.

Melberg, D. B. (1980). The effects of the handicapped and nonhandicapped tutor on the academic achievement of the economically disadvantaged adolescent tutor and the elementary age tutee (Doctoral dissertation, University of Wisconsin, 1980). *Dissertation Abstracts International, 42*(02), 659A.

Mercer, C. D., Campbell, K. U., Miller, W. D., Mercer, K. D., & Lane, H. B. (2000). Effects of a reading fluency intervention for middle schoolers with specific learning disabilities. *Learning Disabilities Research and Practice, 15*(4), 179–189.

Meyer, B.J.F., & Rice, G. E. (1984). The structure of text. In P. D. Pearson, R. Barr, M. L. Kamil, & P. Mosenthal (Eds.), *Handbook of reading research* (pp. 319–351). White Plains, NY: Longman.

Miller, S. P., & Mercer, C. D. (1993). Mnemonics: Enhancing the math performance of students with learning disabilities. *Intervention in School and Clinic, 29*(2), 78–82.

Moats, L. C. (2005, March). *Teaching reading is rocket science: What effective teachers know and do.* Presentation at CORE Leadership Conference, Oakland, CA.

Montague, M., & Applegate, B. (1993). Middle school students' mathematical problem solving: An analysis of think-aloud protocols. *Learning Disability Quarterly, 16,* 19–30.

National Reading Panel (NRP). (2000). *Teaching children to read: An evidence-based assessment on the scientific research literature on reading and its implications for reading instruction* (NIH Publication No. 00-4754). Washington, DC: U.S. Department of Health and Human Services, National Institute of Child Health and Human Development.

National Institute of Child Health and Human Development (NICHD). (2000). *Report of the National Reading Panel. Teaching children to read: An evidence-based assessment of the scientific research literature on reading and its implications for reading instruction: Reports of the subgroups* (NIH Publication No. 00-4754). Washington, DC: U.S. Government Printing Office. Also available on-line: http://www.nichd.nih.gov/publications/nrp/report.htm.

Northwest Regional Educational Laboratory. (2001). *6 + 1 trait writing.* Retrieved December 31, 2002, from http://www.nwrel.org/assessment/department.asp?d=1

Overton, T. (2003). *Assessing learners with special needs: An applied approach* (4th ed.). Upper Saddle River, NJ: Merrill Prentice Hall.

La Pray, M., & Ramon, R. (1969). Word list: Quick gauge of reading ability. *Journal of Reading, 12*(4), 305–307.

Rakes, G. C., Rakes, T. A., & Smith, L. J. (1995). Using visuals to enhance secondary students' reading comprehension of expository text. *Journal of Adolescent and Adult Literacy, 39*(1), 46–54.

Reschly, D. (1992). Special education decision making and functional/behavioral assessment. In W. Stainback & S. Stainback (Eds*.), Controversial issues confronting special education: Divergent perspectives* (pp. 286–301). Needham Heights, MA: Allyn & Bacon.

Richard-Amato, P. (1996). *Making it happen: Interaction in the second language classroom.* White Plains, NY: Longman.

Roach, J. C., Paolucci-Whitcomb, P., Meyers, H. W., & Duncan, D. A. (1983). The comparative effects of peer tutoring in math by and for secondary special needs students. *The Pointer, 27*(4), 20–24.

Rosenshine, B., & Stevens, R. (1984). Classroom instruction in reading. In P. D. Pearson (Ed.), *Handbook of reading research* (pp. 745–798). New York: Longman.

Samuels, S. (1979). The method of repeated readings. *Reading Teacher, 32*(4), 403–408.

Schmidt, J. L., Deshler D. D., Schumaker, J. B., & Alley, G. R. (1989). Effects of generalization instruction on the written language performance of adolescents with learning disabilities in the mainstream classroom. *Journal of Reading, Writing, and Learning Disabilities International, 4*(4), 291–309.

Schumaker, J. B., Deshler, D. D., Alley, G. R., Warner, M. M., Clark, F. L., & Nolan, S. (1982). Error monitoring: A learning strategy for improving adolescent academic performance. In W. M. Cruickshank & J. W. Lerner (Eds.), *Coming of age: Selected papers from the 18th International Conference of the Association for Children and Adults with Learning Disabilities* (pp. 170–183). Syracuse, NY: Syracuse University Press.

Schumaker, J. B. (2002). *The theme writing strategy.* Lawrence: University of Kansas.

Schumaker, J. B., & Lyerla, K. D. (1991). *The paragraph writing strategy.* Lawrence: University of Kansas.

Schumaker, J. B., Nolan, S. M., & Deshler, D. D. (1985). *The error monitoring strategy.* Lawrence: University of Kansas.

Schumaker, J. B., & Sheldon, J. B. (1998). *Fundamentals in the sentence writing strategy.* Lawrence: University of Kansas.

Scruggs, T. E., & Mastropieri, M. A. (1989). Mnemonic instruction of learning disabled students: A field-based investigation. *Learning Disability Quarterly, 12,* 119–125.

Seidenberg, P. L. (1989). Relating text-processing research to reading and writing instruction for learning disabled students. *Learning Disabilities Focus, 5*(1), 4–12.

Short, E. J., & Ryan, E. B. (1984). Metacognitive differences between skilled and less skilled readers: Remediating deficits through story grammar and attribution training. *Journal of Educational Psychology, 76,* 225–235.

Simons, S. M. (1991). *Strategies for reading non-fiction.* Eugene, OR: Spring Street.

Singer, H., & Donlan, D. (1982). Active comprehension: Problem-solving schema with question generation for comprehension of short stories. *Reading Research Quarterly, 17,* 166–185.

Singh, R. K. (1982). Peer tutoring: Its effects on the math skills of students designated as learning disabled (Doctoral dissertation, American University, 1981). *Dissertation Abstracts International, 42,* 4693A.

Stein, N. L., & Trabasso, T. (1982). What's in a story? An approach to comprehension and instruction. In R. Glaser (Ed.), *Advances in instructional psychology* (Vol. 2, pp. 213–267). Hillsdale, NJ: Erlbaum.

Thorndyke, P. W. (1977). Cognitive structures in comprehension and memory of narrative discourse. *Cognitive Psychology, 9*, 77–110.

Torgesen, J. K. (2005, March). *Dyslexia, and other things that make it difficult to learn to read proficiently.* Keynote presentation at meetings of the Utah Branch of the International Dyslexia Association, Salt Lake City, Utah.

Torgesen, J. K., Rashotte, C. A., & Alexander, A. (2001). Principles of fluency instruction in reading: Relationships with established empirical outcomes. In M. Wolf (Ed.), *Dyslexia, fluency, and the brain* (pp. 333–355). Parkton, MD: York Press.

Troia, G. A., Graham, S., & Harris, K. R. (1999). Teaching students with learning disabilities to mindfully plan when writing. *Exceptional Children, 65*(2), 235–252.

U.S. Department of Education. (2002). No Child Left Behind Act of 2001. Retrieved June 15, 2005, from http://www.ed.gov/policy/elsec/leg/esea02/index.html

Wagner, T. (1995). What's school really for, anyway? And who should decide? *Phi Delta Kappan, 76*(5), 393–399.

Weaver, C. A., & Kintsch, W. (1991). *Effects of topic familiarity and training in generative learning activities on poor readers' comprehension of comparison/contrast expository text structure: Transfer to real-world materials.* Paper presented at annual meeting of International Reading Association, New Orleans.

Wilkinson, G. S. (1993). *Wide Range Achievement Test—Revised (WRAT3).* Wilmington, DE: Jastak Associates.

Wong, B. (1997). Research on genre-specific strategies for enhancing writing in adolescents with learning disabilities. *Learning Disability Quarterly, 20*, 140–159.

Wren, S., & Watts, J. (2002). *The Abecedarian Reading Assessment.* Retrieved August 10, 2005, from http://www.balancedreading.com

Xin, Y. P., & Jitendra, A. K. (1999). The effects of instruction in solving mathematical word problems for students with learning problems: A meta-analysis. *Journal of Special Education, 32*, 207–225.

Yopp, H. K. (1992). Developing phonemic awareness in young children. *Reading Teacher, 45*(9), 696–703.

Ysseldyke, J. E., & Algozzine, B. (1995). *Special education: A practical approach for teachers.* Boston: Houghton Mifflin.

STUDENTS WITH MODERATE TO SEVERE DISABILITIES (LOW-INCIDENCE)

Historically, the needs of students with moderate to severe disabilities have been the last to come to the attention of policy makers in education. Originally, some were enrolled in public schools but were not appropriately educated, and large numbers remained at home or were inappropriately placed in residential facilities.

As progress was made in establishing public policy at the state and federal levels to benefit students with mild disabilities, parents and advocates for school-age individuals with more severe disabilities began to demand educational services for this group of children as well. As this movement gained momentum, the public debate centered around what would constitute education for this group as the instructional needs of many students with moderate to severe disabilities fell more in the areas of self-help skills and learning to communicate or behave appropriately in public settings than academics in the traditional sense.

Initially, public policies focusing on education for this group were what came to be labeled permissive legislation. That is, legislation made it permissible for states and local districts to expend public funds on providing special education for learners with moderate to severe needs. However, school districts were under no obligation to do so. Thus, while this was a beginning, it was still up to parents and advocates to convince local boards of education to offer appropriate special education services for this group. The response was slow at first. One of the contributing factors was the low incidence of students with moderate to severe disabilities. This posed particular problems in rural communities, where it was difficult, both from a staffing and a financial standpoint, to deliver services to a few students, often at different age levels. Therefore, only large population centers were in a position to be responsive to the growing demand for services for students with low-incidence disabilities, and they were often reluctant or unable, due to a lack of qualified teachers.

One of the most significant movements that benefited the development of special education programs for all students with disabilities, but particularly those with moderate to severe needs, was the reorganization of school districts into larger units—cooperatives and intermediate units—which represented larger populations and, therefore, a larger tax base to support programming. As this occurred, the movement to mandate programs and services for all students with disabilities became more feasible, and the history of special education began to change.

As a side note, to some extent, public policy began to shape education for students with visual and hearing impairments earlier than for other groups of students with moderate to severe disabilities. Views continue to vary on why this was the case. However, some of the reasons were related to the fact that the public understood disabilities such as blindness and deafness better than they did cognitive and developmental disabilities, which were mainly hidden—unseen. Additionally, beyond the core disability, the instructional needs of these students did not seem to set them apart as much as other individuals with moderate to severe disabilities because they represented a wider range of cognitive abilities.

Unlike with students with mild to moderate disabilities, it is far more difficult for beginning special education teachers to predict the attributes of the students with moderate to severe disabilities they may find assigned to their classes. The same is true for general education teachers in inclusion settings. In general, as the severity of a disability increases, the probabilities increase that the individual presents unique instructional needs and therefore requires more services.

As a person preparing to teach in special education, you have an obligation to be informed about the instructional implications of students with disabilities at all levels of severity. This is no small challenge. Asking you to develop a broader knowledge base on learner characteristics and teaching strategies adds to your professional responsibilities. To that end, most special education teacher training programs offer structured introduction, overview, or foundations courses in which books like the one you are studying are used to provide background information on all disabilities.

Part III focuses particularly on background information on the disability groups identified in the Individuals with Disabilities Education Act (IDEA) as low-incidence and possessing moderate to severe disabilities. They include students with cognitive and developmental disabilities, autism spectrum disorders, deafness and hard of hearing, and visual impairments. A separate chapter has been included that focuses on the instructional needs that are common to many students within all these groups. Thus, chapter 14 is designed for beginning teachers who plan to teach in general education or in special education for students with mild to moderate disabilities who also need to understand the characteristics and exceptional learning needs of students with moderate to severe disabilities. This chapter addresses topics that generalize across disability groups included in Part III. Examples include communication skills, self-determination, community resources, alternative assessments, and universal design for learning.

Cognitive and Developmental Disabilities

Sean J. Smith

Individuals with mental retardation can benefit from support and services nearly within days of their birth. Thus, our understanding of the disability and its causes and our ability to identify the disability as soon as possible have direct consequences on how and what we can provide in terms of direct intervention and support. Consider the experiences of Luke and Ellie in the following cases studies.

The instruction and overall approach to the growth and development of students with cognitive and developmental disabilities have undergone significant changes in classrooms across the country in recent decades. In the past, many students with these disabilities were

CASE STUDIES

Luke

Teresa and John were excited and couldn't wait for the birth of their first child. Having married two years ago when they were both 25, they couldn't wait to start a family. The pregnancy had been uneventful and the sonogram indicated that their first would be a boy. When their little boy finally arrived, they named him Luke. Luke had a normal delivery and was healthy in every way. However, the pediatrician who visited the hospital room suggested Luke be tested for Down syndrome. While his heart appeared to be fine, his facial features, the folds in his hands, and the displacement between his big toe and the rest of his toes indicated he might have this syndrome. Sure enough, two days later the pediatrician called Teresa and John at home to confirm that Luke had Down syndrome. Through the tears, Teresa and John began to worry about what would happen next. Over the past two days, they had learned from the nurses in the hospital as well as from family and friends that this disability could be quite debilitating. In addition, they had learned that it often meant other health concerns. Teresa and John were scared and weren't sure where to turn.

Fortunately, like many parents of infants with Down syndrome, they quickly learned about services available to them and their son. Thanks to coordination by a local health agency, Luke was soon receiving regular service from a speech pathologist and a physical therapist, as well as an occupational therapist. By the time he was 3 months old, Luke had his own Individual Family Service Plan, an early childhood educator who worked closely with Teresa and John, and services at least once a week from varied service providers. All this was organized around Teresa's and John's busy work and family schedule and was provided on their living room floor. By the time Luke was ready for preschool, he had received three years of fairly intense home-based support at no cost to his parents. This support was critical in the development of skills he would need to transition successfully to an inclusionary preschool program.

(continued)

continuing case studies

***

Ellie

About the time Luke was born, a college friend of Teresa's, Joanne, and her husband, Craig, were expecting their first child. Joanne's pregnancy had been uneventful, and through their sonogram she and Craig learned that they were expecting a little girl, whom they planned on naming Ellie. A month prior to Joanne's delivery date, she was involved in an automobile accident and ended up delivering Ellie within a day. Born quite small and in need of oxygen, Ellie spent her first three weeks of life in the hospital's neonatal unit. There, she began to gain weight and, finally, about the time of the original due date, Ellie was allowed to go home with Joanne and Craig.

Joanne and Craig were not certain what to expect from their firstborn but worked hard to provide Ellie with a safe and supportive home. At her 18-month pediatric appointment, the pediatrician expressed minimal concern about the fact that Ellie wasn't walking and her speech was a bit delayed. By the time Ellie was 2 years old, Joanne and Craig were actively trying to understand why Ellie was delayed in meeting almost every milestone. While their pediatrician was not concerned, Craig and Joanne looked to family and friends for answers. It wasn't until Ellie was nearly 2½ years old that Joanne's Mommy's Day Out provider suggested she have Ellie tested through a Parents as Teachers program offered by the local public school system. Through this program, Ellie was found to have significant delays in speech; by the time she was 3 years old, Ellie was receiving speech services once a week. By the time she was in kindergarten, teachers were expressing concerns of a development delay and suggesting further testing. It wasn't until the end of her first-grade year that Ellie was found to have a disability under the area of mental retardation. By this time, Ellie's teachers were suggesting a more self-contained setting to meet the specific needs of her disability and to provide services she had not received during the early part of her development.

taught in separate, isolated placements or even in institutional environments. Today, a significant number of these students are taught in the general education environment for a portion, if not the majority, of the instructional day. This change is the result of increased emphasis on including all students in the general education setting.

And placement is only part of the equation. Better understanding of cognitive disabilities, as well as increased expectations for what individuals with cognitive disabilities are capable of doing, has led to significant alterations in educational programs and subsequent outcomes for students with cognitive disabilities. Revisions in educational outcomes have translated into more independence and expanded self-determination on the part of individuals in mapping out their life and career expectations. In turn, these changes have enhanced the quality of life for persons with cognitive disabilities and started to alter society's perception of these individuals and their capabilities. We are entering a time in the history of the education of students with cognitive disabilities at which we are truly "pushing the envelope" in terms of what is possible for them.

In this chapter you will learn the various definitions of cognitive and developmental disabilities, characteristics of the disability, and its causes. You will learn how students with cognitive disabilities are typically served in schools and how they are identified for services. The chapter concludes with an overview of ways to develop and implement educational programs that enhance access to the general education curriculum for students with cognitive disabilities.

Definition of Mental Retardation

Because the term used in the federal definition—as well as by state and local education agencies— is *mental retardation* (MR), we will use this term here in referring to individuals with cognitive and developmental disabilities.

Current Federal Definition

The identification of MR in school-age children has not been altered significantly for more than 20 years. The definition of MR in the Individuals with Disabilities Education Act (IDEA) (2004) is the same as the definition presented in the 1983 manual published by the American Association on Mental Deficiency (AAMD), which reads as follows:

> *Mental Retardation refers to significantly subaverage general intellectual functioning existing concurrently with deficits in adaptive behavior and manifested during the developmental period that adversely affects a child's educational performance. (34 C. F. R, Sec. 300. 7[b][5]) (U. S. Office of Education, 1977, p. 42478)*

The diagnostic manual of the AAMD (known today as the American Association on Mental Retardation [AAMR]) has clarified the components of the definition as follows (AAMD, 1983, p. 11):

General intellectual functioning: is based on results from an individually administered intelligence test by a qualified person.

Significantly subaverage: was originally defined as having an IQ score of about 70 or below (that is 2 standard deviations below the mean for the specific test used). Grossman (1983) states that 70 is intended as a guideline, allowing the score to be extended upward to 75, depending upon the reliability of the test used. Previous definitions of MR had extended the IQ score to as high as 85 or below.

Deficits in adaptive behavior: is defined as displaying significant limitations in the ability to meet age-appropriate cultural standards effectively in learning, personal independence, and social responsibility.

Developmental period: is defined as the time between the moment of conception to the age of 18.

AAMR's Definition

The definition of MR included in IDEA is one of at least seven definitions that professional and governmental agencies have adopted since the early 1950s. In 1992, the ninth edition of the AAMR handbook on definition and classification of MR (Luckasson et

Note

The 1992 definition of MR by the AAMR has changed the way people think about mental retardation. The meaning of the term continues to develop and evolve with subsequent definitions.

al., 1992) introduced a *functional definition* and classification system intended to link "mental retardation" to a system of supports and to move the diagnostic process away from its historic reliance on levels of deficit identified by performance on an IQ test. This effort marked a significant departure from previous AAMR efforts to define and determine what constitutes MR. Indeed, some educators and researchers argue that this definition, with its emphasis on present functioning, represents a shift in the conceptualization of the disability and the services needed to address the needs of individuals with MR.

In this definition, MR is defined not as something that a person *has* or something that is a characteristic of the person but, rather, as a state of functioning such that limitations in functional capacity and adaptive skills must be considered within the context of environments and supports. Luckasson et al. (1992) noted that "mental retardation is a disability only as a result of this interaction" (p. 10); that is, only as a result of the interaction between the functional limitation and the social context—the environments and communities in which people with intellectual disability live, learn, work, and play. Thus, AAMR's reconceptualization of MR places considerable emphasis on the interaction between the person with the disability and the context in which that person lives, learns, works, and plays.

Another implication of AAMR's 1992 definition of MR is that the degree of the disability is not a fixed trait but may change over time and across environments. More important, the level of retardation is significantly affected or determined by the level of supports that are generic to the specific environment. Thus, if the individual only needs supports that are commonly available to typically developing peers, no special supports are necessary and the diagnosis of retardation would be deemed inappropriate. Even though only four states adopted the 1992 definition and associated criteria for determining if a student has MR (Denning, Chamberlain, & Polloway, 2000), the definition and diagnostic protocols embodied in the revised definition offered the field a new paradigm from which to identify students, focusing on the instruction and overall support necessary for students with MR to prosper in school and community environments.

In 2002, the AAMR offered a subsequent definition:

> *Mental retardation is a disability characterized by significant limitations both in intellectual functioning and in adaptive behavior as expressed in conceptual, social, and practical adaptive skills. This disability originates before age 18.*

The 2002 definition is based on five assumptions essential to the application of the definition:

1. Limitations in present functioning are considered within the context of community environments typical of the individual's age peers and culture.
2. Valid assessment considers cultural and linguistic diversity as well as differences in communication and sensory, motor, and behavioral factors.
3. Within an individual, limitations often coexist with strengths.
4. An important purpose of describing limitations is to develop a profile of needed supports.
5. With appropriate personalized supports over a sustained period, the life functioning of the person with MR generally will improve.

Each of these assumptions calls for supports to improve the likelihood of the individual functioning successfully in everyday environments. Supports refer to the services, resources, and personal assistance that improve the way a person functions—how he or she develops, learns, and lives. Supports range from *intermittent* (provided from time to time) to *pervasive* (constant).

The classification and support schemes in the 1992 and subsequent 2002 AAMR definitions are founded on the assumption that categorization based on the support needed is better than categorization based on IQ because it (a) implies that individuals with MR can achieve positive outcomes with appropriate support services, (b) avoids reliance on a single IQ score, and (c) may result in descriptions that are more meaningful when considered in combination with adaptive skills (discussed later in the chapter).

Unfortunately, AAMR's call for an end to the traditional classifications of mild, moderate and severe, to be replaced by classification according to levels of supports (i.e., intermittent, limited, extensive, pervasive), has had limited response. Many local school districts continue to use the levels of retardation while largely ignoring the levels-of-supports model.

The AAMR, related professionals, and parents argue that the way an individual is classified affects how he or she is perceived and, thus, educated. If a child is seen as what he or she cannot do (i.e., IQ scores) instead of the support he or she needs to succeed, the program of education, curriculum and instructional practices, and preparation for adulthood/transition will be affected negatively. For example, if Francis, a student with Down syndrome, is seen first as a child with language and cognitive delays, his program will emphasize what he cannot do and not on what he can accomplish. If history is a guide, Francis would end up in a segregated self-contained classroom and his limitations would intensify his separation from his typically developing peers. As a result, his transition to adulthood, too, would involve a segregated setting away from the general society in work, living, and overall community involvement.

Defining Developmental Disabilities

In 1997, IDEA added the term *developmental delay*, often associated with MR, as a separate category by which to classify children through the age of 9. Developmental delay is often the term of choice for early intervention programs, where it is not possible or beneficial to apply one of the classification categories to a child who exhibits functional and adaptive delays. As of 1997, schools can use the term *developmental delay* for children through age 9, at the discretion of the state or district, whenever a child is exhibiting delays significant enough to require intervention in one or more of the following areas:

- Physical development
- Cognitive development
- Communication development
- Social or emotional development
- Adaptive development

Although a child identified as having a developmental delay may be identified subsequently as having MR, this designation does not automatically transfer the classification. Instead, a developmental delay prior to the age of 9 may be altered subsequently to a classification of a learning disability, a speech and language disability, or possibly no disability at all. Regardless, the term *developmental delay* is being applied increasingly and may represent a less stigmatizing label for children with MR prior to the age of 10.

Computers are an excellent way to help students develop their communication skills.

Prevalence

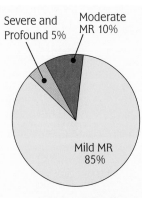

Severe and Profound 5%

Moderate MR 10%

Mild MR 85%

A majority of people who are MR are classified as mild.

If we consider the theoretical distribution of IQ scores based on the normal curve, we would expect 2.27% of the population to fall two standard deviations or more below average, which would put those individuals within the intellectual domain of an individual with MR. But it is difficult to obtain an accurate prevalence rate for MR because it is directly related to the way MR is defined. Because the definitions vary, the reported rates are inconsistent, ranging from less than 1% up to 3% of the general population. Perhaps most useful for educational purposes is the 0.96% rate reported in the U.S. Department of Education's (2003) *Twenty-Fourth Annual Report to Congress*. Further, reports indicate that 85% of this population consists of students who are considered to have mild MR. About 10% are considered to have *moderate* levels of retardation, and an additional 5% are at *severe and profound* levels.

During the 2002–2003 school year, these percentages translated to 614,433 students with MR, ages 6 to 21, receiving special education services. Interestingly, since 1990, the number of students with learning disabilities has increased at three times the rate of the number of students with MR. Some would argue that students who previously were identified as having MR are now being found eligible for special education services under the category of learning disabilities. Regardless, the number of students identified as having MR has remained static over the past decade, and since 1975 has actually decreased.

Most of the new cases are identified during the school years, as contrasted to early intervention or post-school years (U.S. Department of Education, 2003). Thus, the clinical diagnosis of mild MR seems to be age-dependent, with most of the cases being diagnosed after school environments place challenges or demands on the individual. An exception is severe retardation, which is identified much earlier because of the noticeable gap between the individual's functioning and typical development. Severe/profound retardation usually is identified soon after a child enters an early intervention program.

Causes of Mental Retardation

The causes of MR must be considered specific to two overlapping populations: (a) mild MR associated with lower socioeconomic status, and (b) severe MR, more typically linked to biological causes. Depending upon the individual, however, there is a connection between nature and nurture. For example, a child's disability that results initially from a biological cause may be compounded by environmental factors. This seems to be true when considering that mothers who have not finished high school are four times more likely to have children with mild MR than are mothers who have completed high school. Why? We are not certain. A variety of factors, including genetic and socioeconomic (e.g., poverty, malnutrition), may be involved. What we do know is that the exact cause of the disability is known in less than half of the cases. And cultural and social factors play a significant role. In the following discussion we will look at genetic, environmental, and toxic factors.

Genetic/Chromosomal Factors

Disorders resulting from genetic and chromosomal abnormalities comprise one group of biological causes of MR. The most widely known of these chromosomal conditions is Down syndrome. A more recently identified chromosomal disorder, which came to light in the 1980s, is Fragile X syndrome. This is the most common inherited cause of MR. Several other genetic or chromosomal causes are under investigation.

Down Syndrome

In the most common cause of Down syndrome, an infant is born with three, rather than two, copies of the 21st chromosome (known medically as trisomy 21). Normally, a person has 46 chromosomes (23 pairs), half of which are inherited from each parent. Children with Down syndrome, however, have cells that usually contain 47 chromosomes, the extra one being a third chromosome 21. This extra genetic material in infants with Down syndrome is what disrupts their physical and cognitive development.

Down syndrome results from genetic and chromosomal abnormalities.

The cause of Down syndrome remains a mystery. Although it can happen to anyone, scientists do know that women ages 35 and older have a significantly increased risk of giving birth to a child with Down syndrome. A 35-year-old woman has a 1 in 350 chance of conceiving a child with Down syndrome. By age 40, this number jumps to about 1 in 100. By age 45, the odds are 1 in 30. Because younger women give birth more often, however, most babies with Down syndrome are born to younger mothers.

Williams Syndrome

Another genetic disorder, Williams syndrome, results from the deletion of material in the seventh pair of chromosomes. The IQ of the population of individuals with Williams syndrome ranges from about 40 to 100, with a mean of around 60. Attendant problems range from lack of coordination to light muscle weakness, to heart defects, MR, and occasional kidney damage. No two individuals with Williams syndrome have exactly the same problems.

Fragile X

The most common inherited form of MR is Fragile X, affecting about one in 1,200 males of all racial and ethnic groups. It can cause a range of mental impairment from mild to severe, with many typical features and symptoms. It is associated with the X chromosome in the 23rd pair of chromosomes. In males, the 23rd pair consists of an X and a Y chromosome. In females, it consists of two X chromosomes. This disorder gets its name because the bottom of the X chromosome is pinched off in some of the blood cells.

Phenylketonuria

Phenylketonuria (PKU) is a birth defect caused by a recessive gene found in both parents. A specific enzyme needed to break down the protein known as phenylalanine is lacking. Some babies have excessive levels of this protein and, when untreated, this can lead to brain damage. Fortunately, PKU is fully treatable by a special diet and can be detected by a simple blood test. In most, if not all, states, this test is required prior to the baby leaving the hospital.

Environmental Factors

The role of the environment as a whole in promoting or restricting the development of a child has received attention. An example is the Head Start program, which seeks to provide early intervention for children at risk for delays because of environmental factors. Key considerations for potential causes of MR include (a) poverty; (b) health problems often associated with nutritional deficiencies, lack of resistance to disease, and inadequate health care; and (c) limited educational opportunities (or environmental stimulation). Although poverty and MR may be linked, we should keep in mind that the overwhelming majority of individuals growing up in poverty do not have MR (Taylor, Klein, Minich, & Hack, 2000).

Like the other disabilities discussed in this book, MR can result from brain injuries sustained during birth or incurred in childhood, as well as premature birth. Trauma to the fetus during birth can occur when the baby's position makes normal delivery difficult or when labor is prolonged or complicated. Infants who are born prematurely often have an underdeveloped nervous system and may not be able to catch up in development after birth.

Toxic Factors

Today's world is complicated by the use of vaccines, chemicals, and other products intended to improve our life and lifestyle. Yet, while we benefit in many ways from these products, there is much we do not know about their potential negative effects on people. For example, the lawn-care industry has spawned a great number of products to reduce weeds and keep our lawns green. At the same, these chemicals could be having a negative impact on children, animals, and the overall environment, of which we are unaware.

Chemicals

Chemicals that are used to support and enhance everything from the clothes we wear to the food we eat can have detrimental impact on human development. About 80,000 new synthetic chemicals have been approved for use in the United States since World War II. The use of chemicals globally increased from 1 million tons per year in 1930 to 400 million tons per year in 1998. An estimated 2,000–3,000 new chemicals are registered each year. Chemicals are used every day in the United States, and in many areas we have come to depend upon them.

Despite the many benefits, some of these chemicals have been proven to cause, and others are suspected of contributing to, developmental disabilities. Still others may contribute to health problems. We have no idea what effects the vast majority of chemicals and chemical combinations are having on our current and future health, and on the health and development of future generations (AAMR, 2004).

Testing of individual chemicals is deficient; only a few have undergone comprehensive safety assessments. Remarkably, in the United States today, before chemicals are introduced into society, there is no mandatory testing of their potential to cause harm. Therefore, when you buy a product off the shelf that contains chemicals, no one—neither the government, nor the manufacturer—has evaluated its potential to cause you harm. None of the 15,000 chemicals used most commonly has been tested for toxicity in the combinations in which they occupy the shelves of your local stores.

So chemicals are out there. For us, the question is: What do we know and what don't we know about toxic chemicals and their possible connection to MR and developmental disabilities? During the winter of 2004, a group of manufacturers, policy makers, and disability advocates convened and articulated the following concerning chemicals and mental retardation (AAMR, 2004):

- We know that some *neurotoxicants* can affect the brain and nervous system development of children.
- We know that the developing brain is uniquely vulnerable to toxic chemical exposures.
- We do not know the extent to which neurotoxicants may be implicated in causing MR.
- We know that fetal exposure to higher levels of neurotoxicants—alcohol and other solvents, PCBs, and heavy metals (mercury and lead)—can result in MR and other neurodevelopmental disorders.
- We know that exposure to several known environmental neurotoxins (such as lead, mercury, PCBs, solvents such as alcohol and toluene, and tobacco smoke) can disrupt development of the human brain and, depending on the dose, results

in permanent limitations in intelligence, learning, attention, memory, comprehension, language acquisition, written and verbal communication, behavior, and socialization skills.

Fetal Alcohol Syndrome

Alcohol in the mother's blood passes through the placenta and enters the embryo or fetus through the umbilical cord (McCreight, 1997). Even if consumed in moderation, alcohol is implicated in what is called *fetal alcohol syndrome* (FAS). Through a number of biological means, alcohol affects the size, shape, and function of the cells that form the brain, heart, kidneys, and all the other body organs and systems. At any time during pregnancy, the mother's drinking can affect these organs and systems. Children born to mothers who ingested alcohol during their pregnancy may be born with MR, heart defects, drooping eyelids, and other facial anomalies.

Assessment

The multidisciplinary team (such as the classroom teacher, special educator, school psychologist, speech pathologist, parents, administrator, occupational or physical therapist, and school counselor) has two important functions in assessing a student: (a) to determine whether the student meets the criteria of MR (i.e., to assess the student's intelligence and measure his or her adaptive skills) and, if so, (b) to determine the child's program needs.

Intelligence

Of the many types of intelligence tests (IQ tests) available, two of those used most commonly in schools today are the Stanford–Binet—Fourth Edition (Thorndike, Hagan, & Sattler, 1986) and the Weschler Intelligence Scale for Children-Third Edition (WISC-III) (Wechsler, 1991). Both of these instruments are administered verbally, allowing the student to communicate an understanding without the challenge of giving a written response. Both tests elicit information about the child's intellect by dividing the student's mental age (the age level at which the student is functioning) by the student's chronological age and multiplying by 100.

IQ tests such as the Stanford–Binet and the WISC-III are considered reliable and valid instruments. Thus, based on the test score, a team can better understand the student's ability and begin to develop interventions or programs suitable for his or her academic needs. As the AAMR (2002) definition emphasizes, however, determining MR solely according to IQ is unwise. Among several reasons for caution, three are noted here:

1. The concept of intelligence is a construct. Therefore, although it may seem to be precise and accurate, it is an inference based on observed performance and therefore can change.
2. An IQ test is "a snapshot in time," a measure of a specific child at a specific point in time. From this information, we make inferences on performance and ability, but IQ scores have been known to change. The younger the child, the less valid and reliable is the test.
3. What we learn from IQ tests is often not directly applicable to the development and subsequent implementation of educational objectives and related

instruction for a student. Instead, teacher-administered, criterion-referenced assessments measuring specific curricular skills are generally more useful in identifying and planning meaningful instruction for individual students.

Adaptive Behavior

Adaptive behavior is the collection of social and practical skills that people have learned so they can function in their everyday lives. Significant limitations in adaptive behavior negatively influence a person's daily life and affect his or her ability to respond to a given situation or to the environment. For a student to be found eligible for services under the category of MR, the team must identify clear deficits in adaptive behavior. Determining the level of adaptive skills is important in identifying the disability and also for determining the supports an individual may require for success in school, work, and the community.

A number of instruments are used to assess the adaptive behavior of school-age children. On these standardized measures, significant limitations in adaptive behavior are operationally defined as performance at least two standard deviations below the mean of either (a) one of three types of adaptive behavior—conceptual, social, or practical—or (b) an overall score on a standardized measure of conceptual, social, and practical skills.

An example of such instruments is the AAMR's Adaptive Behavior School-School (ABS-S) (Lambert, Nihira, & Leland, 1993). Also widely used is the Vineland Social Maturity Scale (Doll, 1965). A more recent tool, developed in the early 1990s, is the Assessment of Social Competence (ACS) (Meyer, Cole, McQuarter, & Reichle, 1990).

We should note that, even with these and other norm-referenced instruments, measuring adaptive behavior is difficult. In large part, reaching agreement on what is considered appropriate behavior is problematic because what is considered appropriate in one situation or by one group may not be considered appropriate in or by another.

Characteristics of Students With Mental Retardation

The two major characteristics of MR are (a) limitations in intellectual functioning and (b) limitations in adaptive behavior. We will mention speech and language characteristics that impact both intellectual and adaptive limitations, although this is also a separate and specific need.

Limitations in Intellectual Functioning

Intelligence refers to a student's general mental capability for solving problems, paying attention to relevant information, thinking abstractly, remembering important information and skills, learning from everyday experiences, and generalizing knowledge from one setting to another. As has been discussed, intelligence is measured by intelligence tests and a student is regarded as having MR when his or her IQ score is approximately two standard deviations below the mean.

In many schools today, students with an IQ score of 55–70 (about 85% of the MR population) would be considered mildly mentally retarded, those with an IQ level between 35–40 and 50–55 would be included in the moderate MR classification (about

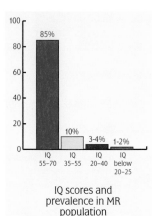

IQ scores and
prevalence in MR
population

10% of individuals with MR), students with an IQ level between 20–25 and 35–40 would be considered severe MR (about 3%–4% of individuals with MR), and an IQ level below 20 or 25 would be considered profound MR (about 1%–2% of persons with MR). Regardless of the precise IQ score, students with MR typically have impairments in intellectual functioning, including problems with attention, memory, generalization, and motivation.

Attention

In any learning situation, attention to task is crucial to learning. Students with MR have difficulty in the three major components of attention: attention span (length of time on task), focus (blocking out distracting stimuli), and selective attention (discrimination of important stimulus characteristics; Smith, 1997). This requires training these students to be aware of the importance of attention and to learn how to actively monitor its occurrence.

Memory

One of the most consistent findings is that people with MR have difficulty remembering information. A distinction usually is made between short-term and long-term memory. Information being recalled after a period of days, months, or longer is referred to as being in *long-term memory*, whereas information stored from a few seconds to a few hours is said to be in *short-term memory*. Once information is learned, it generally is retained over the long term regardless of whether the person has a disability. The inability of individuals with MR to attend to tasks, as well as their limited ability to use rehearsal strategies or adequate rehearsal activities, limits their ability to place information in their short-term memory (Nunn & Nunn, 1993).

Individuals with MR also have problems with *working memory*, which involves the ability to keep information in mind while simultaneously doing another cognitive task. An example of working memory is someone trying to remember an address while listening to instructions on how to get there.

Generalization

Generalization refers to the ability to transfer learned knowledge or behavior in one task to another task and to make that transfer across different settings or environments. Individuals with MR typically have difficulty generalizing the skills they have learned in school to their home and community settings, with their differing cues, expectations, people, and environmental arrangements. This is because their home and community settings often are more complex and have more distractions and irrelevant stimuli than their classrooms.

A number of behaviorally oriented strategies have been developed to help these learners overcome their deficits in generalizing the skills they learn. Factors that seem to facilitate generalization include varying the setting, the time of day, the materials, and the people working with a student (Westling & Fox, 2000). For example, community-based instruction helps learners minimize their problems with generalization by allowing them to practice skills in environments where they are expected to use these skills.

Motivation

A great deal of research has been conducted on the motivation of individuals with MR, and the research consistently reveals that a student's low motivation often results from a history of failure. A lack of motivation also has been described as a lack of self-direction or the inability to self-direct. Because of an intensive history of failure, many individuals with MR begin to lose confidence, which causes them to rely on the leadership and skill of others. This low motivation or distrust in their own abilities leads to a problem-solving style called *outer-directedness*—distrusting one's own solutions and looking excessively to others for guidance (Paris & Winograd, 1990). This is a special concern for students with MR because outer-directedness can make them vulnerable to control by others.

Another characteristic of self-direction or motivation involves the cause-and-effect relationship between a person's behavior and life events. *Locus of control* is a personality characteristic in which people judge how much they think they control life events that directly affect them. People with an *internal locus of control* believe they are the reason for their success or failure, whereas people who feel they have little or no control over their lives demonstrate an *external locus of control* (Wehmeyer, Agran, & Hughes, 1998). Individuals with MR tend to be more dependent upon others, less trusting of their abilities, and more motivated by extrinsic reinforcers. This can be complicated when they are treated differently by parents and teachers because of their cognitive delay, which reinforces their dependence on others.

Limitations in Adaptive Behavior

In addition to limitations in intellectual functioning, individuals with MR have significant limitations in adaptive behavior as expressed in their conceptual, social, and practical adaptive skills. Individuals without disabilities demonstrate adaptive behavior in meeting environmental expectations. Examples of adaptive behaviors include the following:

- Skills needed to adapt to one's living environment
- Self-direction
- Choice-making
- Problem solving
- Goal setting and attainment
- Self-observation
- Self-awareness
- Home living
- Functional academics

For example, some individuals with MR have difficulty taking care of their personal needs. In most cases, they can learn to care for their personal needs at least as well as the general population without disabilities. Because of the diversity of individuals with MR, these skills vary and the intensity of the training required to help them master the related skill likewise will vary. Too, a person's age as well as cultural expectations and environmental demands affect adaptive behavior.

To determine a student's adaptive behavior capacities, teachers and other professionals attend to the student's conceptual skills, social skills, and practical skills. A student may have a combination of strengths and needs in any or all of these areas.

Self-Determination

Self-determination means "acting as the primary causal agent in one's life and making choices and decisions regarding one's quality of life free from undue external influence or interference" (Wehmeyer, 1996, p. 24). Being a causal agent means being able to take action to cause things to happen in one's life. Thus, self-determined people shape their future; they do not depend on random luck to cause good things to happen to them (Wehmeyer, Palmer, Agran, Mithaug, & Martin, 2000). Self-determination incorporates many skills, including choice-making, decision making, problem solving, and goal setting (Wehmeyer, Lance, & Bashinski, 2002).

Self-Regulation

Self-regulation is a broad term referring to an individual's ability to manage his or her own behavior. People with MR have difficulties with *metacognition*, which is closely connected to the ability to self-regulate. Metacognition refers to a person being aware of the strategies necessary to perform a task, knowing how to use the strategies, and being able to evaluate how well the strategies are working.

Repeated failure can lead to *learned helplessness*, a term reflecting the belief that failure will result from even the most extraordinary efforts. A student's repeated experiences of failure lead to an expectation of failure.

Speech and Language

Speech and language problems occur with frequency among students with MR. Speech problems most often involve difficulties with articulation—the pronunciation of words. Common articulation errors are substitution, omission, addition, or distortion of sounds. Language disorders that typically accompany MR include delayed language development and restricted or limited active vocabulary.

Among students with mild MR whose speech and language needs are more pronounced, other factors contribute to the challenge. For example, in children with Down syndrome, the higher prevalence of childhood ear infections can lead to hearing impairments, which may cause poor articulation and contribute to further delay in the acquisition of language. And children with Down syndrome tend to have motor challenges as a result of the characteristic protruding tongue, which can compound their language difficulties.

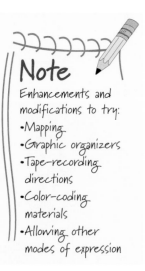

Note

Enhancements and modifications to try:
- Mapping
- Graphic organizers
- Tape-recording directions
- Color-coding materials
- Allowing other modes of expression

Research-Based Interventions and Best Practices

What do "research-based practices" entail? First, curriculum and instructional design must address "best" instruction for all. Design tools and powerful strategies include teaching to BIG ideas, integrating curriculum strategically, teaching learning strategies in conspicuous ways, creating scaffolds for student learning that are thoughtful and aligned with individual needs, priming background knowledge so new learning connects meaningfully to what is already known, and providing review judiciously (more for some and less for others) with specific feedback. Explicit enhancements to curriculum and instruction for hard-to-teach students utilize mapping, advance organizers, analogies, and graphic organizers. Regardless of excellent curriculum design and instructional delivery, some students need accommodations or modifications to the planned instruction because they lack prerequisite skills or knowledge, or because they learn at a different rate than peers.

Some students also need specialized, supplemental instruction characterized by intensity, control of task difficulty with targeted, explicit feedback, working in small groups, and learning through multiple models of mediated learning. Further, the environment or setting in which instruction takes place must be structured to facilitate learning and allow collaboration among many instructional experts. Below, we offer a select example of research-based practices that have been shown to be effective for individuals with MR.

General Classroom Setting

The emphasis on standards-based curriculum has led to the development and implementation of adaptations for students with MR. Without modifying or supplementing the curriculum to meet the needs of the individual student, students with MR are not able to be included successfully in standards-based instruction and subsequent state assessments. Whenever possible, the student should participate in the same activities as the rest of the class. Successful adaptations may enhance a child's functioning.

Instructional Adaptations

Instructional adaptations begin with changes in how a teacher delivers instruction. Often, all that may be necessary to enable the student to participate in the elementary classroom activity is to modify directions or create more structure in the lesson. Modifications might include offering auditory or tactile cues or tape-recording the directions to encourage independence.

Material Adaptations

Adapting instructional material to fit the needs of students with MR is another important consideration. Examples of modifications are using pictures to support instruction, developing cue cards to structure a lesson, enlarging print or highlighting critical components, altering the position of the material to emphasize

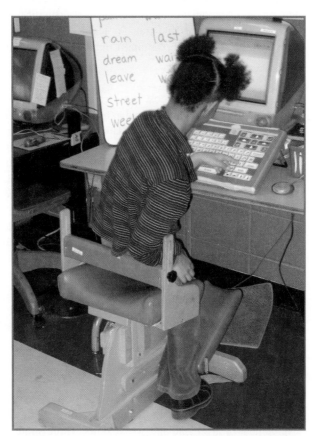

Spelling words written on a large dry-erase board, an adaptive keyboard, and a specially designed chair all help to support the instruction of this learner in a general classroom setting.

critical concepts, color-coding materials to assist with short- and long-term memory development, using manipulatives or hands-on materials to assist in constructing meaning, or organizing learning centers where students can practice what they learn.

Response Adaptations

Response adaptations are essential for many students with MR. If students are not able to complete lessons as assigned for the entire class, even with modifications, teachers must consider assigning less work or allowing students to demonstrate mastery of completion in other ways (e.g., speaking, drawing). For many students, simply breaking the task into smaller units is effective. For written assignments such as reports or journals, students might be given the opportunity to substitute oral presentations. For content-area coursework, students may be allowed to use pictures or artwork to demonstrate their understanding of the material. Also, the versatility of the computer offers countless alternative response modes.

Systematic Instruction

As we have discussed, students with MR frequently have problems with attention, memory, and generalization, which makes it difficult for them to acquire information, retain learned material, and transfer learned material to new situations. These challenges require some level of support in most learning situations.

Generalization

As mentioned, one of the most significant challenges these students face involves generalization—the ability to apply what has been learned in one setting to another setting, possibly with another instructor. This is especially critical in the functional skills included within the K–12 environment, which are intended to prepare the student for home, community, and work environments. If students cannot transfer skills across settings, the educational program is significantly challenged.

One of the most effective ways to foster generalization is to teach the skills in the setting where students will use them, such as the general education setting with same-aged peers, or in the community setting where the student lives and potentially will work. Five specific generalization strategies include (Giangreco, 1998)

1. using multiple examples in your instruction,
2. teaching relevant/functional behaviors,
3. teaching students to self-monitor for generalization,
4. implementing the same strategy across settings, and
5. programming for generalization.

Memory and Attention

Students with MR often do not succeed in the general education setting because they have difficulty discriminating between what is and what is not important in the instructional task. The ability to discriminate within the learning context is essential to the development of academic and social skills. Three strategies for enhancing discrimination are as follows (Hamill & Everington, 2002):

1. *Reinforcing the correct response.* Direct and immediate reinforcement of correct responses calls attention to the correct response in a positive manner.

2. *Highlighting the desired response.* Color-coding, auditory cues, and picture prompts are ways to highlight the correct responses.
3. *Teaching responses to natural cues.* Students are taught to respond to cues in the environment rather than the teacher's prompts or instructions.

Motivation

Research comparing individuals with MR against their typically developing peers has found that individuals with MR have a greater tendency to approach a new situation with an expectation of failure. People who expect to fail tend to set lower goals, expend less effort in given tasks, and fail to attempt new tasks. As mentioned, these characteristics can create a condition called *learned helplessness.* Four strategies for promoting motivation, and thus success in learning situations, include the following (Henley, Ramsey, & Algozzine, 1999):

1. *Minimizing the errors.* Attempt to arrange the materials and instruction so the student will make only correct responses.
2. *Frequently using descriptive praise and reinforcement for correct responses and attempts.* Students who have experienced frequent failure need more reinforcement; descriptive praise is one of the most effective and easiest ways to accomplish this.
3. *Promoting positive attitudes in others* regarding students' abilities.
4. *Employing multilevel instruction* that allow teachers to individualize instruction within group instruction.

Self-Determination Skills

Individuals who are self-determined make their own decisions and are in control of their lives. Presenting students who have MR with choices and encouraging their skills in making choices will facilitate their attaining a satisfying quality of life. To be self-determined, students need to develop an understanding of who they are and learn to advocate for themselves (Wehmeyer, Lattin, Lapp-Rincker, & Agran, 2003). To become effective self-advocates, students must be able to communicate their needs and desires to others.

Teaching students self-determination and self-advocacy skills is a complicated process. Some guidelines to consider are the following:

1. Being mindful that control should reside with the student, involve students whenever possible in all decisions that have a direct impact on them.
2. Provide students with opportunities to make choices and to identify and voice their preferences.
3. Foster reciprocal friendships to enhance appropriate and meaningful interaction with peers and individuals within the community.
4. Use appropriate questioning techniques.

Altering Content

When a student cannot perform the tasks in the standard curriculum, even with modifications in instruction, materials, or responses, it may be appropriate to identify alternative, related tasks within the same content area or to alter the content. This does not mean "watering down" the content. Instead, a related skill is identified in the content area, enabling students to progress at their own rate and at the same time work with others. For example, in a language arts class, one student may be working on sentence structure while another is writing an essay.

When making adaptations in the academic content, teachers should refer to the assessment data collected on a given student to understand his or her level of academic functioning. Understanding the student's level allows for the development of effective parallel assignments that individualize instruction while simultaneously meeting the needs of the entire class. Science is a content area that lends itself well to multilevel instruction, as, for example, the teacher can assign tasks of differing levels of difficulty to science experiments.

In altering content for the student with MR in the general education classroom, the teacher might present material in a manner applicable to the child's personal life, incorporating familiar names and objects into instructional stories and math problems. Or the teacher could use personal photographs and objects with which the student can easily identify, to offer a context for the learner.

The teacher could extend this application of content to the student's experiences outside of school. Connections with the community expand the curriculum and at the secondary level also enhance the transition from the school-based experience to a permanent community-based environment.

Another strategy is to use games to reinforce the general curriculum. Bingo is a popular favorite, along with television game shows such as "Wheel of Fortune" and "Jeopardy." Combinations of color, photographs, and games can help the student understand complex concepts.

Worksheets continue to be used for students to practice newly learned materials, and also to evaluate students' progress and understanding. Although worksheets have limitations for students with MR, they can be adapted to connect course content to a practical context, thereby motivating the learner. For example, reading the newspaper in a social studies class can engage students' interest because it informs them about people and events in their own community.

Structuring the students into small, cooperative learning groups also can facilitate access to the content during elementary, middle, and secondary instruction. Students with MR can participate effectively in science labs, as mentioned, if the labs are modified to include real-life, hands-on explorations that are multisensory and organized so the students with MR are paired with more accomplished students from whom they can benefit from role modeling. Also, they might be encouraged to show their accomplishments in alternative ways.

Access to the General Education Curriculum and Settings

The reauthorization of IDEA in 2004 extends the principle of access to the general education curriculum for all students by combining the 1997 amendments to IDEA with the critical features of No Child Left Behind. This means that all children have to be included in state assessments and requires that children with disabilities be provided meaningful access to the curriculum and a standard against which to be measured annually. IDEA further specifies that a student's IEP has to include the program modifications or supports necessary to attain annual goals, to be involved in and progress in the general education curriculum, and to participate in all state and local assessments that measure the student's achievement.

In including students with MR in the standards-based curriculum, applied academic, community-referenced programs emphasize hands-on activities that students find meaningful. These kinds of curricula may be valuable for students with MR and also for typical students because the content is presented in a way that directly connects with the student's experience. This approach enhances generalization, offers ample opportunities for cooperative activities with typically developing peers, and prepares students for skills they will need as adults.

Likewise, applied curricula directly connect the standards-based content and the context in which that content is used in the real world. While giving students real-world connections, using authentic activities also allows the teacher to observe the students' actual level of skill acquisition. The student's performance provides a valuable tool for determining how the student is progressing in an applied curriculum. Understanding a student's appropriate skill level is critical in subsequent curriculum development, instruction, and, finally, local and statewide assessments.

Meeting the overall developmental needs of individuals with MR is not a simple task. Significant planning and effective instruction will be necessary to meet their needs while also addressing the concerns of the larger group of students. Schools that operate with an inclusive philosophy are better able to meet the needs of all students. Similarly, applied curriculum for a targeted group makes the learning relevant to the students—a critical need in today's schools. Making connections to post-school outcomes provides direct connections to community settings and furthers the transition and success for individuals after they complete their formal schooling.

Summary

Individuals with cognitive disabilities have unique needs that, if addressed appropriately, can result in a meaningful education with typically developing peers. Through academic and adaptive skill development, individuals with cognitive disabilities can and should be involved in their overall growth. Likewise, through self-determination and self-regulation these individuals can shape their future through choice-making, decision-making, problem-solving, and goal-setting activities. To achieve this success, educators must identify and include unique instructional, material, and response adaptations in the student's IEP and overall educational program. Finally, information and training of school personnel and peers are vital to enhance opportunities and necessary supports for students with MR to maximize their potential.

References

American Association on Mental Retardation (AAMR). (1992). *Mental retardation: Definition, classification, and systems of support.* Washington, DC: Author.

American Association on Mental Retardation. (AAMR). (2002). *Mental retardation: Definition, classification, and system support* (10th ed.). Washington, DC: Author.

American Association on Mental Retardation (AAMR). (2004). *Pollution, toxic chemicals, and mental retardation: A national blueprint for health promotion and disability prevention.* Washington, DC: Author.

Denning, C. B., Chamberlain, J. A., & Polloway, E. A. (2000). An evaluation of state guidelines for MR: Focus on definition and classification practices. *Education and Training in Mental Retardation and Developmental Disabilities, 35*(2), 226–232.

Doll, E. A. (1965). *Vineland Social Maturity Scale.* Circle Pines, MN: American Guidance Service.

Giangreco, M. (1998). *Quick-guides to inclusion 2.* Baltimore: Paul H. Brookes.

Grossman, H. J. (Ed.). (1983). *Manual on terminology in mental retardation* (1983 rev. ed.). Washington, DC: American Association on Mental Deficiency.

Hamill, L., & Everington, C. (2002). *Teaching students with moderate to severe disabilities: An applied approach for inclusive education.* Columbus, OH: Merrill.

Henley, M., Ramsey, R. S., & Algozzine, R. F. (1999). *Characteristics of and strategies for teaching students with mild disabilities* (3rd ed.). Boston: Allyn & Bacon.

Lambert, N., Nihira, K., & Leland, H. (1993). *Adaptive Behavior Scale–School* (2nd ed.). Austin, TX: Pro-Ed.

Luckasson, R., Coulter, D. L., Polloway, E. A., Reiss, S., Schalock, R. L., Snell, M. E., et al. (1992). *Mental retardation: Definition, classification, and systems of supports.* Washington, DC: American Association on Mental Retardation.

McCreight, B. (1997). *Recognizing and managing children with fetal alcohol syndrome/fetal alcohol effects: A guidebook.* Washington, DC: Child Welfare League of America.

Meyer, L. H., Cole, D. A., McQuarter, R., & Reichle, J. (1990). Validation of the Assessment of Social Competence (ASC) for children and young adults with developmental disabilities. *Journal of the Association for Persons with Severe Handicaps, 15,* 57–68.

Nunn, G. D., & Nunn, S. J. (1993). Locus of control and school performance: Some implications for teachers. *Education, 113,* 636–640.

Paris, S. G., & Winograd, P. (1990). Promoting metacognition and motivation of exceptional children. *Remedial and Special Education, 11*(6), 7–15.

Smith, J. D. (1997). Mental retardation as an educational construct: Time for a new shared view? *Education and Training in Mental Retardation and Developmental Disabilities, 32*(3), 167–173.

Taylor, H. G., Klein, N., Minich, N. M., & Hack, M. (2000). Middle-school-age outcomes in children with very low birthweight. *Child Development, 71,* 1495–1511.

Thorndike, R. L., Hagen, E. P., & Sattler, J. M. (1986). *Technical manual, Stanford–Binet intelligence scale* (4th ed.). Chicago: Riverside.

Wechsler, D. (1991). *Wechsler Intelligence Scale for Children* (3rd ed.). San Antonio, TX: Psychological Corp.

Wehmeyer, M. (1996, December). Student self-report measure of self-determination for students with cognitive disabilities. *Education and Training in Mental Retardation and Developmental Disabilities,* 282–293.

Wehmeyer, M., Agran, M., & Hughes, C. (1998). *Teaching self-determination to students with disabilities: Basic skills for successful transition.* Baltimore: Paul H. Brookes.

Wehmeyer, M. L., Lance, G. D., & Bashinski, S. (2002). Achieving access to the general curriculum for students with mental retardation: A curriculum decision-making model. *Education and Training in Mental Retardation and Developmental Disabilities, 37,* 223–234.

Wehmeyer, M. L., Palmer, S., Agran, M., Mithaug, D., & Martin, J. (2000). Promoting causal agency: The self-determined learning model of instruction. *Exceptional Children, 66,* 439–453.

Wehmeyer, M. L., Lattin, D., Lapp-Rincker, G., & Agran, M. (2003). Access to the general curriculum of middle-school students with mental retardation: An observational study. *Remedial and Special Education, 24,* 262–272.

Westling, D. L., & Fox, L. (2000). *Teaching students with severe disabilities* (2nd ed.). Upper Saddle River, NJ: Merrill.

U.S. Department of Education. (2003). *Twenty-fifth annual report to Congress on the implementation of the Individuals with Disabilities Education Act: Data analysis systems* (DANS). Washington, DC: U.S. Government Printing Office.

U.S. Office of Education. (1997). Implementation of Part B of the Education of the Handicapped Act. *Federal Register, 42*(163), 42474–42518.

Autism Spectrum Disorders

11

Brenda Smith Myles, Anastasia
Hubbard, Terri Cooper Swanson,
Ronda L. Schelvan, & Alison Simonelli

In this chapter we will overview *autism spectrum disorders*— definitions, characteristics, causes and prevalence, research-based interventions and practices, and strategies and supports that facilitate access to the general education curriculum and settings.

Definition

Autism spectrum disorders (ASD) are complex, lifelong pervasive developmental disorders, which include autism, Asperger Syndrome (AS), and pervasive developmental disorder–not otherwise specified (PDD–NOS). Individuals with ASD have difficulty with a triad of impairments that severely impact

CASE STUDIES

Rosemarie

Rosemarie, a child with autism, has limited verbal skills, which makes it difficult for her to communicate her wants and needs. For example, to request something, she will take an adult by the hand, walk him or her to an area in the classroom where she wants to go, and then wait for the adult to begin a series of "20 questions" (visually and verbally) to determine what she wants. Often Rosemarie will show her frustration by crying or grabbing the adult's hand. Or she will repeat the phrase "Do you want a cookie?", which the teacher has come to interpret as Rosemarie's way of requesting something not limited to food.

Changing activities can be stressful for Rosemarie, who might drop to the floor and whine instead of moving to a different location. During free-time, she positions herself away from the other students and invariably repeats the activity of connecting Legos™ in sets of three in red–yellow–blue order. When Rosemarie is not actively engaged in an activity, she frequently makes a quiet humming noise.

***

James

James, a middle-school student with Asperger Syndrome, began speaking at the same age as his peers, but he didn't use speech fluently until the age of 5. Although he has never been to England, his speech resembles that of an Englishman speaking formally and precisely. Academically he is at grade level or above, but his social skills are limited. Specifically, he lacks the skills to initiate, maintain, and terminate conversations. His special interest of vacuum cleaners borders on an obsession, which tends to discourage his peers from interacting with him because that is essentially the only subject about which he continually wants to talk.

(continued)

continuing case studies

In the hallway, between class periods, if someone asks James, "Do you have the time?" (meaning "What time is it?"), he interprets the question literally and responds, "No, I am on my way to Mr. Desmond's class and I cannot be late!" or, "Yes, I have the time. I have a new watch. It even has a calculator, a stopwatch, and an alarm."

At other times James "polices" the hallway, pointing out rule infractions and reminding other students of the behaviors appropriate during passing times or attempting to talk about his special interest, vacuum cleaners. Sometimes James becomes anxious and rocks back and forth in his chair or flaps his hands in front of his face. Interactions and behaviors such as these get James labeled as an "odd duck."

their ability to interact with others (Wing, 1996). According to the *Diagnostic and Statistical Manual of Mental Disorders,* 4th Edition, Text Revision (DSM-IV-TR) (American Psychiatric Association [APA], 2000), these impairments include

1. impairments in social interaction;
2. impairments in communication; and
3. restricted repetitive and stereotyped patterns of behavior, interests, and activities.

Characteristics

The term *autism* was first used by Leo Kanner (1943) in the 1940s to describe 11 children in his psychiatric practice who had difficulty relating to others and preferred to be left alone. He found that these children shared a variety of unique symptoms and behaviors that affected their ability to interact with others, including (a) problems relating to others; (b) difficulties with language and speech; (c) developmental delays; (d) difficulties with changes in the environment; and (e) stereotypic, repetitive actions and other peculiar motor movements.

In 1944, Hans Asperger published his seminal work on four boys from his clinical practice who also exhibited distinctive characteristics, which he labeled "autistischen psychopathen." Asperger identified the major traits within this disability as (a) social isolation and awkwardness, (b) self-stimulatory responses, (c) insistence on environmental sameness, (d) normal intellectual development, and (e) normal communication development. He reported that the individuals he studied did not have autism as defined by Kanner. The exceptionality Asperger reported on is currently termed *Asperger Syndrome.*

PDD–NOS is diagnosed when an individual has difficulty with the triad of impairments mentioned for ASD in general, but does not meet the diagnostic criteria for a specific pervasive developmental disorder, such as autism or Asperger Syndrome. For example, an individual may have the characteristics of Asperger Syndrome but with delayed language development. Because these characteristics do not meet all of the criteria for Asperger Syndrome, the diagnosis is PDD–NOS.

Note

PDD–NOS and Asperger Syndrome, as well as autism, fall on the autism spectrum but have distinctive characteristics unique to their disorder.

Individuals with autism, AS, and PDD–NOS are all on the autism spectrum and therefore are affected by the triad of impairments proposed by Wing (1996), but each has individual characteristics that must be treated accordingly. As a result, even though you may work with a number of students with ASD, each student will function at a different level and have differing skills.

The four major characteristics of ASD involve social interaction; communication; restricted repetitive and stereotyped patterns of behaviors, interests, and activities; and sensory–processing issues.

Social Interaction

Students with ASD have difficulty understanding nonverbal behaviors, such as eye-to-eye gaze, facial expressions, body posture, and gestures. For example, they may not be able to make eye contact during conversation or they may stare inappropriately. And because of their difficulty recognizing and interpreting others' body language and facial expressions, they might not notice gestures such as shaking one's head to indicate "yes" or "no." As a result, children with ASD may appear aloof or avoidant.

Individuals with ASD also have difficulty with developmentally appropriate spontaneous or make-believe play. For example, during free-time play, Rosemarie connects Legos in sets of three in red–yellow–blue order. She does this every day without variation. By comparison, a typical child may play with Legos daily but would likely build a different representative object and might participate in this activity with peers.

Communication

Students on the autism spectrum display a variety of difficulties with communication. Many people with autism have limited verbal ability, and often their language development does not meet typical milestones. Individuals with AS, conversely, have typical language development but may have difficulty initiating or maintaining a conversation with others (APA, 2000). Often when attempting to take part in a conversation, persons with ASD display idiosyncratic and repetitive language. In the case study, James speaks formally and precisely, which is not typical of teenagers in general. Rosemarie sits away from her peers during free-time because she does not know how to converse with other children.

Restricted Repetitive and Stereotyped Patterns of Behavior, Interests, and Activities

Students with ASD often display repetitive, restricted, and stereotyped interests, activities, and patterns of behavior. Many are significantly preoccupied with a special interest that is not typical of same-age peers either in focus or intensity. For example, a 13-year-old boy like James is preoccupied with vacuums, whereas a typical 13-year-old boy would more likely be interested in action movies, comics, and 13-year-old girls.

Some individuals with ASD have a need to repeat actions, such as going through a door twice before they can enter a room. Others, especially if they are excited or nervous, display repetitive and stereotyped motor movements, such as hand flapping, body rocking, repeated touching of specific objects, and repeating words or sentences.

Frequently, children with ASD appear to adhere inflexibly to nonfunctional routines or rituals. For example, they may have to finish an activity before they move to another one even though the teacher has told them to stop and the next activity is their favorite school subject. Rosemarie shows her frustration with change by dropping to the floor and whining instead of going on to the next activity. James reveals his strict adherence to rules by pointing out rule infractions to his peers.

Sensory Processing Issues

In addition to the triad of impairments, many individuals with ASD display a myriad sensory processing issues that negatively impact their daily lives (Asperger, 1944; Ermer & Dunn, 1998; Ghaziuddin, Butler, Tsai, & Ghaziuddin, 1994; Gillberg, 1989; Kanner, 1943; Myles et al., in press; Wing, 1991. Individuals with sensory processing issues can be either hypersensitive (more sensitive) or hyposensitive (less sensitive) to things in their environment. In the case studies, when Rosemarie is not actively engaged in an activity, she quietly hums, and when James becomes frustrated, he rocks in his chair and flaps his hands. Because of these sensory sensitivities, an individual with ASD might be easily distracted, have difficulties in focusing on what is most important and sitting still, and may even seem to be disobedient or defiant to avoid a sensory experience.

Causes and Prevalence

ASD is a complex disability whose cause is not fully understood. According to Gillberg and Coleman (2000), "Autism is an etiologically heterogeneous entity caused by many different diseases; it is a final common pathway syndrome based on the fact that there are only a finite number of ways for so young a brain to react to injury" (p. 301). Here we will briefly overview three areas commonly discussed as possible causes: genetics, brain differences, and environmental factors.

Genetics

Researchers focusing on the genetic factors in ASD suggest that no single genetic factor is responsible for causing ASD; rather, multiple genetic factors seem to intricately connect to form a wide range of developmental malfunctions. Although studies have shown that genes might be the cause of ASD, the degree of exhibited symptoms varies across families (Gillberg & Coleman, 2000). Evidence also suggests a high frequency of ASD among siblings, compared to other disabilities (Yirmiya, Shaked, & Erel, 2001).

Brain Structure Differences

Differences in brain structure in individuals with ASD have been investigated. For example, differences in the brains of individuals with ASD have been found in (a) the cerebellum, which serves motor coordination, balance, and cognitive function (Courchesne et al., 2001; Piven, Saliba, Bailey, & Arndt, 1997; Ryu et al., 1999); and (b) the frontal lobe and temporal lobes, which are involved in cognitive and social functions (Carper & Courchesne, 2000; Pierce & Courchesne, 2001; Piven, Amdt, Bailey, & Anderson, 1996). Researchers also have found fewer cells, higher cell density, or less volume in the brains of individuals with ASD than in neurotypical individuals (Aylward et al., 1999; Kemper & Bauman, 1998).

Environmental Factors

One of the most controversial factors as possible causes of autism is that of immunizations, particularly the measles, mumps, and rubella (MMR) vaccination (Wakefield et al., 1998). Studies refuting the autism–vaccination link have been reported (Dales, Hammer, & Smith, 2001; Stratton, Gable, Shetty, & McCormick, 2001).

As illustrated, ASD is a complex disability whose cause is not fully understood. Besides, the prevalence of ASD is not definitively known. The DSM-IV-TR (APA, 2000) reports a prevalence rate of autism of 5 per 10,000 while declining to report definitive data on AS in this regard. Others have reported prevalence rates ranging from 57 (Scott et al., 2002) to 108 (Kadesjo, Gillberg, & Hagberg, 1999) in 10,000.

Regarding gender, the DSM-IV-TR (APA, 2000) reported that autism is four to five times more likely to occur in males than in females, and that males are five times more likely than females to be diagnosed with AS. Kadesjo et al. (1999) reported a male-to-female ratio of 9:1 in ASD, and Scott et al. (2002) reported a 4:1 ratio.

Assessment and Evaluation for Special Education and Related Services

ASD is generally diagnosed using diagnostic criteria presented in DSM-IV-TR (2000), but the diagnosis is not simple because of the considerable variation in symptomology. Briefly, ASD is diagnosed through a multidisciplinary process consisting of (a) a review of developmental and family histories; (b) administration of diagnostic tests; (c) observations in multiple settings; and (d) assessment of skills, behavior, and other previously identified areas of challenge.

Assessment for program planning typically goes beyond administration of measures designed to identify characteristics of ASD. When attempting to develop a program plan for a student with ASD, the following areas are generally assessed:

1. Cognitive challenges
2. Adaptive behaviors
3. Sensory issues
4. Developmental concerns
5. Behavioral issues
6. Speech and language development
7. Preacademic/academic needs

Research-Based Interventions and Best Practices

Each child with ASD is different and presents with different needs. Therefore, we have to look at each student individually when selecting the best interventions, also taking into consideration the classroom environment. Several empirically based interventions may be used in the classroom to facilitate social interaction and promote independence for students with ASD (Heflin & Simpson, 1998). We will discuss the use of visual supports, priming, Social Stories™, structured teaching, and applied behavior analysis.

Visual Supports

Because students with ASD tend to process visual information more efficiently than auditory information, instructional and directional information should be provided in a visual format. Visual supports are an effective way to address some of the challenges that students with ASD face, such as processing time, anxiety, organization, and problem solving. These encompass a range of materials from visual schedules and graphic organizers to task cards and pictures or icons that facilitate making choices (Hodgdon, 1995; MacDuff, Krantz, & McClannahan, 1993; McClannahan, 1999). For example, Rosemarie uses a choice board to select free-time activities. Teachers, as well as the students themselves, can create visual supports to help with initiating and maintaining conversations, transitions, and communication between home and school.

Priming

Similar to Rosemarie, most students with ASD struggle with transitions and new situations, becoming anxious and confused. Priming, a strategy by which an adult previews activities prior to their occurrence, is designed to decrease the anxiety that accompanies change and new situations for students with ASD. A teacher, parent, paraprofessional, or peer can prime a student for an entire day or a single activity. In priming, the actual materials that are going to be used during the day/activity are presented to the student. This process could involve looking through a book, skimming through a test, or showing the student a sample of a final product. Priming is easy to use and involves a minimal time commitment (Bainbridge & Myles, 1999; Kamps et al., 1992; Myles & Adreon, 2001; Schreibman, Whalen, & Stahmer, 2000; Wilde, Koegel, & Koegel, 1992; Zanolli, Daggett, & Adams, 1996).

Social Stories™

Another means of helping students make sense of their environment—Social Stories™—addresses a major challenge primarily resulting from their communication and social skills deficits. A Social Story™ is an individualized text or story that describes a specific social situation from the student's perspective. The description may include where and why the situation occurs, how others feel or react, or what prompts their feelings and reactions (Bledsoe, Myles, & Simpson, 2003; Gray, 2000; Gray & Garand, 1993; Hagiwara & Myles, 1999; Kuttler, Myles, & Carlson, 1998; Lorimer et al., 2002; Norris & Dattilo, 1999; Swaggart et al., 1995).

The narrative may be used to describe an upcoming event, provide appropriate social cues, explain a social or an academic routine, or discuss how others will act and feel. For example, James reads a Social Story™ that provides him with topics of conversations and appropriate ways to initiate and terminate conversations. Social Stories™ may be exclusively written documents or may be paired with pictures, audiotapes, or videotapes (Swaggart et al., 1995). They may be created by educators and parents, often with student input.

Structured Teaching

The physical environment plays a role in the learning needs of all students, particularly students with ASD. The TEACCH (Treatment and Education of Autistic and related

Communication handicapped Children) program consists of a method called *structured teaching* (Schopler, Reichler, & Lansing, 1980). In structured teaching, the environment is modified to meet the needs of students (Schopler, Mesibov, & Hearsey, 1995) by (a) placing students away from distractions and high-traffic areas, (b) labeling areas and materials in the room, and (c) utilizing visual schedules.

Rosemarie's classroom environment is ordered using structured teaching. She has a visual schedule of daily events, classroom areas designated for certain activities, independent tasks that she completes following an activity book, and a visual timer indicating the beginning and ending of all tasks.

Applied Behavior Analysis Strategies

The applied behavior analysis (ABA) paradigm contains a number of strategies that have proven helpful to children and youth with ASD. Of these, the most commonly used are (a) incidental teaching, (b) prompting, and (c) discrete trial training (Leaf & McEachin, 1999; Lovaas, 2003).

Incidental Teaching

In incidental teaching, a teacher structures a lesson/learning objective around a child's interests and uses opportunities in the daily routine to promote learning and social interaction (Farmer, 1994; McGee, Morrier, & Daly, 1999). For example, when James began talking about vacuum cleaners during a math lesson on measurement, his teacher suggested that he measure several vacuum cleaner parts as part of his assignment.

Prompting

Prompting involves cueing a student to carry out a specific task. Prompts may be physical, in which a teacher helps a student with the task, or verbal, in which the teacher asks questions or makes statements pertaining to the task.

Another form of prompting is nonverbal. In this least invasive prompt, adults gesture or point to aid a student in completing a task (Maurice, Green, & Luce, 1996).

Discrete Trial Training

Discrete trial training involves breaking down tasks or lessons into easy steps to eliminate ambiguity and extraneous language in an effort to promote learning (Sundberg & Partington, 1998). A discrete trial consists of (a) presentation of a stimulus, such as a teacher instruction; (b) the child's response; and (c) the consequence, which often includes a child-preferred reinforcer (Lovaas, 2003).

Access to the General Education Curriculum and Settings

Students with ASD may be placed in a variety of classroom settings based on their strengths, challenges, and goals. Rosemarie, for instance, is in a self-contained program, whereas James spends time in both a resource room and the general education classroom.

For students with ASD placed in the general education classroom, a combination of (a) students' teams developing an understanding of ASD, (b) structuring the classroom setting, and (c) making modifications to academics should be used to help these students access the general education setting and curriculum, as illustrated below. Because Rosemarie spends most of her day in a self-contained class, her team has to create opportunities and activities for her to be included with her typically developing peers.

Understanding ASD

Many professionals and paraprofessionals who work with students with ASD do not adequately understand the characteristics and best practices associated with this diagnosis, particularly because ASD is a complex disorder yet to be fully understood. School teams, including administrators, must work together to ensure that opportunities are provided to strengthen team members' understanding of ASD.

The general educator who works with a student with ASD, for example, should understand ASD well enough to know that the student's behavior challenges communicate a message such as a lack of understanding, frustration, or a sensory challenge, as opposed to being purposefully cruel or disobedient, and that proactive measures such as priming must be developed to address them (Janzen, 2003; Myles & Adreon, 2001). The general educator also should realize the importance of teaching students with ASD the hidden curriculum, or the knowledge of daily life that most people learn naturally, but in which students with ASD often require direct instruction (Myles, Trautman, & Schelvan, 2004). For instance, many students with ASD do not understand what topics of conversation are acceptable to talk about with their fellow students but not with their teachers.

Perhaps most important, general educators who understand ASD will take the following three actions:

1. Embrace the strengths and challenges of a student with ASD, and build from them to help the student succeed in the general education classroom.
2. Communicate with the student with ASD when possible to try to learn his or her perspective on a situation or, alternately, aim to view the situation from the student's perspective when this level of communication is not possible.
3. Implement age-appropriate accommodations that provide the student with ASD the supports needed without drawing attention to him or her unnecessarily.

Structuring the Classroom Setting

Students with ASD in the general education setting benefit from implementation of visual supports, organizational strategies, and sensory accommodations. Actually, these practices should be considered for *all* students. In nearly every case, strategies that are put into place to aid students with ASD also benefit every other student in the classroom (Janzen, 2003).

Visual supports such as lists, schedules, and maps help students better understand their environment. Organizational strategies, which may include visual supports such as labels, color-coding, and the depiction of boundaries, aid students in understanding where to place and retrieve items, as well as where certain activities should take place (Hodgdon, 1995; Savner & Myles, 2000). Finally, sensory accommodations, such as providing a student with an item to fidget with to help him or her attend to instruction, help students with ASD recognize and accommodate their sensory needs (Brack, 2004; Dunn, 1999).

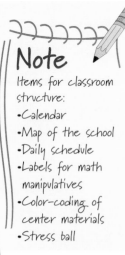

Note

Items for classroom structure:
- Calendar
- Map of the school
- Daily schedule
- Labels for math manipulatives
- Color-coding of center materials
- Stress ball

Making Academic Modifications

General educators should begin to help their students with ASD to access the general education curriculum by addressing the challenges these students have with executive function. This includes the ability to select and organize key information (Dawson & Guare, 2004). Graphic organizers provide an excellent means of recording and organizing information. Students with ASD must be taught how to use and create graphic organizers, and they particularly benefit from being provided with these tools (Dawson & Guare, 2004; Earles, Carlson, & Bock, 1998).

General educators must understand the severe fine- and visual-motor challenges associated with handwriting for individuals with ASD (Myles et al., 2003) and recognize that, although it may be beneficial for the student with ASD to be able to write legibly by hand, in most cases a person only has to be able to handwrite a legal signature. Present-day technology offers students with ASD many alternative options for recording information beyond their signature, such as typing it into computers, creating voice recordings, and making video recordings.

Additional possible accommodations include requiring students to handwrite only key words, using multiple-choice, fill-in-the blank, or true/false items for assessments, allowing students to highlight information/answers, and enabling them to work with a scribe (Myles & Adreon, 2001; Parette & Scherer, 2004). This understanding of handwriting and related accommodations should be applied to all facets of the learning process, including, but not limited to, the following: (a) taking notes; (b) doing homework; and (c) completing assessments such as assignments, projects, and tests (Smith, Alvarado, & Glennon, in press).

Summary

Autism spectrum disorders are complex, lifelong, pervasive developmental disabilities, the cause(s) and prevalence of which are yet to be fully understood. Potential causes relate to genetics, brain differences, and environmental factors. In general, ASD is characterized by impairments in the areas of social interaction, communication, and restricted repetitive and stereotyped patterns of behavior, interests, and activities. Research-based best practices in the ASD field include visual supports, priming, Social Stories™, structured teaching, and applied behavioral analysis-based strategies.

All interventions and strategies implemented with students who have ASD should be tailored to the individual's specific strengths and challenges. Further, helping students with ASD to access the general education curriculum entails a combination of understanding what it means to have ASD, from both the student's personal perspective and the teacher's understanding of the characteristics, structuring the classroom setting and making academic modifications.

References

American Psychiatric Association. (2000). *Diagnostic and statistical manual of mental disorders* (4th ed., text revision). Washington, DC: Author.

Asperger, H. (1944). Die 'autistischen psychopathen' im kindesalter. *Archiv fur Psychiatrie und Nervenkrankheiten, 117,* 76–136.

Aylward, E. H., Minshew, N. J., Goldstein, G., Honeycutt, N. A., Augustine, A. M., Yates, K. O., Barta, P. E., & Pearlson, G. D. (1999). MRI volumes of amygdala and hippocampus in non-mentally retarded autistic adolescents and adults. *Neurology, 53,* 2145–2150.

Bainbridge, N., & Myles, B. S. (1999). The use of priming to introduce toilet training to a child with autism. *Focus on Autism and Other Developmental Disabilities, 14,* 106–109.

Brack, J. C. (2004). *Learn to move ... Move to learn: Sensorimotor early childhood activity themes.* Shawnee Mission, KS: Autism Asperger Publishing.

Bledsoe, R., Myles, B. S., & Simpson, R. L. (2003). Use of a social story intervention to improve mealtime skills of an adolescent with Asperger Syndrome. *Autism: An International Journal of Research and Practice, 7,* 289–295.

Carper, R. A., & Courchesne, E. (2000). Inverse correlation between frontal lobe and cerebellum sizes in children with autism. *Brain, 123,* 836–844.

Courchesne, E., Karns, C. M., Davis, H. R., Ziccardi, R., Carper, R. A., Tigue, Z. D., Chisum, H. J., Moses, P., Pierce, K., Lord, C., Lincoln, A. J., Pizzo, S., Schreibman, L., Haas, R. H., Akshoomoff, N. A., & Courchesne, R. Y. (2001). Unusual brain growth patterns in early life in patients with autistic disorder: An MRI study. *Neurology, 57,* 245–254.

Dales, L., Hammer, S. J., & Smith, N. J. (2001). Time trends in autism and in MMR immunization coverage in California. *Journal of the American Medical Association, 285,* 1183–1185.

Dawson, P., & Guare, R. (2004). *Executive skills in children and adolescents A practical guide and intervention.* New York: Guilford Press.

Dunn, W. (1999). *The Sensory Profile.* San Antonio, TX: Psychological Corp.

Earles, T., Carlson, J. K., & Bock, S. J. (1998). Instructional strategies to facilitate successful learning outcomes for students with autism. In R. L. Simpson & B. S. Myles (Eds.), *Educating children and youth with autism: Strategies for effective practice* (pp. 55–112). Austin, TX: Pro-Ed.

Ermer, J., & Dunn, W. (1998). The sensory profile: A discriminant analysis of children with and without disabilities. *American Journal of Occupational Therapy, 52,* 283–289.

Farmer, V. D. (1994). Increasing requests by adults with developmental disabilities using incidental teaching by peers. *Journal of Applied Behavior Analysis, 27,* 533–544.

Ghaziuddin, M., Butler, E., Tsai, L., & Ghaziuddin, N. (1994). Is clumsiness a marker for Asperger Syndrome? *Journal of Intellectual Disability Research, 38,* 519–527.

Gillberg, C. (1989). Asperger Syndrome in 23 Swedish children. *Developmental Medicine and Child Neurology, 31,* 520–531.

Gillberg, C., & Coleman, M. (2000). *The biology of the autistic syndromes* (3d ed.). London: Mac Keith Press.

Gray, C. (2000). *Writing social stories with Carol Gray.* Arlington, TX: Future Horizons.

Gray, C. A., & Garand, J. D. (1993). Social stories: Improving responses of students with autism with accurate social information. *Focus on Autistic Behavior, 8,* 1–10.

Hagiwara, T., & Myles, B.S. (1999). A multimedia social story intervention: Teaching skills to children with autism. *Focus on Autism and Other Developmental Disabilities, 14,* 82–95.

Heflin, L., & Simpson, R. L. (1998). Interventions for children and youth with autism: Prudent choices in a world of exaggerated claims and empty promises. Part I: Intervention and treatment option review. *Focus on Autism and Other Development Disabilities, 13,* 194–211.

Hodgdon, L. A. (1995). *Visual strategies for improving communication: Practical supports for school and home.* Troy, MI: Quirk Roberts.

Janzen, J. (2003). *Understanding the nature of autism: A guide to the autism spectrum disorders* (2d ed.). San Antonio, TX: Therapy Skills Builders.

Kadesjo, B., Gillberg, C., & Hagberg, B. (1999). Brief report: Autism and Asperger Syndrome in seven-year-old children: A total population study. *Journal of Autism and Developmental Disorders, 29,* 327–331.

Kamps, D. M., Leonard, B. R., Vernon, S., Dugan, E. P., & Delquadri, J. C. (1992). Teaching social skills to students with autism to increase peer interactions in an integrated first grade classroom. *Journal of Applied Behavior Analysis, 25,* 281–288.

Kanner, L. (1943). Autistic disturbances of affective contact. *American Journal of Psychiatry, 103,* 242–246.

Kemper, T. L., & Bauman, M. (1998). Neuropathology of infantile autism. *Journal of Neuropathology and Experimental Neurology, 57,* 645–652.

Kuttler, S., Myles, B.S., & Carlson, J.K. (1998). The use of social stories to reduce precursors to tantrum behavior in a student with autism. *Focus on Autistic Behavior, 13,* 176–182.

Leaf, R., & McEachin, J. (1999). *A work in progress: Behavior management curriculum for intensive behavioral treatment of autism.* New York: DRL Books.

Lorimer, P. A., Simpson, R., Myles, B. S., & Ganz, J. (2002). The use of social stories as a preventative behavioral intervention in a home setting with a child with autism. *Journal of Positive Behavioral Interventions, 4,* 53–60.

Lovaas, O. I. (2003). *Teaching individuals with developmental delays: Basic intervention techniques.* Austin, TX: Pro-Ed.

MacDuff, G., Krantz, P., & McClannahan, L. (1993). Teaching children with autism to use photographic activity schedules: Maintenance and generalization of complex response chains. *Journal of Applied Behavior Analysis, 26,* 89–97.

McClannahan, L. E. (1999). *Activity schedules for children with autism: Teaching independent behavior.* Bethesda, MD: Woodbine House.

McGee, G. G., Morrier, J. J., & Daly, T. (1999) An incidental teaching approach to early intervention for toddlers with autism. *Journal of the Association for Persons with Severe Handicaps, 24,* 133–146.

Maurice, C., Green, G., & Luce, S. C. (1996). *Behavior intervention for young children with autism: A manual for parents and professionals.* Austin, TX: Pro-Ed.

Myles, B. S., & Adreon, D. (2001). *Asperger Syndrome and adolescence: Practical solutions for school success.* Shawnee Mission, KS: Autism Asperger Publishing.

Myles, B.S., Hagiwara, T., Dunn, W., Rinner, L., Reese, M., Huggins, A., et al. (in press). Sensory processing issues in children with Asperger Syndrome and autism. *Education and Training in Developmental Disabilities.*

Myles, B. S., Huggins, A., Rome–Lake, M., Hagiwara, T., Barnhill, G. P., & Griswold, D. E. (2003). Written language profile of children and youth with Asperger Syndrome. *Education and Training in Developmental Disabilities, 38*(4), 362–370.

Myles, B. S., Trautman, M. L., & Schelvan, M. L. (2004). *The hidden curriculum: Practical solutions for understanding unstated rules in social situations.* Shawnee Mission, KS: Autism Asperger Publishing.

Norris, C., & Dattilo, J. (1999). Evaluating effects of a social story intervention on a young girl with autism. *Focus on Autism and Other Developmental Disabilities, 14,* 180–186.

Parette, P., & Scherer, M. (2004). Assistive technology use and stigma. *Education and Training in Developmental Disabilities, 39,* 217–226.

Pierce, K., & Courchesne, E. (2001). Evidence for a cerebellar role in reduced exploration and stereotyped behavior in autism. *Biological Psychiatry, 49,* 655–664.

Piven, J., Amdt, S., Bailey, J., & Anderson, N. (1996). Regional brain enlargement in autism: Magnetic resonance imaging study. *Journal of American Academy of Child and Adolescent Psychiatry, 35,* 530–536.

Piven, J., Saliba, K., Bailey, J., & Arndt, S. (1997). An MRI study of autism: The cerebellum revisited. *Neurology, 49,* 546–551.

Ryu, Y. H., Lee, J. D., Yoon, P. H., Kim, D. I., Lee, H. B., & Shin, Y. J. (1999). Perfusion impairments in infantile autism on technetium-99m ethyl cysteinate dimmer brain single-photon emission tomography: Comparison with findings on magnetic resonance imaging. *European Journal of Nuclear Medicine, 26,* 253–259.

Savner, J. L., & Myles, B. S. (2000). *Making visual supports work in the home and community for individuals with autism and Asperger Syndrome.* Shawnee Mission, KS: Autism Asperger Publishing.

Schopler, E., Mesibov, G. B., & Hearsey, K. (1995). Structured teaching in the TEACCH system. In E. Schopler & G. B. Mesibov (Eds.), *Learning and cognition in autism* (pp. 243–267). New York: Plenum.

Schopler, E., Reichler, R. J., & Lansing, M. (1980). *Individualized assessment and treatment for autistic and developmentally disabled children. Volume II: Teaching strategies for parents and professionals.* Baltimore: University Park Press.

Schreibman, L., Whalen, C., & Stahmer, A. (2000). The use of video priming to reduce disruptive transition behavior in children with autism. *Journal of Positive Behavior Interventions, 2*(1), 3–11.

Scott, F. J., Baron–Cohen, S., Bolton, P., & Brayne, C. (2002). Brief report: Prevalence of autism spectrum conditions in children aged 5–11 years in Cambridgeshire, UK. *Autism, 6,* 231–237.

Smith, S.J., Alvarado, D., & Glennon, G. (in press). Assistive technology. In B. S. Myles (Ed.), *Asperger Syndrome.* Thousand Oaks, CA: Corwin Press.

Stratton, K., Gable, A., Shetty, P., & McCormick, R. (Eds.). (2001). *Immunization safety review: Measles–mumps–rubella vaccine and autism.* Washington, DC: National Academy Press.

Sundberg, M. L., & Partington, J. W. (1998). *Teaching language to children with autism and other developmental disabilities.* Pleasant Hill, CA: Behavior Analysts.

Swaggart, B. L., Gagnon, E., Bock, S. J., Earles, T. L., Quinn, C., Myles, B. S., et al. (1995). Using social stories to teach social and behavioral skills to children with autism. *Focus on Autistic Behavior, 10,* 1–16.

Wakefield, A. J., Murch, S. H., Anthony, A., Linnell, J., Casson, D. M., Malik, M., et al. (1988). Ileal-lymphoid-nodular hyperplasia, non-specific colitis, and pervasive developmental disorder in children. *Lancet, 351,* 637–641.

Wilde, L. D., Koegel, L. K., & Koegel, R. L. (1992). *Increasing success in school through priming: A training manual.* Santa Barbara: University of California.

Wing, L. (1996). *The autistic spectrum: A guide for parents and professionals.* London: Constable and Co.

Yirmiya, N., Shaked, M., & Erel, O. (2001). Comparison of siblings of individuals with autism and siblings of individuals with other diagnoses: An empirical summary. In E. Schopler, N. Yirmiya, & C. Shulman (Eds.), *The research basis for autism intervention* (pp. 59–73). New York: Kluwer Academic/Plenum Publishers.

Zanolli, K., Daggett, J., & Adams, R. (1996). Teaching preschool age autistic children to make spontaneous initiations to peers using priming. *Journal of Autism and Developmental Disorders, 26*(4), 407–422.

Hearing loss

12

Sally Roberts

The heterogeneity of children with hearing loss is likely the most complex factor affecting how they learn and, subsequently, how they are taught. They differ in type and severity of hearing loss, mode of communication, experiences, intelligence, whether they have other disabilities, and in many other ways. If teachers have an image of these differences, they will be able to better adapt their instruction to maximize each child's opportunity for learning. In a world controlled by sound and spoken language, it requires the use of a variety of methods, materials, and strategies to ensure that all children with hearing loss will be able to have a successful and meaningful educational experience. This chapter is designed to help teachers form an image of what it might be like to teach a child with hearing loss. Ideally, this image will be broad enough to reflect the many differences that these children will bring to the classroom.

The Hearing Process

Before we can understand hearing loss, we must know what is involved in hearing—how sound is processed. The hearing process is called *audition*. When we hear sounds, we are really interpreting patterns in the movement (vibration) of air molecules. Sounds are described in terms of their *pitch* or *frequency* (very low to very high) and *intensity*

CASE STUDY: NATHAN

Thirteen-year-old Nathan is in the eighth grade. Nathan and his dad both are profoundly deaf. His mother and sister have full hearing and are fluent in American Sign Language (ASL). This is Nathan's first language, and English is his second language. Although Nathan is above grade level in his sign language skills, his reading and writing skills are at about a fourth-grade level. He attends a public middle school and is mainstreamed for math, science, and history classes. He goes to a resource room for his English class and for remedial reading support from an itinerant deaf educator. Nathan has an educational interpreter for his general education classes but not for the school swim team or meets in which he participates enthusiastically.

Nathan is a bright student who tries hard in school, but he is becoming increasingly frustrated with his reading and writing and is starting to show a lack of motivation in those areas. Noting that Nathan's classes are getting more difficult and his improvement in reading and writing is slowing, his parents are afraid that he will fall further and further behind. Therefore, his IEP team is planning to provide Nathan with more support. He has been assessed formally on an annual basis and has taken the state achievement tests in reading and math every year since the third grade. He took the state writing exam in fifth grade and will be taking it again this year.

or loudness (very soft to very loud). Frequency is measured in *hertz* (Hz), and loudness is measured in *decibels* (dB) (named in honor of Alexander Graham Bell).

Speech has a mix of high and low frequencies and soft and loud sounds. Most of the sounds we hear every day are in the 250 to 6,000 Hz range. Conversational speech is usually at about 45 dB to 50 dB. You have normal hearing if you can hear frequencies between 20 and 20,000 Hz and 0 and 120 dB. A whisper is about 20 dB, and a shout can be as loud at 70 dB. Vowel sounds such "o" have low frequencies, and consonants such as "f" and "sh" have higher frequencies. An individual who cannot hear high-frequency sounds will have a hard time understanding speech. Figure 12.1 gives the frequency of familiar sounds.

Hearing Mechanism

To understand what can go wrong with the hearing process, we have to understand the anatomy of the hearing mechanism, which is divided into the outer, middle, and inner ears.

Outer Ear

The outer ear consists of the *auricle* or *pinna* and the *ear canal*. Its purpose is to collect sound waves and funnel them to the *tympanic membrane*, or eardrum. The vibrating air molecules hit the eardrum and cause it to vibrate.

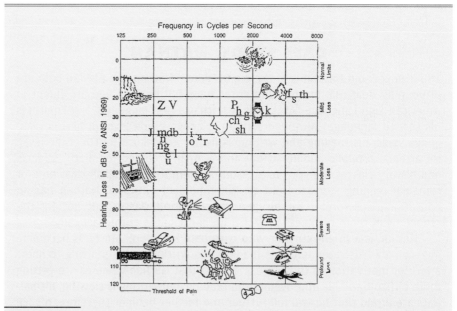

From *Hearing in children* (5th ed.), by J. L. Northern & M. P. Downs (Philadelphia: Lippincott, Williams, & Wilkins, 2002), p. 18. Used by permission.

FIGURE 12.1
Standard Audiogram Showing Frequency of Familiar Sounds

Middle Ear

Located behind the eardrum, the middle ear consists of three little bones, the *malleus*, the *incus*, and the *stapes*. Because of their shape, you may know them as the hammer, anvil, and stirrup, respectively. In combination these bones are called the *ossicular chain*. The vibration of the eardrum transfers energy to the ossicular chain, causing the bones to vibrate and transmit the sound through the middle ear cavity.

Also found in the middle ear is the *eustachian tube*, which extends from the throat into the middle ear cavity. Its primary purpose is to equalize the air pressure on the eardrum when we swallow or yawn. This is why our ears feel plugged when an airplane is landing and yawning helps "open them up."

Note
Ossicular chain:
• Malleus (hammer)
• Incus (anvil)
• Stapes (stirrup)

Inner Ear

The inner ear contains the *cochlea*, a snail-shaped bony structure located just beyond the *oval window*, the membrane that separates the middle and the inner ear. The cochlea houses the *organ of Corti*—the actual organ of hearing—and the *vestibular mechanism*, or semicircular canals, the sensory organ of balance. The cochlea has multiple rows of delicate hair cells that are connected to the auditory nerve. These hair cells are actually sensory receptors for the auditory nerve.

The cochlea is arranged tonotopically, meaning that the hair cells closest to the oval window respond to high-frequency sounds and those at the top (if the cochlea were unrolled) are more sensitive to sounds in the lower frequencies. When the middle ear bones vibrate and transfer the sound waves to the oval window, its vibration moves the fluid in the cochlea across the hair cells, generating impulses to the nerve.

Control of balance is the role of the other structure in the inner ear, the *vestibular mechanism* or semicircular canals. These canals are filled with the same fluid found in the cochlea, and this fluid is highly sensitive to head movements. The vestibular mechanism helps our body maintain its equilibrium and is highly sensitive to motion and gravity.

Figure 12.2 depicts the anatomy of the ear, with a cross-section of the cochlea.

From the inner ear, sound is transported by way of the auditory (eighth) nerve to the temporal lobe of the brain. The route from the ear to the cochlea passes through at least four neural relay stations on its way to the brain. It may help to think of this transfer of sound to the brain as a train trip with stops at several stations along the route. Once sound reaches the auditory cortex, it can be associated with other sensory information and memory, allowing us to perceive and integrate what we have heard (Batshaw, 2002).

Definitions

Normal hearing requires that each of the parts of the ear functions properly. The location and nature of any problem will determine the degree and type of hearing loss. Two terms, *deaf* and *hard of hearing*, are most often used to describe hearing loss based on its severity. *Unilateral* refers to a loss in one ear, and *bilateral* denotes a loss in both ears.

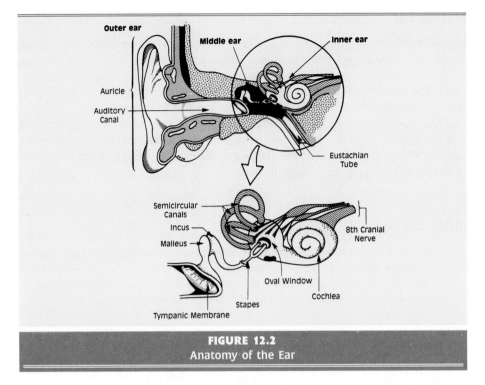

FIGURE 12.2
Anatomy of the Ear

Deaf

The term *deaf* is often overused to describe *all* individuals with hearing loss. The Individuals with Disabilities Education Act (IDEA) defines deafness as

> *a hearing impairment which is so severe that the child is impaired in processing linguistic information through hearing, with or without amplification, which adversely affects educational performance. (300.7(c)5)*

With regard to severity or level of hearing, individuals are considered deaf if they have a hearing loss of 70–90 dB or greater and cannot use their hearing, even with amplification, as their primary means for developing language.

Hard of Hearing

Someone with normal hearing can hear sounds between 0 and 120 dB of loudness. Sounds softer than 0 are too soft to hear and sounds louder than 120 dB cause pain. By contrast, the term *hard of hearing* applies to an individual with a hearing loss in the 20–70 dB range who benefits from amplification and communicates primarily through speaking. That means these individuals cannot hear sounds that are softer than 20 dB but they can hear sounds that are louder than 70 dB. Individuals are considered deaf if sounds must be at least 70 to 90 dB or greater before they can hear them.

Table 12.1 gives a classification system showing the ranges of hearing loss based on severity. For example, someone with a 26 dB loss (sound must be at least 26 dB of loudness before it can be heard) is considered to have a mild hearing loss. Because the range for a mild loss is between 26 dB and 40 dB, anyone with a loss within that range

TABLE 12.1		
Classification of Hearing Loss Levels		
Hearing Loss in Decibels (dB)	**Classification**	**Effect on Ability to Understand Speech**
0 – 15	Normal hearing	None
15 – 25	Slight hearing loss	Minimal difficulty with soft speech
26 – 40	Mild hearing loss	Difficulty with soft speech
41 – 55	Moderate hearing loss	Frequent difficulty with normal speech
56 – 70	Moderate-to-severe hearing loss	Occasional difficulty with loud speech
71 – 90	Severe hearing loss	Frequent difficulty with loud speech
> 90	Profound hearing loss	Near total or total loss of hearing

has a mild loss even though a 40 dB loss is greater than the 26 dB loss. The table also shows the ability to understand speech based on severity of the loss.

Although some people use the term *hearing impaired* to describe a child with a hearing loss, special educators prefer to use "person-first" language. Thus, they would say "the child who is deaf" when referring to students with hearing loss. Others (see the later discussion of the Deaf community) think the term *impaired* has negative connotations and prefer to say *deaf child* (Batshaw, 2002). They are particularly resistant to the term *hearing impaired* because this implies a condition in need of correction or repair. They do not view themselves as needing to be "fixed" or "cured" but, rather, as a distinct cultural and linguistic group (Lane, Hoffmeister, & Bahan, 1996).

Age of Onset

Prelingual deafness means that the hearing loss happened before the child learned language (before age 2). A *postlingual* loss means that it occurred sometime after age 2. Individuals who learned language before their hearing loss have an aural/oral communication problem, not a language problem. Depending on the age when hearing is lost, someone with postlingual deafness has reading and writing skills similar to those of a person who can hear but has a slight delay in learning new language idioms.

Site of Hearing Loss

A hearing loss is also defined based on the location of the problem along the auditory pathway.

There are two primary types of hearing loss, conductive and sensorineural. A *conductive hearing loss* results from a problem in the outer or middle ear, the part of the ear that "conducts sound" to the inner ear. A *sensorineural hearing loss* can occur as a result of damage to the cochlea and/or the auditory nerve. Although a conductive loss can be improved by amplification or medical intervention, a sensorineural loss cannot be treated medically. A *mixed hearing loss* involves both a conductive and a sensorineural problem.

Some individuals have a *central auditory processing disorder*. Although their outer, middle, and inner ear remain intact, there is some problem in the pathway that transmits the signal to the brain. Remember the train trip analogy? Something is happening at one of the various stations on the way to the designation. Consequently, a central auditory processing disorder is not a loss of the ability to hear but, instead, a loss in the ability to process the auditory message.

When we look at Nathan's hearing in terms of each of the classifications, we find that he is considered deaf because he has a profound hearing loss. This means that his loss is 90 dB or greater in both ears. It is a sensorineural loss because the problem is located in his cochlea. In your classrooms you will encounter students with all types of hearing loss—children who are deaf like Nathan and children who are hard of hearing, children with conductive loss and those whose loss is sensorineural.

Characteristics of Hearing Loss

The primary impact of hearing loss on the academic achievement of children relates to the development of spoken language. Research has shown that the IQ range of children who are deaf or hard of hearing is much the same as it is in the general population (Moores, 2001). Thus, their problems academically are probably related more to difficulties with speaking, reading and writing than to their overall cognitive abilities.

Speech and English Language Development

Children are born with an innate ability and desire to learn to communicate. Typical language acquisition for hearing children follows a predetermined sequence that is similar across most languages and cultures. Children usually become native speakers of at least one language just by being exposed to it; no direct instruction is needed. The language development of children who are born deaf or hard of hearing also follows this predetermined sequence; however, they have delays ranging from mild to severe. These delays are a direct result of the inability to process auditory information or lack of exposure to a visually encoded language (Spencer & Meadow–Orlans, 1996). As a consequence, the most debilitating aspect of deafness is not the loss of hearing but, rather, the lack of language that results from receiving an insufficient auditory or visual message.

Delays in speech and language development vary depending on the level of hearing loss and the amount of input the child receives. Even the speech of children with a moderate loss may be affected. Although they may be able to hear speech, they may miss crucial information. If a child is born deaf, most speech will be inaudible even with amplification. Thus, speech reception will be significantly impaired unless the child is an exceptional *speechreader*, and expressive speech will most likely show problems with articulation, voice quality, and tone, making the child difficult to understand.

Academic Achievement

The academic achievement of children with hearing loss depends on their characteristics as well as the characteristics of their parents, teachers, and school programs. We know that these children have specific educational challenges in the areas of reading and writing (Easterbrooks & Baker, 2002). In our case example, Nathan's primary difficulties academically are in these two areas. Communication and education are strongly linked because educational curricula are language based.

Academically, children who are hard of hearing are still among the least appropriately served. The issues and challenges of the group of students with mild and moderate hearing losses are complex and have severe implications for their academic and social success. Their needs are often overlooked and misunderstood. Because these children can hear some things, they may not be immediately referred for services. Accumulated years of misunderstanding what they are hearing can result in grade retention and a gap between their ability and their academic achievement. They also are at risk socially because they may miss the small social nuances in interactions in the school's hallways, cafeterias, and gyms (Easterbrooks & Baker, 2002).

Social and Emotional Development

Congenital deafness is a low-incidence disability; it affects a small percentage of the population. This means that most of the people with whom they will interact will be hearing—including most of their families. According to Stuart, Harrison, and Simpson (1991),

> deafness per se does not determine the emotional and social development of the individual. Rather, it is the attitudes of hearing people that cause irreparable harm to the personality of the deaf person. (p. 124)

Consequently, the social and emotional development of children with hearing loss is affected primarily by two factors: (a) the communication barriers that result from the child's difficulty acquiring oral language, and (b) the preconceived ideas of deafness held by the hearing world. The average hearing person will have difficulty communicating with those who have hearing loss, and deaf children soon become aware of these communication problems as they try to make their wants and needs known. This situation is unsettling for both parties. Deaf children easily feel a sense of isolation and loneliness that gets worse as they realize that others might not be comfortable interacting with them (Scheetz, 2004). They may even begin to see themselves through the eyes of society and develop a feeling of being outsiders in a hearing world.

The Deaf Community and Culture

Deaf people often differentiate between uppercase *Deaf* and lowercase *deaf.* Capital *D Deaf* refers to those who are affiliated with the Deaf community and Deaf culture, and lowercase *deaf* refers to the medical and audiological descriptions of having a hearing loss (Andrews, Leigh, & Weiner, 2004).

Nathan is a member of the *Deaf community*, which represents a diverse group in terms of demographic, audiologic, linguistic, political, and social factors. It encompasses deaf children of hearing and deaf parents, extended family members, individuals who work with people who have hearing loss, and even those who are hard of hearing or "oral deaf" (Singleton & Tittle, 2000). Because Nathan's dad is deaf and uses American Sign Language (ASL), he is considered part of the Deaf community. Even though Nathan's mother and sister both have full hearing, they also are considered members of the Deaf community because they are able to use the language of the community and can interact socially with its members.

Note

Nathan's sister is called a CODA, a term that stands for "children of deaf adults." The term KODA ("kids of deaf adults") is sometimes used for children under age 18. Nathan's sister probably identifies with both the Deaf community and the hearing community.

Deaf culture refers to individuals in the Deaf community who use American Sign Language and share beliefs, values, customs, and experiences. The terminology used by the medical and deaf communities to label individuals with hearing loss reflects two different perspectives. Unless the child with a hearing loss comes from a deaf family, Deaf culture is taught mostly through socialization with their peers. This can start as early as elementary school or as late as adulthood. For the mainstreamed child in the public school, Deaf culture is transmitted through membership in Deaf organizations within the Deaf community, reading histories of famous Deaf people, and exposure to Deaf performing arts (drama and mime) and Deaf artwork. It is recommended that children who are deaf and hard of hearing be exposed to Deaf peers and adults and to Deaf culture.

Prevalence and Causes

Compared to other groups of children with disabilities in our schools, students with hearing loss make up a relatively small group. The U.S. Department of Education (2002) reported that 70,767 children and youth with hearing loss between the ages of 6 and 21 received some type of special services in our public schools in the year 2000–01. Preschool programs (ages 3 to 5) served another 8,395 children. These numbers make up about 1.4% of the total numbers of children served.

Determining the cause of hearing loss is often complicated by a delay in diagnosis, and many causes remain unknown. When a hearing loss is present at birth, it is called a *congenital* loss regardless of the cause. Hearing losses that occur after birth are termed *acquired*. Among the factors that can result in hearing loss are hereditary or genetic factors, an event or injury during pregnancy (prenatal), or injury at or just following birth. Some factors that can cause an acquired hearing loss are trauma, disease, and exposure to excessive noise.

Genetic Causes

Nathan's hearing loss is a result of hereditary deafness. His father is deaf, as are several members of his extended family. Hereditary loss occurs in approximately 1 in 2,000 children. Most genetic hearing loss (80%) is a result of an inherited autosomal recessive gene and is not associated with any type of syndrome. The more than 70 documented inherited syndromes associated with deafness can result in either a conductive, a sensorineural, or a mixed loss (Batshaw, 2002).

Prenatal Factors

Exposure to viruses, bacteria, and other toxins prior to or immediately following birth can result in a hearing loss. During delivery or in the newborn period, a number of complications, such as lack of oxygen (hypoxia), can damage the hearing mechanism, particularly the cochlea.

The major cause of congenital deafness is infection that occurs during pregnancy or soon after the baby is born. Prior to the development of a vaccine, rubella (one of the forms of measles) was one of the leading causes of deafness. The rubella epidemic in the United States in 1964–65 resulted in a huge increase in the incidence of deafness. After the vaccine became available, the incidence decreased considerably. Other prenatal infections that can cause hearing loss include toxoplasmosis, herpes virus, syphilis, and cytomegalovirus (CMV). The most prevalent of these infections is CMV, with an incidence of 5–25 per 1,000 births (Batshaw, 2002). This viral infection is spread through close contact with an individual who is shedding the virus through body fluids. No vaccine is available for protection against CMV, but care should be taken by hand washing and by avoiding contact with individuals who have the disease.

Toxoplasmosis, characterized by jaundice and anemia, results in hearing loss in about 15% of infants born to mothers who have this disease. Pregnant woman should avoid contact with cat feces or raw and undercooked meat, which may be contaminated with this virus. The herpes virus is transferred to the infant as the infant passes through the birth canal. Mothers with genital herpes disease most often deliver by cesarean section to avoid transferring the infection to their infant (National Center on Birth Defects and Developmental Disabilities, 2004).

Premature infants, particularly those weighing less than 1,500 grams (3⅓ pounds), have an increased susceptibility to hypoxia, hyperbilirubinemia, and intracranial hemorrhage, all of which have been associated with sensorineural hearing loss. Other factors associated with congenital sensorineural hearing loss are Rh incompatibility between mother and child and the use of ototoxic drugs.

Rh incompatibility was a much more common cause of hearing loss before the development of anti-Rh gamma globulin (RhoGAM) in 1968. Injection of RhoGAM in the first 72 hours following delivery of her first child will keep the mother from producing antibodies that could harm her later babies. Certain antibiotics are considered ototoxic and can destroy the outer row of hair cells in the cochlea. Physicians, however, can monitor drug levels in the blood to prevent the drugs from reaching toxic levels.

Infections in Infancy and Childhood

Infections in infancy and childhood can lead to a sensorineural hearing loss. For example, bacterial meningitis poses a 10% risk of hearing loss from damage to the cochlea. Unilateral hearing losses have also been seen following mumps, and a bilateral loss can occur as a result of chickenpox and measles.

The most common cause of hearing loss in young children is middle ear disease or acute otitis media (ear infection), in which fluid collects in the middle ear behind the eardrum. This disease can go undiagnosed and, though it does not result in a permanent conductive hearing loss, it can cause hearing to fluctuate in young children during the crucial time they are acquiring speech and language in the first two years of life. In fact, 75%–90% of all young children have at least one ear infection before they are 2 years old.

A blow to the skull can cause trauma to the cochlea that may result in a sensorineural hearing loss. It also can damage the middle ear bones, resulting in a conductive loss. Mild to moderate sensorineural hearing loss can occur from being around excessive noise such as firecrackers and air guns. Transient or permanent sensorineural loss also may result from exposure to very loud sound over time. Using headphones at high intensity levels or attending rock concerts where noise levels can reach 100–110 dB may be damaging. A sustained exposure to sound levels of 90 dB or greater is potentially harmful to the cochlea and should be avoided (Batshaw, 2002).

Assessment and Evaluation for Special Education and Related Services ▪ ▪ ▪ ▪ ▪

Assessment is done initially for diagnostic purposes. Depending on the results, the child is evaluated to determine eligibility for special education and related services and placement.

Diagnostic Assessment

The diagnosis of a hearing loss is made by a combination of professionals, including the child's physician, an *otologist* (a physician who specializes in diseases of the ear), and an *audiologist*. Audiologists have special training in testing and measuring hearing and are able to evaluate the hearing of a child at any age. Audiologists also have the necessary skills to participate in the child's rehabilitation and treatment and to prescribe and evaluate the effectiveness of hearing aids and cochlear implants.

Measuring Hearing Loss

To measure the type and severity of hearing loss, the simplest test of hearing ability is *pure tone audiometry*. Audiologists use a machine called an audiometer, which measures the threshold for hearing at various sound frequencies. A *threshold* is the softest level at which sound can first be detected. The individual listens to a series of beeps, called pure tones, and indicates when he or she can hear them. Responses are recorded on an *audiogram*, a picture of how you hear. It shows how much one's hearing varies from normal if there is a loss (severity), and where the problem might be located in the auditory pathway (type).

The vertical lines on an audiogram represent pitch or frequency (Hz), and the horizontal lines represent loudness or intensity (dB). The top of the audiogram on the left side shows 125 Hertz, a very low-pitched sound. Looking across, each line represents a higher and higher pitch. The critical pitches for speech are 500–3,000 Hz. Going down the left side of the audiogram, the increasing loudness of sound is represented in decibels. The first number listed is minus 10 dB because there is never a complete absence of sound in our world. Moving downward, each number represents a louder and louder sound as though the volume were being turned up on your stereo. Responses to sound are plotted on the graph in terms of how loud a sound must be at each frequency before you can hear it. Every point on an audiogram represents a different sound.

The audiologist tests hearing using air conduction (through earphones). The sound leaves the earphones, traveling through the air in the ear canal, through the middle ear, and to the cochlea in the inner ear. The sensitivity of the cochlea is tested using bone conduction through a small vibrator placed on the bone behind the ear. Sounds presented this way travel through the bones of the skull directly to the cochlea and auditory nerve, bypassing the outer and middle ear. Bone conduction responses are marked on the audiogram with one of two sets of marks that look like [ ] or < >. If the hearing thresholds obtained by bone conduction are the same as by air conduction, there is no blockage of sound in the outer or middle ear and the hearing loss is caused by loss of sensitivity in the cochlea or auditory nerve.

The audiogram in Figure 12.3 depicts Nathan's sensorineural hearing loss, showing a profound loss in both ears. The hearing sensitivity in the left ear is represented by

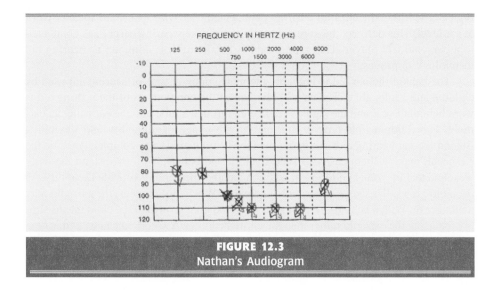

FIGURE 12.3
Nathan's Audiogram

the "X," and the hearing sensitivity in the right ear is represented by an "O." These symbols show Nathan's responses to pure tones presented by air conduction.

The audiologist most likely will perform two additional tests: tympanography and speech audiometry. *Tympanography* is not a hearing test; it is a test of how well the middle ear is functioning and how well the eardrum can move. A small rubber tip is placed in the ear and a little air is pumped into the outer ear canal. If the middle ear is functioning properly, the air causes the eardrum to move. If there is a problem in the middle ear, it may show up as no eardrum movement. For example, very little movement of the eardrum could indicate fluid behind the eardrum as a result of a middle ear infection.

The ability to use speech for communication is a function of two things:

1. The ability to detect the sounds of speech
2. The ability to understand speech

The pure tone audiogram shows how much sound someone can detect, but it does not tell us how clearly speech can be heard. We can make predictions based on the degree and type of hearing loss, but to measure speech discrimination—how well a person can understand speech—special tests are used. For *speech audiometry*, words are presented at different levels of loudness and the person is asked to repeat them. A child with a sensorineural hearing loss may have a problem understanding the words, even when they are loud enough. Generally, the greater the sensorineural hearing loss, the poorer the speech discrimination.

Hearing Aids

Finally, audiologists provide assistance in the selection and use of hearing aids. Hearing aids amplify sound but do not correct hearing. That is, they can make sound louder but not necessarily clearer. Modern hearing aids come in three main types—body aids, behind-the-ear aids, and aids worn inside the ear. The body aids are typically worn on the chest in a harness connected by a wire to a small speaker worn at ear level. This delivers the signal directly, much like wearing earphones connected to a personal CD player. This type of aid is becoming less common as hearing aid technology improves.

The behind-the-ear aid is probably the most common type of hearing aid used by children and adults alike. The case holding all of the components of the hearing aid is worn behind the ear and the signal is delivered through a tube into the ear using an ear-mold. For children, this type of aid has the advantage of durability and flexibility. Behind-the-ear hearing aids are larger than the hearing aids worn completely inside the ear canal, making them easier to keep track of and better able to withstand the daily wear and tear by young children. In addition, behind-the-ear aids provide flexibility. As the child grows, the size of the ear also increases. When this happens, the earmold may no longer fit. With a behind-the-ear aid, accommodating growth of the child means simply replacing the earmold rather than the entire hearing aid. Children can wear this type of aid behind one or both ears. Hearing aids worn inside the ear are customized to fit the size and shape of the ear canal and are used for mild to moderately severe hearing loss. These aids can be damaged by earwax and drainage and are not typically recommended for children.

Cochlear Implants

The *cochlear implant* is becoming more widely used for children with hearing loss. This is an electronic device that is surgically implanted under the skin behind the ear and contains a magnet that couples to a magnet in a sound transmitter worn externally. A surgeon inserts an electrode array into the cochlea to provide direct stimulation to the nerve fibers. A speech processor that can be worn on the body or behind the ear is connected to a headpiece by a cable. Sound is picked up by a microphone and sent to the speech processor, which filters, analyzes, and digitizes the sound into coded electrical signals. These coded signals are sent through a coil across the skin to the internal implanted receiver/stimulator via an FM radio signal. The receiver delivers electrical stimulation to the appropriate implanted electrodes in the cochlea and then carries it to the brain through the auditory nerve.

A cochlear implant does not restore normal hearing or amplify sound. Rather, it provides a sense of sound to individuals who are profoundly deaf and cannot otherwise receive auditory signals. It "gets around" the blockage of damaged hair cells in the cochlea by bypassing them and directly stimulating the auditory nerve (National Institute on Deafness and Other Communication Disorders, 2000).

Educational Evaluation

We conduct educational evaluations of children for a variety of reasons—to determine eligibility for services, to determine placement, to diagnose a problem, to provide feedback, and to plan instruction. The test for eligibility for special education services for children with hearing loss is usually their initial assessment—the hearing test. The test for placement, where the child will be taught, is designed to match the child with the most appropriate setting to receive the services he or she needs. Children who are deaf or hard of hearing also may require specific tests to determine the nature and extent of their disability. This is particularly true if the child has problems in addition to hearing loss.

Testing to provide feedback is important because teachers need to know if their instruction is successful and parents want to know about their child's progress. Finally, assessment is used to guide instruction. It can be as complex as state-mandated testing programs for all students and as simple as a 10-item spelling test. Even though Nathan has a disability, he has still been required to take the state-mandated achievement tests each year.

The assessment of communication involves testing speech and/or sign language skills, depending on the communication modality the child is using. Children with hearing loss are tested on their achievement in all of the academic areas (reading, math, science, social studies, etc.).

Many of the problems we face in assessing children with hearing loss are related to the following (Stewart & Kluwin, 2001):

1. The child is a user of nonstandard English (English is a second language if the child uses American Sign Language to communicate).
2. The child's speech intelligibility is impaired.
3. Many tests that require reading are difficult for the deaf child with reading delays.
4. Standardized achievement tests are rarely norm-referenced with this population.

Fundamental issues that impact deaf education in the face of state-mandated testing include the goals of the state testing system and how deaf students can be accommodated within that system. In recent years, with the greater emphasis on accountability in public schools, states are placing much more emphasis on student performance. This has significant implications for students with hearing loss. Elliot, Kratochwill, and Schulte (1998) identified eight possible accommodations to the state formats for students with disabilities. Using these categories, Stewart and Kluwin (2001) adapted the list and made the accommodations specific for deaf students. Their suggestions include providing assistance prior to testing to teach any new forms of test-taking, providing a longer time period for the assessment, interpreting the directions, and even changing the format and content (rephrasing an item) if this can be done without altering the intent of the question.

Research-Based Interventions and Best Practices

The Commission on Education of the Deaf (COED) (1988) was established by the Education of the Deaf Act of 1986 to study the quality of education for students with hearing loss. The commission reported concern over the lack of progress in reading and other language achievement levels by deaf children over the prior 20 years. According to members of the commission, teachers and researchers had failed to find the proper way to teach literacy skills to deaf students.

Given the increased demand for literacy to be able to function successfully in society today, maybe the problem is that we have failed to keep up with the demand. Greater variety and sophistication of reading and writing is required of today's students than in the past. Consequently, research and best practices in education for students with hearing loss has focused to a large extent on language and literacy.

Early Intervention

A recurring finding across language, social, and academic areas is that early intervention for children with hearing loss and their families is vital. Programs should provide young children with similar peers, role models, and appropriate developmental skills training, as well as support for acquiring communication and language. Early intervention programs also should help parents understand the needs of their child so they can make informed decisions about issues that will affect their future (Marschark, Lang, & Albertini, 2002).

Early access to a language-rich environment is critical. When you consider how much language hearing children have acquired by the time they reach school, it is obvious that parents must make sure that their child is constantly exposed to language from an early age. This means better education for parents concerning strategies to enhance communication with their deaf or hard-of-hearing children whether they use spoken or sign language. Important components of early language and social and cognitive development include getting and maintaining attention, labeling and commenting on objects, and explaining events. Hearing parents need to learn the effective visual communication techniques that deaf parents typically use (Marschark et al., 2002).

Classroom Interventions

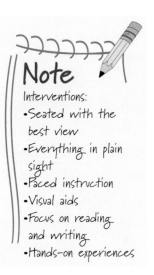

Note

Interventions:
- Seated with the best view
- Everything in plain sight
- Paced instruction
- Visual aids
- Focus on reading and writing
- Hands-on experiences

As a basic consideration, all deaf and hard-of-hearing students must have a clear view of the faces of the teacher and the other students. They should not be seated facing the window, where the glare will make it difficult for them to see. The child should feel comfortable in asking to have his or her seat moved to get a better view. For a deaf student who depends on visual communication (sign language), a teacher must make the field of vision clear and unobstructed so the student can see what the teacher is communicating. When an educational interpreter is used in the classroom, the teacher should pace his or her instruction so it allows the interpreter to complete the message before the teacher moves on. And the teacher should use as many visual aids as possible.

Reading and writing must be given high priority in the classroom. Children should be exposed to hands-on experiences and taught the relationships among concepts and the multiple meanings of words. Visual aids can be used to show links between words and their categories (e.g., animal–dog–golden retriever). All of these seem to be areas in which children with hearing loss lag behind their hearing peers.

Bi-Bi Model

The Star Schools Project (Nover & Andrews, 1998) is a multi-state, distance-learning project to implement and test a proposed bilingual/English as a Second Language model for deaf students who are acquiring and learning two languages—American Sign Language and English. This project is looking at teaching methods for a bilingual/bicultural approach called Bi-Bi to teach language and literacy to students who are deaf and hard of hearing. The model takes the theories and knowledge from English as a Second Language (ESL) research and applies them to deaf education (Easterbrook & Baker, 2002).

Authentic Experiences

Language and knowledge can be gained only when they are presented in ways that are meaningful to children with hearing loss. Many of the traditional language programs are limited in their use with children who are deaf or hard of hearing because they have no connection to the real world, or *authentic experiences* (Clarke, 1983). A list of sentences in a book is relevant only if the child has had experiences that are related to what is described.

Authentic experiences are particularly important for children with hearing loss because they may not have had the same experiences as their hearing peers or had them in the same way. For example, we explain to the hearing child why he or she must put on mittens to go outside ("It's below freezing today and your hands will turn blue!"). For the child with a hearing loss who lacks the language for this explanation, the parent may put on the mittens without explanation. When the child later encounters a written sentence about freezing temperatures, he or she will have had no authentic experience with this situation.

Integration of Vocabulary Development

The process of integrating vocabulary is based on the following principles:

1. Words are parts of related concepts.
2. Words are presented in context.
3. Words are everywhere.

Words occur in bunches. Words do not occur in isolation. They appear in contexts that define the words and their meanings. For example, spring can be a season of the year, a coiled piece of metal, a jump, a small body of flowing water, and many other things. Words are everywhere. Writing appears on toys, on clothing labels, even on cereal boxes! In an integrated approach to vocabulary development, words appear on charts, on bulletin boards, on objects in the room, and so on.

Opportunities for Self-Expression

Self-expression is a large part of learning in a classroom. This approach involves providing an opportunity for the student to practice verbal skills and to define and refine ideas. The teacher allows the student to convert the information in his or her head into another form and then express it. Self-expression will show the depth and direction in which the information has been processed.

Deaf Role Models

If the only adults in their world have hearing, it may be difficult for children with hearing loss to visualize their capabilities and to create a goal for their future (Stewart & Kluwin, 2001).

Children with hearing loss should have the opportunity to meet and interact with deaf adults. Role models can be a positive example of adult behavior, and they also can show the children what they can become.

Shared Reading

Teachers and researchers at the Clerc National Deaf Education Center at Gallaudet University developed a Shared Reading Project (Schleper, 1997), which depends heavily on the use of ASL and fluency in signing, as well as a knack for reading signs. The methods were gained from watching how deaf adults read to deaf children, emphasizing the importance of dramatization, connecting the English sentences with the way they are signed in ASL, and engaging the children in the reading process.

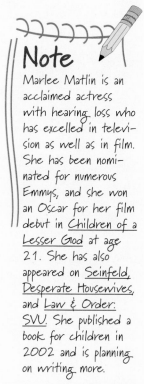

Note

Marlee Matlin is an acclaimed actress with hearing loss who has excelled in television as well as in film. She has been nominated for numerous Emmys, and she won an Oscar for her film debut in Children of a Lesser God at age 21. She has also appeared on Seinfeld, Desperate Housewives, and Law & Order: SVU. She published a book for children in 2002 and is planning on writing more.

Educational Quality

When the Commission on the Education of the Deaf (COED) assessed the quality of all educational services provided to students with hearing loss, their 1988 report, *Toward Equality*, concluded that the present status of education for persons who are deaf in the United States is unsatisfactory. Their major recommendations emphasized promoting English language development and recognized the "unique needs" of students who are deaf, requesting that service providers take these needs into account when developing IEPs.

Finally, the commission urged the Department of Education to reconsider the emphasis of IDEA on the least restrictive environment. They requested that educators focus on appropriateness of the placement of each student with hearing loss, taking into consideration the child's need to be taught by, and be able to interact with, others who use the same mode of communication.

In direct response to the commission's report, the federal government issued new policy guidelines relative to the education of students who are deaf. The guidelines pointed out that "any setting, including a regular classroom, that prevents a child who is deaf from receiving an appropriate education that meets his or her needs, including communication needs, is not the LRE (least restrictive environment) for that child" (Department of Education, 1992, p. 49275). These guidelines have been interpreted to mean that, for students with hearing loss, the least restrictive environment may not be the general education classroom. Consideration of appropriate placement must include a priority placed on the child's communication needs.

Educational Placement

Based on these guidelines, it is clear that access to communication is critical when deciding educational placement for students with hearing loss. There is a wide range of placement options. More and more children with hearing loss are being educated in general education classrooms. They may be receiving special services, including classroom amplification by an FM sound–field system, audiological evaluation, speech/language therapy, resource support from a trained deaf educator, instructional accommodations, and an educational interpreter.

The most recent IDEA legislation (2004) has expanded the related-services area to include greater access to interpreting services in the classroom. The law now identifies that interpreting services would include, but not be limited to, oral transliteration services and cued language services, as well as sign language interpreting.

Another placement option is a special classroom in the public school with other students who are deaf or hard of hearing. The teacher is usually a trained deaf educator, and the students may be included with their hearing peers for some academic subjects or for art, music, or physical education.

The final placement option would be considered a segregated setting. The deinstitutionalization movement has had an impact on the education of students who are deaf or hard of hearing. Prior to the 1980s, most students with hearing loss (particularly those who were deaf), were educated in large residential schools for the deaf or in separate public or private day schools. They often entered those schools at age 5, learned to communicate from their peers and deaf adults who worked at the schools, made lifetime friendships, met their spouse, and settled in the area to live and work. This educational setting was the basis for developing and perpetuating the Deaf community and

Deaf culture. Passage of the Education of All Handicapped Act in 1975, and its accompanying mandate for placement in a "least restrictive environment," has changed the nature and prevalence of these residential and day programs.

With the wider range of placement options in public schools, enrollment in residential schools has declined and many have closed, although members of the Deaf community and some professionals in the field of deafness continue to advocate for the right to choose this placement option (Moores, 2001). No matter what the educational placement, several issues continue to impact education for students with hearing loss. These relate largely to the communication options discussed below.

Communication

Communication is a critical aspect of typical development for all children. It is the way we interact with others and learn about the world around us. Often, children with hearing loss do not have full access to communication until they are well past the age deemed important for language acquisition.

Four approaches are commonly used to teach communication skills to students with hearing loss: the auditory–verbal approach, the oral approach, the manual approach, and total communication, which includes a combination of the other three. Cued speech is an alternative to natural sign languages and signed systems that is used

Assistive technology can greatly help communication, as demonstrated by this student who wears an auditory hearing device while his teacher wears a microphone to amplify her speech.

as a supplement to spoken English. There is a long history of controversy surrounding which approach is the most appropriate. Ultimately, no single method meets the needs of all children. The most recent IDEA (2004) legislation stipulates that the IEP team must consider the variety of languages and communication modes that a child who is deaf or hard of hearing might use in the educational setting.

Auditory–Verbal Approach

The auditory–verbal approach emphasizes amplification of sound and helping the child use his or her residual hearing, through early identification and subsequent amplification or cochlear implant. This approach helps children learn to use their residual hearing through *auditory training* to enhance listening skills and use speech to communicate.

Oral Approach

The oral approach also emphasizes the use of amplified sound and using residual hearing to develop oral language. In contrast to a strictly auditory–verbal approach, though, this method allows for the use of visual input (i.e., speechreading) to augment the receipt of auditory information. The speechreader watches the speaker's lip movements, as well as facial and body gestures, to aid in understanding what is being said. This skill is extremely difficult to master because such a small amount of what is said is actually visible on the lips.

Manual Approach

The manual approach to teaching communication promotes the use of the child's intact visual modality to get information. It emphasizes *sign language*, complex combinations of hand movements to convey both words and concepts. Manual communication encompasses several different sign systems, each with its own proponents.

American Sign Language (ASL)

In the case study, Nathan uses ASL, the most widely used sign language among deaf adults in North America. Although some individual ASL signs have comparable English words, its signs are meant to represent concepts rather than individual single words.

Fingerspelling

Fingerspelling is a form of manual communication that uses a hand representation for all 26 letters of the alphabet. Figure 12.4 shows the American manual alphabet.

Variations of ASL

The primary sign systems used in the United States are Pigeon Signed English (PSE), Seeing Essential English (SEE), Signing Exact English (SEE2), and Signed English. Users of PSE employ a basic ASL sign vocabulary but often rely on things such as initialization to convey meaning. For example, the sign for *eat* can be made with the letter *L* tapping the mouth to indicate the word *lunch*. As in spoken English, English-based sign systems use minimal inflection and a basic subject–verb–object word order. They also use markers to indicate plurals, possessives, tenses, adverbs, adjectives, and so on.

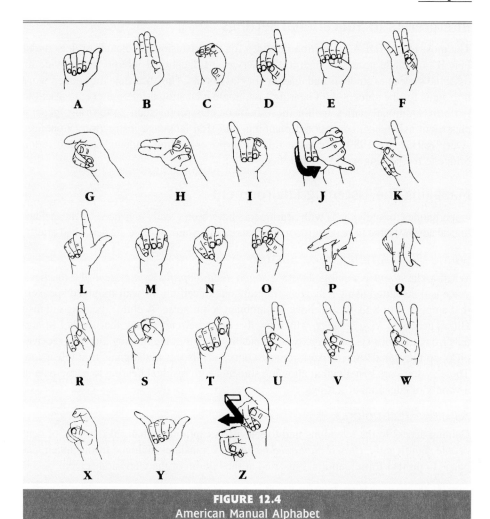

FIGURE 12.4
American Manual Alphabet

Total Communication

The philosophy behind *total communication* is to combine as many sources of information as possible, involving sign and spoken language and support for residual hearing. Thus, this approach encompasses amplification, speechreading, speech training, reading, and writing in combination with signs.

Cued Speech

An alternative to natural sign language and English sign systems is *cued speech*. This is a supplement to spoken English intended to make its features fully visible (LaSasso & Metzger, 1998). Because many sounds look the same on the lips when they are pronounced, cued speech uses 36 different cues to clarify the 44 different sounds in English. Placement of the cues on the face also indicate vowels and consonants. This is very different from sign languages that provide information about meaning rather than about sound.

Interpreters in Educational Settings

The most recent IDEA legislation provides for an expansion of related services under Part B to include access to interpreting services. Educational interpreters provide an essential service to students and teachers in classrooms. They translate the spoken word into signs for the student with hearing loss. Some educational interpreters are asked to perform additional duties within the school or classroom, such as tutoring, general classroom assistance, educational planning, and sign language instruction (Stuckless, Avery, & Hurwitz, 1989). The educational interpreter is often students' communication bridge to the hearing world around them.

Managing the Listening Environment

Opportunities for individuals with hearing loss have been greatly enhanced by the technological advances that have occurred in the past decade. Some of these are described briefly.

Sound–Field Amplification System

When a classroom is equipped with a *sound–field amplification system*, the teacher's voice is transmitted using a lavaliere microphone to ceiling- or wall-mounted speakers that amplify it to 8 to 10 dB above the ambient room noise. A child's hearing aid also allows access to *loop systems*, which involve closed-circuit wiring that sends FM signals from an audio system directly to an electronic coil in the hearing aid. The receiver picks up the signals much like a remote control sends infrared signals to a television. These systems are beneficial in allowing students with residual hearing to participate in a variety of educational settings.

Assistive Technology

Gaining access to the telephone and to television captioning changed the lives of deaf people significantly. *Closed-captioned technology* translates dialogue from spoken language to printed form (captions) inserted at the bottom of the television screen.

Telecommunication Devices

The modern *telecommunication device for the Deaf (TDD)* allows individuals to send, receive, and print messages by phone. A typewriter converts letters into electrical signals and sends them via modem through the phone lines. A modern telecommunications device that is taking the deaf world by storm is the two-way pager. The equivalent of the cell phone for people with hearing loss, these devices provide mobile communications to hard-of-hearing and deaf consumers.

Computers and the Internet

Personal computers have provided individuals with hearing loss access to information in ways never thought possible. They can provide instructional support to students, including learning sign language. A computer system (C-print) developed by the National Technical Institute for the Deaf (NTID) gives individuals using a software-equipped laptop computer real-time translations of the spoken word. Students with hearing loss can attend a lecture, watch an interpreter without having to look down to take notes, and view the simultaneous written text of what is being said.

Video Relay Services

Video relay services (VRS) enables a deaf or hard-of-hearing person to make a telephone call via an Internet video connection. VRS enables conversations in sign language to take place at approximately normal speed. An interpreter translates the caller's ASL into speech for the hearing user and speech into ASL for the deaf user. It is free to everyone and requires only a personal computer, a Web camera, and a high-speed Internet connection.

Accommodations

Many of the accommodations you will make to serve your students with hearing loss will benefit everyone in your classroom. Slowing the pace of your lecture for an interpreter is helpful for all students, as is providing written explanations for everything you say orally. Scripts and outlines for movies and videotapes, as well as projecting a visual presentation of material, makes learning clearer and more enjoyable. Teaching deaf history and culture will bring a whole new dimension to your social studies curriculum. Finally, when you facilitate social and learning interactions by pairing your deaf or hard-of-hearing student with a hearing "buddy," both will benefit.

Summary

Even though only 1.4% of school children have a hearing loss, the heterogeneity of this group of children poses a challenge to teachers. Among the factors that affect the learning of these children are the type and severity of the loss, age of onset, site of the loss, mode of communication, experiences, intelligence, and whether any other disabilities are present. The major classifications are *deaf* and *hard of hearing*, and the causes can be either genetic or acquired.

The initial assessment is done for diagnostic purposes, The primary test is pure tone audiometry to produce an audiogram. Two additional tests that the audiologist performs are tympanography and speech audiometry. Following diagnosis, the hearing loss might be mitigated by a variety of hearing aids or a cochlear implant.

Educational evaluations are conducted to determine eligibility for services and placement. Results will be used to match the child with the most appropriate setting and to guide instruction. The Commission of Education of the Deaf has studied the quality of education for students with hearing loss and have made suggestions for early intervention and classroom interventions. In the classroom, the primary consideration is speech and language development. Among the possibilities are the Bi-Bi model, authentic experiences, integration of vocabulary development, opportunities for self-expression, deaf role models, shared reading, and interpreters.

The four approaches used most commonly to teach communication skills to students with hearing loss are the auditory–verbal approach, the oral approach, the manual approach, and total communication. Technology has greatly enhanced the learning opportunities for deaf and hard-of-hearing students. Innovations include the sound–field amplification system, closed-captioning, TDDs, computers and the Internet, and video relay services.

References

Andrews, J. F., Leigh, I. W., & Weiner, M. T. (2004). *Deaf people: Evolving perspectives from psychology, education, and sociology.* Boston: Pearson Education.

Auditory–Verbal International. (2000). *Principles of auditory–verbal practice* [Online]. Retrieved January 15, 2005, from http://www.auditory-verbal.org

Batshaw, M. L. (2002). *Children with disabilities* (4th ed.). Baltimore: Paul H. Brookes.

Clarke, B. R. (1983). Competence in communication for hearing impaired children: A conversation, activity, experience approach. *British Columbia Journal of Special Education, 7*, 15–27.

Commission on Education of the Deaf. (1988). *Toward equality: Education of the deaf.* Washington, DC: U.S. Government Printing Office.

Easterbrooks, S. R., & Baker, S. (2002). *Language learning in children who are deaf and hard of hearing: Multiple pathways.* Boston: Allyn & Bacon.

Elliot, S. N., Kratochwill, T. R., & Schulte, A. G. (1998). The assessment accommodation checklist: Who, what, where, when, why, and how? *Teaching Exceptional Children, 3*(2), 10–14.

Gallaudet Research Institute. (2002). *Literacy and deaf students* [Online]. Washington, DC: Author. Retrieved January 16, 2005, from http://gri.gallaudet.edu/literacy/

Joint Committee on Infant Hearing. (2000). Year 2000 position statement: Principles and guidelines for early hearing detection and intervention programs. *American Journal of Audiology, 9*, 9–29.

Lane, H., Hoffmeister, R., & Bahan, B. (1996). *A journey into the Deaf-World.* San Diego, CA: Dawn Sign Press.

LaSasso, C. J., & Metzger, M. A. (1998). An alternative route for preparing deaf children for BiBi programs: The home language as L1 and cued speech for conveying traditionally spoken languages. *Journal of Deaf Studies and Deaf Education, 3,* 265–289.

Marschark, M., Lang, H. G., & Albertini, J. A. (2002). *Educating deaf students: From research to practice.* New York: Oxford University Press.

Moores, D. F. (2001). *Educating the deaf: Psychology, principles and practices* (5th ed.). Boston: Houghton Mifflin.

National Center on Birth Defects and Developmental Disabilities. (2004). *Hearing loss* [Online]. Atlanta, GA: Author. Retrieved November 28, 2005, from http://www.nih.gov/nidcd/health/coch.htm

National Institute on Deafness and Other Communication Disorders. (2000). Cochlear implants. *Health information: Hearing and balance* [Online]. Retrieved January 15, 2005, from http://www.nih.gov/nidcd/health/pubs_hb/coch.htm

Nover, S., & Andrews, J. (1998). *Critical pedagogy in deaf education: Bilingual methodology and staff development* (Star Schools Project Grant No. R203A70030-97, Report No. 2). Santa Fe, NM: New Mexico School for the Deaf.

Scheetz, N. A. (2004). *Psychosocial aspects of deafness.* Boston: Pearson Education, Inc.

Schleper, D. (1997). *Reading to deaf children: Learning from deaf adults.* Washington, DC: Pre-College National Mission Programs.

Singleton, J., & Tittle, M. (2000). Deaf parents and their hearing children. *Journal of Deaf Studies and Deaf Education, 5*(3), 221–236.

Spencer, P., & Meadow-Orlans, K. (1996). Play, language, and maternal responsiveness: A longitudinal study of deaf and hearing infants. *Child Development, 67,* 176–191.

Stuart, A., Harrison, D., & Simpson, P. (1991). The social and emotional development of a population of hearing-impaired children being educated in their local mainstream schools in Leicestershire, England. *Journal of the British Association of Teachers of the Deaf, 15*(5), 121–125.

Stuckless, E. R., Avery, J. C., & Hurwitz, T. A. (1989). *Educational interpreting for deaf students: Report of the National Task Force on Educational Interpreting.* Rochester, NY: National Technical Institute for the Deaf, Rochester Institute of Technology.

U.S. Department of Education. (1992). Deaf students education services: Policy guidance. *Federal Register, 57*(211) (Friday, October 30, 1992), 49274–49276.

U.S. Department of Education. (1992). Guidelines for educational programs for deaf students, *Federal Register, 57*(211), 49275–49276.

U.S. Department of Education. (2002). To assure the free appropriate public education of all children with disabilities. *Twenty-fourth annual report to Congress on the implementation of the Individuals with Disabilities Education Act.* Washington, DC: U.S. Government Printing Office.

Visual Impairments

13

Rosanne K. Silberman & Jane Erin

Visual Impairment

Definitions ■ ■ ■ ■ ■ ■

Visual impairment refers to a measured loss of any of the visual functions such as acuity, visual field, color vision, or binocular vision (Barraga & Erin, 2001). The Individuals with Disabilities Act (IDEA) Amendments of 1997 (PL 105-17) define visual impairment, including blindness, as "an impairment in vision that, even with correction, adversely affects a child's educational performance. The term includes both partial sight and blindness" (34 C.F.R. 300.7 ([c]]13]).

Legal blindness is a standard used to determine eligibility for specialized rehabilitation or educational services. A person who is legally blind has a central visual acuity of 20/200 or less in the better eye with best correction, which means that he or she can see an object at 20 feet that a person with normal vision can see from 200 feet away. A person also is considered legally blind if the visual field is restricted to 20 degrees or less, which is like peering through a narrow tunnel.

A person with *low vision* refers to someone who has a significant visual impairment but also has significant usable vision. Educationally, this characterizes an individual who is severely visually impaired even with prescribed corrective lenses, but whose visual function may be improved through the use of compensatory visual strategies, optical aids, non-optical aids, and environmental modifications (Corn & Koenig, 1996).

Blind is a functional definition used primarily by educators to describe someone who is totally blind or has light perception (awareness of light) without projection (the

CASE STUDY: NANCY

Nancy is a 16-year-old high school junior with low vision. When she is wearing her glasses with thick lenses, she can read regular print from 6 inches away and can find a paper clip from about 8 inches away. Visually impaired since birth, she recently lost more vision and no longer can see the whiteboard in school. Although Nancy is average-looking and neat, her wardrobe, which her mother purchases, is out of style, particularly in comparison to the clothes her fashion-conscious peers wear.

She has no siblings, and her parents prefer that she spend time with peers in her own home. Nancy has one best friend and sometimes invites friends to her home for parties and sleepovers. She would like to participate in the swimming program at the YMCA on Saturdays, but her parents don't want her to travel alone by bus because she may miss her stop.

A certified itinerant *teacher of students with visual impairments* (TVI) comes to the school for an hour three times a week. Nancy performs at grade level academically but has difficulty with mathematics because she is unable to see the graphs and equations in the text and no longer can read her own writing. Because she reads more slowly than her classmates, she has to spend most evenings and weekends doing homework. Recently she

(continued)

began to learn Braille, which may give her a reading option in the future if her vision continues to worsen.

The State Commission for the Blind has provided the school with a videomagnifier system that accompanies the computer with voice output in the library. In addition, Nancy just had a low-vision evaluation and the low-vision specialist gave her a telescopic lens for looking at the whiteboard and other distant objects. Nancy has not tried this optical aid yet in school. Her itinerant teacher orders many of her textbooks and leisure reading material in recorded format. Because Nancy is taking home economics, she and the itinerant teacher met with the home economics teacher to determine how to adapt the oven dials and make it easier for Nancy to use materials on highly reflective surfaces that produce glare. As a career goal, Nancy hopes to attend college and become an English teacher.

ability to locate the light source). Children who are blind learn primarily through their tactual and auditory senses rather than through vision (Huebner, 2000). People can be either *congenitally blind* (born blind or losing vision in infancy) or *adventitiously blind* (losing vision in childhood or adulthood as a result of disease or trauma). Those who are congenitally blind do not have the opportunity to develop the ability to retain visual memory, whereas those who are adventitiously blind usually retain visual memory that aids in acquiring skills, particularly those related to mobility.

Characteristics of Visual Impairments

The development and learning of children who are blind or who have low vision are affected by the type and severity of their vision loss, as well as by the presence of additional disabilities. Most children with visual impairments (85%) have sufficient usable vision to assist them in learning. Only about 15% have no vision, and these children learn through touch and hearing. The number of children with visual impairments and additional disabilities ranges from 50%–75% of the total number of those with visual impairments. The most common disabilities represented in this group are mental retardation, learning disabilities, neurological disabilities, and auditory impairments (deaf-blindness) (Hatlen, 1998).

Blindness or low vision impacts learning in all areas of development. These areas include motor development, concept development, communication skills, and social interactions.

Motor Development

Infants with visual impairments often exhibit motor delays during the early stages of development. Sighted infants develop head control and rotation by lifting their heads and looking around, which enables them to build upper-body rotation and head control.

Because infants with little or no vision are not aware that objects exist beyond their reach, they are not motivated to reach for or move toward objects. To motivate them to initiate locomotor activities such as crawling and walking, they need both touch and sound stimuli, numerous opportunities, and encouragement (Silberman, Bruce, & Nelson, 2004; Warren, 2000).

Children and youth with visual impairments often have low muscle tone and inadequate *proprioception* (sensory awareness of the body's position in space). This may result in poor posture and a wide gait. Without early experiences in movement and active play, they may also have later difficulties with weight control, physical stamina, and coordination.

Concept Development

Children and youth who are blind or have low vision, particularly those who are born blind or lose their vision early in life, have information-gathering deficits. Without vision, children must use their other senses to learn about concepts and objects that sighted people experience visually. These may include concepts/objects such as the height of trees and buildings, colors, and the moon and stars.

The sense of hearing provides clues as to distance and direction, but it does not provide any ideas about specific features such as size and shape. For example, a child with low vision can hear the sound of a bird and detect its location but cannot determine its physical characteristics. A 6-year-old girl who is blind might be able to describe many things about automobiles, including traffic jams and the price of gasoline, but she may not know how many wheels a car has, perhaps because she has not had the opportunity to explore the outside of a car.

The sense of touch can help a blind child understand concrete concepts, but some objects are inaccessible to tactual observation. For example, mountains and rivers are too large to be touched as a whole; flies and ants are too small to access directly, and butterflies and spiderwebs are too fragile to be touched. Other objects, such as boiling water and campfires, are too hot to touch, and those in liquid form, such as mercury, are in containers (Lowenfeld, 1981a). Words, sensory cues, models, and real objects are used to teach concepts such as these.

Touch also does not enable the person who is blind to scan the environment to gain knowledge. Only what is reachable at arm's length can be perceived. Thus, a student who is blind going to a store to shop or to a concert or football game will miss out on a variety of experiences the sighted student has. He or she is dependent on others to explain and interpret the experience.

Communication Skills

Blindness or low vision affects the development of language in infants and young children in several ways. Without the ability to see facial expressions and use eye gaze and gestures such as pointing, children with visual impairments are unable to use these early visual communication cues with their parents to direct their attention and convey messages. These children also may be unaware of the meaning of events and routines. For example, without vision they may not be aware that Daddy is putting on his coat to go outdoors.

When a parent refers to an object in the environment such as a ball or a shovel, the sighted child shows his or her understanding by looking at it. The parent continues to

Note

Concepts and objects that are not tangible must be taught by a combination of words, sensory cues, models, and real objects. Sense of touch is essential for a person with a visual impairment.

expand the concepts related to the object and thereby helps the child increase his or her vocabulary and linguistic concepts. Parents of children with visual impairments tend to provide only the names of objects or requests for objects without any additional enriched information because the child gives them little or no feedback or indication that he or she understands or is interested. This tendency for overlabeling thus prevents the child with visual impairments from acquiring increasingly complex language patterns. Other comparisons between children who are sighted and children with visual impairments show that the latter ask more questions, change the topic to focus on their own interests, and relate more to adults in communication than to their peers (Fazzi & Klein, 2002; Lueck, Chen, & Kekelis, 1997).

Social Interactions

As indicated earlier in the chapter, a child with little or no vision is unable to rely on visual signals such as eye gaze and smiling by parents, siblings, and peers in social exchanges. Without being able to imitate these behaviors, these children also are unable to return these cues, so their social interactions are limited and sometimes misinterpreted (Sacks & Silberman, 2000). This can precipitate negative attitudes toward the child and result in his or her becoming socially isolated.

As the child with a visual impairment gets older, the lack of facial expressions and other nonverbal cues tends to send a message of disinterest or apathy to sighted peers. How others react to and interact with the child with a visual impairment affect his or her ability to develop a positive self-concept, a sense of independence, and opportunities for further experiences to develop social competence.

Without vision, initiating and maintaining social contact is difficult. With just a glance, children who are sighted can greet a classmate, show interest, and know when to take turns or respond to a peer. Children who are blind or who have low vision, by comparison, may have difficulty monitoring the attention of peers and may not know if someone is talking directly to them or when a classmate joins or leaves them. As a result, these children may initiate conversation when no one is near. Sometimes children who are blind or have low vision use physical contact such as a tap on the arm in place of eye contact in their social interactions—a behavior that may hinder friendship because some children who are sighted do not want to be touched.

Some children with visual impairments exhibit repetitive forms of physical activity such as rocking, head-turning, and eye-pressing. These self-stimulatory behaviors or mannerisms are socially inappropriate and, although they may begin as patterns in response to stress or intense involvement, they become habitual. With behavior modification and contracts between the student, the teacher in the general education classroom, and sometimes peers, these behaviors can be reduced and sometimes omitted altogether (Mar & Cohen, 1998).

Prevalence and Causes

Children with visual impairments represent a low percentage of the school-age population—fewer than 1 child in 1,000. According to a 2004 annual survey (American Printing House for the Blind, 2006), 57,199 legally blind students were enrolled in school programs. The decision to provide special education service as a result of visual impairment is based on whether the child is unable to benefit from the general curriculum without adaptations. Many children who qualify are not legally blind and therefore would not be counted in the APH survey, so the number of children receiving educational service is much higher than the American Printing House survey indicates.

It is important for general education teachers and others on the team responsible for instruction of a child with a visual impairment to know the etiology of the child's impairment and the implications that impact instruction in the classroom.

Refractive Errors

Refractive errors are caused by a defect in the eye's ability to focus light rays on the retina and usually can be corrected by eyeglasses or contact lenses. Individuals with severe refractive errors, however, may be visually impaired even after correction. Refractive conditions include the following:

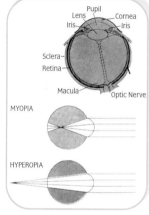

Anatomy of the eye

1. *Myopia,* or nearsightedness, in which light rays focus in front of the retina. Myopic students can see near objects clearly, but they have difficulty seeing distant objects.
2. *Hyperopia,* or farsightedness, in which the eyeball is too short and light rays focus behind the retina. Students with hyperopia cannot see near objects clearly. They may have difficulty reading and often complain of eyestrain or fatigue during tasks that require near vision.
3. *Astigmatism,* in which vision is distorted because of the irregular curvature of the cornea.

Eyeglasses are commonly worn by students and teachers alike to correct any type of refractive error.

Other Conditions

The following eye conditions may result in severe visual impairments that require intervention by TVIs and *certified orientation and mobility specialists* (COMS):

- *Albinism:* A hereditary congenital condition that results in reduced or total lack of pigment throughout the body. *Ocular albinism,* more common in males than females, involves pigmentary differences in the eyes only and is characterized by reduced visual acuity, astigmatism, photophobia, and nystagmus (involuntary movement of the eyes).
- *Amblyopia:* A condition that results in reduced visual acuity in one eye, for which no organic cause is found. Amblyopia may occur when the individual suppresses the image in one eye to avoid double vision or when the eyes have unequal refractive errors. This condition must be diagnosed and treated as early as possible to prevent permanent visual loss.
- *Congenital cataract:* An opacity or cloudiness of the lens that prevents passage of light rays to the retina, creating images that are distorted and hazy. When the lens is removed surgically, the child wears contact lenses, bifocals, or glasses to improve acuity at near and far distances.
- *Congenital glaucoma:* An abnormally developed drainage system that blocks the flow of fluid, increasing pressure in the eye and the size of the eyeball. If not treated, glaucoma damages the optic nerve and can lead to permanent visual loss or blindness.
- *Cortical visual impairment (CVI):* A reduction in vision resulting from damage to the posterior visual pathways or visual cortex of the brain (occipital lobe). Although children with CVI have intact eye structures, the visual systems of the brain are unable to interpret what the eyes see. As a result, their visual functioning varies depending on levels of sensory input and fatigue. They avoid eye contact, prefer colored objects, use touch rather than vision to identify objects, and prefer familiar, quiet environments (Gense & Gense, 2005; Silberman, Bruce, & Nelson, 2004). CVI is often accompanied by other neurological disabilities.
- *Nystagmus:* Rapid, involuntary movement of one or both eyes, usually accompanied by other ocular disorders. Even though the eyes move, the child sees objects as stationary.
- *Optic nerve atrophy:* A condition characterized by damage to the fibers in the optic nerve so that electrical impulses are unable to travel from the retina to the occipital lobe. Visual characteristics may include reduced visual acuity, field losses, and difficulties with color vision.
- *Optic nerve hypoplasia (ONH):* Incomplete development of the optic nerve that carries visual information to various locations in the brain, especially the occipital lobe. ONH is present at birth and may affect one or both eyes. Visual functioning ranges from normal visual acuity to total blindness. Visual-field loss varies from loss of detailed vision in both central and peripheral fields, in which a child does not recognize people or objects in the periphery, to subtle peripheral-field loss. Some lack depth perception and may be unable to locate objects in space; some have mild photophobia and may squint, lower their head, avoid light by turning away, or resist participating in outdoor activities. ONH often is associated with other neurological abnormalities such as septo-optic dysplasia (SOD) (Hatton, Topor, & Rosenblum, 2004).

- *Retinitis pigmentosa:* An inherited condition in which symptoms usually begin during adolescence and result in progressive deterioration of the retina. Peripheral vision and night vision are affected first. Later the person develops tunnel vision, an extreme reduction in the visual field that leaves only a small circle of vision. The person may become totally blind.
- *Retinopathy of prematurity:* A disorder that can develop in premature infants, characterized by an overgrowth of blood vessels in the retina, which causes visual loss ranging from moderate myopia to total blindness. It is associated with very low birth weight and gestational age. The effect on visual loss of administering oxygen is not known.
- *Strabismus:* A deviation of the eyes that prevents simultaneous focus by both eyes. To avoid seeing double, the child may suppress the vision in one eye, which can result in amblyopia.

Assessment and Evaluation for Special Education and Related Services

Educational assessment for the purposes of placement and instructional decisions should be conducted by a collaborative team in which the TVI plays a major role. The team may include the TVI, the COMS, the general education teacher, the family, and related-services professionals such as the school psychologist, assistive technology specialist, speech–language pathologist, occupational therapist, and physical therapist. Assessments should be comprehensive, broad-based, and ongoing. No single assessment tool should be used by itself.

Components of a comprehensive assessment for learners with visual impairments include functional vision; learning media; intellectual and cognitive abilities; educational achievement; compensatory skills, including communication modes; assistive technology; motor skills and orientation and mobility; social interaction skills, recreation, and leisure; independent living skills; and career education (Barclay, 2003; Heinze, 2000). Several specific assessments are discussed in this section.

Assessment of Functional Vision

The certified TVI or COMS conducts a Functional Vision Assessment (FVA) to document how the child uses vision in typical activities in school and home environments. Some ocular–motor skills that are observed in an FVA are fixation, tracking, shift of gaze, and scanning (Anthony, 2000, 2003). Some teachers conduct additional criterion-referenced procedures to provide them with further information about a child's vision.

One commercial instrument, the Individualized, Systematic Assessment of Visual Efficiency (ISAVE) (Langley, 1998), is used to assess the functional vision of infants, children, and young adults with significant cognitive, neurological, physical, and sensory impairments who cannot respond reliably to standard measures. It is particularly valuable for children who have cortical visual impairment. Another criterion-referenced instrument is the Program to Develop Efficiency in Visual Functioning (Barraga & Morris, 1980), an assessment and developmental curriculum for enhancing visual skills. Recommendations based on results of the FVA and other procedures on how the student uses vision in a variety of environments will be helpful to teachers in designing instructional programs that include strategies for helping to engage the student visually.

Assessment of Learning Media

After conducting an FVA, the TVI should conduct a Learning Media Assessment (LMA) to determine how efficiently a child with a visual impairment uses the visual, tactile, and auditory sensory channels during daily routines (Koenig & Holbrook, 1995). The results will help the team select the appropriate media for reading and literacy activities. For example, a student might use Braille for reading long assignments and use print with an optical aid when reading a label on a CD or a short recipe.

Educational Assessment

Test norms for students who are sighted are not always appropriate for those who have visual impairments. Many instruments contain subtests or items that depend on vision; these should be deleted or modified by providing additional explanations. Further, if a student is given extra time to complete a test or answers the questions verbally, the results cannot be interpreted in the intended manner. Even so, a normed test might be warranted if the results show the student's strengths, weaknesses, and overall performance in comparison with peers in the class. The TVI should explain and interpret to other members of the team the student's incorrect or inadequate responses related to lack of vision.

Because of the low incidence and diversity of the population, few reliable and valid tests have been standardized on learners with visual impairments. Criterion-referenced tests are appropriate informal means of assessing learners with visual impairments. Because these instruments are not standardized, administration procedures can be modified to meet the needs of students with little or no usable vision. Teacher-made checklists, interviews, authentic and performance assessment, and direct observation during typical routines provide valuable information on how successfully the learner with the visual impairment is performing academically and interacting socially with peers in the general education classroom.

Concept Development and Readiness Skills

The Tactile Test of Basic Concepts (Caton, 1976), normed on learners with visual impairments, is the tactile version of the Boehm Test of Basic Concepts (Boehm, 1971). It uses simple geometric forms to assess specific concepts, including those focusing on directionality, which are important prerequisite skills for mobility. The Mangold Developmental Program of Tactile Perception and Braille Letter Recognition (Mangold, 1977) is helpful in both assessing and teaching Braille readiness skills, including tracking skills, coordinated and independent use of the hands for reading, left–right and top–bottom orientation, and introduction of the Braille alphabet characters.

Academic Content Areas

The No Child Left Behind (NCLB) legislation (2001) requires annual academic assessments in reading and math for all students in grades 3–8. Adapted versions of several commercial academic achievement tests used in public schools are available in Braille and large print. These include the Stanford Reading Achievement Tests on a variety of levels, the Stanford Diagnostic Reading Test, and the Iowa Test of Basic Skills. An adapted version of the Key Math Diagnostic Arithmetic Test is available in Braille. These and other adapted versions are published by the American Printing House for the Blind.

Tests should be administered with the adaptations specified on the IEP, including appropriately sized print, Braille, extended test time, lighting and environmental adaptations, and any prescribed low-vision devices. A comprehensive list of assessments for learners with visual impairments can be found in Heinze (2000) and at the website of the Texas School for the Blind and Visually Impaired at http://www.tsbvi.edu/recc/assessment.htm ("Assessment," 2004).

Research-Based Interventions and Best Practices

Because students with visual impairments are few in number and often have multiple disabilities, little empirical research has been done to support instructional approaches. Evidence from student progress data and professional experience, however, supports the practices described here. Lowenfeld (1981b) identified three important principles for appropriate teaching strategies:

1. *Concreteness.* Whenever possible, the teacher should provide real objects for students who are blind or who have low vision to manipulate so they can obtain information regarding shape, size, weight, hardness, surface qualities, pliability, and temperature. Sometimes models are necessary, but students must be made aware that the information is incomplete or distorted in some way. For example, the student does not experience the texture of a banana when using a model.

2. *Unified experiences.* The unit plan of instruction enables students with visual impairments to assimilate and organize separate impressions into a meaningful and unified experience. By going to actual field sites, students can learn the component parts and develop concepts that children who are sighted learn from casual glances. For example, when being taught a unit about shopping in a supermarket, students can go to the supermarket and learn about the organization of stock on shelves, display of items, labeling, and pricing of items. General education content areas such as reading, spelling, and mathematics can be taught in relation to shopping in a supermarket.

3. *Learning by doing.* Students with visual impairments need many opportunities to learn how to do things independently. Although acquiring skills such as these may take them longer because of their inability to imitate, the emphasis should be on providing as little assistance as possible so they can develop self-confidence. If children receive too much unnecessary help, they can reach a state of learned helplessness—the loss of initiative because of the absence of an outcome.

Children and youth with visual impairments also require specific instruction in curriculum areas that typically are not included in the standard general education curriculum. The specific areas, which Hatlen (1996) described as the expanded core curriculum, should be taught by qualified TVIs and COMS. Professionals consider these areas vital for the success of learners with visual impairments.

Communication Modes, Including Braille

Students with visual impairments must receive instruction in literacy in modes that will enable them to read and write. Braille, a tactual system for reading and writing, was developed in 1829 by Louis Braille, a Frenchman who was blind. Braille consists of embossed characters using various combinations of raised dots in a Braille cell, two dots wide and three dots high (see Figure 13.1).

In *uncontracted Braille*, each character stands for a letter, and words are spelled just as they are in print. In *contracted Braille*, letter combinations, parts of words, and words are contracted to save space and increase the reading rate. For example, in contracted Braille, when the letter "e" stands alone, it means the word "every." One character is used instead of five.

Although contracted Braille often is used from the start in kindergarten or first grade to teach reading and writing, it is more complex than uncontracted Braille. One of its major disadvantages is that the Braille symbols and the actual spelling of the word often have no relationship. For example, when a Braille reader (tactually) sees the letter "x" alone, it refers to the word "it"; when the letters standing alone are "xf," the word is "itself." Thus, children who are blind in a general education class have a more difficult time learning to read than their peers who are sighted. Children who are blind are expected to become literate based on a specific curricular approach rather than on the varying levels of difficulty of the specific words in Braille. Research is being conducted to determine whether contracted or uncontracted Braille is the best teaching approach for beginning readers.

In addition, Braille readers who learn to read contracted Braille in the early elementary grades may have more difficulty learning to spell accurately because they encounter most words in a contracted form. TVIs and general education teachers, therefore, should require these students to spell words in their entirety as well as in contracted form.

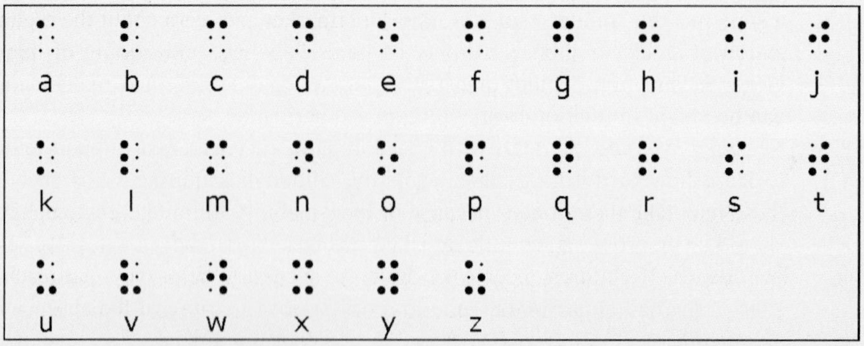

FIGURE 13.1
Braille Alphabet

This student reading Braille is fully included in a general education classroom with support from an itinerant teacher.

Braillewriter
circa 1900

Young students learn to write in Braille at the same time as they learn to read it. They first use the *Braillewriter*. In mid-elementary school, when they are proficient in reading Braille and have sufficient manual dexterity, they often are introduced to the *slate and stylus*, a manual Braillewriting device that can be used for notetaking and brief writing tasks.

Most Braille readers in general classrooms learn to read through the same literacy program as their classmates. When students need a more structured system for learning Braille, they may receive instruction in the reading series *Patterns* (Caton, Pester, & Bradley, 1983), a literacy program designed for early readers who are blind. The stories have an experiential base that does not depend on visual clues, and the vocabulary is related to the complexity of the Braille characters.

Literacy programs are available, too, for older students who lose vision and have to transfer from print to Braille. Academic Braille readers also learn specialized Braille codes such as the Nemeth code for reading and writing mathematics and scientific notation, a code for music, and various codes for foreign languages.

Listening Skills

Because children and youth with visual impairments depend on the auditory channel for much of their learning, they need to develop efficient listening skills. Young children have to learn awareness of sounds, identify their source and location, interpret differences in sounds, follow simple directions, and understand the direct and indirect meanings of words that are easier to learn through vision. Older students need skills in identifying main ideas and critically analyzing content material, developing auditory memory, including recall of important facts, and listening selectively for specific information and in distracting environments.

Orientation and Mobility (O&M)

Instruction in orientation and mobility (O&M), a related service defined in IDEA, should be provided by a COMS to students with visual impairments as required in the IEP. The emphasis should be on developing body image, spatial and positional concepts and environmental awareness; learning the layout of general education classroom and other rooms in school and at home; maintaining contact with the physical environment (e.g., landmarks); moving independently and safely; and using appropriate techniques and devices (Lewis, 2004).

Because O&M instruction should be integrated into all daily activities in home, school, and community environments, the COMS's role is to provide direct instruction to students with visual impairments, as well as strategies for ensuring a safe environment for independent movement, to members of the collaborative team that includes the TVI, the classroom teacher, and others who work directly with the student on a regular basis. An excellent resource for assessing and teaching O&M skills is TAPS (Pogrund et al., 1993).

The following are examples of realistic goals for O&M for students with visual impairments:

- Use visual cues, such as the light from the window, to find the Braillewriter on the shelf (sensory skills).
- Locate the water fountain two doors to the right of the cafeteria, or find the clothing hook that is second from the end (concept development).
- Use auditory clues, such as the sound of computers, to locate the principal's office in the school, or use tactile clues such as the textured wall to locate the gym (environmental awareness).

Human Guide Technique

The human guide technique is used most frequently by children and youths with visual impairments in general education classrooms and other school and community environments. When walking with another person, the student with a visual impairment grasps the sighted person's arm just above the elbow and walks about a half step behind the guide. The student follows the guide's body movements to go from place to place, around obstacles, through narrow passageways, and up and down stairs.

Visual Efficiency

Children with visual impairments can learn to use their vision efficiently through a variety of instructional approaches provided by the TVI, COMS, and low-vision specialist. Ophthalmologists and optometrists who specialize in low vision can also help many children and youth with visual impairments to see better by prescribing optical aids for specific activities. For example, a monocular telescope may enable a student to see the chalkboard, find a friend's house number, or see the pins and score when bowling with friends who are sighted. A magnifier placed directly on a page or inserted on eyeglasses may enable a student to read regular print books in school, a menu at a restaurant, or price tags on clothing in a store.

Environmental factors also play a key role in enhancing the visual efficiency of children and youth who have visual impairments. Environmental modifications can

Teachers can reduce visual clutter in many ways, including using a piece of paper to guide the reader and allow him to focus on one line at a time.

eliminate or reduce visual fatigue, allowing many students to participate in activities more successfully. Specific factors include (Corn, DePriest, & Erin, 2000; Silberman, Bruce & Nelson, 2004)

- lighting (reducing or increasing illumination),
- color and contrast (providing enhanced contrast of objects in the environment),
- glare (reducing interference of glare on visual activities),
- visual clutter (keeping classroom and student's work area simple), and
- size and distance (determining appropriate size of objects presented and distance from the teacher or whiteboard).

Teachers of young children and of students who have additional disabilities should integrate visual-enhancement activities into the general education curriculum. Specific skills such as fixating on objects, tracking moving objects, shifting the gaze from one object to another, and reaching for objects after locating them visually should be taught as part of the child's natural routines throughout the day.

Social Interaction Skills

Children and youth with visual impairments need to develop specific social skills that their peers who are sighted learn through visual observation. Instruction in social interaction skills may include greeting through verbal or gestural means, orienting toward others when speaking, beginning and ending conversations appropriately, choosing clothing that is appropriate for specific activities, and requesting assistance such as transportation to an activity.

Leisure and Recreational Activities

Many recreational activities are easily adapted for children and youth with visual impairments. For example, physical games and activities can be more accessible through the use of guide ropes, tactual or brightly colored markings, beepers, audible balls, and sighted guides. Activities such as swimming and hiking require almost no adaptations. Card games, chess, checkers, and other board games are easily adapted using Braille and enlarged print.

Career Education

Career education for students with visual impairments should begin early and continue throughout their school years. Many students who graduate from high school and college have poor work habits, such as tardiness, disorganization, and inappropriate work-related social skills. Examples of career education competencies that can be taught are the following:

- *Preschool:* Orienting and attending to a speaker; following class rules; putting clothing and supplies where they belong
- *Elementary school:* Following oral or written instructions to order materials from APH; working unassisted on assignments using adaptive tools and materials
- *Middle school:* Identifying and describing roles of major community workers; performing volunteer and paid work for neighbors and family members
- *High school:* Showing well-developed work behaviors such as paying attention to details and performing tasks even when they are difficult or unpleasant

Because of their lack of vision, students with visual impairments do not know the myriad of jobs that are available, and they miss out on the huge amount of information about careers that sighted students acquire. For example, students with visual impairments may not see the librarian at work or a teller counting money in a bank. As part of their educational program, they should be exposed to different career alternatives, develop appropriate work habits, and be given guided work responsibilities and structured experiences that will help them choose an appropriate career (Wolffe, 2000).

Assistive Technology

Students with visual impairments need to learn to use a variety of assistive devices so they can access information. These may include

- videomagnifiers (closed circuit television);
- notetakers with speech, Braille, and print output;
- Braille translation programs;
- computer access through Braille displays or speech programs;
- screen-enlargement programs; and
- digital book readers.

Assistive technology assessment should consider the student's level of functioning and preferred learning medium. Students need instruction in selecting appropriate devices and techniques for using and maintaining them. It can be helpful for students seeking any kind of assistance, whether it's a technical device or something like a monocular telescope, to work into its use gradually, see other people using or modeling it, learn about it in class, or demonstrate it for others.

Independent Living Skills

Children and youth with visual impairments need structured, task-analyzed instruction in daily living skills such as eating, dressing, grooming, preparing food, taking care of their clothing, managing money, and shopping. They do not learn these skills incidentally by observing and imitating their parents, siblings, and peers. Therefore, specific instruction is essential, taking a team approach with the parents as active participants, to help them become self-sufficient.

Access to the General Education Curriculum and Settings

Access to general education requires adaptations and targeted strategies, learning materials and devices geared to children with visual impairments, and assistive technology so these children can access print materials.

Classroom Adaptations and Strategies

The following adaptations and strategies will help general education teachers include children with visual impairments in daily activities with classmates who do not have disabilities (Silberman, Bruce, & Nelson, 2004; Spungin, McNear, & Torres, 2002):

- When approaching a student who is blind or has a visual impairment, always state your name and encourage the students in the class to do the same.
- When addressing a student who is blind, call him or her by name so the student is sure that he or she is the one being called on.
- When the class is using visual materials such as films or pictures, provide brief descriptions of the materials.
- When speaking to a student who is blind, feel comfortable using words such as *see* and *look*. The student sees and looks with his or her hands.
- Avoid standing with your back to the window, as the glare from the window will prevent students with low vision from focusing on you.
- When scheduling daily activities, rotate activities requiring vision with those involving auditory and motor channels, to accommodate the needs of students with low vision who may become fatigued.
- Allow extended time to students with visual impairments for taking exams or completing written reports or assignments in class based on assessed student needs.
- Change seats or student groupings regularly in cooperative learning projects, to enhance opportunities for social interaction betweeen the student who is blind and peers without disabilities.
- Use more than one way to present information in learning centers, on bulletin boards, and other points for information access (e.g., both a recorded and a printed copy of the same book).

Note

As students near adulthood, they must make the transition into more independent living. Adaptations such as larger bank checks with raised lines and personal projection screens can help manage their daily routine.

- Work with the TVI: Include other students in lessons and activities with the student who has the visual impairment, to increase awareness and knowledge of alternative ways of acquiring information.
- Provide the student with visual impairment with three-dimensional concrete objects or models during demonstrations, particularly in science, and have the student nearby, to be able to touch the materials being described to the class.

Learning Materials and Devices

Most curricular materials in public schools emphasize visual features, including pictures, graphs, print, visual formatting, video, and computer software. Access to the general curriculum for a child who is visually impaired depends on availability of adaptive materials that allow enhancement of visual features or use of tactile or auditory media. Because materials often have to be prepared individually, teachers must identify the necessary materials well in advance—usually early in the spring preceding the new school year. The 2004 reauthorization of IDEA requires publishers to provide text materials in a consistent electronic format, that of the National Instructional Materials Accessibility Standard (NIMAS), to lessen the preparation time for materials in alternative formats.

Assistive Technology Devices for Accessing Print Materials in the General Education Classroom

Students with visual impairments can access print materials used in the general curriculum via specialized equipment and software, including the following (Lewis, 2004):

- *Screen reader:* Uses synthesized speech to read text displayed on a computer monitor as the user moves a cursor or types on a keyboard
- *Braille embosser:* Uses a Braille-translation program to emboss a Braille version of the print materials; connected to a computer
- *Screen-enlargement software:* Is installed in a computer to increase the size of characters on the screen, the cursor, the menu, and dialogue boxes
- *Closed-circuit television (CCTV):* Magnifies print material or graphics placed on a viewing stand that can be seen on a monitor
- *Optical character readers (OCRs):* A scanner, connected to a computer, that scans printed material that is converted into a computer text file

Non-Optical Devices to Enhance Visual Functioning in the Classroom

Many children and youth who have low-vision benefit from simple non-optical aids and devices that help them use their vision more efficiently and reduce visual fatigue.

- *Bookstands:* Allow the individual to raise, angle, and/or bring the print closer to the eyes; they reduce postural fatigue caused by bending over to get close to the printed material.
- *Felt-tip pens:* Produce a dark, bold line for creating letters and diagrams. They come in varying widths; black ink usually is preferred.
- *Acetate:* Involves placing yellow acetate over the printed page to darken the print and heighten the contrast with the background paper.
- *Large-print textbooks:* Can be helpful for students who cannot read regular print at close distances with an optical aid. Some students use large print only for

subjects such as mathematics, because of the tiny symbols and tight spacing. Boldness and spacing of letters, the contrast, and paper color and quality also affect ease of reading. Because some children with visual impairments do not benefit from enlarged type, it should be provided only if the team supports the need based on assessment results. Limitations of large-type books are their lack of color, oversize, and reduced availability after the student leaves school.

- *Lighting with rheostats:* Enable the student to increase or decrease the illumination and adjust the angle of light in each room.

Tactual Aids

Children and youth who are blind use a variety of tactual devices and aids for learning. Some learners with low vision also use them along with visual and auditory aids.

- *Braille books:* Produced by transcribers, computers, commercial publishers, and APH. Braille readers should have direct access to a Braille text to allow them to read along with their peers.
- *Braillewriter:* A machine for typing Braille on paper. The machine has six keys, corresponding to the six dots in the Braille cell; a space bar; a back spacer; and a line spacer.
- *Slate and stylus:* A metal frame with openings through which Braille dots are punched with a pointed stylus. The student writes from right to left and turns the paper over to read the Braille.
- *Braille notetaker:* Quiet and portable technological devices that often are no larger than a book. They have many functions, including saving and editing material, linking to printers and computers, and providing auditory feedback; some models have a Braille display.
- *Sewell kit:* Consists of a rubber-covered board on which acetate or paper is placed, allowing the user to use raised lines to represent shapes or graphics with a pen or pointed object.
- *Tactile graphics kit:* Contains tools that produce various types of textured lines and shapes that can be used for drawing graphs and maps for social studies and O&M.
- *Tactual maps and globes:* Have raised surfaces and textures for demonstrating geographic concepts; can be purchased or made from craft materials.
- *Abacus:* A nonelectronic tool, similar to the Japanese soroban, that children who are blind can use for calculation; it has felt backing so the beads do not slip.
- *Braille measuring devices:* Rulers, compasses, protractors, and measuring tapes with raised or Braille markings to allow tactile use during mathematics activities.
- *Templates and writing guides:* Open, rectangular forms made of cardboard, plastic, or metal that enable students to write within boundaries when producing signatures, filling out forms, etc.

An abacus

Devices to Enhance Auditory Functioning

Children and youth with visual impairments use auditory devices, often in combination with tactile and/or visual aids. These include cassette tape recorders, compact disc players, talking calculators and watches, digital text players, and recorded books on CDs or cassette tapes. Also, audible gym equipment such as beeper balls and goal locators enable them to participate in gym activities with their sighted peers.

Resources

Most states have an Instructional Materials Center that distributes materials for visually impaired students. In some states Educational Service Centers or Intermediate Units assist in supplying materials provided by government or nonprofit agencies, including the American Printing House for the Blind, American Foundation for the Blind, Recordings for the Blind and Dyslexic, and the National Library for the Blind and Physically Handicapped.

Placements and Services

Placements and services cover a spectrum from preschool programs to general education classes, special classes, specialized schools for students with visual impairments, and postsecondary services.

Preschool Programs

Programs for infants and children under age 3 are either home-based or center-based. At the preschool level, children attend specialized centers, private preschools, or special public school classes, with services from a TVI as appropriate. Programming encourages development of early motor experiences, language, conceptual skills, and social skills.

General Education Classes

Most students with visual impairments spend some or all of their school day in a general education class with nondisabled peers. These students receive services from a TVI, who usually is an itinerant teacher who travels from school to school and works directly with a student for a few hours a week or serves as a consultant to the educational team.

Special Classes

In this option, students spend most of the day in a special class in the public school building with a highly qualified teacher of learners with visual impairments. Sometimes children with additional disabilities are educated in specialized classrooms taught by other special educators, and the TVI serves as an itinerant teacher or consultant.

Specialized Schools for Students With Visual Impairments

Some students attend specialized schools as day or residential students, where they have access to specially trained personnel, educational materials, and technological aids to meet their unique needs (Lewis & Allman, 2000). Although many students who attend specialized schools have additional disabilities, students whose only disability is visual impairment also may attend because they need services that are not available locally. Many schools also provide short-term intensive instruction on weekends and during summers in areas such as assistive technology, study skills, and career education skills.

Postsecondary Services

Transition planning should begin when the child is 14 years old, and a statement of transition services should be incorporated into the IEP by the time a student is 16—or earlier, if appropriate. Transition planning should involve a team consisting of the student, parents, TVI, COMS, general educator, other special educators if appropriate, and representatives of appropriate adult service agencies (Lewis & Allman, 2000). Work experiences, postsecondary education, travel and transportation, residential options, and mentoring opportunities with adults with visual impairments should be considered in transition planning.

Summary

Although children and youth with visual impairments represent only a small percentage of the overall population, the wide variation in ages and levels of functioning require a broad range of services to help them reach their full educational potential. A collaborative team that includes highly qualified TVIs and COMS must be included in both assessment and curriculum planning to ensure that the unique needs of children with visual impairments are met.

Instructional strategies should address appropriate accommodations and adaptations necessary for students with visual impairments to acquire academic content areas (core curriculum) and specialized instruction in expanded core curriculum areas that include compensatory skills such as communication modes, visual efficiency, social interaction skills, career education, independent living skills, assistive technology, recreation and leisure, and transition. The availability of appropriate adapted materials, including Braille books and low-vision devices, will ensure that this population of learners receives the most successful educational opportunities possible.

References

American Printing House for the Blind. (2006). *Annual report 2005*. Louisville, KY: Author.

Anthony, T. L. (2000). Performing a functional low vision assessment. In F. M. D'Andrea & C. Farrenkopf (Eds.), *Looking to learn: Promoting literacy for students with low vision* (pp. 32–83). New York: AFB Press.

Anthony, T. L. (2003). *Individual sensory learning profile interiew.* Chapel Hill, NC: Early Intervention Training Center for Infants and Toddlers with Visual Impairments (FPG Child Development Institute, UNC-CH.

Assessment. (2004). Retrieved October 5, 2005, from http://www.tsbvi.edu/recc/assessment.htm

Barclay, L. (2003). Expanded core curriculum: Education. In S. Goodman & S. Wittenstein (Eds.), *Collaborative assessment* (pp. 94–121). New York: AFB Press.

Barraga, N. C., & Erin, J. N. (2001). *Visual impairments & learning* (4th ed.). Austin, TX: Pro-Ed.

Barraga, N., & Morris, J. (1980). *Program to develop efficiency in visual functioning.* Louisville, KY: American Printing House for the Blind.

Boehm, A. E. (1971). *Boehm test of basic concepts.* San Antonio, TX: Psychological Corp.

Caton, H. (1976). *Tactile test of basic concepts.* Louisville, KY: American Printing House for the Blind.

Caton, H. R., Pester, E., & Bradley, E. J. (1983). *Patterns: The primary Braille reading program.* Louisville, KY: American Printing House for the Blind.

Corn, A. L., DePriest, L. B., & Erin, J. N. (2000). Visual efficiency. In A. J. Koenig & M. C. Holbrook (Eds.), *Foundations of education: Instructional strategies for teaching children and youths with visual impairments* (Vol. 2, pp. 464–499). New York: AFB Press.

Corn, A. L. & Koenig, A. J. (1996). Perspectives on low vision. In A. L. Corn & A. J. Koenig (Eds.), *Foundations of low vision: Clinical and functional perspectives* (pp. 3–25). New York: AFB Press.

Fazzi, D., & Klein, M. D. (2002). Cognitive focus: Developing cognition, concepts, and language. In R. L. Pogrund & D. L. Fazzi (Eds.), *Early focus: Working with young children who are blind or visually impaired and their families, 2nd ed.* (pp. 107–151). New York: AFB Press.

Gense, M. H., & Gense, D. J. (2005). *Autism spectrum disorders and visual impairment.* New York: AFB Press.

Hatlen, P. (1996). The core curriculum for blind and visually impaired students, including those with additional disabilities. *RE:view, 28,* 25–32.

Hatlen, P. (1998). Foreword. In S. Z. Sacks & R. K. Silberman (Eds.), *Educating students who have visual impairments with other disabilities* (pp. xv–xvi). Baltimore: Paul H. Brookes Publishing.

Hatton, D. D., Topor, I., & Rosenblum, L. P. (2004). Visual conditions in infants and toddlers. In I. Topor, L. P. Rosenblum, & D. D. Hatton (Eds.), *Visual conditions and functional vision: Early intervention issues* (pp. 159–277). Chapel Hill, NC: FPG Child Development Institute.

Heinze, T. (2000). Comprehensive assessment. In M. C. Holbrook & A. J. Koenig (Eds.), *Foundations of education: Vol 2. Instructional strategies for teaching children and youths with visual impairments, 2nd ed.* (pp. 27–59). New York: AFB Press.

Huebner, K. M. (2000). Visual impairment. In M. C. Holbrook & A. Koenig (Eds.), *Foundations of education: History and theory of teaching children and youths with visual impairments, 2nd ed.* (Vol. 1, pp. 55–76). New York: AFB Press.

Koenig, A. J., & Holbrook, M. C. (1995). *Learning media assessment of students with visual impairments: A resource guide for teachers.* Austin: Texas School for the Blind and Visually Impaired.

Langley, M. B. (1998). *Individualized, systematic assessment of visual efficiency (ISAVE).* Louisville, KY: American Printing House for the Blind.

Lewis, S. (2004). Visual impairments. In R. Turnbull, A. Turnbull, M. Shank, & S. J. Smith (Eds.), *Exceptional lives: Special education in today's schools, 4th ed.* (pp. 456–486). Upper Saddle River, NJ: Pearson/Merrill Prentice Hall.

Lewis, S., & Allman, C. (2000). Educational programming. In M. C. Holbrook & A. J. Koenig (Eds.), *Foundations of education: Instructional strategies for teaching children and youths with visual impairments, 2nd ed.* (Vol. 1, pp. 218–246). New York: AFB Press.

Lowenfeld, B. (1981a). Effects of blindness on the cognitive functions of children. In B. Lowenfeld (Ed.), *Berthold Lowenfeld on blindness and blind people* (pp. 67–78). New York: American Foundation for the Blind.

Lowenfeld, B. (1981b). The child who is blind. In B. Lowenfeld (Ed.), *Berthold Lowenfeld on blindness and blind people* (pp. 29–37). New York: American Foundation for the Blind.

Lueck, A. H., Chen, D., & Kekelis, L. (1997). *Developmental guidelines for infants with visual impairment: A manual for early intervention.* Louisville, KY: American Printing House for the Blind.

Mangold, S. S. (1977). *The Mangold developmental program of tactile perception and Braille letter recognition.* Castro Valley, CA: Exceptional Teaching Aids.

Mar, H. H., & Cohen, E. J. (1998). Educating students with visual impairments who exhibit emotional and behavior problems. In S. Z. Sacks & R. K. Silberman (Eds.), *Educating students who have visual impairments with other disabilities* (pp. 262–302). Baltimore: Paul H. Brookes Publishing.

No Child Left Behind Act of 2001, PL 107-110, 115 Stat. 1425, 20 U.S.C. §6301 *et seq.* (2001).

Pogrund, R., Healy, G., Jones, K., Levack, N., Martin-Curry, S., Martinez, C., Marz, J., Roberson-Smith, B., & Vrba, A. (1993). *Teaching age-appropriate purposeful skills:*

An orientation and mobility curriculum for students with visual impairments. Austin: Texas School for the Blind and Visually Impaired.

Sacks, S. Z., & Silberman, R. K. (2000). Social skills. In A. J. Koenig & M. C. Holbrook (Eds.), *Foundations of education: Instructional strategies for teaching children and youths with visual impairments, 2nd ed.* (Vol. 2, pp. 616–652). New York: AFB Press.

Silberman, R. K., Bruce, S., & Nelson, C. (2004). Children with sensory impairments. In F. P. Orelove, D. Sobsey, & R. K. Silberman (Eds.), *Educating children with multiple disabilities: A collaborative approach, 4th ed.* (pp. 425–527). Baltimore: Paul H. Brookes Publishing.

Spungin, S. J., McNear, D., & Torres, I. (2002). *When you have a visually impaired student in your classroom: A guide for teachers.* New York: AFB Press.

Warren, D. H. (2000). Developmental perspectives. In B. Silverstone, M. A. Lang, B. P. Rosenthal, & E. E. Faye (Eds.), *The Lighthouse handbook on vision impairment and vision rehabilitation* (Vol. 1, pp. 325–337). New York: Oxford University Press.

Wolffe, K. (2000). Career education. In A. J. Koenig & M. C. Holbrook (Eds.), *Instructional strategies for teaching children and youths with visual impairments* (2nd ed., Vol. 2, pp. 679–719). New York: AFB Press.

Moderate to Severe Disabilities Instructional Perspectives

14

Edward L. Meyen & Yvonne N. Bui

like the other bridging chapters that conclude each part of the book, chapter 14 is intended to complement the disability-specific chapters. This chapter presents instructional strategies that are applicable to students with moderate to severe disabilities. If you are preparing to teach students with exceptional learning needs, you may have questions about the logic of grouping the chapters in Part III under the heading of Students With Moderate to Severe Disabilities. This is understandable, as learners within each disability group vary in their attributes and needs. For example, in reading the chapters related to moderate to severe disabilities (i.e., cognitive and developmental disabilities, autism spectrum disorders, deafness, and visual impairments), you learned that the conditions characterizing these disabilities result in learners of varying ability, need for specialized instruction, potential for independence, and success in accessing the general education curriculum.

You also have learned that some students with the disabilities described in these chapters do well in inclusion settings and others require more direct and intense interventions to achieve their potential. In addition, as you become familiar with the professional literature, you will encounter instructional resources that are disability-specific. Only in the most recent literature do you see classification of disability groups by descriptive terms such as moderate, severe, or high-incidence and low-incidence.

Placing Disability Groupings in Perspective

In chapter 1, covering the history of special education and the need for legislation to create programs for students with disabilities, we pointed out that one of the major factors contributing to the need for special legislation to mandate educational programs for learners with disabilities was the incidence of students with disabilities. The higher the incidence, or the larger the number of students with a specific disability, the more likely a state was to respond to advocacy efforts to establish special education programs. The same was true at the national level. Within low-incidence groups are those whose disabilities are the most serious. States have been slower to respond by providing special education to meet the needs of these students.

In developing special education programs over several decades, terms referring to levels of severity and levels of incidence have come to be used as a form of shorthand to communicate about groups of learners. These terms, however, convey little about the instructional needs of these students. Instead, what is communicated are the relative numbers and the intensity of interventions required to enhance their educational performance.

Another term you have encountered in the literature and in this book that pertains to classifying groups of students with disabilities is *category*. For a significant period during the 1950s, 1960s, and part of the 1970s, each disability (e.g., learning disabilities, speech and communication disorders, emotional/behaviors disorders, hearing impaired) was considered as a category of disability. Special education programs were developed to serve children based on their disability label (i.e., category), and teacher education programs were structured to prepare teachers to teach students within a specific category. This approach—referred to as categorical programming—was replaced later by noncategorical programming. Now students' instructional needs, rather than the characteristic of learners with a disability, have become the common denominator for determining educational classifications.

Although these classification systems may seem disconnected from learners' instructional needs, they served a useful function at the time they were used. Much of the United States is rural, and these schools typically have only one or two students with a severe disability in attendance. When instructional programming is the focus, schools have to respond to groups of students with common needs. In this context, the population base necessary to yield a sufficient number of students within a disability group and to be able to plan for teachers and interventions for students who share common attributes is paramount.

As interventions have become more powerful and we have learned more about ways to support students with disabilities in inclusion settings, these issues have less significance. More attention now is directed to factors other than disability—such as performance, social adjustment, readiness, and maturity—in determining the appropriateness of placement. This does not minimize the importance of considering the individual needs and learning attributes of students based on their disability, but it does mean that broader groupings and integration are viewed as important in ensuring access to instructional programming for these students. For this reason, in the current literature, information relevant to instruction and the emerging research-based practices tend to be organizing program designs around incidence or level of severity. For the immediate future, low-incidence or moderate to severe classifications will remain part of our nomenclature, if for no other reason than to communicate through existing legislation and policy.

Uniqueness and Similarities Among Students With Moderate to Severe Disabilities ■ ■ ■ ■ ■

Learners with moderate to severe disabilities tend to have more attributes and instructional needs that are specific to their disabilities than do students with mild disabilities. These unique attributes translate into the need for intense interventions and, therefore, special training for teachers. For example, a blind student likely will have to be taught the skills necessary for her to become proficient in generating Braille products and in reading Braille. This same student may not have special needs in terms of the curriculum. Her unique needs are instructional in nature, not content related. Consequently, the general education curriculum is just as applicable to her as to students without a disability. Finally, her unique needs are not necessarily shared with other students who have moderate to severe disabilities.

Taking another case, a student who is deaf may require the use of augmented communication devices or have to be taught sign language as a result of his deafness. These same skills or resources may be applicable to hearing peers or to other students with moderate to severe disabilities. For example, a student with a cognitive disability may be taught sign language as a young child to enhance her communications skills. The use of these skills and tools by individuals with other disabilities is often overlooked by the general public.

Note

In the field of special education, the focus has shifted from labeling the disability to how these students learn and how we as a society can reach them. The person is always placed before any disability he or she may have, which requires educators to be more open-minded and think outside the box in terms of teaching strategies and adaptations.

In another example, the stress experienced by a student with moderate to severe disabilities often evokes behaviors that are inappropriate in social situations or significantly interfere with learning. Thus, although the student does not have a behavior disorder, he may display behaviors not unlike those of a student with an emotional or behavior disorder.

Regardless of their disability, in coping with their frustrations, students may respond to interventions designed to assist students with severe behavior disorders. For example, the positive behavior supports discussed in chapter 5 may apply to students with severe to moderate disabilities even when their primary needs are more unique to their disability (e.g., cognitive disability).

Figure 14.1 illustrates the concept of shared versus unique instructional needs. The challenge for teachers is in determining shared instructional needs. Although these needs are not the same for all learners within a disability group, some generalizations are possible. The proportion of shared and unique needs reflected in Figure 14.1 is merely an approximation. Beginning teachers should become familiar with the shared instructional needs and the interventions that are most likely to generalize across students within the classification.

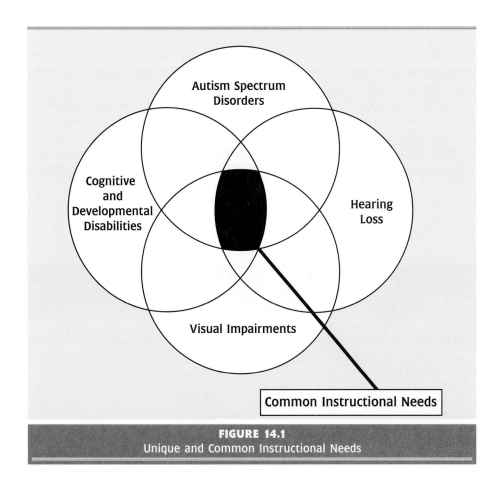

FIGURE 14.1
Unique and Common Instructional Needs

Instructional Strategies
That Generalize

In studying the chapters in Part III pertaining to students with moderate to severe disabilities, you learned that students with different disabilities have attributes that require specialized approaches to instruction. Becoming skilled in meeting these needs requires specific skills and knowledge. Your teacher education program includes extensive preparation in this area. The program also may provide you opportunities to become familiar with instructional strategies and curriculum content that generalize across most students with severe to moderate disabilities. That is important, as you will be expected to be familiar with the needs that are most common in students.

In an attempt to confirm the strategies and content that generalize to diverse groups of students to which beginning teachers should be introduced, we surveyed five teacher educators experienced in preparing teachers to work with students with moderate to severe disabilities. Each participant also was recognized as a contributor to the professional literature in research-based practices for students with moderate to severe disabilities. As a background for the survey, the participants received a description of the purpose and organization of this book and a statement describing our request for input on educational practices that generalize across the instructional needs of students with moderate to severe disabilities. They were asked to relate the five or six educational practices that came to mind as they thought about this group of learners—educational practices that generalize across learners and learning environments.

All participants responded to the survey. The educational practices reported ranged from 5 to 11, with a total of 47. In the open-ended inquiry, the responses varied from a list of explicit practices to descriptive statements that included more than single practices. After eliminating redundancies and consolidating responses that were similar, five topical areas were identified as reflecting the consensus on educational practices that generalize sufficiently to warrant being introduced to beginning teachers.

Table 14.1 lists the topics on which the survey respondents agreed. These topics will be discussed here in a context applicable to beginning teachers, with an emphasis on research-based practices.

TABLE 14.1
Educational Practices That Generalize Across Students
With Moderate to Severe Disabilities

Practices That Generalize	References to Other Chapters in This Book
1. Balancing functional/ general education curriculum	Chapters 10, 15
2. Universal design for learners	Chapters 4, 15
3. Self-determination	Chapters 3, 10, 15
4. Cooperative learning	Chapter 15
5. Alternate assessment	Chapter 1

Balancing Functional/ General Educational Curriculum

For many students with moderate to severe disabilities, especially those with cognitive disabilities, the curriculum has emphasized life skills such as learning how to manage public transportation and buy groceries. This functional approach has been integrated into their individualized education programs (IEP), and teacher education programs have prepared teachers on competencies related to the functional model. At the same time, the curriculum has been largely individualized to accommodate the growth and development of these learners in an effort to ensure that they progress to their potential.

In comparing the typical functional curriculum for students with moderate to severe disabilities with the general education curriculum on an appropriate age-level basis, the differences are clear. These differences are distinguished largely by the academic orientation of the general education curriculum (e.g., reading, math) and the scope of expected outcomes by grade level. In addition, the instructional settings in which the two types of curriculum are delivered vary, with much more of the functional curriculum being implemented in community settings versus the classroom.

As discussed in this chapter and in chapter 1, the passage of NCLB is introducing widespread changes in education. NCLB's emphasis on standards-based instruction as a construct for the general education curriculum and the accompanying accountability system of statewide assessments have significant implications for students with moderate to severe disabilities. Specifically, while offering high academic expectations for all students, a standards-based curriculum does not reflect the curricular elements that are essential to instructional planning for students whose needs require components of a functional curriculum. Nor does the general education setting offer the richness of community-based learning that is critical for students who need a functional curriculum.

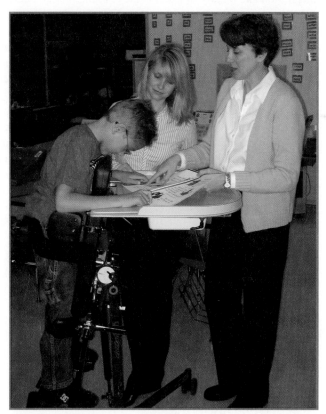

This student works on part of his functional curriculum (i.e., using his stander) while completing a reading lesson from his general education curriculum.

Teaching Context

The challenge for teachers of students with moderate to severe disabilities in an age of standards-based instruction is to ensure that the general education curriculum is balanced with students' functional needs. This does not suggest ignoring the standards and content frameworks of the general education curriculum. Rather, it means that these frameworks must be translated so the standards or the benchmarks and indicators reflect reasonable expectations for students with moderate to severe disabilities. This may involve examining the curriculum used with these students and aligning it with the general education curriculum. The alignment should focus on what the student needs to learn from an analysis perspective, not a predetermined level of outcome. Thus, teachers should be guided by the standards-based general education curriculum from the perspective of content, while advocating for a functional orientation.

Community-Based Instruction

Community-based instruction (CBI) is one popular method that teachers can apply to meet students' functional needs in the community setting. In CBI, students receive opportunities to learn, practice, and apply life skills in the natural settings in which they are expected or appropriate. Examples of functional life skills critical to community integration and quality of life include learning how to balance a checkbook, navigating public transportation, doing laundry at a public facility, and dining at a restaurant.

Generalizing or applying skills learned in a classroom setting to the real-life scenario in the community is difficult for many students with moderate to severe disabilities. Depending on the resources available, within CBI students can either apply the knowledge they learned in an academic setting to real-life settings or actually learn the skills in the natural setting.

Integrating the functional and general curriculum within CBI is a powerful tool to help in the transition of students with moderate to severe disabilities from school to the work environment. IDEA allows students with severe or multiple disabilities to attend school until they are 21 years old. Thus, their school experiences should prepare them for life after school, where they can be integrated into the community and be as independent as possible. For a successful transition, students must gain experience with types of jobs in which they are interested and learn how to access community services and resources.

One way to implement CBI in the secondary grades is for a student with a disability to be fully included in general education classes with peers and also spend some time each day in the community, working at a job or learning about services in the community (Friend, 2005). For example, a high school student with Down syndrome could be in a general education science class in the morning and work part time in the afternoon at the local pet store across town, to which she has to ride a public bus. In the morning, in her biology class, the student learns about animals, and later in the day she can apply this knowledge at her job at the pet store. At the same time, she is learning about how to use public transportation and managing a savings account, where she deposits her paychecks.

Research-Based Practices

Because transferring skills from an artificial setting (e.g., classroom) to an authentic setting (e.g., jobsite) is challenging for individuals with moderate to severe disabilities

Note

Community-based instruction is also commonly known as functional life skills curriculum. CBI is a method of instruction that is designed to incorporate community-working experiences such as banking skills and job training into students' educational programs.

(Westling & Fox, 2000), researchers and practitioners suggest teaching students critical life skills within the natural environments of their homes, places of employment, and communities. For example, a high school student with autism may have an interest in fixing cars. One option would be to have him take two years of auto mechanics classes at school and then apply for a job at an auto repair shop after graduation. Another option would be for him to learn how to fix cars by working for two years at an auto repair shop with support from a job coach. When students learn functional skills at actual job-sites, it positively impacts their learning and generalizing of other skills they will need for employment (e.g., being punctual, being well groomed) and independent living (Dymond & Orelove, 2001).

According to some experts, high school students with multiple/severe disabilities may receive as much as 90% of their educational program in community settings (NICHCY, 2001). This type of on-the-job training makes it easier for students to transition to supported employment (e.g., with a job coach or supervisor) after high school, and later to competitive work in fully integrated settings. This is much preferred over sheltered employment or day activity centers, in which the individuals work in segregated settings on artificial and menial tasks and receive low pay (Smith, 2004).

In some cases, teachers need to teach the relevant skills in an academic setting first and then give the students the opportunity to practice the skills in the community. Learning all the individual skills that go into a task all at once in a real-life scenario can be overwhelming for a student (not to mention very expensive!). To conduct simulations and trials in the classroom requires conducting a task analysis, breaking down the larger task into its subtasks.

For example, to teach the students how to dine in a restaurant, the teacher could set up a mock restaurant in the classroom and teach each skill needed to dine properly at a restaurant: approach the hostess, wait to be seated, read a menu, choose healthy food options, order the meal, use proper table etiquette, ask for the check, calculate the tip, pay the bill, and make sure to get proper change. In setting up mock environments, the teacher should create a look and feel as close as possible to the natural setting to best promote generalization and maintenance of skills to the real-life setting. In the restaurant example, this means getting real menus and table settings, using real money, and so on.

Some research supports this type of learning situation. In one study, students with moderate mental retardation were able to shop for groceries, including using math and problem-solving skills, after two days per week of CBI supplemented by simulation training in the classroom (Morse & Schuster, 2000).

Despite many positive outcomes, CBI poses a few dilemmas and has been subject to criticism. The first issue involves inclusion. If students are receiving a significant proportion of their education in community settings, they typically are not being educated with their general education peers. When implementing CBI, as mentioned, we must balance the students' need for a functional curriculum with access to the general education curriculum.

Universal Design for Learners

Special education has left a major legacy within education by directing attention to learners' individual differences. From the beginning of educational programs for learners with disabilities, the emphasis has been on assessing learners' abilities and needs and subsequently creating instructional interventions to enhance their ability to achieve their potential.

Initially, the approach was general, consisting mostly of grouping learners with similar needs for purposes of instruction, providing specialized equipment when needed, and using the assessment strategies of the day to individualize instruction. Over the years, we have learned much about assessment, instruction, curriculum, behavior, instructional design, and the validation of research-based practices. Teachers now have more knowledge and skills to apply in their teaching. They also are better prepared to determine how best to design instructional experiences for their students with exceptional learning needs.

We have known for a long time that instructional strategies designed for students with specific needs related to a given disability also are useful in teaching learners with other disabilities or learners with no known disability. This is because we have concentrated on creating instructional strategies for students with disabilities that employ the best of teaching, including techniques that engage learners and enhance their ability to generalize their learning to other situations. This is the ultimate goal of education.

Today the profession is undergoing a shift in how we look at the design of teaching methods, curriculum, and instructional resources in the context of meeting the instructional needs of diverse learners—if not all learners. Universal Design for Learning (UDL) is an emerging framework for designing learning experiences and instructional resources. David Rose, co-executive director of the Center for Applied Special Technology (CAST), has been at the forefront in moving the principles of universal design from its origins in the field of architecture to the education of students with disabilities (Tollefson, 2003).

The earlier work of Ron Mace in architecture gave rise to the concept of universal design. Rather than limit the utility and access of physical structures by their designs, Mace got the idea of creating designs that would maximally benefit all users. For example, with regard to accessibility, the focus shifted to accessibility for everyone, including those with disabilities. It had an aim of meeting the needs of all who may use an architectural structure rather than a narrow range of users. Out of these early stages of universal design in architecture evolved a philosophy of design that undergirds much of today's architecture.

In responding to the concept of universal design, CAST had the vision to harness the capacity of digital technologies to build instructional strategies and tools by applying the principles of universal designs to learning. The work of CAST has set the stage for broader application of these principles in education and changed the course of how technology is applied in education. In describing the work of CAST, Rose (with Meyer, 2000) did so in the context of the digital age by emphasizing that digitizing tools and multimedia and hypermedia software have enabled the exploration of electronic alternatives to printed books with "built-in" means of access to address the varied needs of learners.

Rose pointed to an important difference between universal design applied in architecture and universal design for learning by differentiating *access to information* and *access to learning*. Access to learning is important for all learners, but especially for those with moderate to severe disabilities. These learners depend more on others to structure resources, curricula, and experiences in ways that enhance their opportunity to learn. An example of a teaching strategy that adheres to the UDL principle is to demonstrate through modeling while explaining how to complete a task, followed by guided practice.

Note

Universal Design for Learning is, simply put, a reconceptualization of the curriculum so it is accessible and appropriate for students with different learning profiles.

The development of digital instructional resources has had a positive effect on the accommodations required by IDEA that are becoming available for students with disabilities, and in the design features that are being embedded in educational software and materials that are being integrated into the general education curriculum—for example, being able to convert text to audio easily by clicking a command in an e-learning program. This increases opportunities for students with disabilities to benefit from the general education curriculum while offering greater assurance that their curriculum is aligned with national and state curriculum standards. Chapter 15 addresses UDL from the perspective of technology-based instruction.

Teaching Context

Although all educators should understand the principles of UDL, this is especially important for teachers who have primary responsibility for students with disabilities. For UDL, as with any innovation, reform movement, or paradigm shift, we begin with a definition. Over time, new knowledge from experience and research changes the practices of UDL. The outcome becomes improved conditions and generalization of best practices. A popular definition of technology-based UDL is the one developed by the Council for Exceptional Children (1999):

> *In terms of learning, universal design means the design of instructional materials and activities that make the learning goals achievable for individuals with wide differences in their abilities to see, hear, speak, move, read, write, understand English, attend, organize, engage and remember. Universal design for learning is achieved by means of flexible curricular materials and activities that provide alternatives for students with differing abilities. These alternatives are built into the instructional design and operating systems of educational materials-they are not added on after-the-fact. (p. 4)*

In chapter 9 you learned about curriculum and instructional strategies applicable to students with mild to moderate disabilities. In reflecting on the discussion in that chapter related to reading, writing, and math, it becomes apparent that the concept of UDL may be achieved more readily in instructional settings that serve students with mild to moderate disabilities than those that serve students with moderate to severe disabilities. One reason is the closer relationship between curriculum standards as typically implemented in inclusion settings and the instructional needs of students with mild to moderate disabilities. As UDL receives more attention in teacher education and professional development programs, opportunities for involving teachers in the development and/or adoption of materials based on UDL will increase.

For teachers of students with moderate to severe disabilities, regardless of the instructional setting, the challenge is greater, but the need to achieve UDL may be even more significant. For example, for students who have significant sensory impairments, mobility challenges, cognitive disabilities, or other moderate to severe disabilities, teachers are faced with having to translate curriculum standards into content and instructional strategies that meet these students' needs. If a learner is unable to hear or comprehend instructional materials in printed form because of a disability, teaching becomes more complex. In teaching toward a standard set for all learners, you likely will find that for the student with moderate to severe disabilities, you will have to develop, augment, or adapt content and alter your performance expectations, and create alternative approaches to assessing student performance.

Rose (with Sethuraman & Meo, 2000) aptly described the challenge that teachers face in teaching diverse students while making sure that each student develops the skills necessary for success:

> *The traditional curricular toolbox, focused on text with ancillary other media, does not offer sufficient flexibility to meet varied learner needs. Implementing UDL to meet varied learner needs requires assembling a variety of tools, programs, materials and Web sites that can be used in different combinations for different learners and for different teaching purposes. The flexibility comes in part from the collection itself, which enables inherent flexibility of each component. (p. 4)*

When teachers are concerned with the wide array of learners typically found in inclusion settings, they are more likely to locate resources such as those cited by Rose than when they are concerned specifically with students who have moderate to severe disabilities.

Research-Based Practices

No formula or set of detailed resources is available from which to select UDL requirements for specific learners with moderate to severe disabilities. It is a matter of understanding the principles of UDL and applying them to the needs of individual learners. Wehmeyer, Lance, and Bashinski (2002) developed principles applicable to UDL within the context of a multi-level model that is useful for teachers. Table 14.2 presents a modified version of these principles.

This teacher practices using different instructional strategies with technology, focusing on appropriate content and the way her student responds.

TABLE 14.2
Principles, Rationale, and Criteria in Applying Universal Design to Curriculum, Instruction, and Evaluation

Principles/Rationale	Criteria
1. *Flexible use.* From the outset, curriculum, instruction, and evaluation should be designed for students with diverse abilities.	■ Accommodates students with diverse abilities ■ Accommodates students who speak various languages ■ Does not stigmatize students ■ Benefits as many potential users as possible ■ Avoids inconveniencing students with any particular characteristics
2. *Simple and intuitive use.* From the outset, curriculum, instruction, and evaluation should be designed to be as easy as possible to understand and use.	■ Is easy to use ■ Avoids unnecessary complexity ■ Provides clear directions and understandable examples ■ Breaks complex tasks into small steps
3. *Perceptible information.* From the outset, curriculum, instruction, and evaluation should be designed to be readily perceived regardless of environmental conditions or a user's sensory abilities.	■ Communicates information to users independent of environmental conditions and/or users' sensory abilities ■ Highlights essential information ■ Breaks information into comprehensible chunks
4. *Tolerance for error.* From the outset, curriculum, instruction, and evaluation should be designed to minimize the likelihood of error and the negative consequences resulting from error.	■ Avoids punishing students for mistakes ■ Provides ample time to respond ■ Provides immediate and thorough feedback ■ Monitors progress ■ Provides adequate practice time
5. *Reasonable physical, cognitive and psychological efforts.* From the outset, curriculum, instruction, and evaluation should be designed to avoid making a user uncomfortable or fatigued.	■ Presents information that can be completed in a reasonable timeframe ■ Avoids physically, cognitively, and/or psychologically exhausting the user
6. *Size and space for approach and use.* From the outset, curriculum, instruction, and evaluation should be designed to be used in a physically accessible manner.	■ Requires a reasonable amount of space ■ Incorporates accessible materials and learning activities

Source: From *Exceptional Lives: Special Education in Today's Schools* (4th ed.), by R. Turnbull, A. Turnbull, M. Shank, & S. J. Smith (Upper Saddle River, NJ: Pearson Education, 2004), p. 62.

You will want to make these UDL principles an integral part of your teaching philosophy and approach to instructional decision making. Research-based resources and practices will evolve to aid you in making UDL instructional decisions that match the needs of individual learners with moderate to severe disabilities. In the interim, you can build your own repertoire of options that meet the principles of UDL and are applicable to these students. Although this will be basically anecdotal in nature, it has to be systematic. In studying chapter 15, you will note that an emerging resource base of software programs is employing the principles of UDL. Although some are applicable to students with moderate to severe disabilities, most are designed for students whose needs are aligned more closely with the academic offerings of the general education curriculum.

As UDL principles get translated into research-based practices for students with moderate to severe disabilities, some practices that may prove useful to teachers are listed below. Employing these practices should enhance your effectiveness over time in implementing UDL principles with this population of students.

1. Become knowledgeable of the UDL principles.
2. Become skilled in adapting and augmenting content to individual needs.
3. Translate curriculum standards into teaching concepts or skills applicable to your students.
4. Profile your students' learning attributes.
5. Profile the augmentations and adaptations that you develop or adopt.
6. Record the augmentations and/or adaptations that work with given students.
7. Profile the alternate assessments you develop for measuring performance.
8. Collect data on students' responsiveness to the augmentations and adaptations.
9. Focus on content, instructional strategies, technology, and resources/materials.
10. Attend to the learning environment(s) in which you use UDL options successfully.

Self-Determination

Turnbull and Turnbull (2001) have defined self-determination for individuals with significant disabilities as "the means for experiencing a quality of life consistent with one's own values, preferences, strengths, and needs" (p. 56). They point out that the challenge is to develop a self-determined vision of quality of life, actualize the vision, and make adjustments and enhancements over the lifespan. Self-advocacy, goal setting and attainment, decision making, risk-taking, and self-awareness are among the behaviors reflected in curricula and instructional interventions designed to teach self-determination to students with disabilities.

Most of us have approached our lives in this manner without thinking about it in terms of self-determination. Although we have not all been successful, most of us, beginning in childhood, were encouraged to think about what we wanted to do when we grew up. As our ideas evolved, we were reminded of what we had to do to achieve those aspirations. This often involved going to college, attending a technical school, or doing an apprenticeship of some kind. Over time, our preferences or circumstances changed, and we made decisions on those aspects of our lives that we wanted to alter or adjust to attain the quality of life that was important to us at the time—whether it was getting a job with flexible hours so we could pursue an advanced degree, taking a job in another part of the country where we could pursue our love of the outdoors, or other options.

Historically, many children and youth with disabilities have not been encouraged to identify and pursue their aspirations. If their disabilities were in the moderate to severe range, their futures often were influenced by available options, not their aspirations. They typically did not assume an active role in influencing the nature or evolvement of their lives.

Over the past few decades, this situation has begun to change. This is largely because of more effective special education programs, public policy, changes in societal attitudes and values, and, more recently, the influence of those who espouse the principles of self-determination. The self-determination philosophy requires a commitment by teachers to prepare students with disabilities for assuming more active roles in their life decisions.

Through your study of the history of special education, you have become familiar with the early advocacy efforts required to frame legislation and to pass bills into law. As public policy began to change, circumstances changed and educational equity became a reasonable goal for students with disabilities through access to the general education curriculum and the accompanying accountability system, as called for in NCLB.

But much remains to be done for all students to realize equity. Acquisition of self-determination behaviors may well make the difference in closing the gap between what exists and true educational equity. As their aspirations for the quality of life they deserve translate into sources of motivation and confidence, students with disabilities can play a much more instrumental role in determining their own future. Rather than being dependent on advocates and policies to determine their destiny, they can be prepared as self-advocates, capable of making a difference in their lives by communicating their strengths, needs, preferences, aspirations, and values.

CASE STUDY: TERRA

Terra has been blind since birth. Her parents have been highly effective in ensuring that she has had access to needed services at the appropriate times. Terra quickly learned Braille and was responsive to mobility training. She was introduced to technology in preschool and immediately became computer-literate. By the time she was in elementary school, she was adept at using text readers and programs such as *Dragon Speaking Naturally*. When she entered middle school, her achievement level was above average, and teachers were impressed with her independence. Terra was resourceful and timely in submitting assignments. Although her personality is not outgoing, she continues to participate in class discussions. As a result of her academic performance and excellent technology skills, she has consistently met the goals set on her IEP.

Although their daughter's progress was highly satisfying for her parents and teachers, it was becoming apparent to her parents that Terra could do far more than was expected of her. They had created opportunities for her

(continued)

to participate in community activities and had enrolled her in computer application programs offered by the local community college. These were positive experiences for Terra, but her parents were beginning to notice that she often was reluctant to volunteer to demonstrate her skills when presented with opportunities to do so. Nor was she assertive in situations in which an initiative on her part would likely have resulted in additional instruction or opportunities for her to gain enrichment experiences.

As her parents reflected on these observations, they came to realize that the same behaviors characterized Terra's participation in IEP meetings. She accepted the goals set for her and met them fully within the specified time, but she never went beyond them. As important as these behaviors were, her parents were confident that she could do more if she were to become a self-advocate.

Following an IEP meeting, they asked their daughter how satisfied she was with the goals and if she thought she could do more. Terra responded that she could, but when asked why she didn't suggest this during the meeting, she replied that if the teachers were satisfied with her performance, that was good enough for her.

Over the next few days, her parents revisited this discussion and tried to help Terra think through the importance of communicating more directly what she believed she could do or aspire to. Although she understood her parents' perspective, she was quick to tell them that she was not comfortable in boasting about her skills or in disagreeing with her teachers. She was satisfied with doing what was asked of her. Her parents appreciated her attitude but at the same time were looking ahead to the day when Terra would be on her own, going to college and preparing for a career.

In visiting with friends who had a son who was enrolled in a program for students with Asperger syndrome, Terra's parents brought up their concerns and found that they had similar concerns about their son, Kerry, and had been working with his teacher on a self-determination program. As a result of this discussion, Kerry's parents arranged for Terra's parents to meet with the boy's teacher. That started Terra's parents on a fact-finding mission.

They soon learned that children and adolescents with disabilities commonly are not self-advocates or self-motivated. More important, they learned that a number of self-determination intervention programs have proven to be effective. They also learned that because Terra was so successful in the general education curriculum, her teachers had not sensed her need for instruction in self-determination.

The efforts of Terra's parents had a positive outcome. Terra's teachers engaged her in a self-determination program, and her parents supplemented the instruction with their own initiatives. Her parents felt good about the program and also learned that although Terra and Kerry were very different in terms of their disabilities, they shared a common need that could be met by instruction in self-determination.

Teaching Context

Many times throughout your career, you will be asked to explain your teaching philosophy. This may occur in a course, during an interview, in a parent–teacher conference, or in your association with professional colleagues. The assumption is that how you teach and relate to your students, and the decisions you make, are influenced by your teaching philosophy. The anticipated answer to this question is not a detailed description of theory or research-based practices. Rather, it is an expression of the beliefs that form the core of your teaching philosophy.

In writing about self-determination and standards-based reform, Wehmeyer, Field, Doren, Jones, and Mason (2004) make the point that "promoting self-determination has become 'best practice' in the education of students with disabilities" (p. 413). They emphasize that instruction on self-determination should be infused into the curriculum for all students, including students with disabilities. This is a significant statement—placing self-determination in the context of the core beliefs that merit consideration when developing a philosophy of teaching. As such, it gets to the heart of developing independent lifelong learners and individuals capable of participating in curriculum and life decisions.

Wehmeyer et al. (2004) also discuss the knowledge and skills standards included in the performance-based standards of the Council for Exceptional Children that relate to self-determination (see Table 14.3). No single standard addresses self-determination. Rather, the emphasis on self-determination is integrated throughout the standards. This

---

TABLE 14.3
CEC Knowledge and Skills Standards Related to Self-Determination

Instructional Strategies (S)
- Teach individuals to use self-assessment, problem-solving, and other cognitive strategies to meet their needs.
- Use procedures to increase the individual's self-awareness, self-management, self-control, self-reliance, and self-esteem.

Learning Environments and Social Interactions (S)
- Teach self-advocacy.
- Create an environment that encourages self-advocacy and increased independence.

Instructional Planning (S)
- Involve the individual and family in setting instructional goals and monitoring progress.
- Design and implement instructional programs that address independent living and career education for individuals.
- Design and implement curriculum and instructional strategies for medical self-management procedures.

Collaboration (S)
- Assist individuals with exceptional learning needs and their families in becoming active participants in the educational team.
- Plan and conduct collaborative conferences with individuals with exceptional learning needs and their families.

Source: From "Self-Determination and Student Involvement in Standards-Based Reform," by M. L. Wehmeyer, S. Field, B. Doren, B. Jones, & C. Mason, in _Exceptional Children, 70_(4), p. 419. Copyright © 2004.

reinforces the importance of teachers developing competencies for teaching self-determination principles and behaviors.

In examining the instructional terms embedded in the standards cited in Table 14.3, it is clear to see that they are important to the lives of students with moderate to severe disabilities, including skills in problem solving, self-advocacy, self-control, self-reliance, and self-esteem. With proper preparation, opportunities to teach these principles and behaviors can easily be integrated into the instructional program. Although the opportunities for teaching these vital skills are extant in the curriculum, they are not easy for the students to understand and incorporate into their repertoire of daily life skills. Therefore, parents and teachers must engage in purposeful teaching of these life skills and behaviors.

Research-Based Practices

Self-determination represents a relatively recent entry in the special education literature. It is based largely on principles and philosophical beliefs that undergird sound instructional practices with outcomes measured in quality-of-life indices. We can research levels of participation, problem-solving skills, and other behaviors related to self-determination, but the desired impact of these skills—to enhance the ability of individuals to influence the quality of life they later experience—is not easily measured, and re-teaching and reinforcement for applying the skills may be necessary over time. This is in contrast to academic skills such as reading and math, in which learners get immediate feedback from applying their skills in terms of whether they are correct or incorrect.

In reporting on the Self-Determination Synthesis Project funded by the Office of Special Education Programs, authors Karvonen, Test, Wood, Browder, and Algozzine (2004) described the literature base from 1972 to 2000 and their subsequent analysis to determine which interventions had been studied, and with whom. They found that all components of self-determination were reflected in the 51 studies they reviewed. Most of the studies focused on teaching choice-making to individuals with moderate and severe mental retardation or self-advocacy to individuals with learning disabilities or mental retardation. In addition, most of the studies targeted transition-age students (ages 14–21) or adults.

Parents play a significant role in shaping the behavior of their children. For students in general education, the focus of parents tends to be on academics and homework. However, for families of students with moderate to severe disabilities, life skills must receive equal emphasis. Grigal, Neubert, Moon, and Graham (2003) surveyed parents of high school students (16 years and older) with high- and low-incidence disabilities to determine their beliefs about self-determination. They found that the following three factors were significant:

1. IEPs—student participation in IEP meetings, parental beliefs about their child's involvement in IEP meetings, and teaching students how to participate in IEP meetings
2. Student expression of choice and interest, parental beliefs about their child's opportunities to express interests and abilities, as well as to make choices in school
3. Teaching self-determination, beliefs about the values of emphasizing self-esteem in their child's classes, as well as teaching goal-setting and decision-making processes

Teachers must not underestimate the ability of students with moderate to severe disabilities to achieve self-determination skills and behaviors. For these children to become self-advocates will necessitate purposeful efforts by teachers and family members to help them achieve proficiency in self-determination.

Cooperative Learning

As a special education teacher of students with moderate to severe disabilities, several roles may be available to you:

1. You might be assigned to a self-contained classroom (special day class) with a group of students who have varying disabilities similar to the one mentioned in the case study earlier in this chapter.
2. Your students may be in your special day class for most of the school day and mainstreamed into general education classrooms for some periods throughout the day.
3. All of your students may be fully included in general education classes for the entire school day (except for itinerant services) and you are the inclusion support teacher.

Regardless of the class setting, you will have to decide how you want to group the students for instructional purposes to meet their individual needs. Cooperative learning is one form of grouping and instructional strategy that can be implemented for students with moderate to severe disabilities in any type of class setting because it allows students with varying abilities and/or backgrounds to work together as a team to achieve a common goal.

Having students with disabilities work in cooperative learning groups has several advantages:

- In cooperative learning, students work in heterogeneous small groups to meet individual academic needs and goals. Small-group instruction can be utilized in a special day class and/or when students are mainstreamed or fully included in general education classrooms.
- Cooperative learning builds a sense of unity and interdependence in the classroom, as contrasted with an environment based on competition. Students are held accountable for their individual learning as well as the learning of their group members (Johnson & Johnson, 1991, 1999; Kagan, 1990; Wood & Algozzine, 1997).
- Especially if students are mainstreamed or fully included in general education, students with disabilities are integrated into the learning tasks with their nondisabled peers. This may lead to more positive attitudes toward students with disabilities by nondisabled peers, as well as the attitudes of students with disabilities toward themselves (Hallahan & Kauffman, 2003; Slavin, 1991).

Teaching Context

Cooperative learning should not be confused with "group work," in which students work on an activity with arbitrary partners or in small groups. Cooperative learning groups can be organized in at least three ways (Wood, 2002):

1. *Peer teaching*: Students work in pairs on a structured task. This can involve reviewing and testing each other on spelling words or math facts, or working

Note

Advantages to cooperative learning:
- Allows students of varying capabilities to work together as a team
- Builds unity in the classroom
- Fosters interdependence
- Holds students accountable for their team members
- Promotes social acceptance among students with differing abilities

All students can benefit from various forms of peer teaching, whether it's sharing an amusing passage in a book during personal reading time or collaborating on a project for a structured assignment.

together on a computer project (see chapter 9 for a discussion of peer-assisted learning). For example, if a student with cerebral palsy is mainstreamed into a general education class for reading, she could read to a nondisabled peer (and vice versa) to practice fluency.

2. *Group project*: The more common form of cooperative learning involves a small group of three or four students working together on one group project. In this format, every student is involved and contributes to the final outcome. For example, if you have a special day class with a variety of students with disabilities, they can work together to create an art mural or dictate a group story to a paraprofessional.

3. *Jigsaw format*: Similar to the group project, this format involves a small group of students working together toward a common goal. In jigsaw, each student is assigned a specific task to complete for the entire group to meet its goal. For example, in a science project about mammals in a full-inclusion general education class, the student with a hearing impairment might be assigned to research physical aspects about mammals on the computer while the other group members would research other aspects of mammals such as habitat, food, reproduction, and so on. Then all of the group members would bring their information back to the group to develop a final report. A sign-language interpreter could help the student with the hearing impairment report his information to the group.

Regardless of the format, a main distinction between cooperative learning and group work is that cooperative learning is highly structured and systematic, requiring a lot of preparation and planning from the teacher. In cooperative learning, the teacher is

responsible for ensuring that certain structural elements are in place to facilitate interdependence among group members. For example, the teacher has to decide which task
or project the students will work on, how to group the students and assign roles, and
how to monitor and assess individual and group learning.

When deciding which task(s) or project students will engage in, the teacher must
ensure that the task is amenable to cooperative learning. For example, you want to
select a task or project in which interdependence is possible and all students can contribute to the group in a meaningful way. But the task also must create an opportunity
for students with disabilities to learn an important skill or concept. Thus, the cooperative learning format may not be the most efficient method to teach every skill or concept. At times, a direct instruction or whole-group method may be more appropriate.

Other important factors to consider in selecting tasks are state and grade-level standards and the students' individual IEP goals. With limited instructional time available,
teachers have to choose tasks that correlate with state standards and statewide assessments as well as help students progress toward achieving their IEP goals. Finally, teachers have to consider whether students must master any prerequisite academic or social
skills before they can engage in cooperative learning. This may involve setting up some
ground rules about how they are to contribute and support group members, as well as
how to ask for help or resolve conflicts. Once the academic task and objectives have
been selected, the teacher has to define and explain them clearly to the students. Finally,
the student also may have an IEP behavioral or social skills goal that has to be
addressed before developing cooperative learning groups.

Proper assignment of students into small groups may prevent some behavioral
problems and also facilitate the groups in achieving their goals. When assigning students to groups, the first step is to ensure that they are of mixed ability, or heterogeneous. Especially in general education classes, students with disabilities benefit when
group members have varied abilities and are able to support and help them without
doing the work for them (Goor & Schwenn, 1993; Malmgren, 1998; O'Connor &
Jenkins, 1996). Thus, the teacher will have to balance the groups so members will work
well together without one or two students taking over. Individual accountability is
another component of cooperative learning. The first time, the teacher may want to
group students with disabilities with other students whom they know work well
together and support each other.

Once the groups have been selected, assigning specific roles to individual students
will ensure that every member has a role, or job (individual accountability), and that the
group will obtain its goal only if all members are successful in their jobs (interdependence). Many different roles or jobs can be assigned to different group members, depending on the nature of the task. Some of the more common roles are: timekeeper, recorder,
presenter, summarizer, researcher, and artist. For example, a student with autism could
be the artist for the group project. Although matching roles with students' strengths is
important, students should not stay in the same role all the time or be labeled with one
role. Group members and their roles should alternate so students can develop new skills
and learn to work with other students in the class.

Once the task and groups have been assigned, the teacher must decide how to monitor and evaluate the students' progress on the task. Before the students begin, the
teacher has to set expectations for each group member, as well as for the entire group.
Some questions to consider in doing this are the following:

■ What are the learning outcomes for each student?

- Are there set benchmarks to indicate proficiency or mastery for individual students?
- How will the teacher intervene for students who are having difficulty meeting expectations or working with group members?
- What if some students require that certain concepts be reviewed or re-taught?
- What will the final project look like?
- How long will the group project take to complete?
- Is a rubric or criteria available to evaluate the group's final product?

Once these individual and group expectations are set, the teacher has to communicate them to the students so they have a clear idea of the process as well as the final goal. During implementation of cooperative learning, the teacher should be available at all times to assist the groups and answer any questions about the task. Finally, the teacher must provide closure for the lesson and summarize the major points covered during the activity (Johnson & Johnson, 1986).

Research-Based Practices

Over the past two decades, a substantial amount of research has been conducted on cooperative learning and its effect on student learning. Cooperative learning originally was designed for students in general education classrooms. Research supports its effectiveness in increasing academic achievement (e.g., Slavin, 1996) and improving peer interactions (e.g., Slavin, 1991). Also, some research indicates that cooperative learning promotes the inclusion of students with disabilities in general education (e.g., Goor & Schwenn, 1993; Wood, Algozzine, & Avett, 1993).

Still, the results are mixed. The research also indicates that some teachers found cooperative learning to be too prescribed, complex, and unrealistic for the students with disabilities in their classes (Antil, Jenkins, Wayne, & Vadasy, 1998). These teachers preferred to implement a more informal or modified approach to cooperative learning. Other studies have indicated that cooperative learning was not successful with students with disabilities (McMaster & Fuchs, 2002). In one study, less than half of the students with disabilities participated successfully in cooperative learning groups (O'Connor & Jenkins, 1996).

Implementing cooperative learning groups has been especially challenging for students with behavioral issues (Pomplun, 1997). Reviews of studies suggested that cooperative learning strategies that held individual students responsible for learning the assigned material (i.e., individual accountability) and offered group rewards based on the collective performance of all members corresponded to greater success on the cooperative learning assignment (McMaster & Fuchs, 2002; Stevens & Slavin, 1991; Tateyama-Sniezek, 1990).

Note

NCLB and IDEA set guidelines for curriculum and assessment, and it is up to each state (and, ultimately, each individual teacher) how to serve their students in the best possible way.

Alternate Assessment

Chapter 1 introduced you to how NCLB and IDEA have set forth the conditions for standards-based instruction for all students and accompanying accountability measures in the form of statewide assessments. Both of these laws have serious implications for the education of students with moderate to severe disabilities. For example, a review of NCLB makes clear that a major requirement involves translating standards and assessment programs designed for use in general education in a manner that makes them appropriate for students with moderate to severe disabilities. This entails the development of alternate assessments. Although the NCLB sets the parameters, individual states are responsible for determining the alternate assessments to be used.

In preparing to become a special educator, you are sensitive to the importance of ensuring equity for all students. But you know from studying this book that, historically, students with disabilities, particularly those with moderate to severe disabilities, have not always been included in legislation targeted at improving education in the United States. Thus, their inclusion in NCLB may be viewed as a positive step in that it encourages access to the general education curriculum and sets high expectations for students with disabilities along with all other students. In the context of "all" students, students with moderate to severe disabilities present many challenges to teachers, policy makers, and test developers in connection with implementation of NCLB.

The clear mandate from IDEA, too, is to maximize all students' involvement in the general curriculum. Nevertheless, limited attention has been paid as to how to meet these goals for students with intellectual or developmental disabilities (Wehmeyer, Lance, & Bashinski, 2002; Wehmeyer, Lattin, & Agran, 2001).

Through your coursework and your prior personal experiences in education, you know how the needs of students with moderate to severe disabilities vary from those of typical students in general education and, hence, the challenges they face in succeeding in the general education curriculum. Students with disabilities also must participate in statewide testing, and their performance is included in reporting Annual Yearly Progress (AYP). For these reasons, the teacher can anticipate the enormous task that states face in implementing NCLB. At the same time, we must be encouraged by the prospect that society values the idea of increasing opportunities for students of all abilities to gain instruction in the skills and knowledge that contribute to their meeting the standards.

Teaching Context

NCLB requires states to use a documented and validated standards-setting process as they (a) frame academic achievement standards applicable to students with moderate to severe disabilities, and (b) implement accountability programs. The legislation allows for alternate assessments as part of the accountability program and defines who is eligible to take an alternate assessment. This includes students with the most significant cognitive disabilities. The policy limits eligibility to 1% of the students enrolled in the grades tested but does allow for some local variance. The next 2% may take a state's "Modified Assessment."

Both the alternate and the modified assessments are to be based on the state's general assessment standards. This flexibility in creating alternate or modified assessments enhances the opportunity to better align assessments with standards-based curricula for students with moderate to severe disabilities. The task of developing valid and reliable alternate assessments, however, remains complex. Standards-based curricula must be effectively aligned with assessments for the typical student in general education, as well as alternate assessments for students with the most significant disabilities. Because these policies are so new, research hasn't provided much direction. This is especially true for students who have been grouped in this book within the category of having moderate to severe disabilities.

Teachers must know how states will implement the accountability requirements of NCLB as they relate to alternate assessments. The U.S. Department of Education (2005) has published a resource document referred to as *Non-Regulatory Guidance*.

Although designed for policy makers at the state and local levels, it was written in a manner that makes it useful for teachers as well. The document addresses a number of questions that are important to teachers in understanding the relationship between alternate assessments and curriculum alignment.

For instance, in discussing alternate assessments based on grade-level achievement standards, the document emphasizes the requirement that the same content must be addressed and that all students must be held to the same expectations as in the standard assessment. States have to document that the results from alternate assessments based on grade-level achievement standards are comparable in meaning to the results from the standard assessments for the same grade level.

When alternate assessments are based on alternate achievement standards, the curriculum can cover a narrower range of content. For example, the alternate assessments may cover fewer objectives under each content standard. They also may reflect a different set of expectations in the areas of reading/language arts, mathematics, and science than do standard assessments or alternate assessments based on grade-level achievement standards.

The lack of a knowledge base related to alternate assessments and alternate achievement standards places teachers of students with moderate to severe disabilities in the position of having to provide instruction to their students without the benefit of knowing that curriculum alignment is in place or that the alternate assessments are technically valid. This is in contrast to teachers in general education, in which the curriculum is better defined and more likely to be aligned with standards. In addition, the test developers have had years of experience in designing large-scale assessments aligned with general education curricula. This is not the case in curriculum alignment or the development of alternate assessments for students with significant disabilities. Examples of alternate assessments in the form of portfolios, anecdotal records, observation scales, and simulations have to be further developed and validated.

NCLB requires alignment with general education standards. At the same time, IDEA requires that the unique needs of students with disabilities be accommodated—yet, the needs of students with moderate to severe disabilities encompass a broader array of functional skills than are likely to be included in the age-appropriate general education curriculum. Although this does not bring the two laws into conflict, the fact that states must be in compliance with IDEA further complicates the implementation of NCLB for students with moderate to severe disabilities.

Research-Based Practices

While a knowledge base on alternate assessments and alternate achievement standards is emerging, teachers will continue to face serious challenges until more research has been conducted and more experience has been gained with implementation of NCLB as applied to students with moderate to severe disabilities. One way to cope is to collaborate with other teachers and professionals who are trying to align their instruction with the standards-based curriculum. At the same time, beginning teachers should take advantage of new knowledge and research-based practices as these evolve. Finally, they can contribute to the knowledge base themselves by developing alternate assessments that they judge to be appropriate and aligned with the standards-based curriculum.

To some extent, this is similar to what has been occurring, in that teachers of students with moderate to severe disabilities have routinely assumed responsibility for modifying the general education curriculum to meet the needs of these students. In many situations, they have done so with limited specialized resources, and assessments often have taken the form of strategies to demonstrate progress on instructional goals. These may be anecdotal, of a portfolio nature, observations, or work samples. Experience in assessing progress relative to IEP goals also will be helpful.

Much of the alternate assessment literature is limited to primarily portfolio assessments. Research is needed on other forms of alternate assessments to monitor student progress. In assessing the status of the knowledge base on alternate assessments, Wehmeyer, Poggio, and Tindal (2004) couched their appraisal of how little we know about the technical adequacy of alternate assessments in a series of questions:

> *Are we targeting the same standards as general education?*
>
> *And what about generalizability—*
>
> *Can we separate the real performance of students from the judges and the tasks?*
>
> *Are students being judged in a reliable manner, and are alternate tasks consistent?*
>
> *What else improves when students make progress on alternate assessment?*
>
> *And what are the consequences of this system? (p. 19)*

Answers to these questions may be organized as components of validity. This validation process must focus on decision making with equal reach to all types of assessments (portfolios, observations, and performance assessments). Most important, we will have to anchor the process of developing technical adequacy so the measures have impact on instructional programs and classroom practices.

The literature base on alternate assessments will mature over time, and models for curriculum alignment that takes into consideration the unique need of students with disabilities will evolve. We can expect statewide alternate assessments to become valid and technically sound.

Summary

Students with moderate to severe disabilities have many attributes that are unique to their specific disability. For this reason, teacher education programs often offer courses that are specific to a disability. In Part III of this book, information is organized around the disabilities that are referred to as "moderate to severe." Despite their unique needs, these students share some attributes that translate into common needs. That does not mean that everyone who has hearing loss, or is blind, or has autism, or has cognitive deficits, will have the same needs. But many will benefit from instruction in some common curricular areas.

This chapter explored educational practices that tend to generalize across the instructional needs of students with moderate to severe disabilities, including balancing functional/general education curriculum and community-based instruction, universal curriculum design, self-determination, cooperative learning, and alternate assessment. These instructional areas are discussed in more detail elsewhere in the book. In this chapter we have attempted to place them in perspective relative to their appropriateness for students with moderate to severe disabilities. At the same time, we have tried to develop a context couched in standards-based reform, which gives them particular importance and reminds teachers of their responsibilities for ensuring that these common areas of instruction are not overlooked amid the important initiatives to ensure access to the general education curriculum for their students.

References

Antil, L. R., Jenkins, J. R., Wayne, S. K., & Fadasy, P. F. (1998). Cooperative learning: Prevalence, conceptualizations, and the relation between research and practice. *American Educational Research Journal, 35,* 419–454.

Council for Exceptional Children. (1999, Fall). Universal design: Ensuring access to the general education curriculum. *Research Connections in Special Education, 5,* 1–8.

Dymond, S. K., & Orelove, F. P. (2001). *Federal disability terms: A review of state use. Quick Turn Around (QTA).* Alexandria, VA: Project Forum at the National Association for Directors of Special Education.

Friend, M. (2005). *Special education: Contemporary perspectives for school professionals.* Boston: Pearson Education.

Goor, M. B., & Schwenn, J. O. (1993). Accommodating diversity and disability with cooperative learning. *Intervention in School and Clinic, 29,* 6–16.

Grigal, M., Neubert, D. A., Moon. M. S., & Graham, S. (2003). Self-determination for students with disabilities: Views of parents and teachers. *Exceptional Children, 70*(1), 97–112.

Hallahan, D. P., & Kauffman, J. M. (2003). *Exceptional learners: An introduction to special education* (9th ed.). Boston: Allyn & Bacon.

Johnson, R. T., & Johnson, R. T. (1986). Mainstreaming and cooperative learning strategies. *Exceptional Children, 52,* 553–561.

Johnson, D. W., & Johnson, R. T. (1991). *Learning together and alone.* Englewood Cliffs, NJ: Allyn & Bacon.

Johnson, D. W., & Johnson, R. T. (1999). *What makes cooperative learning work?* Retrieved April 12, 2001, from http://www.ebsco.com

Kagan, S. (1990). The structural approach to cooperative learning. *Educational Leadership, 47*(4), 12–15.

Karvonen, M., Test, D. W., Wood, W. M., Browder, D., & Algozzine, B. (2004). Putting self-determination into practice. *Exceptional Children, 71*(1), 23–41.

Malmgren, K. W. (1998). Cooperative learning as an academic intervention for students with mild disabilities. *Focus on Exceptional Children, 31,* 1–8.

McMaster, K. N., & Fuchs, D. (2002). Effects of cooperative learning in the academic achievement of students with learning disabilities: An update of Tateyama Sniezek's review. *Learning Disabilities Research and Practice, 17,* 107–117.

Morse, T. E., & Schuster, J. W. (2000). Teaching elementary students with moderate intellectual disabilities how to shop for groceries. *Exceptional Children, 66,* 273–288.

National Information Center for Children and Youth with Disabilities (NICHCY). (2001, December). *Severe and/or multiple disabilities.* Washington, DC: Author.

O'Connor, R. E., & Jenkins, J. R. (1996). Cooperative learning as an inclusion strategy: A closer look. *Exceptionality, 6,* 29–51.

Pomplun, M. (1997). When students with disabilities participate in cooperative groups. *Exceptional Children, 64*(1), 49–58.

Rose, D., with Meyer, A. (2000, Winter). Universal design for learning. Associate editor column. *Journal of Special Education Technology, 15*(1), 1–7. Retrieved March 22, 2001, from http://jset.unlv.edu

Rose, D., with Sethuraman, S., & Meo, G. J. (2000, Spring). Universal design for learning. Associate editor column. *Journal of Special Education Technology, 15*(2), 1–8. Retrieved March 22, 2001, from http://jset.unlv.edu

Slavin, R. E. (1991). Synthesis of research on cooperative learning. *Educational Leadership, 48*(5), 71–81.

Slavin, R. E. (1996). Research on cooperative learning and achievement: What we know, what we need to know. *Contemporary Educational Psychology, 21,* 43–69.

Smith, D. D. (2004). *Introduction to special education: Teaching in an age of opportunity* (5th ed.). Boston: Pearson Education.

Stevens, R. J., & Slavin, R. E. (1991). When cooperative learning improves the achievement of students with mild disabilities: A response to Tateyama-Sniezek. *Exceptional Children*, 276–280.

Tateyama-Sniezek, K. M. (1990). Cooperative learning: Does it improve the academic achievement of students with handicaps? *Exceptional Children, 56*, 426–437.

Tollefson, J. (2003). Universal design: Harnessing the power of the digital world. *Stratenotes, 12*(2), 1–2. Lawrence: University of Kansas Center for Research on Learning.

Turnbull, R., Turnbull, A., Shank, M., & Smith, S. J. (Eds.). (2004). *Exceptional lives: Special education in today's schools* (4th ed.). Upper Saddle River, NJ: Pearson Education.

Turnbull, A. P., & Turnbull, H. R. (2001), Self-determination for individuals with significant cognitive disabilities and their families. *Journal of the Association for Persons with Severe Handicaps, 26*(1), 56–62.

U.S. Department of Education. (2005, August). *No Child Left Behind. Alternate achievement standards for students with the most significant cognitive disabilities. Non-regulatory Guidance*. Retrieved September 1, 2005, from http: www.ed.gov/policy/elsec/guid/altguidance.pdf

Wehmeyer, M. L., Field, S., Doren, B., Jones, B., & Mason C. (2004). Self-determination and student involvement in standards-based reform. *Exceptional Children, 70*(4), 413–425.

Wehmeyer, M. L., Lance, G. D., & Bashinski, S. (2002). Promoting access to the general curriculum for students with mental retardation: A multi-level model. *Education and Training in Mental Retardation and Developmental Disabilities, 37*(3), 223–234.

Wehmeyer, M. L., Lattin, D., & Agran, M. (2001). Achieving access to the general curriculum for students with mental retardation: A curriculum decision-making model. *Education and Training in Mental Retardation and Developmental Disabilities, 36*, 327–342.

Wehmeyer, M. L., Poggio, J., & Tindal, G. (2004). KU Center on Standards and Assessment Development. Submitted to *Center on Standards and Assessment Development Grant Review, CFDA 84.324U*. Washington, DC: U.S. Department of Education, Office of Special Education Programs.

Westling, D. L., & Fox, L. (2000). *Teaching students with severe disabilities* (2nd ed.). Upper Saddle River, NJ: Merrill.

Wood, J. W. (2002). *Adapting instruction to accommodate students in inclusive settings* (4th ed.). Upper Saddle River, NJ: Merrill Prentice Hall.

Wood, K., & Algonzzine, B. (1997). Introduction: Cooperative learning across the curriculum. *Reading & Writing Quarterly, 13*(1), 1–3.

Wood, K. D., Algonzzine, B., & Avett, S. (1993). Promoting cooperative learning experiences for students with reading, writing, and learning disabilities. *Reading and Writing Quarterly, 9*, 369–376.

PREPARATION FOR THE FUTURE

Part IV

P reparing for the future of educating children and youth with disabilities is a little like the television program *Back to the Future*. Much of what is on the horizon for all of education in the future has already been addressed in the history of special education. That is, we only need to examine past initiatives to find evidence of how policy makers and the profession of special education has dealt with the challenges and opportunities that face all of education today. Special education has often been a pacesetter in anticipating educational issues and responding accordingly. While the responses have not always altered the course of the future, the field has been responsive.

Each chapter in the parts that make up this book offers information and experiences that focus on what teachers need to know to be effective in teaching students with disabilities. The chapters also add to the knowledge base of beginning teachers in an effort to encourage them to continue to build and develop their professional skills. Specifically, this book was designed to enhance professional growth. If you are using the e-book along with this book, it can serve as a way to introduce readers to examples of how a traditional book can, through technology, be transformed into a dynamic teaching tool that is responsive to the learning preferences and styles of users. That in itself is in the spirit of looking toward the future of education in this country.

Predicting issues facing special education in the future depends on one's perceptions. As we conceptualized this book, we explored the various issues in the field and worked with chapter authors to integrate relevant topics into their respective chapters. As the content evolved, it became apparent that two issues have emerged that will greatly influence the future of the field and will become more central to the roles and responsibilities of beginning teachers in the future: technology and professionalism. This is not to suggest that technology and professionalism are universal concerns for all readers. Issues are time-bound and perception-based. But when one steps back and reflects on the many special education issues that appear in the media, that occupy the minds of policy makers, and that are central to the lives of children with disabilities and their families, it is clear that emerging technologies and highly qualified teachers (professionalism) are likely to transpire as common expectations. At a minimum they can change the future for individual learners.

The decision to focus this part on the future on technology and professionalism was not an easy one. However, it was intentionally made early in the planning stages of the book as we were searching for issues that not only generalize across disability groups but also potentially impact on the quality of life for all students with exceptional learning needs. Our decision was influenced largely by the following, professionalism discussed first and then technology.

Professionalism: Becoming highly qualified should be the goal of every beginning teacher. While instructional decisions should be evidence-based, they should also be made out of a commitment and passion by teachers to be the very best that they can be. This goes beyond their personal competence as teachers. They must also be reflective in their collaboration skills, committed as advocates for the children they serve, sensitive to family and community needs, and involved in lifelong professional learning. In many ways, this perspective on professionalism is not more than fulfilling our responsibilities as professional educators engaged in ensuring a quality education for all learners, including those with exceptional learning needs.

In response to advocacy efforts from the profession and parents of children with disabilities, the federal government passed legislation in the early 1950s in support of programs to train professors at the doctoral level for leadership roles in the preparation of special education teachers. Initially, the focus was on personnel preparation in mental retardation. This initiative has since been expanded to cover all areas of disability and, more recently, support for students at most licensure levels in postsecondary education. Yet, special education continues to be one of the areas experiencing the most severe shortages of licensed teachers. This is in part due to expanded opportunities for individuals who in years past may have opted to major in special education. Today the admission requirements to teacher education are equal to or exceed those for other helping professions. The result is that although the pool of individuals pursuing preparation for careers in teaching today is comprised of very able students, the numbers are not sufficient to meet the need.

Technology: One could argue that if professionalism is achieved by all beginning teachers, there is little justification for advocating that attention be given to any other issues such as technology when addressing the future. But another way of looking at technology rather than as an expected proficiency of teachers is to view it as having the potential to dramatically improve the quality of life for all individuals with disabilities. In this context, the responsibility for exploiting the benefits of technology is broadened to include all professionals, families, communities, and the private sector.

It is a rare individual whose daily life has not been dramatically changed by technology. This has not necessarily been by choice. Society has embraced the benefits of technology. The current momentum is driven by consumer response and the expectations of individual users. Young people who have grown up with technology are major contributors to new technologies and the need for applications as they mature and become a dominant segment of our population. In terms of our educational system, however, it is clear that e-learning environments, while emerging, are still in their infancy at all levels of education. This raises the question of what technology holds for persons with disabilities in the future—whether as students or as members of the work force and the community.

Technology in the form of assistive devices has been a mainstay in improving the quality of life for persons with disabilities for decades. Many of the assistive devices of the past would be defined today as low tech. Others, such as communication devices, were high tech, even by the standards of today. Advancements in technology and the emergence of the Internet have greatly altered what technology can offer to individuals with disabilities and their families in the future. Of equal importance will be increased access to education, training, and employment that will evolve from advances in technology and the framing of public policy.

Teachers become key to determining how technology will benefit individuals with exceptional learning needs in the future. They have the advantage of being able to observe children and youth with exceptional learning needs interacting in learning environments and have the knowledge to translate needs into improved teaching–learning strategies. Further, as teachers become more sophisticated in their understanding of technology, they can have a more direct influence on setting priorities for the development of new technologies and communicating how technology can enhance their specific teaching roles while also addressing quality-of-life benefits for all learners.

Emerging Technology

J. Emmett Gardner & Dave L. Edyburn

15

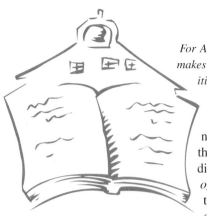

For Americans without disabilities, technology makes things easier. For Americans with disabilities, technology makes things possible.
(National Council on Disability, 1993)

This quote highlights the significance of technology for individuals with disabilities. Historically, the emphasis on technology for individuals with disabilities has been thought of as *assistive technology*—extending the abilities of an individual in ways that provide physical access (e.g., wheelchairs, switches) and sensory access (e.g., Braille, closed captioning). More recently we've come to understand that additional attention must be given to the use of technology for teaching and learning. In this chapter we apply the term *special education technology* to a wide array of applications that relate to what special educators and students with disabilities do. The chapter provides an overview of assistive technology, universal design, instructional technology, and content-based application, as well as the role of the World Wide Web in fostering learning in special education.

Regardless of the specific application of technology, the purpose is always the same: to harness the potential of technology in ways that offer individuals with disabilities increased opportunities for learning, productivity, and independence. Without technology, these opportunities would not be available.

Assistive Technology

Over time, individual success stories have persuaded the U.S. Congress to enact a change strategy utilizing federal policy and major funding initiatives to foster the rapid expansion of research, development, and technology related to individuals with disabilities. The two factors that contributed to passage of these laws are as follows:

1. The apparent value of technology already available in the marketplace for individuals with disabilities
2. The exceedingly small number of people who were benefiting from existing technology

As a result, federal policy has incorporated technology as a mechanism for capturing the potential of technology on an ever-increasing scale.

The potential of technology for individuals with disabilities has been codified into a series of federal laws (the Americans with Disabilities Act, 1990; the Individuals with Disabilities Education Act Amendments, 1997; the Telecommunications Act of 1996; the Assistive Technology Act of 1998). The two laws most relevant for the work of educators are the Technology Related Assistance for Individuals Act (The Tech Act), passed in 1988, and the 1997 reauthorization of the Individuals with Disabilities Education Act.

Defining Assistive Technology Devices and Services

Federal law (IDEA '97 Final Regulations) recognizes two dimensions of assistive technology: assistive technology devices and assistive technology services. These definitions originally were developed as part of the 1988 Tech Act legislation and subsequently have been cited or incorporated into all technology and disability legislation.

> *§300.5 Assistive technology device.*
>
> *As used in this part, Assistive technology device means any item, piece of equipment, or product system, whether acquired commercially off the shelf, modified, or customized, that is used to increase, maintain, or improve the functional capabilities of a child with a disability. (20 U.S.C. 1401(1))*

Although many people believe the term *assistive technology* applies only to computers, in reality assistive technology devices (e.g., adaptive feeding instruments, wheelchairs, vision aids) have a long history in the field of special education and rehabilitation. Estimates suggest that more than 25,000 assistive technology devices have been designed to enhance the life functioning of individuals with disabilities. Given that the operational word in the definition is *any*, some have argued that the definition is so broad that it could include anything. Others have noted that the definition simply reflects the idea that assistive technology solutions may involve no technology (no-tech), low technology (lo-tech), or high technology (high-tech).

A second definition advances a critical component involved in the effective use of assistive technology: Success is dependent not only on having access to a device but also factors involving selection, acquisition, and use of a tool. These ideas are codified in the definition of assistive technology service:

> *§300.6 Assistive technology service.*
>
> *As used in this part, Assistive technology service means any service that directly assists a child with a disability in the selection, acquisition, or use of an assistive technology device. The term includes (a) The evaluation of the needs of a child with a disability, including a functional evaluation of the child in the child's customary environment; (b) Purchasing, leasing, or otherwise providing for the acquisition of assistive technology devices by children with disabilities; (c) Selecting, designing, fitting, customizing, adapting, applying, maintaining, repairing, or replacing assistive technology devices; (d) Coordinating and using other therapies, interventions, or services with assistive technology devices, such as those associated with existing education and rehabilitation plans and programs; (e) Training or technical assistance for a child with a disability or, if appropriate, that child's family; and (f) Training or technical assistance for professionals (including individuals providing education or rehabilitation services), employers, or other individuals who provide services to, employ, or are otherwise substantially involved in the major life functions of that child. (20 U.S.C. 1401(2))*

The definitions of assistive technology device and assistive technology service provide a comprehensive perspective on processes that enable individuals with disabilities to acquire and use assistive technologies that enhance functional capabilities.

Assistive Technology Consideration

The concept of assistive technology consideration is a rather recent development. Its origin can be traced to the Individuals with Disabilities Education Act Amendments of 1997 (Public Law 105-17), which contained a requirement for Individual Education Program (IEP) teams to consider assistive technology (AT) in the development of an IEP:

> The IEP Team shall (v) consider whether the child requires assistive technology devices and services. [Section 614 (d)(3)(B) Consideration of Special Factors.]

Some observers believed that this language reflected a new federal policy, but Golden (1998) argued that it simply formalizes a previous responsibility:

> The IDEA requires schools to provide AT if it is needed for a student to receive a free appropriate public education (FAPE). FAPE can include a variety of services such as special education, related services, supplementary aids and services, program modifications or support for school personnel. AT, just like other components of FAPE, must be provided at no cost to parents. The specific IDEA requirement for schools to provide AT is as follows:
>
> 300.308 Assistive Technology.
>
> Each public agency shall ensure that assistive technology devices or assistive technology services or both, as those terms are defined in 300.5–300.6 are made available to a child with a disability if required as part of a child's (a) Special education under 300.17; (b) Related services under 300.16; or (c) Supplementary aids and services under 300.550(b)(2). (p. 4)

Golden's analysis highlights the critical issue of free appropriate public education (FAPE). Schools are required to provide assistive technology for students who need such tools, if they are necessary for the student to participate in and benefit from a free appropriate public education. The historical implications of this requirement are unquestioned in the context of mobility (e.g., a powered wheelchair) and communication (e.g., an augmentative communication system). Now, however, the requirement explicitly covers all disabilities, and the magnitude of these decisions in the context of high-incidence disabilities often raises a budgetary red flag for administrators. For example, does every student with poor handwriting need a laptop computer? If so, where will the funds come from to pay for this educational need? If not, who will decide which students can benefit from a laptop computer and who can't?

The federal mandate to consider assistive technology means that each IEP team must document, on the IEP, its efforts to consider assistive technology for each student. This legal obligation has created an immense professional development responsibility to ensure that all participants are aware of their duties and have sufficient knowledge and skills to make informed judgments about the value of technology-enhanced performance. As a result, there has been a tremendous need in the field for training and resources.

Note

Examples of assistive technology devices:
- Pool lift
- Automatic doors
- Headwand
- Voice amplification
- Expanded keyboard
- Voice recognition system
- Hearing aid
- Speaker phone
- Magnifier

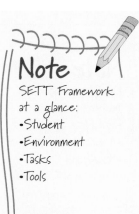

Note

SETT Framework
at a glance:
• Student
• Environment
• Tasks
• Tools

The SETT Framework

The SETT Framework, created by Joy Zabala (1995), focuses the attention of IEP teams on the Student, the Environment, the Tasks required for active participation in the activities of the environment, and the Tools needed for the student to address the tasks. SETT was designed to facilitate gathering and organizing data to enhance assistive technology decision making. This model has been widely adopted and implemented because of the intuitive nature of the four core areas, its ease of use in assessment and decision making, and the fact that the student is the initial and primary focus. In addition, this model illustrates how changes in the environment or the task can fundamentally alter the need for tools—which is the final consideration.

Who Can Benefit?

As school districts seek to implement assistive technology on a systemic basic, an analysis by Golden (1999) can be used to sensitize administrators to the gap between students currently using assistive technology and those who could potentially benefit (see Table 15.1). To arrive at an estimate of the size of the population of students receiving special education that potentially could benefit from assistive technology, she used the diagnostic categories in Missouri to develop conservative projections of the number of students who should be using assistive technology. The estimates were based on the typical types of educational needs that students have in academic areas, study skills, daily living, leisure/recreation, and program accessibility, and insight concerning the types of assistive technology available to address such needs.

The purpose of this exercise is to offer some benchmarks for schools to use in a programmatic evaluation of whether they are adequately addressing assistive technology needs (e.g., if your school has a number of students with visual impairments who

TABLE 15.1 Anticipated Assistive Technology Use	
Disability	**% Expected AT Use**
Deaf and Hard of Hearing	100%
Blind and Visually Impaired	100%
Physical Disability	100%
Deaf/Blindness	100%
Multiple Disabilities	100%
Traumatic Brain Injury	50–75%
Autism	50–75%
Learning Disability	25–35%
Health Impairment	25–35%
Cognitive Disability	25–35%
Speech/Language Disorder	10–25%*
Emotional Disability	10–25%

* Most students who need and/or use augmentative communication devices have an identified disability other than "speech/language," thus the lower projected usage for this diagnostic category.

Source: Golden, D. (1999). Assistive technology policy and practice. What is the right thing to do? What is the reasonable thing to do? What is required and must be done? *Special Education Technology Practice, 1*(1), 12–14.

are not using any assistive technology, you should find out why). The concept of *expectancy benchmarking* offers some intriguing possibilities for guiding the assistive technology consideration process.

Access to Curriculum

A critical consideration associated with the need for assistive technology involves providing access to the curriculum. Although access to the general curriculum was first advanced in the 1997 reauthorization of IDEA, related developments associated with content standards and high-stakes testing set the stage for passage of No Child Left Behind (NCLB). As a result, assistive technology is now directly relevant as a means of providing accessible learning materials to students with disabilities as a necessary means of enhancing grade-level achievement.

Universal Design for Learning

Principles of universal design have emerged from our understanding of the design of physical environments for individuals with disabilities. Perhaps the best example of the success of universal design principles are curb cuts on sidewalks. Originally designed to improve mobility for people with disabilities within our communities, curb cuts go beyond that and improve access for people with baby strollers, roller blades, bikes, and so forth.

More recently, universal design concepts have been applied to computers. For example, the TRACE Center at the University of Wisconsin–Madison has spearheaded conversations between the disability community and technology developers concerning initiatives to include disability accessibility software as part of the operating system. It would provide access as the computer comes out of the box rather than require the person to track down assistive technology specialists to make specialized modifications. Today, accessibility control panels are available on every computer.

Recently, a concerted effort has been made to apply universal design principles to learning. A leader in the area of universal design for learning is the Center for Applied Special Technology (CAST). CAST believes that universal design is a critical issue if students with disabilities are going to be able to access the general education curriculum and subsequently demonstrate high levels of academic achievement. CAST now sponsors the National Consortium on Universal Design for Learning (http://www.cast.org/udl/).

In a class of 30 middle school students, one can anticipate that 5 to 7 students have below-grade-level reading skills, 3 to 5 will have learning disabilities, 1 or 2 may have vision or hearing difficulties, and 1 or 2 might have a primary language other than English. Teachers working with students in inclusion settings face a relentless demand to modify curricular, instructional, and assessment materials. Modifications always will be necessary as a result of technology, media, and materials that are not designed for the range of diversity found in every classroom.

Modifications are reactive. This means that students with disabilities often experience a delay in obtaining information that is readily available to their peers without disabilities. Universal design seeks to alter this paradigm by providing a new way of thinking about access that is proactive rather than reactive.

The promise of universal design suggests that instructional materials can be designed to provide adjustable instructional design controls (think of these as a volume control slider that is adjustable to be off or at some level between low and high). Universal design control panels could be included in all instructional software and be accessed by students and teachers when an adjustment is needed. Just think of it: Do you need reading materials at a lower readability? Just go into the control panel and reset the slider and those materials will be presented. Do you want a glimpse of the future? The following Web sites are representative of resources to explore how rich instructional content can be presented so students can access the level with the appropriate supports they need.

> Ben's Guide to U.S. Government for Kids
> http://bensguide.gpo.gov/

> StarChild: A Learning Center for Young Astronomers
> http://starchild.gsfc.nasa.gov/docs/StarChild/StarChild.html

> Windows to the Universe
> http://www.windows.ucar.edu/

Each of these examples illustrates important components of a universally designed curriculum (e.g., tiered learning materials, text-to-speech support, language translation), but no one example includes all components. As a result, much remains to be done to capture the potential of universal design. To learn more about the principles of universal design, access the online book *Teaching Every Student in the Digital Age: Universal Design for Learning* (http://www.cast.org/teachingeverystudent/).

Instructional Technology Applications

When most people think of technology in special education, they probably envision students with disabilities working with assistive technology devices, such as communicating with peers and teachers using an augmentative communication device, using an Intellitools keyboard to provide alternative access to a computer, or converting text-to-speech using a screen reader while browsing the Web. These devices, products, and/or services improve the functional capacity of students to accomplish tasks.

When we consider the context and activities of students with disabilities in K–12 school settings, the term *instructional technology* is a subtle but noteworthy variation of the assistive technology definition. Instructional technology, which may or may not involve a unique assistive technology device, emphasizes consideration of how technology can be used to enhance students' access to,

An example of an adaptive keyboard

and learning of, content that corresponds to designated curriculum standards and IEP goals. Instructional technology also considers ways to improve the capacity of teachers to deliver effective instruction in classroom and school settings.

Roblyer (2003) views the integration of technology in education as ranging from approaches based on models that are directed or constructivist. The *directed approach* stresses outcomes that focus on remediation of academic areas (e.g., reading, writing, math) in which a student has identified weakness(es). The teacher helps students acquire and become proficient in prerequisite content-related knowledge and skills areas associated with academic/learning tasks, so they can perform the skills with fluency or automaticity (e.g., performing fundamental skills such as decoding and/or recognizing words, performing math facts and operations, keyboarding, retrieving facts from memory). The *constructivist approach* emphasizes obtaining competence in the use and manipulation of information, in which higher-order thinking skills, such as problem solving, analysis/synthesis, decision making, and the development/construction of knowledge and products, are the focus of learning activities.

From a special education standpoint, students with disabilities display a wide range of cognitive and academic strengths and weaknesses associated with the K–12 academic curriculum. Within any curriculum content area, special education students are called on to apply knowledge and skills relevant to both the directed *and* constructivist learning models. More often than not, these students are in general education settings, working alongside peers and on the same assignments. Technology-enhanced methods support their acquisition and understanding/processing of information.

In terms of content area applications such as science, history, and math, there is not a wealth of "special education" software. Rather, there is a range of content-specific programs designed to support learning for *any* learner who may benefit from remediation (i.e., building knowledge and skills) or compensation (e.g., reading level, stronger emphasis on multimedia, content enhancement) that is complementary to traditional teacher/classroom-based instructional methods for given content areas.

The following is representative of technology that can be used with student who have mild disabilities in the content areas of reading, writing, math, and the social and physical sciences. This is followed by a discussion of technology applications for the functional skills of students with mild to moderate cognitive disabilities.

Reading

According to the International Reading Association (IRA) and the National Council of Teachers of English (NCTE), the ability to use technology and information resources, such as libraries, databases, the Web, and multimedia, to acquire and synthesize information to create and communicate knowledge to others (Standard #8 for the English Language Arts) is a fundamental skill that school-age students need to acquire in school (National Council of Teachers of English, 2005). To meet this standard (as well as all 12 of the national standards for English language arts), students with disabilities must develop proficiency in reading and writing.

Reading is one of the most common areas in which students with disabilities demonstrate weaknesses. Yet, it is a skill needed for them to perform efficiently in school. Much of the information that general education students acquire across other content areas (e.g., math, science, social studies, language arts) comes though information presented in books and Web pages. Moreover, reading is a complex behavioral process that does not come easily to some students. It involves sensory perception (e.g.,

> **Note**
>
> Directed approach v. constructivist approach: The directed approach focuses on learning prerequisite knowledge and skills, and the constructivist approach focuses on taking that knowledge and using higher-order thinking skills to manipulate it.

viewing text), the ability to connect letters and words with their spoken sounds (e.g., phonemic awareness and decoding), processing and understanding the meaning of words and sentences (e.g., vocabulary and comprehension), and relating this meaning in terms of prior knowledge and experiences to achieve a functional outcome (e.g., obtaining/learning new information about a subject, how to perform a task, or for personal recreation and enjoyment)—to name but a few of the many facets attributed to the reading process.

With respect to the visual/perceptual components of reading, both the Apple and Windows operating systems, as well as a growing number of software tools that are reading-intensive, are now including accessibility options as part of their system/program preference. These options expand our ability to make easy but fundamental changes in the way text is displayed, such as magnifying the screens or manipulating the size, font, and color of text to fit individual reading preferences.

Text-to-Speech

Among the foremost technology applications for reading are software and hardware tools that aid in converting printed words on paper or in electronic format (e.g., those that normally would be read on a computer screen, such as from a Web page or a CD-ROM encyclopedia) to words that can be heard. This is commonly referred to as "text-to-speech." Instructional technology applications that provide text-to-speech features come in a variety of forms and functions. The more recent operating systems of Apple Macintosh System X and Microsoft Windows allow electronic text to be highlighted and spoken to the user. Further, most documents saved electronically in Adobe Portable Document Format (PDF) can be listened to using the "Read out loud" feature in current versions of Adobe Acrobat and Acrobat Reader (a free download at the Adobe Web site).

A variety of programs provide expanded text-to-speech features from within word processors and/or Web browsers, often working in the background but in combination with traditional software programs. In these programs students can access a variety of features related to the text-to-speech conversion, ranging from being able to select individual words or highlighting sentences and/or paragraphs to be read, to including visual cues that highlight words as they are spoken and allowing individual letters in words to be spelled out. Some programs, such as eReader (CAST), have their own versions of Web browser and/or a word processor. More advanced programs, such as WYNN and JAWS (Freedom Scientific) and Kurzweil 3000 (Kurzweil Educational Systems), include integrated systems that work with scanners so pages from books and handouts can be converted to electronic text, which subsequently can be manipulated (e.g., text-to-speech, and altering the color, type, and size of fonts) or enhanced though other program-related features designed to promote comprehension, such as being able to click on a word and see/hear a dictionary definition/pronunciation and accessing synonyms or antonyms in a thesaurus.

Social and Personal Support

Another area of reading-related technology is support for the social/personal aspects of reading. In this context, the goal is not to teach specific reading-related skills but, instead, to provide varying levels of technology assistance that simply help students access reading materials efficiently.

If a student is certified as having a visual, physical, or severe reading disability that prevents him or her from reading standard print materials, the student may be eligible

Note

The companion e-book to *Exceptional Children in Today's Schools* has a text-to-speech feature in that you can hear any chapter read aloud.

to receive free loans of tapes of books and magazines through the National Library Service for the Blind and Physically Handicapped (NLS), Library of Congress (http://www.loc.gov/nls/index.html). Project Gutenberg (http://www.gutenberg.org/) provides more than 14,000 free electronic versions of classic books, including *Huckleberry Finn* and *Moby Dick*, that can be downloaded into talking word processors or other text-to-speech programs. More and more textbook publishers are providing their textbooks in electronic formats so students can access their social and physical science reading assignments via reading support programs.

Age- and Grade-Appropriate Reading Material

At the elementary school level, a number of illustrated children's storybooks are available in electronic versions that might be read as part of a class or reading assignment. Students can access CD-ROM versions of books like those from the Living Books series (Riverdeep), to read stories such as Dr. Seuss's *The Cat in the Hat* or one of Marc Brown's Arthur series. These programs display individual pages and read the text aloud. Students can move between pages using mouse clicks, arrow keys, or, in some cases, a single switch.

At the middle and high school levels, age-appropriate electronic versions of reading materials are available at lower grade/reading levels but with attention to high interest and vocabulary. For example, a high school student reading at a third- or fourth-grade level can select a variety of classics (e.g., *Treasure Island*, *Black Beauty*, *Little Women*) or high-interest books (e.g., *Ali: The Greatest, Earthquake!, King Tut's Tomb*) from the Start-to-Finish series by Don Johnston. A student using these books receives both a print and an electronic version. The electronic version includes features that allow text to be narrated, individual works spoken, and interactive quizzes to provide feedback on comprehension.

Support in the Reading Process

Programs that support the reading process provide drill and practice and/or forms of computer-assisted instruction (CAI) in phonological awareness, word recognition, vocabulary, spelling, basic grammar, and comprehension skills. Software in this category includes, among others, Edmark Reading Program (Riverdeep), Galaxy Classroom (Riverdeep), the JumpStart reading programs (Knowledge Adventure), the Reader Rabbit series (The Learning Company), Reading for Meaning (Tom Snyder), and the language development programs published by Laureate Learning.

When using reading programs, it is important to distinguish between stand-alone programs to help students achieve fluency and automaticity (e.g., to practice *existing* reading skills) versus programs designed to be instructional in nature, employing forms of computer-supported instruction to introduce and teach reading skills over longer periods of time. These latter programs are larger and more comprehensive, and usually are part of school districts' subscriptions to integrated learning systems. Examples are Read 180 (Scholastic) and the reading components of PLATO Achieve Now (PLATO).

When using technology to improve reading *fluency*, one of the key factors seems to be the extent to which interventions are delivered on a consistent and repeated basis over time (Chard, Vaughn, & Tyker, 2002). Occasional or short-term interventions probably will not be effective.

Given the complexities and domains that comprise the reading process, plus the range of weaknesses of individual students with reading disabilities, there is no guarantee that any software or Web-based reading instruction program will specifically

Note

Some Web sites, such as www.abcteach.com and www.enchanted learning.com, require paid subscriptions but can be a great resource for creating classroom materials.

address all of the unique needs of a given student. Among the software and Web-based tools that aid teachers in creating and personalizing reading-related activities to supplement reading instruction are authoring programs such as IntelliTools Classroom Suite (IntelliTools) and HyperStudio (Sunburst Technology). Also, a variety of programs and Web sites function as tools for creating worksheets (e.g., cloze activities, vocabulary puzzles) for reading-related activities.

Game Formats

Many computer-assisted instruction and drill-and-practice reading programs utilize game formats to motivate students by making the learning environment engaging and including characters the students can easily relate to. Teachers should be particularly sensitive to two potential drawbacks:

1. Avoid selecting *any* educational software using criteria that underemphasize the instructional and content validity in favor of emphasizing its entertainment/motivational features.
2. Be alert to age-appropriateness and avoid content that seems childish or immature, which may embarrass the student.

Writing

Like reading, writing is composed of a variety of elements that student with disabilities often find challenging. Writing entails the physical/mechanical aspect (motor skills related to handwriting and keyboarding), the conceptual areas (the organization and composition of thoughts and content, the expression of information and ideas, grammar), the process of writing (outlining, writing, editing/revising), and the production of text-based products (a paper, a Web site, a report). A variety of technology tools support writing for student with disabilities.

Motor Aids

When considering the physical nature of writing and technology in special education, word processing immediately comes to mind. Given that a variety of students with disabilities demonstrate fine- or gross-motor weaknesses, however, efficient keyboarding, mouse skills, and computer access can be important prerequisites to using word processors and technology-based writing tools effectively.

Students may need to develop their mechanical/sensory skills of typing to be more successful when writing or using instructional software that seeks promptly typed responses or accurately typed and spelled words. Poor keyboarding skills (e.g., slow typing, mistakes/errors, lots of deleting as an attempt to write perfectly) can interfere with the flow of thought expressed in words or in responses that a instructional program rejects. Software programs are available to help students develop typing/keyboarding skills.

Ideally, a keyboarding program should be more than a simple program that asks students to practice typing and get an efficiency score. The program should maintain a record of student progress, provide a systematic way for students to advance in speed and accuracy, and be flexible enough to save their progress in small steps (e.g., they could spend 10 minutes one day and 15 minutes a subsequent day).

Students who have fine- and/or gross-motor weakness and who are unable to use traditional keyboards and/or a mouse to enter text into the computer need alternative means to type and compose. A variety of alternative/adaptive keyboards, such as the IntelliKeys (IntelliTools) and Discover:Board® (Madentec), provide keyboard mouse control and allow for altering the size of keys, the amount of pressure and/or time needed to "press" a key, the locations of keyboard characters (letters, numbers, special characters) so typing can be performed more consistently and reliably. For students who lack the necessary fine- and gross-motor skills to reliably use a keyboard (regular or alternative), program are available that work as, or in conjunction with, word processors. These enable individuals who have one form of reliable, controllable movement (a finger, hand, foot, neck, or eye movement) to use assistive devices, such as single-switch technologies and scanning and/or eye-gaze technology, to control mouse movement and to select keyboard characters and/or prewritten word or phrases.

In its most fundamental form, the ease and flexibility of using a word processor to compose, edit/revise, and publish one's written work in a clear and readable format on a printer or Web page has dramatically relieved the mechanical/physical aspects associated with handwriting and editing/rewriting of assignments in print form. Of course, a crisp print-out, even though it represents a more readable version than a student's handwritten paper, does not necessarily mean that the written product is grammatically or conceptually correct. When considering technology and writing for students with disabilities, teachers often look to a number of additional technology tools that coincide with using a word processor as a way to support clearer expression of students' ideas in writing.

Some students find that they are unable to compose/write when their entire means of feedback is limited to reading words on the screen. For these students, talking word processors, such as CO:Writer Solo (Don Johnston) and IntelliTalk 3 (IntelliTools), allow students to hear while they are typing and/or review what they have typed. This may consist of hearing letters, words, sentences, and paragraphs, and any combination thereof, when words are mouse-clicked, sentences are highlighted, or automatically after a period or return key is typed to end a sentence or a paragraph.

The cognitive task of retrieving words is difficult for some students. Some word processors and programs, operating in the background of word processors, provide a feature called *word prediction*. Programs such as CO:Writer Solo and IntelliTalk 3 can interpret the initial letters typed by a student and apply rules of grammar and language to predict a list of words that most likely will occur next in the sentence. For example, a student, who has weak keyboarding skills and is a terrible speller reaches a point in writing where he needs assistance in continuing the idea, "One of my [favorite] foods is ..." He types the letter *f* and a list of words pops up on the screen that includes "**f**amily," "**f**avorite," and "**f**riend." The student clicks on "favorite" and it gets inserted into the sentence. Word prediction is extremely effective because it reduces the burden of having to type every individual letter in a word.

In other cases, word prediction reduces the cognitive load of having to remember how an entire word is spelled beyond its first few letters. In still other instances, it can retrieve words even if they are misspelled, because it can be set to apply phonetic spelling rules. For students who have problems in the production end of writing, word prediction is an invaluable tool.

Speech-to-text programs that interface with word processors and other software programs allow students to dictate their ideas using headsets with microphones. This feature satisfies both the physical (e.g., typing) and composing aspects for student whose typing is so inefficient or error-prone that it interferes with smooth expression of thought. When selecting and using any speech-to-text program, the teacher should

This student is completing an assignment with a speech-to-text program, speaking aloud his answers into a microphone instead of typing them on a keyboard.

allow the user sufficient learning time to develop competency. Typically, each user must first train the speech-to-text engine to recognize the unique characteristics of the speaker's voice. Factors such as speed of dictation, clarity of speech, and background noise also affect accuracy and reliability of speech recognition.

Conceptual Support

The keyboarding or assistive technology need of some students is secondary to their need to translate their thoughts and ideas into written products that are clear, rational, and organized. Various programs, such as Inspiration (Inspiration Software) and Draft:Builder Solo (Don Johnston), allow students to take notes, brainstorm ideas, visually reorganize their ideas using concept mapping and specialized outlining features, and convert/paste this information into word processors as written products. These programs enable writers to view how their ideas are chunked and the proposed paths and sequence of their written ideas. Some programs have features that highlight information and issue prompts to help students expand these statements into sentences and paragraphs.

Technology can also provide conceptual environments that arouse students' interest, creativity, and motivation to write. These programs (such as Storybook Weaver Deluxe 2004 and The Amazing Writing Machine by Riverdeep), typically used with students in the elementary grades, provide high-interest characters and/or themed content, prompts to generate ideas, initial plot lines, and pictures and graphics that elicit and sustain student writing.

Alternative Communication

A major function of writing involves the communication of ideas and enhancing information presented to others. Educators should keep in mind the many alternative ways by which writing can be considered with respect to other technology-related tasks in school. This may mean the following:

- Using e-mail between students to encourage clarity of writing
- Using word processing to create group and/or shared writing projects such as class newspapers, bulletin board postings, a class cookbook (e.g., every student writes a favorite family recipes), or a collection of poetry (e.g., every student composes a Haiku)
- Using presentation software such as PowerPoint as a reasonable accommodation for students who are not yet adept at formal writing, as an alternative to submitting a formal paper
- Providing students with hardware substitutes for traditional computers—personal digital assistants (PDA) or lightweight, stand-alone keyboards/word processors such as a Dana by AlphaSmart—to type notes or compose lines/sentences/paragraphs at their desk for later transfer into a computer/word processor

Tools that support the writing process should be used in combination with word processing plus the teaching of more traditional writing strategy instruction (MacArthur, 1996). Some sources of additional elaboration on the use of technology to support literacy (e.g., writing, reading, and communication of ideas) in classroom settings can be found in Castellani and Jeffs (2001), MacArthur, Ferretti, Okolo, and Cavalier (2001), Okolo, Cavalier, Ferretti, and MacArthur (2000), and Quenneville (2001).

Math

The National Council of Teachers of Mathematics (NCTM) characterizes the teaching and learning of K–12 mathematics as having two domains:

1. *Content standards*: areas of math that students need to learn (numbers and operations, algebra, geometry, measurement, and data analysis and probability)
2. *Process standards:* areas that emphasize *how* students acquire and apply math content (e.g., through problem solving, reasoning and proof, communication, connections, and representation)

According to the NCTM, "Technology is essential in teaching and learning mathematics; it influences the mathematics that is taught and enhances students' learning" (National Council of Teachers of Mathematics, 2006).

Technology and math are a natural match. Allowing students to use calculators to help with *any* math calculation is one of the most fundamental low-tech examples that comes to mind. For *learning* about math, numerous computer programs are designed to provide students interactive learning environments that involve acquiring understanding of math content and processing standards. These programs cover a range of the following:

- Providing virtual math manipulation environments
- Using visual representations (e.g., graphs or charts) to foster understanding and interpretation of numerical information
- Reading and interpreting charts and graphs
- Learning algebra concepts

- Using decimals
- Using spreadsheets

Two areas of instructional technology and math have been particularly successful with students with mild disabilities:

1. *Drill and practice* to help students develop automaticity of math facts
2. *Anchored instruction* to develop problem solving and higher-order math thinking skills

Drill and Practice

Drill-and-practice software to develop fluency and automaticity of math numbers and basic operations is one of the more empirically validated areas of directed math instruction and technology for students with disabilities. Drill-and-practice programs range from simple (e.g., flash cards) to more complex versions that keep track of student mastery and errors and automatically (and/or under teacher control) adjust features such as rate (of trials and allowable response time), feedback/reinforcement, and difficulty level based on student performance.

Often these programs employ educational game formats and use familiar role models/characters and multimedia embellishment to promote intrinsic motivation. The selected programs should include strong monitoring and record keeping of student progress, as well as features that provide summaries of students' performance that teachers, students, and parents can readily understand.

Anchored Instruction

Software programs based on the anchored instruction model have shown promise with low-achieving students and those with mild disabilities. Anchored instruction (Cognition and Technology Group, 1990) is linked to the concepts of situated and authentic learning, in which multimedia and video are used to anchor the presentation and application of concepts—in this case, math—within exploratory and interactive problem-solving environments. Unlike traditional software programs using animated characters drawn by artists, the anchored instruction programs often include video segments depicting living people (e.g., students with or without disabilities, teachers, friends, store clerks, workers) performing activities such as having to solve a math or science problem related to real-life circumstances.

Typically, these programs use videodisk technology or digital video files to visually chronicle an event ranging in length from 3 to 15 minutes. At the end of the video is a set of questions that require students to perform math calculations and apply higher-order thinking/math reasoning skills. Imbedded in the stories are facts and variables that are necessary during the problem-solving phase. Students can efficiently review the video as often as necessary to gather information, and they may work individually or in small groups to make decisions and reach conclusions based on their math reasoning.

Anchored instruction has indicated improvement in the procedural math skills of low-achieving students and those with mild disabilities (Bottge, 2001; Bottge & Hasselbring, 1993). For direct teaching of computational skills and basic math understanding, students may require more explicit instruction in addition to anchored instruction (Bottge, Heinrichs, Chan, Mehta, & Watson, 2003).

The Social Sciences

Social studies is much more than simply learning historical facts and current events. Many of the social studies learning activities in which students with disabilities participate involve higher-order thinking skills, such as analysis, synthesis, generalization, and decision making, or using technology.

The National Council for the Social Studies (NCSS) (http://www.socialstudies.org/standards/) standards state that social studies education should provide students content related to thematic strands. Five of the 10 NCSS strands are as follows:

- Learning and understanding cultures
- People, places, and environments
- Power, authority, and governance
- Global connections
- Civic ideals and practices

The NCSS believes that a principal role of technology in education is to provide access to cross-disciplinary and multidisciplinary content pertaining to social studies.

One component of social studies instruction is teaching students underlying facts and concrete concepts that apply to social studies. Think of this as learning the *who*, *what*, *when* and *where* of social studies content. At the elementary school level, a variety of software programs provide student ways to interact with social studies-related content, often applied in the context of exploring geographic areas or topics (e.g., "The Rainforest," "South Africa, and "World War II"), in which students experience related content as a means of reinforcing or expanding their understanding of that content.

In contrast to the somewhat limited, static, and reading-concentrated environment of textbooks, the Web and CD-ROMs offer access to large sources of information and also are conducive to dynamic searching for information. For example, primary source documents, such as the Declaration of Independence, can be accessed from http://www.archives.gov/national_archives_experience/charters/

Creativity is an important part of any curriculum. This student enjoys making a valentine for a special school art project.

declaration.html. And historical diaries of North American women from the colonial years to 1950 are available from http://www.alexanderstreet2.com/NWLDlive/.

To enhance the understanding of relationships in more visual formats, spreadsheets and graphing programs can be used to illustrate trends such as population growth over time, or how the populations of villages, towns, cities, and metropolitan areas differ based on education and economic levels. Timeline programs offer ways to more conceptually and temporally illustrate differences and similarities in historical and current events. Mapping software can provide quick access to geographical locations and features, to help embellish/illustrate geographical concepts.

In keeping with the universal design principle that multiple sources of information representation are helpful for student with disabilities, many Web sites and CD-ROMs incorporate pictures, illustrations, maps, sound, and video clips that students can access via hyperlinks. It's one thing to read the words of a famous speech and quite another to watch and listen to an excerpt of Dr. Martin Luther King speaking his "I Have a Dream" speech on the steps of the Lincoln Memorial (http://www.cnn.com/interactive/us/0201/king.speech/embed.html).

Using CD-ROMs, students can search 1,285 issues of *National Geographic* magazines for examples of Egyptian mummy (112 years of *National Geographic* magazine, Encore), or watch video and pictures depicting different cultures (e.g. *Eyewitness History of the World*, Global Software Publishing). Another example of a Web site using universal design principles relative to social studies is the Windows to the Universe—History and People (http://www.windows.ucar.edu/tour/link=/people/people.html), which allows students to review content scaled to beginner, intermediate, or advanced reading/comprehension levels.

Simulation Programs

One popular technology application is the use of simulation programs, which promote learning through the application of already learned knowledge and skills, and observing the consequences of decisions in a simulated context. Students manipulate historical or contemporary information relative to real or compressed time events, often taking on roles and interacting with nonfictional or reality-based characters. Simulation programs are designed with the flexibility to allow students to work individually or in small, cooperative learning groups. Online simulations are designed to foster collaboration and communication between students in multiple locations, using e-mail and online discussions.

Inquiry-Oriented Activities

Some Web-based applications combine social studies content with inquiry-oriented activities that use higher-order thinking skills. The scaffold/metaphor of using virtual field trips or Web-based scavenger hunts is a method to obtain Web-based information to answer study questions. Another form of Web-based learning is using WebQuests (http://webquest.sdsu.edu/). What may make WebQuests helpful for students with disabilities, especially those who have attention or processing deficits, is that they present information and Web links using a structured and organized instructional model that is social studies–friendly. WebQuests are applicable to many different curriculum areas, but because they emphasize a model of Web-based instruction focusing on inquiry-oriented activities, they are particularly applicable to promoting the learning and experiencing of social studies content.

The Physical Sciences

The National Science Education Standards (NCES) (http://books.nap.edu/html/nses/) views specific technologies as a set of integral tools and instruments that students use to develop their abilities and understanding of science. The NCES portrays the knowledge and skills of natural science to understand underlying scientific facts and concepts, develop scientific knowledge as it relates to grade-level understanding and natural science domains (e.g., physical science, life science, earth and space science), and ability to participate in inquiry-based learning, in which students must experiment with and apply scientific information to make decisions and answer questions and/or find solutions to hypotheses.

Software and CD-ROMs

Examples of instructional technology applications as they relate to physical science instruction are similar to those described for social science applications. Science-themed software enables students to explore and experience science-related content as a means of reinforcing or expanding understanding of a particular content. Some programs are designed specifically to promote inquiry-oriented thinking. In these programs, students role-play scientists who are tasked with exploring and having to make decisions that affect ecosystems such as the ocean or a rainforest, or even the solar system.

Science is often heavy on reading, which is not advantageous for students who have mild disabilities—given that reading is one of the most common areas of expressed weakness. Therefore, in terms of understanding factual as well as some of the conceptual aspects of science that are more abstract, numerous CD-ROMs and Web sites present and enhance science facts, concepts, and principles by providing interactive multimedia embellishment of this information. As examples, observing a video or animation of meiosis or mitosis will further understanding of cell division, and seeing an animated example of plate tectonics can help a student understand how a tsunami develops.

Also, spreadsheets and graphing programs can help students see relationships more clearly. Side-by-side charts or graphs can illustrate how factors in some areas influence other factors.

Concept mapping software can also be useful in helping student construct understanding of relationships between variables and factors that make up scientific concepts. They can examine pre-created concept maps, or create their own representations of concepts by mapping variables and factors as part of a class activity.

Simulation Programs

Simulation programs are traditionally associated with laboratory science, in which students manipulate variables and explore things in nature, observing and learning from the consequences of their experimentations. Simulation programs enable students to experiment with things in virtual learning environments that use multimedia to accurately depict the way things appear visually in the real world.

For example, in the area of biology, students can virtually dissect a frog or simulate looking at objects through different types of microscopes. In chemistry, they can virtually mix chemicals, experiment with adding catalysts, and observe the results without fear of poisonous or dangerous consequences. In physics, they can experiment with creating virtual electronic circuits without concern for getting shocked or destroying equipment if they make mistakes.

Adaptive Technologies

In some instances, students with fine- or gross-motor disabilities can use adaptive technologies such as single-switch or an expanded keyboard to control cursor/mouse movement, and virtually manipulate objects on screen in ways they normally could not do because of limited or nonexisting keyboarding/mouse skills. In another context, there are ways to connect scientific instruments so data that originally had to be hand-copied or translated into alternative formats can be entered directly into a software display and graphed in formats that are more visually understandable to some students.

Functional Skills

For student with moderate to severe cognitive disabilities, the technology can be applied with additional accommodations. Consideration always should be given to software that is age-appropriate (e.g., not using kindergarten-themed software to teach basic number concepts to 16-year-olds). Also, the reading level should be appropriate, adapted to be consistent with the student's cognitive knowledge and skills.

Applications are being developed continually to teach functional skills to individuals who are more intellectually challenged. Some videotapes teach self-help skills using video modeling and prompting (Norman, Collins, & Schuster, 2001). Interactive computer programs teach grocery shopping and purchasing skills (Ayers & Langone, 2002; Mechling, 2004; Mechling, Gast, & Langone, 2002; Wissick, Lloyd, & Kinzie, 1992), and functional discrimination skills (Langone, Shade, Clees, & Day, 1999). In addition, a few programs have been designed to promote career education and self-determination. One of these, the multimedia program Choose and Take Action (Sopris West), queries individual preferences related to areas such as working alone or in a group, working inside or outside, wearing a uniform or not, and so forth. The program then displays video clips of various employment settings that most closely match their preferences, as a means to help students identify specific jobs they would like to explore through practical experiences in their community.

Technology and Content Areas in Special Education

Although content areas provide a relatively straightforward organizer, they are not the only category that is useful when considering instructional technology applications pertaining to students with disabilities. Edyburn (2000, 2001, 2002, 2003) has identified more than 100 examples of instructional characterizations in the special education literature. Generally, these fall into the categories of providing students access to the curriculum, learning and applying knowledge, and using technology to address specific academic outcomes. Gardner, Wissick, and Edyburn (in press) discuss technology applications purely from the perspective of instructional outcomes applicable to creative learning activities within any curricular area (e.g., differentiated instruction, thematic units, instructional scaffolds). Okolo (2000) provides a solid overview of content areas with emphasis on instructional outcomes. Pugaliese's (2002) *Stages* is an alternative assessment model that matches the cognitive and language skills of students who have mild disabilities with instructional software programs.

Note

Even though a thirteen-year-old might still be learning the alphabet, the literature and software used to teach him or her still needs to be age-appropriate. Sesame Street characters might not appeal to this adolescent as they would to a typically developing four-year-old learning the alphabet.

Supporting Instruction
Using Web-Based Tools

In addition to providing an information resource for special educators, the Web has been used to support instruction in a variety of ways. Among strategies that utilize Web-related activities and/or tools that provide accommodations and scaffolding of student learning are the following (Gardner & Wissick (2005):

- Working to achieve some degree of proficiency in html and Web design, and using this knowledge to design instructional activities on the Web that provide structure and sequence for students with mild disabilities. Examples in this area include creating WebQuests and Web pages and applying principles of universal design in areas such as selecting appropriate reading levels.

- Making use of online tools that allow teachers who do not know how to write html to organize/scaffold Web-based information, such as sequencing/ordering Web sites, adding prompts or annotations that offer specific directions for tasks to be completed at or with a specific Web site. Examples of tools that help teachers create these types of accommodations are the free online tools TrackStar (http://trackstar.4teachers.org/trackstar/index.jsp) and Web Worksheet Wizard (http://wizard.4teachers.org/), and the low-fee software TourMaker© (http://www. tramline.com/tm/index.htm).

- Providing supplemental, non-Web-based supports outside the computer/Web environment. These include developing worksheets and checklists to add sequence and structure, developing supplemental "how-to" handouts, students completing Web activities as members of a small, cooperative group, and preteaching learning strategies that can be applied at specific points during Web-based learning.

- Including Web-based tools that create versions of traditional learning activities to supplement schoolwork. Web sites such as the Discover School Teaching Tools (http://school.discovery.com/teachingtools/teachingtools.html), FunBrain (http://www.funbrain.com/), Quiz Lab (http://www.quizlab.com/), and 4Teachers.org's (www.4teachers.org) QuizStar and RubiStar allow teachers to create online or printable versions of puzzles, rubrics, quizzes, worksheets, vocabulary words, etc.

- Taking advantage of features in software programs that require little effort on the teacher's part to add structure during Web-based learning. Examples include customizing browsers ahead of Web activities by bookmarking Web sites; creating folders of bookmarks, and adding links to a browser's toolbars, or links to Web resources that are generic but commonly associated with day-to-day Web-activities (such as user-friendly search engines, online dictionaries/encyclopedias, and tools such as TrackStar). Another strategy is to use word processors that allow documents to be created listing Web sites as *hotlists*—word processing documents that contain active hyperlinks. Students open the documents, and when displayed links are clicked, they launch a browser and take the individual directly to the specified Web site.

When accessing a Web site containing special education information and teaching methods, teachers should pay close attention to the validity and authority of the source.

According to Bakken and Aloia (1998), special educators should evaluate the quality of information presented on Web sites by considering the following areas:

- *Content (quality, accuracy, and scope)*
- *Completeness (adequacy of coverage, omissions)*
- *Clarity (ease of use, quality of writing)*
- *Connections (number and quality of hyperlinks)*
- *Corroboration or credibility (documentation of sources, or inclusion of other sources to complement the information provided)*
- *Currency (timeliness of information, up-to-date references).* *(p. 52)*

Note

It is always important for teachers to stay on top of the cutting-edge research and technology developments in the field.

Ongoing Professional Development

Being an educator requires constant professional development. Technology is a fundamental component of the professional and instructional productivity toolkit that teachers use to perform their day-to-day responsibilities. New and revised technology applications in special education—be they assistive devices or instructional applications, universal design, legal considerations, or emerging trends and issues—will continue to become available at a rapid pace. The science of technology and teaching is showing no signs of slowing in its development of new knowledge and skills. Therefore, a commitment to engaging in ongoing professional development is essential for teachers interested in capturing the potential of special education technology for their students.

It is getting easier and easier for educators to gain access to professional development resources to learn new knowledge and skills related to special education and special education technology application. From a practical standpoint, you simply go to a phrase-friendly search engine such as Google and enter a statement combined with the word "tutorial" and the topic you are interested in (for example "tutorial in positive behavior support," or "tutorial on using DreamWeaver," or "tutorial for creating an [iMovie] or [WebQuest]").

Further, the product support Web pages of many of the companies that have developed software and hardware products offer tutorials to help teachers learn how to use their products. A number of public-school-based and university-based offices, centers, and organizations have Web pages linked to tutorials developed in-house and/or lists of links to tutorials published at other Web sites. Teachers should review a variety of them and choose the tutorial that seems to organize content and sequence learning in a manner that makes sense to their learning preferences.

Summary

The marketplace continues to produce dazzling products. Increased attention must be devoted to monitoring these new developments and assessing their relevance and impact for students with disabilities. Although the effect of a disability is often reflected in low academic achievement and failing grades, little systemic efforts are devoted to identifying new technologies that could serve as a powerful intervention for struggling students.

Current laws and regulations governing assistive technology involve only two definitions: (a) assistive technology devices and (b) assistive technology services. These components are two legs of a three-legged stool. Missing from assistive technology federal policy is an appropriate emphasis on the *purpose* of assistive technology—to enhance performance and learning. We sometimes forget that approximately 80%–85% of students in special education have mild disabilities that affect their ability to learn and process information. When IEP teaching reaches the checkbox on whether assistive technology has been considered, far too many students with mild disabilities are not experiencing well thought-out consideration. IEP participants are failing to include instructional technology as part of larger assistive technology consideration process, and many students therefore are not receiving the full benefits of technology accommodations or enhancements to which they are legally entitled.

Some view assistive technology as a blank-check legal mandate that requires schools to purchase devices and services with the hope that they will work for a specific student. Because federal regulations do not specify a process involving the systematic collection and evaluation of data, assistive technology decisions frequently are made without evidence that assistive technology actually improves a student's academic performance. Without data and decision-making guidelines, it is not possible to equitably discern who can benefit from specific assistive technologies and who cannot. As a result, there is an urgent need for research and development to create protocols for measuring assistive technology outcomes and understanding rubrics for decision making.

So what should we anticipate seeing more of in the coming years with respect to special education technology? Hasselbring (2001) predicts smaller, faster, cheaper technologies, in the form of personal computing devices that will enable teachers to apply what we know about the science of learning to deliver instruction, feedback, and guidance any time, any place.

In the special education classroom of tomorrow, students with mild disabilities possibly will be able dictate their assignments 100%, and when editing their text, be prompted in ways to structure their writing that produce more effective communication of their thoughts and creative ideas.

Finally, when considering the use of technology to support instruction, we need to always keep the perspective that good instruction is essentially good instruction. Instructional technology applications represent a tool that special educators can use to enhance the functionality of delivering instruction. The importance lies not in the device or software but in how it's used—by you, the educators—to achieve instructional and learning outcomes and objectives.

References

Ayers, K. M., & Langone, J. (2002). Acquisition and generalization of purchasing skills using a video enhanced computer-based instructional program. *Journal of Special Education Technology, 17*(4), 15–28.

Bakken, J. P., & Aloia, G. F. (1998). Evaluating the world wide web. *Teaching Exceptional Children, 30*(5), 48–53.

Bottge, B. A. (2001). Reconceptualizing math problem solving for low-achieving students. *Remedial and Special Education, 22*, 102–112.

Bottge, B. A., & Hasselbring, T. S. (1993). A comparison of two approaches for teaching complex, authentic mathematics problems to adolescents in remedial math classes. *Exceptional Children, 59*, 556–566.

Bottge, B., Heinrichs, M., Chan, S., Mehta, Z., & Watson, E. (2003). Effects of video-based and applied problems on the procedural math skills of average- and low-achieving adolescents. *Journal of Special Education Technology*, *18*(2), 5–22.

Castellani, J., & Jeffs, T. (2001). Emerging reading and writing strategies using technology. *Teaching Exceptional Children*, *33*, 60–67.

Chard, J. D., Vaughn, S., & Tyker, B. (2002). A synthesis of research on effective interventions for building reading fluency with elementary students with learning disabilities. *Journal of Learning Disabilities, 35*(5), 386–406.

Cognition and Technology Group at Vanderbilt University. (1990). Anchored instruction and its relationship to situated cognition. *Educational Researcher*, *19*(3), 2–10.

Edyburn, D. L. (2000). 1999 in review: A synthesis of the special education technology literature. *Journal of Special Education Technology, 15*(1), 7–18.

Edyburn, D. L. (2001). 2000 in review: A synthesis of the special education technology literature. *Journal of Special Education Technology, 16*(2), 5–25.

Edyburn, D. L. (2002). 2001 in review: A synthesis of the special education technology literature. *Journal of Special Education Technology, 17*(2), 5–24.

Edyburn, D. L. (2003). 2002 in review: A synthesis of the special education technology literature. *Journal of Special Education Technology, 18*(3), 5–28.

Gardner, J. E., & Wissick, C. A. (2005). Web-based resources and instructional considerations for students with mild cognitive disabilities. In D. Edyburn, K. Higgins, & R. Boone (Eds.), *Handbook of special education technology: Research and practice* (pp. 668–718). Milwaukee, WI: Knowledge by Design Press.

Gardner, J. E., Wissick, C. A., & Edyburn, D. L. (in press). The technology enhancement of curriculum, instruction, and assessment. In J. D. Lindsey (Ed.), *Technology and exceptional individuals* (4th ed.). Austin, TX: Pro-Ed.

Golden, D. (1998). *Assistive technology in special education: Policy and practice*. Reston, VA: CASE/TAM.

Golden, D. (1999). Assistive technology policy and practice: What is the right thing to do? What is the reasonable thing to do? What is required and must be done? *Special Education Technology Practice*, *1*(1), 12–14.

Langone, J., Shade, J., Clees, T. J., & Day, T. (1999). Effects of multimedia instruction on teaching functional discrimination skills to students with moderate/severe intellectual disabilities. *International Journal of Disability Development and Education*, *46*, 493–513.

MacArthur, C. A. (1996). Using technology to enhance the writing processes of students with learning disabilities. *Journal of Learning Disabilities*, *29*, 344–354.

MacArthur, C. A., Ferretti, R. P., Okolo, C. M., & Cavalier, A. R. (2001). Technology applications for students with literacy problems: A critical review. *Elementary School Journal*, *101*, 273–378.

Mechling, L. C. (2004). Effects of multi-media, computer-based instruction on grocery shopping fluency. *Journal of Special Education Technology, 19*(1), 23–34.

Mechling, L. C., Gast, D., & Langone, J. (2002). Computer-based video instruction to teach persons with moderate intellectual disabilities to read grocery aisle signs and locate items. *Journal of Special Education, 35*, 224–240.

National Council of Teachers of English. (2005). *Standards for the English Language Arts.* Retrieved January 9, 2005, from http://www.ncte.org/about/over/standards/110846.htm

National Council of Teachers of Mathematics. (2006). The technology principle. Retrieved January 27, 2006, from http://standards.nctm.org/document/chapter2/techn.htm

National Council on Disability. (1993). *Study on the financing of assistive technology devices and services for individuals with disabilities*. Washington, DC: Author.

Norman, J. M., Collins, B. C., & Schuster, J. W. (2001). Using an instructional package including video technology to teach self-help skills to elementary students with mental disabilities. *Journal of Special Education Technology, 16*(3), 5–18.

Okolo, C. M. (2000). Technology for individuals with mild disabilities. In J. D. Lindsey (Ed.), *Technology and exceptional individuals* (pp. 243–301). Austin, TX: Pro-Ed.

Okolo, C. M., Cavalier, A. R., Ferretti, R. P., & MacArthur, C. A. (2000). Technology, literacy, and disabilities: A review of the research. In R. Gersten, E. Schiller, & S. Vaughn

(Eds.), *Contemporary special education research: Syntheses of the knowledge base on critical instructional issues* (pp. 179–250). Mahwah, NJ: Erlbaum.

Pugliese, M. (2002). *Stages: Software solutions for special needs.* Dedham, MA: Assistive Technology.

Quenneville, J. (2001). Tech tools for students with learning disabilities: Infusion into inclusive classrooms, *Preventing School Failure, 45*(4), 167–170.

Robyler, M. D. (2003). *Integrating education technology into teaching.* Columbus, OH: Merrill Prentice Hall.

Wissick, C. A., Lloyd, J. W., & Kinzie, M. B. (1992). The effects of community training using a videodisc-based simulation. *Journal of Special Education Technology, 11*(4), 207–222.

Zabala, J. (1995). *The SETT framework: Critical areas to consider when making informed assistive technology decisions.* Retrieved November 28, 2005, from http://sweb. uky.edu/~jszaba0/SETTintro.html.

Professional Development Resources

Software and Hardware References

The following references are associated with specialized software or hardware cited by name. Readers should note that over the past few years, a number of software publishers have merged but have chosen to maintain their original name with affiliation to their new parent company.

The Amazing Writing Machine by Riverdeep Interactive Learning Limited
   https://www.riverdeep.net/products/other/amazing_writing_machine.jhtml
AspireREADER 4.0/eReader 3.0 by CAST Universal Design for Learning
   http://www.cast.org/products/ereader/
Choose and Take Action by Sopris West
   http://www.sopriswest.com/support/CTA_docs/default.asp
CO:Writer Solo by Don Johnston Inc.
   http://www.donjohnston.com/catalog/cow4000dfrm.htm
Discover:Board by Madentec
   http://www.madentec.com/
Draft:Builder Solo by Don Johnston Inc.
   http://www.donjohnston.com/catalog/draftbuilderd.htm
Edmark Reading Program by Riverdeep Interactive Learning Limited
   https://www.riverdeep.net/products/edmark_reading_program/index.jhtml
Galaxy Classroom by Riverdeep Interactive Learning Limited
   http://www.riverdeep.net/galaxy/index.jhtml
HyperStudio 4.5 by Sunburst Technology, Inc.
   http://store.sunburst.com/ProductInfo.aspx?itemid=176444#complete
Inspiration by Inspiration Software, Inc.
   http://www.inspiration.com/productinfo/inspiration/index.cfm
IntelliTools Classroom Suite by IntelliTools, Inc.
   http://www.intellitools.com/products/
IntelliKeys by IntelliTools, Inc.
   http://www.intellitools.com/
JAWS for Windows screen reader by Freedom Scientific Learning Systems Group
   http://www.freedomscientific.com/fs_products/software_jaws.asp
JumpStart Learning System by Knowledge Adventure
   http://shop.knowledgeadventure.com/DRHM/servlet/ControllerServlet?Action=
   DisplayCategoryProductListPage&SiteID=adventur&Locale=en_US&Env=
   BASE&categoryID=922900

Kurzweil 3000 by Kurzweil Educational Systems
http://www.kurzweiledu.com/products.asp

Laureate special needs software by Laureate Learning Systems
http://www.llsys.com/professionals602/products/prodsby/prodindex.html

Living Books Library by Riverdeep Interactive Learning Limited
https://www.riverdeep.net/products/living_books/library.jhtml

Neo by AlphaSmart
http://www3.alphasmart.com/products/neo.html

PLATO Achieve Now by PLATO Learning
http://www.plato.com/products.asp?cat=Instructional&mark=elem&subj=
reading&ID=137

Read 180 by Scholastic
http://teacher.scholastic.com/products/read180/

Reading for Meaning by Tom Snyder Productions
http://www.tomsnyder.com/products/product.asp?SKU=RFMRFM

Reader Rabbit by The Learning Company (now owned by Riverdeep)
http://www.readerrabbit.com

Start-to-Finish Libraries by Don Johnston Inc.
http://www.donjohnston.com/catalog/stfd.htm

Storybook Weaver Deluxe 2004 by Riverdeep Interactive Learning Limited
http://rivapprod2.riverdeep.net/portal/page?_pageid=353,157846,353_157847&_
dad=portal&_schema=PORTAL

WYNN Literacy Software Solution by Freedom Scientific Learning Systems Group
http://www.freedomscientific.com/LSG/products/wynn.asp

Web Sites

Special Interest Groups

Special Education Technology Special Interest Group (SETSIG) within the International
Society for Technology in Education (ISTE): http://www.iste.org/setsig/

Technology and Media (TAM) Division of the Council for Exceptional Children (CEC):
http://www.tamcec.org/

Access to General Information

About Special Education: http://specialed.miningco.com/

Disability Resources on the Internet: http://www.disabilityresources.org/

Internet Resource for Special Children (IRSC): http://www.irsc.org

LD OnLine: http://ldonline.org

Special Education Resources on the Internet (SERI): http://seriweb.com/

National Dissemination Center for Children with Disabilities (NICHCY):
http://www.nichcy.org/

Instructional Information and Teaching Resources

4Teachers: http://www.4teachers.com

Education World: http://educationworld.com

Blue Web'N: http://www.filamentality.com/wired/bluewebn/

Discovery School: http://school.discovery.com

Education Planet: http://www.educationplanet.com/

Kathy Schrock's Guide for Educators: http://discoveryschool.com/schrockguide/

Project ACCESS Tutorials: http://web.utk.edu/~access/tutorials.html

eLearning Design Lab: http://elearndesign.org/resources.html

PBS TeacherSource: http://www.pbs.org/teachersource/teachtech/tutorials.shtm

WebTeacher: http://www.webteacher.org/

Eduscapes Technology Tutorials for Teachers: http://eduscapes.com/tap/topic76.htm

Integrating Literacy and Technology in the Classroom:
http://www.reading.org/resources/issues/positions_technology.html\

Information on Technology and Special Education

AbilityHub Assistive Technology Solutions: http://www.abilityhub.com/
Assistive Technology Training Online Project (ATTO): http://atto.buffalo.edu/
ABLEDATA: http://www.abledata.com/
Closing the Gap: http://www.closingthegap.com
Cheryl Wissick's Web Toolboxes: http://www.ed.sc.edu/caw/toolbox.html
Education World's Assistive Technology:
    http://www.educationworld.com/special_ed/assistive/index.shtml
Apple Accessibility: http://www.apple.com/accessibility/
Microsoft Accessibility: http://www.microsoft.com/enable/

Books

The following books provide additional opportunities to learn about special education technology applications:

Alliance for Technology Access. (2004). *Computer resources for people with disabilities: A guide to exploring today's assistive technologies, tool, and resources for people of all ages* (4th ed.). Alameda, CA: Hunter House. Also available free online at: http://www.ataccess.org/resources/atabook/s00/s00-01.html.

Belson, S. I. (2002). *Technology for exceptional learners: Choosing instructional tools to meet students' needs.* Boston: Houghton Mifflin.

Bryant, D. P., & Bryant, B. R. (2003). *Assistive technology for people with disabilities.* Boston: Allyn & Bacon.

Church, G., & Glennen, S. (1992). *The handbook of assistive technology.* San Diego, CA: Singular Publishing.

Edyburn, D., Higgins, K., & Boone, R. (Eds.). (2005). *The handbook of special education technology: Research and practice.* Milwaukee, WI: Knowledge by Design Press.

Lindsey, J. (Ed.) (in press). *Technology and exceptional individuals* (4th ed). Austin, TX: Pro-Ed.

Male, M. (2003). *Technology for inclusion: Meeting the special needs of all students.* Boston: Allyn & Bacon.

Ulman, J. G. (2005). *Making technology work for learners with special needs.* Boston: Allyn & Bacon.

Journals That Publish Articles on Special Education Technology

Assistive Technology Outcomes and Benefits
Closing the Gap Newsletter
Computers in the Schools
Educational Technology
Educational Technology Research and Development
Journal of Computing in Teacher Education
Journal of Educational Computing Research
Journal of Special Education Technology
Journal of Research on Technology in Education
Journal of Technology and Teacher Education
Learning and Leading with Technology
Special Education Technology Practice
Technology and Learning

Professional Expectations for the Profession

16

Mary Brownell, Anne G. Bishop,
Dimple Malik, & Lisa K. Langley

Teaching students with disabilities in the public schools has become an increasingly complex, yet rewarding, professional endeavor. Unlike any period in history, special and general education teachers are expected to have a deep knowledge base and a vast array of skills that will allow them to respond to the public call for all students to achieve—and achieve to a high degree. In addition, general and special education teachers are expected to work together with other professionals and parents to help students with disabilities and their nondisabled peers achieve at grade level or beyond. Further, classrooms of today reflect the changing cultural and linguistic diversity of our nation, requiring greater understanding of students and their families.

Gone are the days when special educators worked primarily alone in self-contained settings, teaching only their curriculum of choice. Today's teachers are expected to work collaboratively to support all students in meeting state-mandated academic standards, using evidenced-based practices.

CASE STUDY: TERRY

Like many special education teachers across the country, Terry co-teaches with her fourth-grade general education colleague, Vicky. Together they serve 21 students, 9 of whom have learning disabilities. Terry is a novice teacher, entering her second year of teaching, and Vicky is a veteran, having taught for six years. They volunteered to participate in the first co-teaching situation in their elementary school. The school tends to be traditional, and some teachers are skeptical about the concept of inclusion. Yet, with the support of their principal, Terry and Vicky decide to forge new territory. Even though they are optimistic, Terry and Vicky realize that challenges lie ahead.

A vast majority of their students participate in the federal lunch program and, like many students who live in poverty, are far behind in school. The school's student population is becoming increasingly linguistically and culturally diverse. Hispanic families are moving to the school district to provide labor on the numerous ranches and farms in the area. Many families are not native-English speakers and live in considerable poverty. The combination of language and poverty issues often means that these children need more learning support in school. Among the English Language Learners whom Terry and Vicky have in class is Juan, who also has a documented learning disability. He entered fourth grade unable to read.

Not only the students with learning disabilities in Terry and Vicky's classroom struggle to learn. Terry and Vicky work daily to address the needs of all their students, realizing that all their students are expected to meet high state proficiency standards. Terry and Vicky must teach their students to engage in higher-order thinking skills, such as reaching conclusions, while

(continued)

> ## continuing case study of Terry
>
> also teaching basic reading skills. Simultaneously, the two teachers are figuring out how to work together and draw on each other's strengths. On the one hand, Vicky has taught only general education and does not always focus on providing explicit and well-structured instruction for students with disabilities. Terry, on the other hand, has special education training and knows research-based strategies for helping students with disabilities learn, but she realizes that she knows little about the general education curriculum. Together, they work to blend their specialized knowledge to help all their students.
>
> Terry and Vicky must do a lot of negotiating and planning as a team. Moreover, they must communicate with parents whose backgrounds vary considerably from their own. They know they have little hope of being successful with their students if they cannot work well with their parents.

The case study of Terry reflects many of the changes that are occurring in our nation's schools. More than ever before, special education teachers are being asked to meet high instructional standards, work with increasing numbers of students of diversity, collaborate, and have a basic understanding of the general education curriculum. Understandably, many special education teachers look for support to address these challenges. Also, many people enter the profession not fully prepared or certified for the job because they are responding to the numerous teaching vacancies resulting from the critical shortage of special education teachers. For them, learning on the job takes on a whole new meaning. Therefore, it is particularly important to understand the professional expectations for special educators today and develop a plan to meet these standards.

The Changing Landscape of Special Education

We begin this chapter by providing a snapshot of the changing landscape of special education, which has redefined the roles and responsibilities of special education teachers. Specifically, the changing landscape of special education encompasses

- the call for *educational accountability* and the important legislation that followed,
- the call for *evidenced-based teaching* and *effective schools*,
- the increasing focus on the *inclusion* of students with disabilities in the general education classroom,
- the changing demographics of our *increasingly diverse schools*, and
- the *impact of the teacher shortage* in special education.

Educational Accountability

Educational expectations and opportunities for students with disabilities have changed dramatically since enactment of the Education for All Handicapped Children Act

(EHA) in 1975 (renamed the Individuals with Disabilities Education Act, IDEA, in 1990). As you may recall from chapter 1, this hallmark legislation guaranteed a *free and appropriate education* for all students with disabilities. Public outcry to improve our educational system and the federal mandates that followed have significantly advanced educational opportunities for all students. As a result, the rights and opportunities for students with disabilities have also improved, impacting how schools serve our students. Special education teachers must understand the impact of these more recent laws and the public sentiment that led to these dramatic changes.

Since the early 1980s, the public has been concerned with the academic progress of all school-age students, especially compared to the achievement of students from other industrial nations. The popularity of the report *A Nation at Risk* (National Commission on Excellence in Education, 1983) symbolized the national concern over a declining educational system. Many believed that to regain our competitive edge in a globalized economy, educational reform was the answer. The public outcry resulted in federal legislation that has had a dramatic impact on our schools.

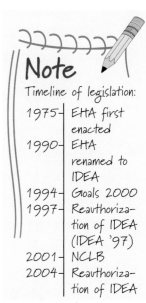

Note

Timeline of legislation:

1975- EHA first enacted

1990- EHA renamed to IDEA

1994- Goals 2000

1997- Reauthorization of IDEA (IDEA '97)

2001- NCLB

2004- Reauthorization of IDEA

Goals 2000: The Educate America Act (PL 103–227, 1994)

Goals 2000 was the first response to the escalating displeasure with public schools. The mandate created education goals relating to school readiness, school completion, student academic achievement, leadership in math and science, adult literacy, safe and drug-free schools, professional development, and parental participation. This act addressed public school children in general and required states to establish plans for meeting specific national education goals. State policymakers responded by implementing reform policies that held schools accountable for student progress. Specifically, students had to meet yearly curriculum goals, as mandated by state policy, and be tested on those goals through state performance assessments. Hence, the concept of *standards-based reform* was born. Goals 2000 set the stage for subsequent laws that eventually would move toward including students with disabilities into the accountability system.

The inclusion of students with disabilities in the standards-based reform movement had a slow start. As general education programs were strengthened, students in special education often were held to individual educational goals and, consequently, different standards. This approach had the unintended consequence of lowering standards and expectations for the students with disabilities. As a result, many secondary students with disabilities did not achieve the academic and life outcomes valued in the special education community. Policymakers, the general public, and parents of students with disabilities were frustrated with these outcomes, as federal and state expenditures on programs for these students were, and have continued to be, considerable.

Two critical legislative mandates directly impacted the education of students with disabilities. The Individuals With Disabilities Education Act of 1997 (IDEA '97) and the reauthorization of Title 1 of the Elementary and Secondary Act (No Child Left Behind Act of 2001, NCLB) realigned our expectations for students with disabilities and altered how special education teachers provide instruction.

Individuals with Disabilities Education Act 1997 (IDEA '97)

The reauthorization of IDEA (IDEA '97) strengthened academic expectations and accountability for students with disabilities, bridging the gap that too often has existed between what students with disabilities learn and what is required in the general education curriculum. Prior to 1997, federal law did not specifically address involving students with disabilities in the general education curriculum, nor did it mandate inclusion in the state and districtwide assessment programs. With IDEA '97, students in special education were expected to receive instruction with their general education peers, and their scores from state assessment tests were evaluated. Teachers such as Terry and Vicky work to develop a new set of skills in response to these new expectations for students and teachers.

No Child Left Behind Act of 2001 (NCLB)

The No Child Left Behind Act of 2001 (NCLB) established a more comprehensive accountability system for all schools and students. This act requires annual tests in grades three through eight and at least one test in high school. More important, the majority of students with disabilities are expected to meet the same high performance standards as their nondisabled peers and be included in the state assessments. The assessments are directly related to the curriculum standards established by each state. The term *high-stakes testing,* commonly used to define this method of accountability, has placed increasing pressure on teachers and schools to improve their educational practices.

The performance of individual schools on state assessment tests is reported publicly, and schools are rewarded or sanctioned accordingly. High-performing schools may be rewarded financially, while low-performing schools face reductions in funds, loss of students to voluntary transfers, public exposure, and, in some cases, closure. Student accountability is also critical, as promotion and graduation hinge on passing these assessments. It is important to understand both the importance of holding all students to the same high standards and the unique challenges presented to students with disabilities and their teachers.

With appropriate *accommodations,* students with disabilities must reach *adequate yearly progress* (AYP). Adequate yearly progress is defined by states to gauge the progress of all public school students, regardless of their socioeconomic or ethnic status, disability, or limited English proficiency. To graduate with a regular diploma, students with disabilities must meet AYP proficiency. Only a small percentage of students with significant cognitive disabilities participate in alternative assessments. The message of the AYP component of the NCLB legislation is that all students will be accounted for in the public schools that serve them, and the achievement gap that has existed for many of our students will be addressed.

Because many students with disabilities, even those with high-incidence disabilities, are functioning below grade level academically, these tests pose significant challenges for special educators who are responsible for student performance. To help students with disabilities succeed, special educators have to be armed with a host of ideas, strategies, and accommodations to use with an increasingly diverse student population. To be considered highly qualified, they must work toward developing these skills and knowledge. They must be ready and willing to work with colleagues and families to help develop instructional plans that will best serve students with disabilities. They often have to remind themselves that restructuring their roles takes time. But they must not lose sight of their daily mission—to provide an engaging, challenging, individualized education for all of their students.

Evidenced-Based Teaching and Effective Schools

In the eyes of the public, the quality of teachers and schools is paramount in the achievement of our nation's children. Educational researchers have documented that students achieve more if schools and teachers are engaging in high-quality practices. Considerable evidence demonstrates that certain schools and teachers get better results. These *effective schools* are characterized by much professional collaboration, community involvement, ongoing commitment to learning instructional strategies that work, clear expectations for student learning and behavior, and continuous reflection on the progress students are making. Teachers who are more capable of securing student achievement gains demonstrate similar qualities, are highly knowledgeable about the subjects they are teaching, and engage in classroom practices that are supported in the research on teaching and learning. Clearly, teachers and schools that employ research-based practices have improved student outcomes.

This research on teacher and school effectiveness has created high public expectations. Policymakers and parents expect teachers to know about the subject they teach and engage in practices that promote effective instruction in that subject. NCLB legislation embraces this standard, insisting that all schools be accountable for hiring, developing, and retaining such teachers, including those who teach students with disabilities. Schools recognize the importance of employing teachers who are highly knowledgeable and skilled as they enter this new era of high achievement standards for all students. Thus, new special educators will have to ready themselves to meet this demand for quality.

The Inclusive Schools Movement

During the early implementation of IDEA, the individual needs of special education students were met by providing separate opportunities and settings. Students were segregated and, unfortunately, often received an inferior education. In the 1980s, parents of students with disabilities became disenchanted with special education. They wondered how their children would acquire the skills to live and work in the community without having access to the general education curriculum in environments that included all students. They believed it was their children's basic civil right to be educated with their peers.

> **Note**
> Even general education teachers who aren't specifically going into the field of special education need to be knowledgeable about the law and how to include special education students in their classroom.

This inclusive classroom consists of same-age peers who are all working on social, academic, and artistic skills together.

In response to this public discontent, Madeleine Will, assistant secretary for special education at the time, proposed that education of students with disabilities should occur in the general education classroom, with cooperation between general and special educators. This 1980s reform was known as the *regular education initiative (REI)*. The *inclusive schools movement* began with the goal of placing students with disabilities in classrooms with same-age peers in the hope that they would acquire more age-appropriate social and academic skills.

The inclusive schools movement has been slow to develop over the last two decades. As a result of the changes we have discussed, however, there has been a marked acceleration of students with disabilities being educated alongside their nondisabled peers. The mandate to include students with disabilities, along with expectations that they will meet high standards in the general education curriculum, requires collaboration among the experts. This can be achieved only through parents collaborating with special educators, classroom teachers, and related-services providers who are highly qualified.

The Diverse Classroom

As you learned in chapter 2, the cultural and ethnic diversity of the United States is growing faster than it has in 200 years. Over the past 10 years, the number of English Language Learners (ELLs) enrolled in K–12th grades has nearly doubled (U.S. Department of Education, 2001). More than a third of the nation's children belong to minority groups, and more than 12 million children live in poverty. Clearly, children who are living in poverty, particularly those from culturally and linguistically diverse backgrounds, face the greatest obstacles in school. Often these students are placed in special education. Substantial evidence indicates that students from certain ethnic groups are overrepresented in special education, particularly in the areas of mental retardation and emotional or behavioral disturbances. This has profound implications for the profession, as the representation of culturally and linguistically diverse students in special education, already large, is apt to grow even larger.

These changing demographic patterns mean that general and special education teachers alike must be prepared to work with an increasingly diverse student population. To provide appropriate support, special educators will have to understand each child's unique background. With many changes in how students in special education are served and the increasingly diverse student population, the education of students with disabilities requires considerable expertise on the part of all professionals involved.

The Critical Shortage of Special Education Teachers

One of the most important challenges of our educational system is the shortage of qualified special education teachers. Further, schools are experiencing a dramatic shortage of special education teachers from diverse cultural backgrounds. As a result, principals are often faced with placing uncertified special educators in the classroom. This shortage has led to creative preparation programs and state/district initiatives to "train up" prospective teachers who are interested in special education, often in a short time.

These efforts include *alternative preparation programs* that provide opportunities to complete certification requirements while teaching, or a reduced level of coursework before entering the classroom. Districts recognize the importance of providing ongoing education and support for special education teachers entering through these routes.

Note

Teach for America, founded in 1989 by Wendy Kopp as part of her undergraduate senior thesis, is a fast-track training program that places recent college graduates in low-income communities to help make a difference in their schools.

Thus, there is a resurgence of well-crafted *induction programs* at the state and district levels to provide formal and informal support to new teachers. A high level of support for teachers in poor urban and rural areas is particularly critical, as they have the highest teacher turnover rates.

In reality, no preparation program, intensive or quick, can prepare teachers with all of the knowledge and skills required to address the new academic expectations for students with disabilities. Therefore, new and veteran special education teachers and general educators alike must respond with ongoing professional training and participate in opportunities to mentor and support one another. As teachers entering this profession, you will be in high demand, and many general educators and administrators will welcome your expertise and dedication to the students who need highly qualified teachers the most. By working collaboratively with your colleagues, you can provide the high-quality education that students with disabilities deserve.

The case of Terry and our description of the changing educational landscape make it clear that special education teachers will have to know and be able to do a great deal to ensure student success. Special educators must be familiar with the general education curriculum and how to help a diverse population of students gain access to it. This requires knowledge about academic standards, instructional and assessment strategies, and the characteristics and development of students with disabilities. Gaining this knowledge occurs over time. The authors of previous chapters in this book have discussed the knowledge that beginning special educators must have to address the needs of students within the specific type of disability.

Understanding and Upholding Expectations for the Profession

At this point, we will explore the principal professional responsibilities and expectations for all beginning and veteran special educators. This means adhering to curriculum standards and providing individualized education, as well as maintaining the professional standards of our profession.

Adhering to Curriculum Standards and Providing Individualized Education

The demands created by federal and state policies for students to meet high academic standards and the charge under IDEA to simultaneously provide an *individualized curriculum* may seem confusing to beginning special educators. After all, students with disabilities have been identified primarily because of their failure to succeed in the general education setting. Access to the general education curriculum, however, does not mean that students with disabilities have to participate in the curriculum in the same ways as their general education peers. "Access" means that students with disabilities require exposure to the knowledge and skills outlined by the state standards but may need multiple types of accommodations and different instructional interventions to meet those standards.

For example, a high school student with a moderate reading disability could participate successfully in an earth science class and meet all of the content standards, with the appropriate accommodations. Support could include access to the textbook on audiotape, study guides for each chapter, and an extended testing period.

Teaching to curriculum standards requires that special educators develop *foundational knowledge* and skills. First, special educators have to be familiar with the curriculum standards for their state and realize that these apply to every student with a disability. *State curriculum standards* usually cover core academic areas, such as reading, writing, mathematics, science, and social studies, as well as standards in other areas, such as physical education, drivers' education, and visual arts. State departments of education publish such standards on their Web sites and often give guidance to schools and teachers addressing those standards.

Second, teaching to curriculum standards requires special and general educators to be knowledgeable of

- the curriculum materials and instructional strategies that support learning,
- *assistive technology* and instructional accommodations that can be used to design learning environments that enable students to meet curriculum standards, and
- how to develop an *individualized education program* (IEP) that incorporates grade-level content standards.

A partnership between special education teachers and general education teachers is essential. Although special education teachers often are not as familiar with curriculum as their general education colleagues, they usually have more understanding of effective instructional strategies and accommodations. Through careful collaborative work, together they have the knowledge and skills to help students with disabilities meet state curriculum standards.

Maintaining the Professional Standards of Our Profession

All professions have organizations that set standards for their members. Our professional standards are designed to provide guidance to those who are responsible for preparing teachers. The Council for Exceptional Children (CEC), the leading organization for the special education profession, has developed standards to guide the preparation and evaluation of beginning special education teachers. These standards are organized around the core knowledge and skills that CEC believes are essential for delivering successful special education. Beginning special education teachers and those who are preparing to become special education teachers should use these standards as a point of reflection to determine if they are acquiring the skills and knowledge they need to responsibly serve students with disabilities.

Although a thorough description of the individual standards is beyond the scope of this chapter, we provide information about the key knowledge and skill areas articulated in the standards. For a more thorough listing and explanation of these critical areas, we refer you to the CEC standards.

Much of the knowledge and skills described next has been addressed in previous chapters of this book. Thus, this book provides a beginning point for acquiring the professional knowledge needed to become a successful special educator. After reading the following sections, you will quickly realize that the knowledge and skill needed to be a successful special educator go well beyond the information presented in this book.

Foundational Knowledge

As a primary source of advocacy for students with disabilities, special educators must understand the moral, legal, philosophical, and theoretical bases for special education

Note

CEC has many special interest divisions that focus on specializations in the field, such as behavioral disorders, giftedness, early childhood, cultural and linguistic diversity, and learning disabilities.

practice. You will have to understand that your job is about providing educational access and opportunity to students. The civil rights movement for persons with disabilities and the passage of the EHA in 1975 were intended to ensure the right of individuals with disabilities to learn and participate fully in mainstream society. Special educators have the primary responsibility for helping students and parents understand their legal rights. To be advocates, special educators must understand the needs of families and their children and their vulnerability within the complex educational system. This is particularly true for families with different cultural beliefs and those who live in poverty.

Many parents, regardless of their background, do not have the essential knowledge and confidence to advocate for their child's needs. Therefore, the special education teacher will have to help them communicate their dreams and desires for their child. To advocate for families and serve students successfully, special educators must understand the *continuum of services* and health care supports available and how to design effective learning environments. This knowledge is essential to ensuring an appropriate education in the *least restrictive environment.*

For instance, special educators must understand that they can serve students in *pull-out instruction* within the general education classroom, as opposed to separating students from their peers. They can use paraprofessionals to work individually with students who have more significant disabilities in general education classrooms, giving these students the opportunity to receive the appropriate curriculum with their nondisabled peers. Understanding the theories behind special education practice also enables special educators to design better instruction and learning environments. Research in cognitive and behavioral psychology has been important in designing interventions and classroom environments that effectively address the needs of students with disabilities.

Knowledge of Individual Learners

Instruction designed to meet the individual needs of students with disabilities is central to defining an appropriate special education program. To respond to students' individual needs and simultaneously ensure their access to the general education curriculum, special educators must understand typical child development and how students with disabilities may differ. Special educators also need to understand the educational implications of developmental differences to determine how to help students achieve state standards. For instance, special educators working with students with learning disabilities have to be aware that these students may not have the organizational skills necessary to summarize information from text and, thus, they may have to be taught a learning strategy to accomplish this skill.

Knowledge about culture and family also provide insight into how students with disabilities learn and the supports they need to achieve successful outcomes. In chapter 2 you learned that many special education teachers have backgrounds that are dissimilar from those of their students and that these differences can create communication problems with families and students. To be effective, special education teachers must be aware of cultural differences and how families perceive the role of schools and special education in their child's life.

Knowledge of students' medical issues is also crucial to maximizing their productivity during school. Special educators will have to understand how various medical conditions influence students' academic and behavioral performance, and the supports available to deal with students' health needs. For example, special educators may have to know how a student with an attention disorder responds to various medications so they can inform the parents and doctors about the effectiveness of these medications. Or special educators may have to understand how to care for and treat a student with AIDS so everyone can remain healthy. In both instances, special educators require knowledge of a student's medical needs and the support of parents and the medical team.

Instructional Planning, Assessment, and Delivery of Individualized Instruction

Special educators play a vital role in planning, evaluating, and carrying out the day-to-day instruction of students with disabilities. Special educators and other critical members of the team must

- assess students' progress,
- design instructional plans based on the knowledge acquired from assessments,
- use effective instructional strategies to carry out instructional plans, and
- use assessments to evaluate the success of their efforts and plan for the next steps.

To begin this instructional cycle, special educators must be aware of the formal assessments used to initially identify students for special education and understand the information generated by these assessments. For example, special educators often are responsible for interpreting test results to general educators and parents.

Second, because formal assessment usually provides only general information about the student's strengths and needs, special educators, to make additional instructional

This teacher often uses individual instruction with her students with learning disabilities in order to ensure they grasp the concepts and understand the assignments.

decisions, must understand how they can follow up with more informal, classroom-based assessments. The curriculum-based assessments and observation systems described in earlier chapters are excellent tools for making daily instructional decisions about children, and special educators should have extensive knowledge of these tools.

To respond appropriately to information generated from assessments, special educators need information about effective instructional strategies. Special educators are primarily responsible for helping general education teachers determine how to design instruction in ways that address the needs of students with disabilities or provide direct instruction to these students. Special educators must be familiar with, and capable of using, multiple interventions proven effective through educational research for students with disabilities. In addition, they must be able to match interventions to needs identified through formal and informal assessments.

Information about using evidence-based interventions has been presented in previous chapters. The U.S. Department of Education also provides resources for teacher through the Educational Resources Information Center and the Office of Special Education Programs (see www.eric.ed.gov/ and www.ed.gov/about/offices/list/osers/osep/index.html).

Designing Effective Learning Environments

Most students need well-designed environments to learn effectively, maintain what they have learned, and generalize their learning to new situations. Like many students, students with disabilities learn best when their classrooms are free from distractions, their individual learning needs are respected and addressed, and they have opportunities to apply their learning to novel problems and situations. If students with disabilities, in particular, do not have access to well-designed learning environments, they are unlikely to make learning progress.

As indicated in chapter 5, students with disabilities at times demonstrate more extreme behavior problems than their nondisabled peers and often require a well-constructed learning environment. Special educators need to know how to

- create effective classroom management systems;
- provide appropriate behavioral supports;
- teach social skills;
- provide opportunities for the students to practice social skills with nondisabled, same-age peers;
- respond respectfully to how culture is influencing the student's behavior;
- use crisis management skills.

In addition, because they are perceived as having expertise with students who have behavioral issues, special educators are often asked to be a resource to their general education colleagues in this area.

Students with disabilities, too, often have difficulty generalizing their learning to new environments. This is especially a concern with students who have more severe cognitive disabilities. Special educators know that it is best for students to practice what they are learning in natural environments to promote generalization. Two places where students with disabilities will need to use their academic, functional, and social skills are the general education environment and the student's community. To make these environments accessible to students with disabilities, special educators have to understand

- how to help students access the general education curriculum,

- types of supports students will need to learn effectively in the community,
- how to teach students to advocate for their needs.

Fostering Communication and Literacy Skills

In reading this book, you know that most students with disabilities are challenged in their ability to communicate ideas and desires and become literate adults. Special educators must become experts in communication and literacy. Specifically, special educators must understand how communication and literacy develops and how second-language issues can influence the communication and literacy skills of students with disabilities. To effectively teach, special educators must have knowledge of research-based strategies for teaching oral expression, vocabulary (both functional and academic), reading, writing, and spelling. In addition, special educators must be aware of the technological advances available to support the literacy and communication needs of students with disabilities.

Fortunately for special educators, numerous Web sites and publications are available for assistance in these areas. For instance, the National Reading Panel provides an excellent guide on the research informing best practice in reading instruction, and the Center for Applied Special Technology (CAST) provides research-based information about how to design literacy instruction (and other types of instruction) that promote the learning of students with disabilities. In addition, considerable information about research-based practices in literacy can be found through the U.S. Department of Education and the Office of Special Education Programs. Furthermore, the chapters in this book provide a framework for communication and literacy instruction that special educators can build upon.

Collaborating With Professionals and Parents

Since the inception of IDEA, *collaboration* with other professionals and parents has been considered the cornerstone of effective special education. Today, an increasingly diverse student population and multiple changes in legislation have underlined its importance, as inclusion and universal academic standards for all students cannot be actualized when teachers work in isolation. Determining how state curriculum standards can be applied to students with disabilities requires creative problem solving and considerable knowledge. This means that special educators, general educators, related-services personnel, and parents must work together.

Schools of today are recognizing the importance of collaborative environments. Teachers are working in a variety of collaborative structures to serve students with disabilities. Examples of these structures are

- *co-teaching*, in which a special and general education teacher work together to serve students;
- *teacher assistance teams*, in which special educators, general educators, and principals come together to serve students;
- *building-based teams*, in which grade-level, interdisciplinary, and multidisciplinary teams plan instructional strategies and explore curricular options;
- *consultative teams*, in which specialists in specific academic areas and classroom teachers work together to implement innovative strategies.

Even though many schools have moved toward greater professional collaboration, parents of children with disabilities—and particularly minority parents living in

Note

Web sites to know:
- National Reading Panel www.nationalreading panel.org
- Center for Applied Special Technology www.cast.org
- U.S. Department of Education www.ed.gov
- Office of Special Education Programs www.ed.gov/about/ offices/list/osers/ osep/index.html

These teachers collaborate on a math lesson, having two forms of visual cues to illustrate 6:00. One teacher leads the lesson while the other teacher is available to assist those students who may need additional help.

poverty—are often left out of the collaboration equation. Parents are excluded from collaboration for complex reasons. For instance, parents may hold different ideas of what it means to be involved in their child's education, or their experiences with school may be unpleasant. Some parents believe they will be unable to communicate with teachers. Confronting these challenges and engaging parents in collaboration is essential. Collaboration with families is required under IDEA, and a comprehensive, well-planned, family–school partnership fosters student achievement.

Effective collaboration requires strong interpersonal skills, knowledge of teaching and students, time, and understanding of different perspectives. Good communication skills, such as the ability to listen and negotiate, are imperative. Many schools have an underlying expectation that special educators enter the school with the knowledge and skills to collaborate effectively to address students' needs. To address this common expectation, beginning special education teachers must make sure that they are acquiring some of these skills during their preparation programs or advocate for collaboration training at the school district.

Engaging in Professional and Ethical Practice

The professional responsibilities and ethical obligations of special educators are well defined and immensely important. Special educators are the key to ensuring that students with disabilities have access to a free and appropriate education program that is delivered in the least restrictive environment. In addition, they are crucial in designing instruction and learning environments that will allow all students with disabilities to meet high curriculum standards and participate in state assessments. In these roles, special educators ensure that the students' IEPs are appropriate and help other team members understand the supports that students will need to successfully operational-ize the IEP.

As advocates for students with disabilities, special educators have an ethical responsibility to be aware of and understand important legislation—including IDEA and NCLB—that guides and impacts the education of these students. Further, special educators must know how states are translating federal legislation into policy and prac-tice. They must be knowledgeable of the curriculum standards for their state and how students with disabilities are included in those standards. And special educators have to understand the accommodations available to students with disabilities in high-stakes testing.

Providing high-quality education to students with disabilities requires special edu-cators to be committed to research-based practices. Students with disabilities must have access to well-designed instruction, based on research. To be successful, special educa-tors have an obligation to learn about research-based interventions and use them in the classroom. Just as we would expect to visit a doctor who is well versed in the latest health-care research, parents should expect their child to be taught by professionals who are well versed on the latest research.

Appropriate professional demeanor requires that special educators have integrity in their interactions with families, students, and other professionals. Special educators must be sensitive to families' needs and try to have realistic expectations of them, rec-ognizing that having a child with a disability can be stressful on the family. Parents may find the medical or behavioral needs of their child overwhelming. Or families may lack financial resources and an adequate social support network to meet their child's needs. Further, special educators must understand that families and students with disabilities have certain guarantees of privacy, and that they are not free to share confidential infor-mation about students and their families unless it affects how special education services are provided.

Finally, special educators must realize the importance of interacting professionally with general education colleagues, paraprofessionals, and related-services personnel. Respectfully resolving disagreements and supporting the efforts of other school staff members involved in the education of students are essential to securing the cooperation needed to serve students with disabilities successfully.

Surviving and Thriving as a Beginning Special Education Teacher

Working in a complex educational system that continuously requires teachers to meet higher accountability demands is challenging for even the most experienced teachers. New special education teachers sometimes feel overwhelmed as they enter the class-room alone for the first time and realize the enormity of what they are expected to do. Beginning special education teachers are simultaneously faced with trying to learn the complex job of teaching, coming to understand the inner workings of school, figuring out the complex system of special education, dealing with the learning and behavior challenges that many students with disabilities present, and ensuring that their students meet high standards.

Even though the job seems enormous, beginning special educators can find the support to survive and even thrive in their first few years of teaching. When special

Note

"My first year as a special education teacher was so over-whelming, but it also made me realize that these kids were what made my job worthwhile. Even now I'm rewarded in dif-ferent ways every single day in the classroom."

—Marie Tate, a veteran teacher in Omaha, Nebraska

educators enter their school, they should begin building a social support network. New special educators should seek out friendly colleagues, in both general and special education, who seem knowledgeable and devoted to helping all students succeed. In addition, new special education teachers should not hesitate to ask their colleagues or the principal to help them when they are uncertain of how to approach specific problems with students or parents or need assistance in improving their skills.

Beginning special educators also must find ways to support their ongoing learning. New special educators quickly learn that, on the first day on the job, they cannot know everything about instructing and serving students with disabilities. To develop their knowledge and remain current about special education practice, policy, and research, special educators would do well to participate in their professional organizations and other professional activities. The Council for Exceptional Children and other professional organizations hold annual conferences that teachers can attend to acquire more knowledge about serving students with disabilities. These professional organizations also maintain Web sites and publish journals. School districts also offer professional development workshops for special educators. Our advice to beginning special education teachers is to take advantage of every opportunity they have to learn.

Beginning special educators must develop realistic expectations for themselves and focus on strategies that will help them cope with the inevitable stresses involved in teaching. Beginning special educators who recognize that they can accomplish only so much in one day and delight in their small accomplishments will feel more satisfied and less stressed. A strong social support network is an inoculation against stress. Beginning teachers must figure out how to solve problems or let them go. Determining those situations that can be changed through problem solving and those beyond their control will help beginners cope with daily stress. Focusing on the positive aspects of teaching also will help beginning special educators persist. Teaching students with disabilities is a rewarding job. Rejoicing in students' progress, no matter how small, helps beginning special education teachers realize the importance of what they do.

You probably chose to enter the special education teaching profession because of your commitment to individuals with disabilities. Remember this as you move forward in the profession, sharpening your knowledge and skills. Recognize that the move to becoming highly qualified is a conscious choice, and you must take the initiative to grow and change. Fortunately, you will be surrounded by other dedicated professionals who are equally committed and actively seek opportunities to work together and contribute to the education of students with disabilities. If you begin your career as an advocate for each of your students, you are well on your way to being a highly qualified teacher.

Summary

The changing landscape in education is impacting the way teachers teach, their need for professional development on a continuous basis, and, most important, their responsibility to students with diverse educational needs. These changes are due in part to new public policies at the national level and the dramatic shifts in demographics occurring across the country. Embedded within these demographic shifts are challenges related to meeting the instructional needs of students with disabilities. With inclusion applying to all children, every teacher can expect to have specific responsibilities for some children with disabilities.

It is important for beginning teachers to understand current and emerging reforms in public education in terms of how they affect the education of children and youth with disabilities. When reforms are backed by legislation, teachers must know their obligations to the students as well as to the schools. They also need to know where to seek assistance in translating legislation into a framework that can help them interpret their professional responsibilities along with understanding the professional standards that guide the profession. Finally, of equal importance is a commitment to professional and ethical practices.

No other human service field focusing on children and youth seems so beset by changes and challenges at the moment as the education of children and youth with disabilities. Learning environments are changing, and public policies seem to be in a state of constant change. Despite a serious teacher shortage, national policy requires that all children be taught by highly qualified teachers. At the same time, resources in support of education are not equal across the country and competition for scarce public resources continues to increase. The challenges for teachers are many, but so are the opportunities to make a difference in the lives of children with disabilities and their families. Having made a career decision to teach, the issue is now to prepare yourself for the challenges as well as the opportunities.

References

National Commission on Excellence in Education. (1983). *A nation at risk: The imperative for educational reform.* Washington, DC: Author.

U.S. Department of Education. (2001). *Twenty-third annual report to Congress on the implementation of the Individuals with Disabilities Education Act.* Washington, DC: Author.

Glossary

Ability grouping: The gathering of students into separate sections according to their basic competence or achievement in a specific area of study; often determined on the basis of academic achievement or performance on standardized tests.

Ableism: Refers to the beliefs that it is better or superior not to have a disability than it is to have one and that it is better to do things the way that people without disabilities do.

Acceleration: A program option for gifted education based on competence rather than age as the criterion for determining a student's access to curricula and academic experiences.

Accessibility: Accessibility is a key issue for individuals with disabilities. Accessibility can be physical (such as having ramps on buildings), programmatic (such as having a sign language interpreter at a meeting), or attitudinal (which is gaining acceptance into society by the general public).

Accessible: Free of barriers to attainment.

Accommodations: Changes made in testing materials and/or instructional procedures that "level the playing field" for students with disabilities.

Acquired hearing loss: A loss that occurs at any time after birth.

Acquisition: Receiving specific tools, such as software or hardware, to assist the student in using technology.

Activity-based assessment (*also called play-based assessment*): Activity-based or play-based assessments are conducted for young children in their natural environments, such as a preschool classroom.

Acuity: Keenness or sharpness of perception.

Acute: Severe, intense.

Adequate Yearly Progress: Adequate Yearly Progress is defined by states as a set measure of academic progress for all public school students, regardless of their socioeconomic or ethnic status, disability, or limited English proficiency.

AD/HD: Attention deficit/hyperactivity disorder.

Adventitiously blind: Loss of vision that occurs in childhood or adulthood as a result of disease or trauma. Someone who is adventitiously blind usually retains visual memory that aids in acquiring skills, particularly those related to mobility.

Affective filter: This mechanism controls how much input the learner receives and is converted into knowledge. It deals with how emotional factors such as attitude, motivation, and anxiety control the rate of developing a second language.

Age-appropriate: Designation for assistive tools and strategies developed to be used with children and adults at different and specific developmental stages.

Alternate assessments: A type of assessment, based on the state's general standards, reserved for 1% of students with the most significant disabilities. An example of an alternate assessment is a student portfolio.

Alternative preparation: Teacher preparation that allows one to obtain a teaching credential without having to follow the traditional college preparation route. It may feature a shorter preparation period, reduced coursework, extended practice in the field, etc.

Amblyopia: A condition that results in reduced visual acuity in one eye, for which no organic cause is found; may occur when the individual suppresses the image in one eye to avoid double vision or when the two eyes have unequal refractive errors.

American Foundation for the Blind (AFB): AFB is a multiservice agency that publishes professional materials, operates a technology center, conducts research, and advocates for people with visual impairments.

American Printing House for the Blind (APH): APH produces educational aids and materials for students with visual impairments. APH receives federal support that allows each state to receive materials distributed on a per-pupil basis. APH maintains a centralized catalog of Braille, recorded textbooks, and large-type textbooks for loan.

American Sign Language (ASL): The sign language used by members of the Deaf community; has the same vocabulary as English but a different grammatical structure.

Anchored instruction: A case-study or other problem situation designed for students to apply concepts and knowledge in order to explore theories of curriculum content.

Anemia: A disorder in which the blood has too few red blood cells or too little hemoglobin.

Annual Yearly Progress (AYP): Based on the provisions of the No Child Left Behind Act of 2001, schools must report their progress on an annual basis on the number of students (large group and subgroup) meeting state standards based on the statewide assessments.

Antecedent: Refers to the action immediately preceding a behavior.

Antisocial behavior: Pattern of behavior that violates widely held social norms and brings harm to others (e.g., stealing, lying).

Anxiety: Refers to persistent and irrational fear that can become focused on specific situations (such as separation or social contact with strangers) or that may be generalized and pervasive.

Applied Behavior Analysis: A paradigm that contains a number of strategies that have been proven to be helpful for students with ASD. Some of these strategies include incidental teaching, prompting, and discrete trial training.

Appropriate education: This principle of PL 94-142 is based on the notion that an appropriate education is one that is individually tailored and designed to fit each student with a disability and one in which the student benefits from the instruction. In order to meet the requirements of an appropriate education, states and local school districts must develop an IEP for each student with a disability aged 3 through 21 and an IFSP for infants/toddlers under the age of three.

Articulation: The management of tongue and lip movements to form specific speech sounds (phonemes) in association with teeth and the mouth cavity.

Artificial setting: A controlled academic environment such as the classroom where students with disabilities learn a skill such as auto mechanics. Students must then transfer those skills to the real-life setting such as an auto body shop.

ASHA: The American Speech-Language-Hearing Association is the professional, scientific, and credentialing body of audiologists, speech–language pathologists, and speech, language, and hearing scientists.

Assisted living: In an assisted living situation, the individual with a disability may live with roommates and receive limited supports from an agency.

Assistive technology: Refers to any item, equipment, or product that can be used to increase, maintain, or enhance the functional capabilities of students with learning disabilities. Assistive devices that help access information include videomagnifiers, screen readers, and digital book readers.

Asthma: A respiratory system disorder that results in difficulty in breathing in reaction to allergens and irritants in the environment.

Astigmatism: A refractive error in which vision is distorted because of the irregular curvature of the cornea.

Audiogram: A graphic representation of an individual's response to sound in terms of frequency (Hz) and loudness (dB).

Audiologist: A specialist who assesses hearing ability and determines and fits appropriate amplification.

Audiometer: An electronic device used to detect a person's response to sound.

Audition: The act or sense of hearing.

Auditory training: A training approach for individuals with hearing loss emphasizing the use of amplified sound and residual hearing by teaching listening skills.

Auditory–verbal approach: A training approach for individuals with hearing loss that uses a structured system of strategies that rely only on the sense of hearing to provide access to language information.

Augmentative and alternative communication (AAC): An integrated group of components, including the symbols, aids, strategies, and techniques to enhance communication.

Auricle/pinna: The top of the external ear; it channels sound into the ear canal.

Authentic assessments: Checklists, observations, interviews of students, informal reading inventories, scales, and portfolios are examples of authentic assessments. They can be developed by teachers and used to provide descriptive information about their students' skills and abilities.

Authentic setting: A real-life environment (such as a grocery store, laundromat, or restaurant) where students with disabilities learn a skill such as food shopping in the natural environment rather than in an artificial setting such as the classroom.

Autism spectrum disorders (ASD): A set of complex, lifelong developmental disorders, which include autism, Asperger Syndrome (AS), and pervasive developmental disorder–not otherwise specified (PDD-NOS).

Automaticity: Refers to the ability to identify words quickly, accurately, and effortlessly at the word level.

Bacterial meningitis: An infection of the meninges, the three membranes enveloping the brain and the spinal cord.

Basal reading series: A graded series of textbooks written specifically to emphasize the sounds of letters in the words of the text.

Biological risk factors: These types of risk factors are intrinsic to the child and include being born prematurely or a diagnosed medical disorder such as seizures.

Bipolar disorder: Refers to major mood disorders characterized by both manic and depressive episodes.

Blind: Functional definition used primarily by educators to describe someone who is totally blind or has light perception without projection.

Blindness: The condition of being totally blind or having light perception without projection.

Braille: Tactual system for reading and writing developed in 1829 by Louis Braille, a Frenchman who was blind. Braille consists of embossed characters using various combinations of raised dots in a Braille cell, two dots wide and three dots high.

Braille display: A feature that provides a temporary tactile display of a small segment of a Braille document; produced by plastic pins that are electronically activated in a row of open cells. The display can be attached to a computer or included on a Braille note taker.

Braille note taker: Quiet and portable technological devices that have many functions, including saving and editing material, linking to printers and computers, and providing auditory feedback. Some models have a Braille display.

Braille printer   *see Embosser*

Braillewriter: A machine for typing Braille on paper. The machine has six keys, corresponding to the six dots in the Braille cell; a space bar; a back spacer; and a line spacer.

Categorical: A method of educational classification where children are grouped based on their specific disability label (i.e., category) for instructional purposes and/or for teacher education programs and certification.

Catheterization: The procedure used to remove urine by or for individuals who lack control of bladder function.

Center for Applied Special Technology (CAST): A nonprofit organization that strives to increase the learning opportunities for all students (and especially those with disabilities) through the research and development of resources and strategies that are technology-based and innovative.

Central auditory processing disorder: A hearing loss that occurs as a result of a problem in the pathway from the cochlea to the brain.

Cerebellum: The part of the brain that controls motor coordination, balance, and cognitive function.

Cerebral palsy: Central nervous system disorder in which damage occurs to the area of the brain responsible for muscle coordination.

Certified Orientation and Mobility Specialist (COMS): An expert who is trained and professionally certified by the Academy for Certification of Vision and Rehabilitation and Education Professionals (ACVREP). This specialist conducts functional vision assessments, manages orientation and mobility assessments, and instructs students in skills related to body image, movement, and travel with and without devices, including the long cane.

Challenged: A term currently used in place of disability in an attempt to minimize the negative connotations of the term *disability*.

Chromosomal disorder: A condition caused by an absent or defective gene or by a chromosomal aberration.

Chronic: A long-term illness or disorder.

Chunked (chunking): A term used to designate a distinct piece of curriculum content that can be learned or studied quickly and nonsequentially.

Closed captioning: The translation of dialogue for a television program into printed words (captions or subtitles), which are then converted to electronic signals that can be inserted into a blank space at the bottom of the picture.

Closed-circuit television (CCTV, *also called videomagnifier*): Magnifies print material or graphics placed on a viewing stand that can be seen on a monitor.

Cochlea: A snail-shaped structure that houses the organ of hearing.

Cochlear implant: An electronic device that is surgically implanted to provide access to sound by bypassing the damaged or destroyed hair cells in the cochlea, allowing the user to perceive sound.

Code switch: The ability to go back and forth between language forms and dialects, depending on the social context.

Codified: Arranging a set of best practices or rules into an organized system.

Cognitive behavioral interventions: Strategies designed to change thoughts or thought patterns that result in observable behavior change.

Cognitive disabilities: A chronic condition characterized by significant impairment in functioning in both intelligence and adaptive skills that is manifested before age 18 and results in substantial functional limitations in three or more life activities.

Collaboration: An interactive process that enables people with diverse levels of expertise to generate creative solutions to mutually important problems.

Communication: An interactive cognitive and social process in which a message is conveyed from one person to another.

Communication delay: A slower rate of language or speech skills acquisition, according to developmental norms, but development does follow a predicted order.

Communicative competence: Capacity for using speech and language to learn how the world operates; to receive, analyze, organize, and store information; to share information with others through a cultural value system; to adjust to listener characteristics.

Community-based instruction (CBI): A method of instruction that is designed to incorporate community-working experiences such as banking skills and job training into students' educational programs. In CBI, students receive opportunities to learn, practice, and apply life skills in the natural settings in which they are expected or appropriate.

Community setting: Work, leisure, or home environments where individuals will transition upon completion of secondary education.

Comprehension: Understanding the meaning of spoken and written language.

Computation: The retention and use of basic math skills, such as addition, subtraction, and math facts.

Concomitant traits: Traits that exist concurrently. Typically one can be positive (e.g., comprehends abstract concepts) and one can be negative (e.g., omits details).

Conduct disorder: Refers to repetitive, persistent patterns of behavior that violate the rights of others or social norms and rules, including aggression, destruction of property, deceitfulness, or theft.

Conductive hearing loss: A loss as a result of a problem in the outer or middle ear that impedes the efficient conduction of sound.

Congenital: Present at birth.

Congenital cataract: An opacity or cloudiness of the lens that prevents passage of light rays to the retina, creating images that are distorted and hazy.

Congenital glaucoma: An abnormally developed drainage system that blocks the flow of fluid, increasing pressure in the eye and the size of the eyeball; if not treated, can damage the optic nerve and lead to permanent visual loss or blindness.

Congenital hearing loss: A loss that is present at birth.

Congenitally blind: Being born blind or losing vision in infancy prior to developing the ability to retain visual memory.

Consequence: Refers to the action immediately following a behavior.

Continuum of services: Refers to the full range of alternative placements from least restrictive to most restrictive that a school can use to serve students with disabilities; the continuum includes regular classrooms in neighborhood schools, resource rooms, self-contained classes, special day schools, residential schools, hospital settings, and homebound instruction.

Contracted Braille: The literary Braille code, which includes numerous symbols for letter combinations and words; for example, "sd" represents the word *said*, and the letter "k" by itself represents *knowledge*. The contracted system was developed in the early 1900s to shorten the length of Braille materials and increase reading efficiency.

Cooperative learning: A form of grouping and instructional strategy that requires students with varying abilities and/or backgrounds to work together as a team to achieve a common goal.

Cortical visual impairment (CVI): A reduction in vision resulting from damage to the posterior visual pathways or occipital lobe; visual systems of the brain are unable to interpret what the eyes see.

Criterion-referenced tests: Tests that compare the performance of a student on a particular skill in a specific area such as math against a set criterion. The criterion might be a percentage score or number correct.

Cross-grade programs: A grouping structure where students are grouped according to their abilities (without regard to grade level) and taught the given subject in separate classrooms.

Cued speech: A technique that facilitates the development of oral communication by combining eight different hand signals in four different locations, thereby providing additional information about sounds that are not easily identified by speech reading.

Culturally responsive teaching: Refers to the usage of cultural knowledge, prior experiences, and performance styles of students who are diverse to make learning more appropriate and effective for them; it teaches to and through the strengths of these students.

Culture: The ideas, symbols, behaviors, values, and beliefs that are shared by a human group. Culture can also be defined as a group's program for survival and adaptation to its environment.

Curriculum-based assessments: Informal tests that are directly tied to the curriculum that students are being taught and therefore can provide an accurate measure of the students' progress.

Cytomegalovirus (CMV): A virus that may cause very few symptoms in adults or it might resemble mononucleosis. In the fetus, however, it can lead to severe malformations.

Deaf: A hearing loss greater than 70–90 dB that results in severe oral speech and language delay or that prevents understanding spoken language through hearing.

Deafblindness: A multisensory impairment wherein the person is both deaf and blind (although the person does not have to be completely deaf and blind to be considered deafblind).

Deaf community: Individuals who are Deaf, who share a culture, attitudes, and set of beliefs, and who use American Sign Language to communicate.

Deaf culture: A pattern of beliefs, values, and experiences that are characteristic of individuals in the Deaf community.

Decibel (dB): The unit used to express how loud sound is.

Demographics: Information from a variety of sources used to create a broad profile of any community. May include population trends, age, gender, race or ethnicity, education, income, crime rates, voting statistics, and occupations. Obtain this information through U.S. Census Bureau, Chamber of Commerce, development offices, or the U.S. Postal Service.

Depression: The loss of interest or pleasure in almost all normal activities lasting for at least two weeks.

Developmental delay: A classification term defined in the 1997 reauthorization of the Individuals with Disabilities Education Act for use with children ages 3–9 and identified by documentation of a delay in development of physical, cognitive, communication, social/emotional, and/or adaptive skills.

Developmental milestones: Behaviors or skills identified as emerging at specific ages during early childhood development.

Diabetes: A metabolic disorder in which the body does not either produce sufficient insulin or use insulin effectively.

Diagnostic process: The process followed by a school's multidisciplinary team to identify a specific disability through the use of norm-referenced tests, direct observation, work samples, home visits, and related data collection.

Diagnostic protocols: Specific tests and tools administered in a manner to determine eligibility for services under special education.

Dialects: Rule-governed, predictable, and linguistically equal variations from standard American English used by identified ethnic, regional, or age groups.

Differentiation: A curricular approach in a gifted program; includes acceleration, complexity, depth, challenge, and creativity.

Direct instruction: A type of teaching method where the concept, skill, or strategy is taught in an explicit and structured manner. Direct instruction is typically led by the teacher.

Disability: Denotes a specific condition such as a heart ailment, loss of limb, or paralysis.

Discrete trial training: The process of breaking down tasks or lessons into easy steps; consists of presentation of a stimulus, waiting for a response from the child, and then a consequence.

Disproportionate representation: This occurs when there is a significantly higher or lower percentage of students who receive special education services in a certain group than their percentage of the school population as a whole. Disproportionality can refer to either over or under the level representative of the general population.

Double jeopardy: Refers to the increased negative effects on a child's development from the interactions of biological and environmental risk factors. For example, a child with a low birth weight who is raised in a poverty setting would be considered to be in a double-jeopardy situation.

DSM-IV-TR: Diagnostic and Statistical Manual of Mental Disorders, 4th Edition, Text Revised.

Dyscalculia: Difficulty in learning to solve mathematical problems.

Dysfluency: Refers to the interruption in the flow of speaking characterized by atypical rate, rhythm, and repetitions in sounds, syllables, words, and phrases.

Dysgraphia: Difficulty in learning to write.

Dyslexia: Difficulty in learning to read or in learning to recognize and understand written words.

Ear canal: The channel through which sounds flow to the middle ear.

Early childhood special education (ECSE): Under IDEA, early childhood special education services are required for preschool children with developmental disabilities from age three until entry into public school. The goal of ECSE is to change children's developmental trajectories by remediating delays caused by developmental disabilities and to prevent secondary disabilities from developing.

Early intervention (EI): Under IDEA, services for children from birth to age three are called early intervention services and include educational, physical, speech and language, nutritional, and psychological services for infant, toddlers, and their families.

Ear mold: A custom-fit device made of soft plastic that attaches to a behind-the-ear (BTE) hearing aid to deliver sound from the aid to the ear.

Educational accountability: Demands from policy makers and the public to hold schools accountable for student progress.

Embosser (_also called Braille printer_): A device that reproduces in Braille information that is stored in a computer's memory. This equipment enables people who do not know Braille to type into the computer and produce Braille output.

English language learner (ELL): A student who comes from a home where another language besides English is spoken.

Enrichment: Modification of curriculum to provide more depth and breadth than is provided through the standard curricula.

Environmental risk factor: This type of risk factor is external to the child and includes poverty, physical abuse and neglect, and parental drug and alcohol abuse.

Epilepsy: A condition in which an individual has recurring seizures.

Ethnic group: A microcultural group or collectivity that shares a common history and culture, common values, behaviors, and other characteristics that cause members of the group to have a shared identity.

Eustachian tube: A structure that extends from the throat to the middle ear cavity and allows for the equalization of pressure and drainage of fluid.

Evidence-based teaching: Proven practices that have been created based upon research findings.

Exceptional: Refers to children with handicapping conditions and special abilities requiring instructional modifications and/or special education.

Executive functioning: The ability to select and organize key information.

Expanded core curriculum: Curriculum areas that typically are not included in the standard general education curriculum, including visual efficiency, social interaction skills, career education, and independent living skills, that should be taught by COMS or TVIs.

Expectancy benchmarking: A concept designed to help school administrators determine how many students in their school population could potentially benefit from assistive technologies.

FAPE   *see Free Appropriate Public Education*

Fetal alcohol syndrome: A condition resulting from the ingestion of alcohol by the mother during the prenatal period, which results in the child being born with cognitive delays, abnormal facial features, organ defects, and reduced physical size throughout life.

Fetal exposure: Conditions impacting the development of the fetus during the prenatal stage of the child's development.

Fingerspelling: A form of manual communication that incorporates all 26 letters of the English alphabet with each letter signed independently.

Fixed trait: A condition specific to an individual and not alterable during his or her developmental period.

Flexible grouping: The practice of grouping students according to ability and/or achievement levels that allows for student movement and fluidity depending on their level of interest and progress.

Fluency: The ability to speak and write a language correctly.

Fluency disorder: A broad term used to describe various speech disorders, one of which is stuttering.

FM Sound Field system: The teacher's voice is transmitted from a lavalier FM microphone to ceiling- or wall-mounted speakers which amplify it 8 to 10 dB above ambient room noise. In this way all the children, regardless of seat location and the direction the teacher is facing, are able to hear the teacher.

Foundational knowledge of special education: The broad understanding and fundamental knowledge about special education that covers special education philosophy, laws, policies, and issues and how this knowledge influences what occurs within the special education arena.

Free appropriate public education (FAPE): PL 94-142 mandated that all states must provide students with disabilities between the ages of 3 and 21 a free and appropriate public education in order to receive federal funds.

Full inclusion: This refers to a philosophical belief held by many special education advocates today that general and special education should be merged and that all students with disabilities should be fully integrated into the general education setting and be educated with students without disabilities.

Functional: Basic capacity specific to learning, behavioral development, social/emotional development, and adaptive skills development.

Functional behavioral assessment (FBA): An evaluation procedure that identifies the consequences (purpose the behavior serves), the antecedents (triggers of the behavior), and setting events (context) that maintain inappropriate behavior; this information is gathered to assist education professionals with education plans for students with disabilities.

Functional curriculum: Emphasizes teaching students concrete and practical skills (e.g., self-help, cooking) rather than abstract theories or academic knowledge. May be taught in the community setting.

General education classroom: The general education classroom would be considered the full inclusion model for students with disabilities because the student's instructional needs would be primarily accommodated in the general education classroom with peers who do not have disabilities. Students in this placement may also receive additional special education or related services within or outside the general education class as long as they spend at least 80% of the school day with their nondisabled peers in the general education setting. The general education teacher is the student's primary teacher.

General education curriculum: The grade-level curriculum (e.g., language arts, math, science, social studies) that is designed for students whose primary instruction is presented by a general education teacher.

Genetics: Pertaining to or carried by genes, the basic unit of inheritance.

Gifted: Refers to those students who display high performance ability in intellectual, creative, artistic, leadership, or specific academic areas.

Gifted and talented student: One identified for special programming based on local or state criteria for students with abilities or talents above those possessed by the majority of students.

Goals 2000: The Educate America Act: Federal legislation that called for educational reform, challenging states to establish state standards and assessments.

Group home: In a group home living arrangement, a group of people with disabilities live in a house in the community where they are usually supported by paid live-in staff. While group homes provide better lifestyle outcomes than more segregated options such as institutions or nursing homes, many people who live there remain segregated from the community at large.

Group project: Within cooperative learning, this grouping structure involves a small group of three or four students working together on one group project. In this format, every student is involved and contributes to the final outcome.

Group work: An activity where a small group of students are assigned to work together. There are typically no assigned or specified roles.

G/T: An abbreviation to refer to gifted and talented students or programs.

Handicap/handicapped: This term describes the consequences of a disability. Children who were considered handicapped in the 1970s represented a wide range of children with conditions requiring instructional modifications or special education, but not including the gifted and the talented. Currently, use of the term *handicapped* is discouraged because it refers to the person instead of the condition of having a handicap.

Hard of hearing: Term used for individuals with losses in the better ear of 25–70dB who benefit from amplification and communicate primarily through spoken language.

Hearing aid: An assistive listening device for individuals with hearing loss. It has a microphone and an amplifier that makes the sound louder.

Hemiplegia: Paralysis on one side of the body.

Herpes virus: A virus leading to symptoms that range from cold sores to genital lesions to encephalitis; it can cause fetal disabilities in early infancy.

Hertz (Hz): The unit used to express the frequency of sound. The measurement is in terms of the number of cycles that vibrating molecules complete per second.

Hidden curriculum: The daily life knowledge that most people learn naturally throughout life.

Higher-level thinking skills: Skills that emphasize critical thinking and abstract concepts such as analysis, synthesis, and evaluation.

High-incidence: A term used to represent a large number (over 100,000) of students with a specific disability. Typically, disabilities within the mild to moderate range fall in this category. For example, learning disabilities is considered a high-incidence disability because of the large proportion of students in this group relative to all students with disabilities.

High-stakes assessment: This refers to public policy in some states to determine students' promotion or graduation based on one single indicator (e.g., statewide assessment). An example of a high-stakes assessment is a high school exit exam.

High-stakes testing: Tests that are used to reward and sanction schools according to student test results, in an effort to improve student, teacher, and school performance.

Human guide technique: The technique where the student with a visual impairment grasps the sighted person's arm just above the elbow and walks about a half step behind the guide, following the guide's body movements.

Human immunodeficiency virus (HIV): A virus that affects an individual's immune system, interfering with the body's ability to fight off infections.

Hyperbilirubinemia: Excessive accumulation of bilirubin in the blood resulting in jaundice.

Hyperopia: Farsightedness; a refractive error in which the eyeball is too short and light rays focus behind the retina.

Hypertonicity: Excessive muscle tone.

Hypotonicity: Too little muscle tone.

Hypoxia: Decreased availability of oxygen during pregnancy, labor, delivery, or after birth; it can result in death or brain damage.

IDEA   *see Individuals with Disabilities Education Act*

IEP   *see Individualized Education Program*

Incidence: Incidence refers to the number of children who at some time in their lives might be considered exceptional.

Incidental learning: Learning that occurs informally.

Incidental teaching: This occurs when a teacher structures a lesson or learning objective around the interests of the student.

Inclusion: The practice of educating students with disabilities with their nondisabled peers in a general education classroom.

Inclusive schools movement: A reform movement designed to restructure general education classrooms so they better accommodate all students, including those with disabilities.

Incongruity: A direct opposition or mismatch between the teacher's and students' cultural backgrounds and/or behavior, expectations, values, etc.

Independent living: In an independent living situation the individual with a disability does not receive any formal services or supports and is expected to perform all functions of daily living independently.

Individualized curriculum: A curriculum that is suited to address the individual needs of the learner.

Individualized Education Program (IEP): A written legal document that describes an educational program designed to meet that child's unique needs. By law, it must contain information regarding the student's present performance, annual goals, participation procedures in assessments, and participation in general education classrooms, as well as other pertinent information concerning the student's educational goals and needs.

Individualized Family Service Plan (IFSP): This is a written document that is the centerpiece for early intervention services under IDEA. After conducting appropriate assessments, the IFSP must include the infant's or toddler's strengths and needs in five areas: cognitive, motor, social or emotional, adaptive, and communication skills. It also must include a statement of the family's resources, priorities, and concerns related to enhancing the development of the infant or toddler, as well as an outline of the proposed services for the child and family and specific goals, objectives, and corresponding timelines.

Individualized health care plans: A detailed plan that includes information about an individual student's specialized health care needs, procedures, emergency care procedures, record of training and monitoring, etc.

Individuals with Disabilities Education Act (IDEA): Replaced PL 94-142, the Education for All Handicapped Children Act. IDEA is a federal law stating that to receive funds, every school system in the nation must provide a free, appropriate education for every child between the ages of 3 and 21, regardless of how serious the student's disability is.

Individual Transition Plan (ITP): When students receiving special education services turn 16, they are required to have an individual transition plan, which may be part of their IEP or a separate document. The ITP is to set goals for the transition process to postsecondary settings.

Induction programs: Instructional support programs that aid teachers new to the educational field. They are usually initiated at the school district level.

Informal assessments: Most informal assessments are developed by teachers or others to assess how well a student is mastering particular skills or knowledge related to classroom instruction. They are not used to compare a student's performance against the performance of other students.

Instruction: The use of certain techniques and delivery systems in the classroom to provide appropriate curricula.

Instructional technology: The theory and practice of using various technologies for learning and instruction.

Insulin: Hormone that controls the level of glucose in the blood.

Integrated environments (*also called supported or competitive employment*): In this type of work environment, individuals with disabilities work in regular jobs in the community alongside workers without disabilities, such as working in a fast-food restaurant.

Integration in existing generic programs: In this type of recreational program, the individual with a disability chooses an existing traditional, age-appropriate recreation program, and an integration specialist or other professional identifies and ameliorates discrepancies between the skill requirements of the program and the individual's capabilities and develops appropriate supports.

Intellectual functioning: Level of intellectual capacity an individual has applicable to learning.

Intelligence testing: Intelligence testing increased in 1916 with the revision of the Stanford–Binet Intelligence Scale. This test made it possible to differentiate students by ability level and identify children as having mental retardation. Today these tests remain a major factor in the diagnosis and placement of many exceptional children in special education programs, although there is question of discrimination toward students from diverse backgrounds.

Interdisciplinary services: In order to provide family-centered services for infants and toddlers with disabilities, this generally requires a model of joint collaboration from multiple professionals from a variety of fields. For

example, it is not uncommon for an early intervention team to be interdisciplinary and include a social worker and physical, speech, and occupational therapists, as well as pediatricians and nurses.

Intermediate Educational Unit (IEU): An IEU is an organizational structure between the local education agency (LEA) and the state education agency (SEA). The IEU provides varying services; some have taxing powers, and others obtain funds from SEAs and by contracting with LEAs. In some states IEUs were created specifically to serve special education programs.

Interpreter: An individual who translates the spoken message into sign. Oral interpreters silently repeat with clear lip movements the message of the speaker. A transliterator provides word for word translation using signs in English word order.

Interventions: To act on another person's behalf in order to change a particular behavior.

Intracranial hemorrhage: A neurological complication of extremely premature infants where the immature blood vessels bleed into the brain.

Intrinsic motivation: A term used to describe a moment when the incentive to act comes from within the student.

Isolated placements: Practice of excluding children from the general education classroom and, instead, educating them in a separate room and/or building for the entire school day.

Jaundice: A yellowing of the complexion and the whites of the eyes resulting from hyperbilirubinemia.

Jigsaw format: Within cooperative learning, this grouping structure involves a small group of students working together toward a common goal. In jigsaw, each student is assigned a specific task to complete for the entire group to meet its goal.

Language acquisition: The subconscious occurrence of acquiring a language resulting from participating in natural communication.

Language disorder: Difficulties with syntax, morphology, phonology, semantic content, and/or pragmatics.

Large-scale assessments: Assessments such as statewide tests used to assess the performance of students by grade level in meeting national and/or state standards.

Learned helplessness: A term that refers to a condition where a person believes that no matter what the effort he or she puts forth, failure will result.

Least restrictive environment (LRE): A requirement under IDEA that states students with disabilities, to the maximum extent possible, must be educated in the general education classroom, with appropriate aids and supports, along with their nondisabled peers in the school they would attend if not disabled, unless a student's individualized education program states otherwise.

Legal blindness: Having a central visual acuity of 20/200 or less in the better eye with corrections (meaning that the person can see an object at 20 feet that a person with normal vision can see from 200 feet away); also if the visual field is restricted to 20 degrees or less.

Level of supports: Integral to the AAMR classification scheme that focuses on the amount of support needed for someone with mental retardation to function in his or her environment as completely as possible; levels are (1) intermittent, (2) limited, (3) extensive, or (4) pervasive.

Local education agency (LEA): An LEA is the public board of education or other public authority within a state that maintains administrative control of public elementary or secondary schools in a city, county, township, school district, or other political subdivision of a state. An LEA has the primary responsibility for implementing and delivering appropriate educational programs and services for all exceptional children and youth. The LEA must be in compliance with state and federal regulations.

Loop systems: Closed-circuit wiring that sends FM signals from an audio system directly to an electronic coil in the hearing aid.

Lower socioeconomic status: A term used to identify the economic status of a family or individual based on income and need. For school districts, this status makes one eligible for free or reduced lunch and related supports available through the school system.

Low-incidence: A term used to represent a small number (less than 100,000) of students with a specific disability. Typically, disabilities within the moderate to severe range fall in this category. For example, hearing impairment is considered a low-incidence disability because of the small proportion of students in this group relative to all students with disabilities.

Low vision: Describes someone who has a significant visual impairment but also has significant usable vision.

LRE *see Least restrictive environment*

Magnifier: A device placed directly on a page or inserted on eyeglasses to enable a person to see and read.

Mainstreaming: The placement of a student with a disability from a segregated, special education setting to a general education setting for specified intervals (e.g., academic, lunch, art) during the school day.

Manual approach: Teaching the use of sign language for communication.

Maternal Rh incompatibility: A condition that occurs when a baby with Rh+ blood is born to a mother with Rh- blood. This leads to a breakdown of red blood cells in the baby. Injecting the drug RhoGAM into the mother can prevent this condition.

Mediational strategies: A process where alternative modes of support are made available to engage a student in the learning experience.

Metacognition: A person's awareness of what strategies are necessary to perform a task and his or her ability to use self-regulation strategies.

Mild mental retardation: Term used to identify the degree of delay in an individual with mental retardation. Those with mild mental retardation make up about 85% of the MR population and have an IQ level between 55 and 70.

Mild to moderate disabilities: Students with disabilities such as learning disabilities, emotional/behavior disorders, speech and language impairments, or mild mental retardation are often, as a group, referred to as learners with mild to moderate disabilities. The same groups may also be identified as high-incidence.

Mixed-ability grouping: A grouping format where students are assigned to groups based on different or heterogeneous ability levels.

Mixed hearing loss: A combination of a conductive and a sensorineural hearing loss.

Moderate mental retardation: About 10% of the mentally retarded population is considered moderately retarded. Moderately retarded individuals have IQ scores ranging from 35 to 55.

Moderate to severe disabilities: A broad group of specific disabilities related to the students' ability level and need for specialized services. This group may include students with cognitive and developmental disabilities, autism spectrum disorders, hearing loss, and visual impairments.

Modification: A change in the curriculum or test that alters the learning expectations or construct of what is being measured.

Modified assessment: A type of assessment based on the state's general standards reserved for the next 2% of students with the most significant disabilities after the 1% who are allowed to take alternate assessments. An example of a modified assessment is allowing a student to use a calculator on a math computation test.

Monocular or monocular telescope: A portable telescope that helps people see things that are larger or farther away (a chalkboard or whiteboard, a friend's house, etc.).

Morphology: The study and use of morphemes—the smallest units of meaning in any language, such as prefixes, roots, and suffixes—to build words.

Motivation: A typical trait of G/T students; they tend to pursue independently topics of interest, enjoy challenging activities, and persevere until a task is completed.

Multicultural education: Multicultural education incorporates the idea that all students—regardless of their cultural, ethnic, and/or racial characteristics, exceptionalities, gender, sexual orientation, and social class—should have an equal opportunity to learn in school. It comprises at least three items: an idea or concept, an educational reform movement, and a process.

Multidisciplinary team: A team made up of professionals from varying disciplines (e.g., educators, parents, physical therapists, physicians, counselors) who work together to develop an individualized education program (IEP) that describes the educational goals for a student with disabilities.

Multilevel classes: A grouping structure where students in the same grade are divided into groups on the basis of ability and instructed in different classrooms for one subject or the entire day.

Myopia: Nearsightedness; a refractive error in which light rays focus in front of the retina.

NAGC: Acronym for the National Association for Gifted Children.

National Library for the Blind and Physically Handicapped: A branch of the Library of Congress that produces recorded materials for recreational reading. Cassette tapes or digital books are distributed free of charge by regional libraries to children, youth, and adults with visual impairments and to others who are unable to read regular print.

NCLB   _see No Child Left Behind Act_

Negative reinforcement: The withdrawal or deferral of an aversive event or stimulus, contingent upon the display of a specific behavior, that increases the probability that the behavior will be repeated.

Neural tube: The embryonic tissue in a fetus that develops into the central nervous system including the spinal cord and brain.

Neurochemical: Refers to the chemical make-up and activities of the nervous system.

Neurotoxicants: A class of biological poison resulting from the byproduct of living organisms (plants, bacteria) that can cause direct damage to the neuro-development of individuals.

NICHCY: National Information Center for Children and Youth with Disabilities.

No Child Left Behind Act (NCLB): A federal law intended to ensure that all children reach challenging standards in reading and math and to close the academic achievement gap by race and class. NCLB is a landmark in education reform designed to improve student achievement and change the culture of America's schools via accountability of results, emphasizing what works for students based on scientific research, expanded parental options, and expanded local control and flexibility.

Noncategorical: A method for educational classification where students are grouped for instructional purposes and/or for teacher education programs and certification based on the learners' characteristics, rather than specific disability labels (i.e., category).

Nondiscriminatory evaluation: This principle of PL 94-142 includes assessing the abilities and needs of the individual student in order to plan for an appropriate education based on each student's strengths, weaknesses, and exceptional learning needs. States and local school districts must assess students in a manner that is both unbiased and nondiscriminatory.

Nonverbal behaviors: These are behaviors that are not verbal, including eye-to-eye gaze, facial expressions, body posture, and gestures.

Nonverbal communication: The act of transmitting information from one person to another without speaking, typically including body language.

Normalization: The principle of normalization was introduced in the early 1970s. The principle called for emphasizing normal environments and behavior and set the stage for the improvement of public attitudes towards persons with mental retardation. The incorporation of normalization as a public policy had a significant impact on deinstitutionalization and the growth in special education programs.

Norm-referenced tests: Tests that are designed to collect and validate data on the performance of large numbers of individuals by grade or age. These tests are used when it is important to compare the results of individuals to the performance of students of a similar age or grade level.

Nystagmus: Rapid, involuntary movement of one or both eyes, usually accompanied by other ocular disorders; even though the eyes move, the person sees objects as stationary.

Obsessive–compulsive disorder: Refers to recurrent and persistent ideas, impulses, or behaviors that are not voluntarily produced and are experienced as senseless or unwanted (e.g., excessive, repetitive thoughts or excessive hand washing).

Occipital lobe: Visual cortex of the brain.

Ocular albinism: Involves pigmentary differences in the eyes and is characterized by reduced visual acuity, astigmatism, photophobia, and nystagmus; more common in males.

Ocular-motor skills: Eye motor skills such as fixation, tracking, shift of gaze, and scanning.

Ophthalmologist: A physician that specializes in ophthalmology, the branch of medical science that deals with the eye and its structure, functions, and diseases.

Oppositional defiant disorder (ODD): Refers to behaviors (lasting at least six months) that are negativistic, hostile, and defiant and are unusual for the individual's age and developmental level. ODD refers to temper tantrums, arguing, and noncompliance that result in significant social, academic, or occupational impairment.

Optical character readers (OCR): A scanner, connected to a computer, that scans printed material which is then converted into a computer text file.

Optic nerve: Either of the pair of nerves that conducts visual stimuli to the brain.

Optic nerve atrophy: A condition characterized by damage to the fibers in the optic nerve so that electrical impulses are unable to travel from the retina to the occipital lobe; visual characteristics include reduced visual acuity, field losses, and difficulties with color vision.

Optic nerve hypoplasia (ONH): Incomplete development of the optic nerve that carries visual information to various locations in the brain, especially the occipital lobe; present at birth and may affect one or both eyes; visual functioning ranges from normal visual acuity to total blindness.

Optometrist: A specialist licensed to examine eyes for defects and refraction faults as well as prescribe correctional lenses and exercises.

Oral approach: A training approach for individuals with hearing loss that emphasizes the development of speech and auditory skills through a combination of speech reading and using residual hearing.

Organ of corti: Consists of multiple rows of hair cells that are the actual receptors for the auditory nerve.

Orientation and mobility (O&M): A service defined in IDEA whereby the person develops body image, learns spatial and positional concepts and environmental awareness, learns the layout of the general education classroom and other rooms in school and at home, maintains contact with the physical environment (e.g., landmarks), moves independently and safely, and uses appropriate techniques and devices.

Orthography: Concerned with letters and their sequences in words.

Ossicular chain: The three small bones in the middle ear (malleus, incus, and stapes—also known as the hammer, anvil, and stirrup) that transmit the sound vibrations through the middle ear cavity to the inner ear.

Otitis media: An infection in the middle ear.

Otologist: A medical specialist who deals with the ear and its diseases.

Ototoxic: Affects the organs or nerves involved in hearing or balance.

Oval window: An opening in the bone between the air-filled middle ear cavity and the fluid-filled inner ear; a thin membrane covers it.

Paradigm: A framework from which a person acts and interacts with their surroundings.

Paraeducators (*also called paraprofessionals*): Individuals trained to assume the role of an assistant to professional educators and provide support under supervision. In educational settings they provide a variety of instructionally related services to children.

Paralysis: Loss of control of muscles or nerves that control the muscles, interfering with voluntary control.

Paraplegia: Loss of voluntary control of both legs.

Parent and student participation: This principle of PL 94-142 emphasizes the rights that parents have of being informed of their child's progress, allowing them to express their concerns and having them become full participants during discussions and decisions (including IEP meetings) related to their child's educational program. Additionally, parents have the right to access or challenge the content of their child's school records through the Family Educational Rights and Privacy Act (FERPA).

PCBs: A group of compounds directly involved in the electricity and mining industries that, when exposed to the food chain and water supply, can cause significant developmental damage to humans.

PDD-NOS: Refers to pervasive developmental disorder–not otherwise specified, an autism spectrum disorder.

Peer mediation: A conflict resolution intervention in which trained students help their peers solve conflicts in a formal situation.

Peer teaching: Within cooperative learning, this grouping structure involves students working in pairs on a structured task. This can involve reviewing and testing each other on spelling words or math facts or working together on a computer project.

Peer tutoring: Involves students assuming an instructional role with another student. In applying peer tutoring, students with or without disabilities may take on the role of the tutors or tutees with grade-level peers or younger students.

Performance-based standards: A set of professional standards established by the Council for Exceptional Children for special education teachers to demonstrate their knowledge and skills.

Perinatal: At birth.

Person-Centered Planning (PCP): In this type of service delivery model, the student with the disability and his or her family assert more control over the student's educational programs. This involves creating a vision for the person's future and then determining how that vision will be realized (e.g., action plans).

Phobia: Any irrational and debilitating fear.

Phoneme: A phoneme is the smallest unit of speech sound, such as /b/.

Phonemic awareness: The knowledge that language can be broken down into smaller segments; involves skills such as breaking sentences into words, breaking words into syllables and sounds, and recognizing and producing rhyming words.

Phonics: To be proficient in phonics, learners must understand and use letter–sound correspondence to read or decode written words. Phonics instruction enhances early spelling and accelerates the rate at which children learn to read new words in text.

Phonological awareness: Being mindful of the association between letters and the sounds they represent within a word.

Phonology: The study of patterns of speech sounds.

Photophobia: Sensitiveness or intolerance to light.

Play-based assessment *see Activity-based assessment*

Portfolio: Individual collections of students' work that are compiled over time. A portfolio might include samples of complete work, work in progress, checklists, teacher observations, and journal entries.

Portfolio assessment: A type of assessment that consists of a collection of a student's work samples to show progress over time.

Positive behavior support (PBS): An approach to school management that allows school personnel to define effective routines and procedures, maintain a positive school climate, and provide a safe and orderly learning environment. PBS includes facilitating successful functioning in the school, classroom, and other specific locations and is conducted at individual student levels.

Positive reinforcement: The introduction of a perceived reward, contingent upon the display of a specific behavior, that increases the probability that the behavior will be repeated.

Postlingual loss: A hearing loss that occurs after speech and language develops (after the age of 2).

Poverty: This term is defined by the federal government using the number of people in the household and the number of related children under 18. The threshold differs for different combinations of adults and dependents.

Pragmatics: The application of syntactic structure, morphology, and semantic content to varied listeners and settings in life situations.

Prelingual hearing loss: A hearing loss that occurs prior to speech and language development (before the age of 2).

Prereferral intervention: These are activities that are designed to increase the classroom teacher's capacity to instruct and manage students who are a challenge to teach, thereby reducing unnecessary and inappropriate referrals for special education services.

Prereferral team: An informal, collaborative, multidisciplinary team that works with general education teachers to design strategies to teach students with difficult behavior in the general education environment; the purpose is to avoid inappropriate referrals to special education and to support teachers taking ownership of difficult-to-teach students. The term used to designate the prereferral team varies from school to school.

Primary disability: A principal cluster of language, speech, and/or hearing characteristics that meets criteria for services under federal and state guidelines for special education.

Priming: A strategy in which an adult previews activities for a student prior to their occurrence.

Problem solving: The ability to solve problems that require analytical and reasoning skills.

Procedural due process: If the parents/guardians of students with disabilities feel the SEAs and LEAs are not complying with the law, they have the right to protest on behalf of their children. Under this principle, LEAs must obtain informed parental consent before they can evaluate or place any student into a special education program,

and they must give parents a copy of their procedural safeguards.

Proficiency: Having the ability to complete a task skillfully.

Prompting: Cueing a student either physically or verbally in order to help him complete a task.

Psychoeducational: Refers to an approach to education that takes into account unconscious motivations of students and focuses intervention on assisting students in gaining insight into their behavior.

Pull-out instruction: Supplemental instruction that occurs often outside of the regular classroom for an individual student or small group.

Punishment: Refers to consequences that reduce the future probability of the display of a specific behavior. Punishment takes the form of response cost (i.e., removal of something valued) or aversive conditioning (i.e., presentation of an aversive stimulus).

Quadriplegia: Loss of voluntary control of all four limbs.

Quality of life: This concept refers to an important outcome of the transition process for students with disabilities—to attain a quality of life that is satisfying and that meets their needs after they leave the school setting. A quality-of-life approach tries to look at the person as a whole and determine if his or her life is satisfactory to the individual.

Race: Refers to the attempt by physical anthropologists to divide human groups according to their physical traits and characteristics. This has proven to be very difficult because human groups in modern societies are highly mixed physically. Consequently, different and often conflicting race typologies exist.

Reading comprehension: Involves the ability of the learner to understand meaning from text.

Recordings for the Blind and Dyslexic: A nonprofit agency located in Princeton, New Jersey, that produces and lends recorded textbooks for students in educational programs. The texts are produced on cassette or in digital formats.

Recreational services: Recreational or leisure services are an important component of a student's transition process toward independence and integration into the community. An increasing research base indicates that services and supports in typical recreational settings may be the best way of achieving meaningful quality-of-life outcomes for persons with disabilities and may replace more group- and center-oriented services such as the Special Olympics.

Referral form: A written statement that specifies the student's behavioral or academic difficulties and experiences and explains how these difficulties interfere with the student's learning.

Refractive errors: Problems in vision, such as myopia, hyperopia, and astigmatism, that are caused by a defect in the eye's ability to focus light rays on the retina; can usually be corrected by eyeglasses or contact lenses.

Regular education initiative (REI): A philosophy that maintains that general education, rather than special education, should be primarily responsible for the education of students with disabilities.

Rehabilitation: Restoring a person to a predetermined level of health.

Related services: These are additional services required by students with disabilities in order to access the specially designed instruction to meet their individual learning needs. Without these additional services, many students with disabilities would not benefit from instruction or could be placed in more restrictive environments. Related services may be either direct (such as speech therapy) or support services (such as transportation).

Remediation: Correcting a deficiency in the student's knowledge in a particular content area.

Research-based practices: Curriculum and instructional methodologies based on empirical (includes data) research studies.

Residual hearing: The amount of remaining hearing.

Resource specialist program: Students with disabilities in this placement receive special education and related services in the resource room for 21–60% of the school day. Generally, students with disabilities attend the resource room for 1–2 hours each day individually or in small groups to receive more individualized instruction from a resource specialist teacher.

Retinitis pigmentosa: An inherited condition in which symptoms usually begin during adolescence and result in progressive deterioration of the retina (peripheral vision and night vision are affected first; then tunnel vision develops; then the person might become totally blind).

Retinopathy of prematurity: A disorder characterized by an overgrowth of blood vessels in the retina, which causes visual loss ranging from moderate myopia to total blindness (can develop in premature infants and is associated with very low birth weight and gestational age).

Ritalin®: A prescribed medication used to treat disorders of inattention.

Rubella *(also called German measles)***:** A viral infection that causes a mild fever and skin rash. If a woman in the first three months of her pregnancy gets this disease, it can lead to severe birth defects.

Rubric: A technique used in grading the performance (e.g., a work sample) of a student. Developing a rubric involves creating descriptions of different levels of performance and then assigning a value to each level. A rubric might include values from one through five, with a rating of one indicating that the student did not demonstrate an understanding of the task.

Schizophrenia: A psychotic disorder characterized by distortion of thinking, abnormal perception, and bizarre behavior and emotions lasting at least six months.

Screen-enlargement programs: Software that enables the user to enlarge computer images to the size the viewer prefers, including menus and associated information that cannot be enlarged using a standard word-processing program.

Screen-enlargement software: Installed on a computer to increase the size of characters on the screen, the cursor, the menu, and dialogue boxes.

Screening: Formally planned procedures, administered by the school or district staff, that every student goes through, including vision tests, hearing tests, or large-scale assessments related to academic skills.

Screen reader: Uses synthesized speech to read text displayed on a computer monitor as the user moves a cursor or types on a keyboard.

Secondary disability: Refers to the additional difficulties experienced by a child that are related to or an outcome of ineffective interventions or interactions from the child's primary disability.

Seizure: A sudden burst of electrical activity in the brain that changes the individual's alertness or behavior.

Selective attention: The ability to focus on relevant stimuli without being distracted by irrelevant environmental factors.

Self-advocacy: The ability to support oneself, rather than being dependent on others, by communicating one's strengths, needs, preferences, aspirations, and values.

Self-control: The ability to control one's behaviors, actions, and thought processes.

Self-determination: Experiencing a quality of life that matches one's own values, choices, needs, and strengths. Some of the components of self-determination include self-advocacy, goal setting and attainment, decision making, risk-taking, and self-awareness.

Self-esteem: One's perceptions of self-worth.

Self-regulation: Refers generally to a person's ability to control his or her own behavior; an area of difficulty for individuals with mental retardation.

Self-reliance: The ability to rely on one's judgment, knowledge, and actions.

Semantic content: Culturally based concepts and vocabulary.

Semantic map: The visual representation or graphic organizer of the relationship between a central concept/topic and meaningful links to other related words.

Semantics: Study of the meaning of language (i.e., vocabulary).

Sensorineural hearing loss: A permanent loss as a result of damage in the inner ear involving the cochlea or the auditory nerve.

Sensory accommodations: Making accommodations according to the individual sensory needs of the student, such as providing the student with a fidget toy or allowing the student to jump on a mini-trampoline.

Septo-optic dysplasia (SOD): A neurological abnormality whereby symptoms may include blindness in one or both eyes or nystagmus.

Severe and profound mental retardation: Those who have severe and profound mental retardation are considered to make up about 5% of the MR population (3–4% for severe, 1–2% for profound). Severely retarded individuals have IQ scores of 20 to 40, and profoundly retarded individuals have IQ scores below 20 or 25.

Severe discrepancy: The student does not achieve commensurate with his or her ability in one or more academic areas even after receiving appropriate instruction.

Shaken baby syndrome: Internal head injuries caused by violent shaking of baby; often results in brain damage or death.

Sheltered environments: In this type of work environment, individuals with disabilities work in nonintegrated groups (only with people with disabilities) where they are usually paid below minimum wage for contract work such as stuffing envelopes.

Sign systems: Systems of communication that use visual equivalents of oral language.

Silent period: The lag time between when second language learners begin to understand messages in a new language and when they are actually able to produce the new language.

Simulation training: Replicating real-life scenarios in a classroom setting by breaking down and analyzing the tasks.

Slate and stylus: A manual Braille writing device that can be used for note taking and brief writing tasks; consists of a metal frame with openings through which Braille dots are punched with a pointed stylus.

Socially maladjusted: Refers to students who may be considered emotionally disturbed; delinquent behavior and predelinquent behavior are considered to be forms of social maladjustment.

Social Stories: An individualized text or story that describes a specific social situation from the point of view of the child.

Special class/special day class (SDC): Students in an SDC are self-contained, meaning that the other students in the class have similar learning or behavioral needs. These students receive special education and related services outside of the general education classroom for more than 60% of the school day, although they may be mainstreamed into the general education class for certain periods of the day or be pulled out for additional services. In this placement, the special education teacher is the primary source of instruction and is responsible for the students' entire curriculum across all content areas (e.g., reading, math, science, social studies).

Special education: IDEA defines special education as specially designed instruction at no cost to the parents to meet the unique needs of students with disabilities. The education should be individualized and provided in various settings with related services if necessary.

Special education technology: The use of any technologies by a special educator or student with disabilities to help counterbalance the student's ability to access curriculum and learn at a level equivalent to that of a student without disabilities.

Specific learning disabilities: A disorder in one or more of the basic psychological processes involved in understanding or using language, spoken or written, that may manifest itself in an imperfect ability to listen, think, speak, read, write, spell, or do mathematical calculations, including conditions such as perceptual disabilities, brain injury, minimal brain dysfunction, dyslexia, and developmental aphasia. The term does not include learning problems that are primarily the result of visual, hearing, or motor disabilities, mental retardation, emotional disturbance, or environmental, cultural, or economic disadvantage.

Speech audiometry: Words presented at different levels of loudness to assess a person's speech discrimination.

Speech disorders: Difficulties with articulation (the way phonemes are pronounced), fluency (speech rate, rhythm), or voice (pitch, volume, and quality).

Speechreader: An individual who is able to understand what is being spoken by looking at the lips and facial movements of the speaker.

Speech reading/lip reading: Interpreting a speaker's words by watching his or her lips and facial movements without hearing his or her voice.

Spina bifida: A congenital disorder that occurs when the neural tube does not completely close during fetal development, resulting in loss of control of the lower part of the body.

Standards-based instruction: A teaching process that uses state or national standards (i.e., grade-level content standards), benchmarks, indicators, and assessments to guide teaching.

Standards-based reform: Policies that hold schools accountable for adequate student and school progress, based on uniform educational content standards.

Stanford–Binet Intelligence Scale: A standardized test that assesses intelligence and cognitive abilities in children and adults aged 2–23.

State curriculum standards: Content standards of learning for students within a particular state that guide teacher instruction.

State education agency (SEA): In each state there is a department of education with a unit dedicated to special education programs. The SEA also monitors compliance of local districts in meeting state and federal requirements.

Strabismus: A deviation of the eyes that prevents simultaneous focus by both eyes; to avoid seeing double, the child may suppress the vision in one eye, which can result in amblyopia.

Structured teaching: This occurs when the environment is modified to meet the needs of students with autism spectrum disorders.

Support: Support is a broad term that encompasses services to help individuals with disabilities function successfully in the community. Support services may include accommodations and modifications in a college setting or services in a living or work environment.

Supported living: In this type of living environment, persons with disabilities live where and with whom they want, for as long as they want, with the ongoing supports needed to sustain that choice. Supported living may involve a person living in his or her own house or apartment with a variety of supports based upon his or her needs.

Supported or competitive employment   *see Integrated environments*

Syndrome: A collection of two or more features that result from a single cause.

Syntactic structure: Organization of phrases and clauses within a specific word order; differs across languages and dialects.

Syntax: Refers to grammatical structure in sentences and paragraphs.

Synthesized speech: The computerized production of phonemes into words based on a variety of programming formats. Synthetic speech devices give students with visual impairments direct access to information through voice output and are available as either hardware or software. Examples of computer speech access programs are JAWS and Window-Eyes.

Syphilis: A sexually transmitted disease that can cause an intrauterine infection in pregnant woman and result in severe birth defects.

TDD/TTY   *see Telecommunication devices for the deaf*

Teacher of students with visual impairments (TVI): A specialist who is trained and certified to work with students who are blind or have low vision. TVIs work in various placements, including specialized schools, disability-specific classes, resource rooms, and inclusive classes, as an itinerant teacher/consultant in public and private settings. TVIs conduct specialized assessments such as the Functional Vision Evaluation and Learning Media Assessment, provide direct instruction in expanded core curriculum areas directly related to visual impairment (such as Braille and daily living skills), and provide materials and adaptations needed for the student to access the general education curriculum.

Technology-enhanced performance: A term used to describe a student's achievement when technological devices have been used to meet the objectives.

Telecommunication devices for the deaf (TDD/TTY): Telephones with screens and keyboards that allow people who are deaf to communicate with others.

Telescopic lens: A monocular or monocular telescope; a portable telescope that helps people see things that are larger or farther away (a chalkboard or whiteboard, a friend's house, etc.).

Teratogens: A foreign agent that interferes with fetal development (e.g., radiation, German measles, toxoplasmosis).

Text structure: The organizational features that serve as a frame or a pattern to help readers identify important information, make logical connections between ideas, facilitate understanding, and summarize text.

Tonotopically: The hair cells in the cochlea are arranged according to sound frequency, with the higher frequency responders closest to the oval window (outside the coiled cochlea) and the lower frequency responders at the top (inside the coil).

Total communication: An instructional method for teaching communication skills to individuals with hearing loss that incorporates oral, auditory, manual, and written components.

Toxoplasmosis: An infectious disease caused by a microorganism. It can cause severe fetal malformations.

Transactional model: The transactional model suggests that biological and environmental risks interact to determine developmental outcomes and that an appropriate environment as well as an intact biological and genetic makeup contributes to maximal outcomes. These transactions—the interactions between the child and his parents or caregivers—are the building blocks of early cognitive, motor, and social–emotional development.

Transition: Refers to the change process from when a student with a disability leaves the K–12 school system and prepares to enter adult life.

Traumatic brain injury: Damage to one or more parts of the brain as a result of physical insult.

Triad of impairments: Commonly seen with students with autism spectrum disorders; includes impairments in social interaction, communication, and restricted repetitive and stereotyped patterns of behavior, interests, and activities.

Tsunami: A very large wave that is put into motion by an earthquake that begins under the ocean.

Tympanic membrane: A thin layer of skin at the end of the external ear canal.

Tympanography: The measurement of the flexibility of the eardrum (tympanic membrane) as an indicator of a middle-ear infection or fluid in the middle ear.

UDL   *see Universal Design for Learning*

Uncontracted Braille: The basic Braille code that includes one symbol for each letter of the alphabet, along with punctuation and composition signs.

Unilateral and bilateral hearing loss: A unilateral hearing loss is one that occurs in one ear only; bilateral loss occurs in both ears.

Universal Design for Learners: An educational design that allows different learners (e.g., students with disabilities) access to information and access to learning.

Universal Design for Learning (UDL): A reconceptualization of the curriculum so it is accessible and appropriate for students with different learning profiles.

Universal precautions: The use of hygienic routine and emergency care providing practices for all individuals to protect the privacy of individuals who have contagious diseases.

Vestibular mechanism: Structure in the inner ear containing three semicircular canals filled with fluid. It is very sensitive to movement and helps the body maintain balance and equilibrium.

Videomagnifier (*also called closed-circuit television*): A system with a camera that enlarges visual materials on a television monitor. By moving print material on a sliding table underneath or beside a camera with an adjustable zoom lens, the user views material enlarged on a television monitor.

Visual impairment: Refers to a measured loss of any of the visual functions, such as acuity, visual field, color vision, or binocular vision.

Visually impaired: Having visual impairment; having a measured loss of any of the visual functions, such as acuity, visual field, color vision, or binocular vision.

Visual supports: Presenting information to a student in a visual way, such as with visual schedules or graphic organizers.

Vocabulary: Spoken and written words of a language (i.e., semantics).

Vocational instruction: Giving students with disabilities job training or related job skills (e.g., mechanics) that they will need to be employable in the job market.

Weschler Intelligence Scale for Children—Third Edition: A norm-referenced intelligence test used widely across the United States to determine a student's intelligence.

Whole-group: A grouping format where the students are instructed in a large-group setting.

Whole language approaches: Combined listening, speaking, reading, and writing lessons integrated around a thematic unit using a common vocabulary across tasks.

Within-class cluster grouping: A grouping structure where the teacher forms ability groups within the classroom and provides appropriate instruction based on the students' abilities.

Word prediction: A feature utilized by some specialized software programs that predicts upcoming words in a sentence based upon what has already been written.

Working memory: Information that is currently available in memory for working on a problem.

Zero exclusion: In this type of recreational program, therapeutic recreation specialists and generic recreation program leaders collaborate to design programs that meet the needs of all participants, with or without disabilities.

Zero reject: This principle of PL 94-142 basically forbids states and local school districts from excluding students with disabilities from educational programs. All students with disabilities (between the ages of 3 and 21) have the right to full educational opportunities and a free, appropriate public education. The zero reject principle ensures that all students with disabilities have access to public education.

Name Index

Subject Index